Praise for *Natural Law: 5 Views*

There once was a day when the knowledge derived from the natural law stood at the center of Western thought and culture. The eclipse of the natural law tradition is yet another sign of the confusion and rebellion that increasingly mark the present age. This important volume, skillfully edited by Ryan Anderson and Andrew Walker, does not attempt to settle all the issues related to natural law. It does succeed, however, in reviewing the landscape and clarifying many important arguments. This lively volume should be both welcomed and read.

—R. Albert Mohler Jr., president, Centennial Professor of Theology, The Southern Baptist Theological Seminary

Natural Law: Five Views is an invaluable treatment, by an assemblage of superb scholars, of the diversity of approaches to natural law and the variety of philosophical and theological issues that arise in connection with it.

—Edward Feser, professor of philosophy, Pasadena City College

The natural law tradition has witnessed a resurgence in American intellectual circles, where its appeal is now more ecumenical than ever. So this volume has a crucial and timely job to perform—and it performs magnificently. It brings together some of the best contemporary minds on the topic and in the format that is most conducive to careful but bracing debate. This is academic exchange at its best, shedding light on—and contributing to—the dominant philosophical current in Western thought for over two millennia.

—Sherif Girgis, associate professor of law, Notre Dame Law School

This book would have been unimaginable a generation ago. Most twentieth-century Protestants neglected their own natural law traditions and believed that natural law was only a Roman Catholic idea, at best. In recent years, natural law has been returning to its rightful place as a universal Christian doctrine—although it has not quite arrived. For those wishing to get a sense of the ideas and debates circling around natural law, this book will prove to be an illuminating resource. The authors manage to be both collegial and polemical and in doing so invite readers to join a perennial discussion about truly important issues for those pursuing a faithful Christian life in a fallen world.

> —DAVID VANDRUNEN, Robert B. Strimple Professor of Systematic Theology and Christian Ethics, Westminster Seminary California

"Does not nature itself teach you?" asks the apostle Paul. In a world at war with nature and nature's God, this is a crucial question. But what is nature? How does it teach? And why does it matter? The five scholars in this book represent five approaches to those questions. For those who have welcomed the renewal of natural law thinking among Christians, this book is a timely and illuminating discussion of God's design in nature and the moral obligations he places upon us.

> —JOE RIGNEY, fellow of theology, New Saint Andrews College

Natural Law

5 VIEWS

Michael Pakaluk
Joel D. Biermann
Brad Littlejohn
Melissa Moschella
Peter J. Leithart

Ryan T. Anderson and
Andrew T. Walker, *general editors*

CRITICALPOINTS

ZONDERVAN ACADEMIC

Natural Law: Five Views

Copyright © 2025 by Andrew T. Walker, Ryan T. Anderson, Melissa Moschella, Michael Pakaluk, W. Bradford Littlejohn, Joel D. Biermann, Peter J. Leithart

Published in Grand Rapids, Michigan, by Zondervan. Zondervan is a registered trademark of The Zondervan Corporation, L.L.C., a wholly owned subsidiary of HarperCollins Christian Publishing, Inc.

Requests for information should be addressed to customercare@harpercollins.com.

Zondervan titles may be purchased in bulk for educational, business, fundraising, or sales promotional use. For information, please email SpecialMarkets@Zondervan.com.

Library of Congress Cataloging-in-Publication Data

Names: Pakaluk, Michael, 1957- author. | Biermann, Joel D., author. | Littlejohn, W. Bradford, author. | Moschella, Melissa, 1979- author. | Leithart, Peter J., author. | Anderson, Ryan T., 1981- editor. | Walker, Andrew T., 1985- editor.

Title: Natural law : five views / Michael Pakaluk, Joel D. Biermann, Brad Littlejohn, Melissa Moschella, Peter J. Leithart ; Ryan T. Anderson and Andrew T. Walker, general editor.

Description: Grand Rapids, Michigan : Zondervan Academic, [2025] | Series: Critical points series | Includes index.

Identifiers: LCCN 2024051588 (print) | LCCN 2024051589 (ebook) | ISBN 9780310128656 (paperback) | ISBN 9780310128663 (ebook)

Subjects: LCSH: Natural law--Religious aspects--Christianity. | Christian ethics. | Christianity--Philosophy. | BISAC: RELIGION / Christian Theology / Ethics | PHILOSOPHY / Ethics & Moral Philosophy

Classification: LCC BR115.L28 P35 2025 (print) | LCC BR115.L28 (ebook) | DDC 241/.2--dc23/eng/20241213

LC record available at https://lccn.loc.gov/2024051588

LC ebook record available at https://lccn.loc.gov/2024051589

Unless otherwise noted, Scripture quotations are taken from The Holy Bible, New International Version®, NIV®. Copyright © 1973, 1978, 1984, 2011 by Biblica, Inc.® Used by permission of Zondervan. All rights reserved worldwide. www.Zondervan.com. The "NIV" and "New International Version" are trademarks registered in the United States Patent and Trademark Office by Biblica, Inc.® • Scripture quotations marked NASB are taken from the New American Standard Bible®. Copyright © 1960, 1971, 1977, 1995 by The Lockman Foundation. Used by permission. All rights reserved. www.lockman.org. • Scripture quotations marked ESV are taken from the ESV® Bible (The Holy Bible, English Standard Version®). Copyright © 2001 by Crossway, a publishing ministry of Good News Publishers. Used by permission. All rights reserved.

Any internet addresses (websites, blogs, etc.) and telephone numbers in this book are offered as a resource. They are not intended in any way to be or imply an endorsement by Zondervan, nor does Zondervan vouch for the content of these sites and numbers for the life of this book.

All rights reserved. No part of this publication may be reproduced, stored in a retrieval system, or transmitted in any form or by any means—electronic, mechanical, photocopy, recording, or any other—except for brief quotations in printed reviews, without the prior permission of the publisher.

Published in association with the literary agency of Wolgemuth & Associates, Inc.

Cover design: Tammy Johnson
Cover image: © MicroStockHub / Getty Images
Interior design: Kait Lamphere
Interior typesetting: Sara Colley

Printed in the United States of America

25 26 27 28 29 TRM 5 4 3 2 1

Contents

Introduction, by Ryan T. Anderson and Andrew T. Walker vii

1. The Classical Understanding of Natural Law, by Michael Pakaluk . . . 1
    a. Biermann Response 27
    b. Littlejohn Response 32
    c. Moschella Response 38
    d. Leithart Response 43
    e. Rejoinder 48
2. A Lutheran Understanding of Natural Law, by Joel D. Biermann . . . 57
    a. Pakaluk Response 82
    b. Littlejohn Response 87
    c. Moschella Response 93
    d. Leithart Response 99
    e. Rejoinder 105
3. Reformed Natural Law, by Brad Littlejohn 111
    a. Pakaluk Response 140
    b. Biermann Response 145
    c. Moschella Response 150
    d. Leithart Response 156
    e. Rejoinder 161
4. The "New" Natural Law, by Melissa Moschella 169
    a. Pakaluk Response 202
    b. Biermann Response 207
    c. Littlejohn Response 212
    d. Leithart Response 218
    e. Rejoinder 224
5. Anti–Natural Law, by Peter J. Leithart 233
    a. Pakaluk Response 257
    b. Biermann Response 263
    c. Littlejohn Response 268

d. Moschella Response............................ 274
e. Rejoinder..................................... 280
Concluding Remarks, by Ryan T. Anderson and Andrew T. Walker... 287

List of Contributors 289
Scripture Index.... 291
Subject/Author Index 293

Introduction

RYAN T. ANDERSON
AND ANDREW T. WALKER

Mention "natural law," "natural law tradition," or "natural law theory" generally to philosophers, lawyers, and scientists, and you may receive any of the following replies:

- "That's just academic jargon for smuggling in God-talk."
- "Do you mean the casualty of Oliver Wendell Holmes Jr.?"
- "Natural law is just a sophisticated way that social conservatives speak to justify their bigotry."
- "Aristotle defended slavery on the basis of natural law."
- "It did not survive the fact-value dichotomy set in motion by Hume and eventually by Darwin's naturalism."

If one were to raise those same categories among Christian theologians, historians, and ethicists, you may receive an additional set of incredulities:

- "It's just a Catholic thing."
- "It relies too heavily on the autonomous reason of fallen humanity."
- "Natural law dilutes the uniqueness of Christian revelation into a generic theory of morality that non-Christians could affirm."
- "It persuades no one."
- "Why rely on natural law when we have God's revealed Word?"
- "Even natural lawyers disagree among themselves on what the natural law is and what the full scope of its entailments are."

Yet natural law voices and natural law theory refuse to go away. Despite the attempts by the academy, secularism, and even some in the church to put natural law into the dustbin of history once and for all, it persists. There is a reason that it is sometimes referred to as one of the cluster of concepts known as the *philosophia perennis* (perennial philosophy).

The Need for the Natural Law

It persists, we suspect, because at the exact moments when enlightened society believes it has moved beyond moral superstitions, events or ideas proliferate reminding individuals of all stripes that some moral accounting is called for. In other words, secular society is apt to espouse a very academic subjectivism, relativism, and agnosticism. Yet when confronted with circumstances that demand interpretation outside what subjectivism and relativism can provide, people often reflexively defer to some remnant of morality "written on their hearts" (Rom 2:14–16).

Whether or not human beings can explain the origins and intelligibility of a moral order they presuppose in their daily lives, we are irrepressibly moral beings who make moral pronouncements. Ironically, in our age, those who espouse no religious system are often the most zealous and indignant in protesting supposed *in*justices—and yet can give no satisfactory account of, or justification for, justice. All of this suggests that despite our attempts to deny universal moral objectivity, we cannot evade it. The crematoriums of Nazi concentration camps are not events one can be indifferent about. Whether a horrendous mass shooting or debates about which family structures best enable human flourishing, natural law finds a way to reassert itself.

The consequences of getting the natural law correct in all its finer details is less important than the outcomes of denying the natural law altogether. Undermining the natural law, even through academic subtlety, can reap a whirlwind of consequences that few are willing to say aloud until they do. Consider a TED Talk given by one of today's most famous public intellectuals, Yuval Noah Harari. In a talk on *homo sapiens*, Harari went on to offer these remarks about human beings and the supposed "rights" we insist upon in political communities:

Many, maybe most, legal systems are based on this idea of this belief in human rights. But human rights are just like heaven or God. It's just a fictional story that we've invented and spread around. It may be a very nice story. It may be a very attractive story. We want to believe it, but it is just a story. It is not a reality. It is not a biological reality. Just as jellyfish, woodpeckers, and ostriches have no rights, *Homo sapiens* have no rights. Take a human and cut him open and look inside. You find their blood, and you find the heart, lungs, and kidneys. But you do not find there any rights. The only place you find rights is in the fictional stories humans have invented and spread around. The same thing is also true in the political field. States and nations are also like human rights and like God and like heaven. They too are just stories. A mountain is a reality. You can see it. You can touch it. You can even smell it. But Israel and the United States, they are just stories. Very powerful stories, stories we might want to believe very much. Still, they are just stories. You cannot really see the United States. You cannot touch it. You cannot smell it.[1]

In one minute, Harari attempted to systematically destroy the only remaining moral system modernity has left—its preoccupation with rights. But he revealed how shallow of a philosopher he is—assuming empiricism is the only valid approach to real knowledge. In a world where the Holocaust, genocides, legalized abortion, the killing fields of the Khmer Rouge, and the Nanking Massacre have claimed millions and millions of lives in the twentieth century alone, one would believe that daring to question the existence of human rights would be *verboten*. But Harari's statement demonstrates how the academic landscape after the scientific revolution has unceremoniously gutted morality of any objective grounding or transcendent horizon. Even still, secular humans demand the full panoply of rights in accordance with a sense of unbounded autonomy. Yet we do so in view of a horizon that negates the intelligibility of these rights obtaining any normative poise.

For Harari as with other materialists, rights are merely contrivances and fables meant to make life on this planet more habitable. Sure, they may

---

1. Yuval Harari, TED Talk, January 23, 2024, https://x.com/glenscrivener/status/1749839206 761832821. The speech is an expanded version of this article authored by Harari, "Why Humans Run the World," June 16, 2015, TED.com, https://ideas.ted.com/why-humans-run-the-world/.

be useful. But for Harari, rights in themselves are merely nighttime fairy tales meant to pacify and lull. To put this in the words of C. S. Lewis in *The Abolition of Man*, one of the most important natural law treatises ever written, "In a sort of ghastly simplicity we remove the organ and demand the function. We make men without chests and expect of them virtue and enterprise. We laugh at honour and are shocked to find traitors in our midst. We castrate and bid the geldings be fruitful."[2] That is the paradox of modern secularism shorn of the natural law: the rights-talk imbued with deep moral significance is evacuated of all objective moral standards.

Secularism and moral skepticism have ceded the world to an eloquent moral barbarism. And many are simply saying this out loud now: without the natural law and its grounding in some notion of objectivity, rights are illusory and mere pleasantries and contingencies hanging in thin air. We both believe the only satisfactory account for moral objectivity is grounded by divine warrant. Only if human beings are moral agents duty bound to a transcendently ordered natural law can rights be grounded in something outside of human exigencies. Rights gain ultimate intelligibility against a backdrop of God creating us as image bearers meant to pursue human goods in accordance with his divine plan. From an ultimate vantage point, true rights require theological justification: natural law is the foundation of natural rights, and natural law has a natural law giver.

Divine teleology, then, is the need of the hour. In our view, Christianity best supplies that moral superstructure. We think this need helps explain the justification for the book you have before you since the Christian moral tradition has reflected deeply on the ideas of natural law, objective morality, and human goods. As we will see, though, there are quite different accounts of natural law from a Christian perspective.

A Primer on Natural Law Theory

What is the natural law? Simply put, it is the moral law accessible to human reason. A cognitive and realist branch of moral philosophy, natural law theory holds that there is an objective account of the good(s) that human beings should strive to attain in accordance with their end as beings who possess a rational nature.

2. C. S. Lewis, *The Abolition of Man* (New York: HarperCollins, 1974), 26.

Natural law theory refers to two domains of inquiry. In the first instance, it refers to the existence of a moral *order* governed by moral laws concerning objective rights and objective wrongs. Second, it refers to the rational agent's *grasp* of that moral order through the faculty of reason. As rational agents, we are beings whose nature allows us to participate in that order. The ultimate aim of natural law, however, is to enable human beings and the communities and institutions they form to achieve their *telos*, or the end or purpose for which their capacities direct them toward. Natural law as a *theory* purports to explain the origins of the natural law, the mind's grasp of that law, and our ability to actualize the human good.

Natural law also considers the justifications for making the distinction between right and wrong actions. An action is deemed "good" in proportion to the action's conduciveness to promote well-being. An action is deemed "wrong" in proportion to that action's impeding the fulfillment of one's well-being. While natural law theory can become very technical (as any discipline invariably can), it need not be complex. At root, the natural law proffers an account of morality that all human beings can, in principle, access—despite our fallenness. Non-Christians rely on the natural law all the time, as C. S. Lewis points out in the appendix to *The Abolition of Man*.

While natural law theory touches upon all aspects of morality and seeks to address a range of complex issues, from the nature of marriage to whether intentional killing is ever permitted, we must stress that the natural law is ultimately about practical reason's grasp of human goods and our ability to actualize those goods in our daily choices. When parents (Christian or non-Christian) care and sacrifice for their children's welfare, they are promoting the good of family well-being. Similarly, non-Christians who follow the Golden Rule (Matt 22:37–39; Luke 6:31) in returning a lost possession to someone demonstrate a sense of duty that springs from their own intuitive sense that if something of theirs was lost, they would want it returned too.

As this volume's authors all consider themselves Christian, it is worth reflecting, however briefly, on how the Christian tradition has evaluated and promulgated natural law theory with regard to its origins, knowledge, content, and utility.

Concerning the origins of the natural law, virtually all accounts of natural law are theistic in nature. Various natural law theories introduce

God's place in the overall theory in different sequences. Still, God is seen as the animating force for bringing the natural law into existence. Deducing the logic of the natural law is straightforward. For an objective moral order to exist, the moral order could not have spontaneously brought itself into existence. Moral obligation does not create itself. The fact of the natural law requires explanation: a divine lawgiver who stands outside the moral order must order its existence and operation. Among the views expressed in this book, the question of origins is the least controversial. Every view represented in this volume affirms the divine origins of the natural law. Where debate enters into consideration is the extent to which natural law can still be known by fallen and sinful human beings, the exact content of the natural law, and why Christians would invoke the natural law.

Concerning questions of knowledge of the natural law, Christians insist that there is a law written on the heart that God inscribes onto every human being's conscience (Rom 2:14–16). There are truths we can deny verbally, even when we know them internally, including that stealing, murder, and cheating are wrong. Even those who engage in such conduct, the natural law teaches, have some knowledge of their wrongdoing (even if they do not *feel* guilty)—and even when they claim they don't know such truths exist or don't believe in objective morality. The first principles cannot be blotted out. The most axiomatic truth of the natural law is that *good is to be pursued and evil is to be avoided.* That stands as the indemonstrable and self-evident claim of the natural law upon which all other moral reasoning builds. As the views of this book will demonstrate, whether knowledge of the natural law retains as much consensus or viability after humanity's descent into sin is a major point of disagreement. The extent to which special revelation is required to have any degree of confidence in the moral law is one of the central debates of natural law theory. There are also important considerations related to the relationships between theology and philosophy and between special revelation and general revelation. Both of us believe that theology and philosophy are mutually reinforcing pillars that reflect two media of God's revelation. When each discipline is properly conducted, neither contradicts the other, but they complement one another in arriving at the same truths through different modes of transmission, though revealed theology can see more (those truths that we can only know through revelation) and see more clearly (even those truths that in principle are accessible to reason).

Concerning the content of the natural law, it is knowledge of human goods and moral norms through practical reason that allows individuals to order their behavior to obtain those goods. For example, though there are many reasons why one may choose to visit an art museum, natural law would hold that human beings are creatures driven by beauty and aesthetic appreciation. Individuals will commune with one another purely for the sake of enjoying one's company; hence, sociability and friendship comprise the broader contours of the natural law. The decision to exercise is not merely a decision to keep one's waistline trim. It is organizing the whole of one's life to pursue health and protect one's bodily existence. A father's daily sacrifice to care for his family is not burdensome. Rather, the natural law tradition would hold that pursuing the conditions that cause a family to prosper is intrinsically value action that serves to strengthen the good of marriage and family life. At bottom, acting to pursue *any* activity that is truly good for *its own sake* as the irreducible motive for acting suggests that the activity at hand relates to the natural law in either a primary or secondary manner. Of course, debate persists about whether certain goods or ends are truly good, noninstrumental, and rightfully ordered in the human's pursuit of them. For example: While money and pleasure are considered worth having by many today (and indeed our society seems obsessed with maximizing both), we would both argue that money and pleasure are not ends in themselves. If they are pursued as though they are their own ends, they lead to the deprivation or counterfeit of true human goods—for example, the good of marriage and family and how one's vocational skill fulfills their sense of worth and contribution, not simply how much money it earns them.

Certain moral norms and principles govern our actions in pursuit of human goods to ensure we do so in a fully reasonable, hence moral, way. We may view the Golden Rule, "Do to others as you would have them do to you" (Luke 6:31), as one moral principle included in the natural law to ensure fairness in our pursuit of human flourishing. Similarly, one may refer to the Pauline principle that one may never do evil so that good may come about (Rom 3:8)—articulated several centuries earlier by Plato's Socrates when he said that it is better to suffer injustice than to commit injustice.[3]

---

3. Plato, *Gorgias*, 469b. See https://www.perseus.tufts.edu/hopper/text?doc=Perseus%3Atext%3A1999.01.0178%3Atext%3DGorg.%3Asection%3D469b

Only *doing* evil, *committing* injustice, corrupts one's character and fails to follow the way of Christ.

Concerning the question of the natural law's utility, great debate enters here as well. Regardless of whether one believes the natural law is a device for moral persuasion or whether one believes natural law is useful for its ability to inform the Christian's understanding of the moral shape of creaturely existence, we can be reasonably confident of this: the natural law provides a lowest common denominator for moral discourse and moral consensus in an age where a multiplicity of ideologies and religions all vie for people's attentions and affections. In other words, apart from a realized eschaton, natural law is the inevitable moral grammar of this age such that Christians will find themselves utilizing it whether they like it or not. That may be frustrating to some. We, however, believe it presents Christians with an opportunity, an entry point to then bring the full scope of Christians ethics to bear with vital urgency in all of today's most pressing moral debates. Moreover, natural law can help Christians better understand revelation and apply it to new questions that Scripture may not directly address. It provides a moral bilingualism: Christians can speak both theologically and philosophically. Natural law is never a replacement for theological ethics. It demonstrates our ability to do both. All of this culminates in what we believe is the most important aspect of natural law's utility: to better understand *why* God has revealed and commanded what he has. A theological ethic that grasps how the creaturely good is grounded in God's plan for the world is an ethic we should all strive to better understand.

Neither of us want the Bible cited any less in public debates; our belief in the necessity of the natural law, however, is that once religious beliefs are dismissed by an interlocutor, moral debate still needs to continue. Public policies will be debated among a diverse set of people and legislators. How will such debate occur when differing accounts of divine revelation are rejected by some? We believe this is where the natural law is unavoidably relevant. And while it is true that those who are likely to dismiss special revelation may be just as likely to dismiss anything natural as well, that does not stop us from having to do the hard work of engaging in reasonable moral debate about what best prospers human beings.

Five Views of the Natural Law

It is only proper to delimit the scope of this project. After all, it is not only Catholics, Lutherans, and Presbyterians who affirm the natural law. Anglicans, Baptists, and the Orthodox affirm it as well. In designing the framework of this volume, however, the editors chose Christian intellectual streams that are meant to capture the broad array of natural law schools on offer: classical natural law, Lutheran natural law, Reformed natural law, new natural law, and anti–natural law. Allow us to give very brief overviews of how these various schools and the contributors who represent each view differentiate themselves.

Classical Natural Law

Michael Pakaluk's chapter on "The Classical Understanding of Natural Law" does not pretend that there was ever any single monolithic teaching regarding ethics in the classical world of Athens and Rome. Instead, Pakaluk highlights the classical teachings about nature, human nature, and society that cultures influenced by Judaism and Christianity appropriated as their own—namely, a discerning process of what to accept or reject from the classical world in light of biblical revelation. Pakaluk stresses that human nature for classical thinkers was not some attempt at crass empiricism, and thus when we are thinking about human nature and humans' natural setting, we're not to engage in a quest for a "state of nature" devoid of social, political, and economic life, à la Rousseau or Locke, but to see that these institutions are necessary entailments of human nature and thus constitute humanity's natural—that is, fully human—setting. Human existence outside of social, political, and economic institutions sufficient to enable our flourishing is not natural. Pakaluk continues with an exploration of what proper self-love and a life of virtue entailed and how the natural law is naturally promulgated in both its content and lawfulness. He concludes with a reflection on Aristotle and Cicero's teaching that friendship entails regarding someone else as a "another self."

Lutheran Natural Law

Lutheran theologian Joel Biermann's chapter showcases a paradoxical approach to the natural law. For Biermann, the natural law exists but cannot be understood apart from its ability to awaken sinners to their need for Christ. Biermann argues that Lutheranism, though assuming the natural law's givenness, has never taken keen interest in an overarching system of natural law as a standalone concept integral to Lutheran theology. Why? While affirming a strong concept of natural law as an abiding reality hardwired into creation order (especially as refracted through the Decalogue), Biermann holds that the natural law is merely instrumentally beneficial to its fulfillment in Christ. Natural law as a standalone category, while conceptually fine as far as the idea itself is concerned, should remind humanity of its fallenness. In this, the natural law—like all law—indicts, condemns, and draws sinners to their knees. Biermann admits that the Lutheran view amounts to a "soft voluntarism" since the natural law is merely an expression of a sovereign God over his creation. The astute reader will detect in Biermann's chapter not an aversion to the natural law *per se*, but an aversion to the natural law where its application seeks to gain more than what can reasonably be hoped for when deploying it.

Reformed Natural Law

In Brad Littlejohn's chapter, he corrects the mistaken claim that Reformed theology is opposed to natural law by demonstrating how suffused the Reformed tradition was with natural law categories, particularly the Reformed scholastics. Citing an array of figures from John Calvin to Girolamo Zanchi to Johannes Althusius to Herman Bavinck, Littlejohn argues that the Reformed tradition understands the natural law not primarily through a rationalist lens, but through extended reflections on how God's created order communicated through what the Reformed tradition commonly refers to as general revelation, which allows for principles of right and wrong to be deduced as humankind interacts within God's world. From the 1621 *Synopsis of a Purer Theology*, Littlejohn approvingly defines the natural law as "the light and direction of sound reason in the intellect, informing man with common notions to distinguish right from wrong, and honorable from shameful—so that he may understand what he should do or shun" (p. 114). The attentive reader will see the significant overlap between Reformed and Thomistic categories of natural law as Littlejohn demonstrates an abundance of semantic and conceptual similarities between the two traditions. Littlejohn draws the reader to understand the natural law primarily as a metaphysical reality before focusing on the epistemological questions it raises.

New Natural Law

Carrying forward the tradition started by Germain Grisez, Joseph Boyle, John Finnis, and Robert P. George, Melissa Moschella's chapter articulates the new natural law theory (NNLT) and its emphasis on the mind's grasp of basic human goods as animating reason for human action rather than a primarily speculative project based on questions of human nature that arise from metaphysics. To be clear, while not antimetaphysical, what distinguishes Moschella's chapter from other chapters in the volume is the new natural law tradition's emphasis on practical reason. For this reason, NNLT is an intellectualist and cognitive theory of the natural law that does not advert preeminently to metaphysical conceptions of the divine to foreground its major tenets. As Moschella states in her chapter, NNLT is concerned with identification of human goods as eudaimonistic and the identification of specific moral norms that allow for those goods to be actualized. As Moschella summarizes, "An act is intelligible—it is a genuinely human act—if it is chosen with the purpose of directly or indirectly instantiating a basic human good" (p. 181). God is the ultimate explanation for all existence, including the existence of humans, the goods that fulfill human nature, and the natural law that directs our actions. According to Moschella, we can know quite a bit about these penultimate matters before adverting to their ultimate grounding.

Anti–Natural Law

It is fair to ask whether Peter Leithart is truly "Anti–Natural Law," as his chapter title suggests, or if he's actually opposed to certain atheological accounts of natural law, as his chapter argues. Early in his essay, he explains: "I am anti-*theories* of natural law that eliminate or bracket revealed Christian theology. Such theories claim to know the origin, shape, and end of nature and human nature without reference to the Creator, the image of God, the Spirit, or Jesus. Since the sixteenth century, such theories have been predominant among both secular and Christian thinkers" (p. 233–34). After describing several concrete weaknesses that he sees in atheological accounts of natural law, Leithart turns to an extended discussion of Thomas Aquinas's discussion of law in *Summa Theologiae*, noting the theological and biblical setting and framework for Thomas's presentation. Next, Leithart offers a challenge to the concept of nature and whether it can do the work that atheological natural law theories try to make it do. Is nature primarily about a given, an original, or an ideal? Is natural opposed to conventional, unnatural, or supernatural? Can our understanding of nature exist apart from the cultivation of nature? And how does any of this mesh with the biblical account of creation? And for that matter, of sin and redemption? Leithart concludes: "When natural law is uprooted from its biblical-theological framework, Christians must regard it as a heap of theoretical fragments that retains its semblance of coherence only by surreptitious borrowings from divine law" (p. 256).

Conclusion

How should we think about whether natural law exists and what its utility is, considering the diversity of viewpoints about it as a theory and all its various contours? The fact that there is a multiplicity of perspectives testifies, we think with a tinge of irony, to the enduring reality that a natural moral law exists and that various traditions attempt to articulate it and theorize about it. Rather than outright contradiction issuing from the viewpoints represented in this volume, we think the various traditions harmonize in bearing witness to an account of the natural law in compelling ways, fitting each tradition's respective approach to questions of objective morality.

Amid the disagreements, all the views represented here affirm that the natural law—though natural, earthly, and creaturely—is still a product of eternal law. Nature, in other words, is born of grace from the start.

Today some Christians aver that the West's return to the natural law will determine our future viability, while others argue that our dismissal of it will lead to flourishing. Various debates roiling even conservative Catholicism and Protestantism hinge upon how the natural law is to be realized in law and protected by constitutional writ. The editors of this volume write as confessional Christians (Catholic and Protestant). We believe that the natural law *can* persuade individuals who do not share our beliefs. At the least, we believe that it can neutralize the more strident forms of progressive thought that often view their own explanatory power with solipsistic triumph. Whether it will is left to be decided by contextual matters that are determined by individualized debates and conversations. Regardless of its persuasive power, both of us are convinced of the need for Christians to have more familiarity and facility with natural law categories—not primarily to persuade the potentially unpersuadable, but for Christians to better understand the logic and coherence of how we believe God has ordered the moral universe.

CHAPTER 1

The Classical Understanding of Natural Law

MICHAEL PAKALUK

My task is to give an exposition of the natural law as understood within the classical framework. I begin, therefore, by saying what I mean by the "classical framework" and then go on to say what is meant within this framework when one claims that there is a natural law. From there I will discuss the content, promulgation, and authority of the natural law so conceived.

The Classical Framework

By the "classical framework" we are *not* to understand some kind of basic philosophy, conceived of as dominant, say, at high periods of Athens and Rome, which through some kind of blind force produced an impetus that lasted centuries until its energy dissipated. The classical world had a tremendous diversity of thought. Consider the four schools of Hellenistic philosophy: Stoic, Epicurean, Skeptical, and Peripatetic. It would have baffled an observer in imperial Rome to propose that these diverse outlooks constituted a single framework.

I mean, then, the deliberate culling out and appropriation by cultures animated by Jewish, Christian, and Islamic beliefs of views in the classical world about nature, human nature, and society that were esteemed as truthful in light of those beliefs. Historically, this classical framework has not been confined to classical periods but has continued to have force insofar as classical sources were regarded as important in education. For example, the education of the American founders was strongly classical, and so were their beliefs. Clerics, lawyers, and civil servants in England and the British Empire were shaped immensely by this "classical framework" through at least the mid-nineteenth century.

This classical framework gained its life and coherence not simply by the culling and appropriation of views regarded as congenial and truthful but also by the strenuous rejection of views from the classical world regarded as false, deceptive, and harmful. Examples from the tradition include St. Augustine's arguments against academic skepticism and Boethius's arguments against fate as an irrational necessitation.

Regarding natural law, the important classical sources, selected out and appropriated as particularly truthful, would be the philosophical writings of Cicero (especially *De Legibus*), Aristotle's *Nicomachean Ethics*, and the *Corpus Iuris Civilis* compiled under the Emperor Justinian. These sources were interpreted in light of the Decalogue, which was regarded as a restatement within divine law of the basic principles of natural law, as well as the two commandments of charity—love of God and love of neighbor as oneself—which have been regarded since Christ as somehow the origin and source of natural law (Matt 22:37–40). Note that the obligation to honor God, publicly as well as in private, was regarded as plainly within the natural law, not a distinctive viewpoint of faith that could be put aside without peril to the integrity of the natural law.

The tradition strenuously rejected the view that all obligation was solely "by convention," that only expedience (or pleasure) mattered for action to the exclusion of a real *bonum honestum*, and that human beings are by nature at war with one another. Thrasymachus in the *Republic* and Callicles in the *Gorgias* represent standard positions that, it was believed, had to be refuted by adherents of natural law.

Today some might prefer to turn to literature and history to illustrate natural law, say, Anna throwing herself under a train, Raskolnikov's tormented conscience, the Lincoln-Douglas debates, or Nuremberg. The classical world could cite Antigone, and it had its occasional witness from history too, such as Socrates' walking away from the Thirty. But in general, reflections on the natural law proceeded as if those sorts of illustration were hardly necessary, on the grounds that evidence for the natural law was abundant and ordinary.

As in other matters, St. Thomas Aquinas in *Summa Theologiae* shows a great mastery of all of the main sources and harmonizes them with great skill; hence, it is reasonable for an inquirer to look first of all to him for a representation of this classical view of natural law. The account I give here is heavily indebted to Aquinas. Moreover, when a text sometimes needs to be cited to corroborate that a position falls within the classical understanding, I regard it as convenient to cite Aquinas rather than the sources on which he in turn depends.

The Purpose of a Theory of Natural Law

Today we perhaps bring to the topic of natural law the supposition that it is a neutral meeting place for persons of goodwill that can serve as a starting point for rational persuasion as regards controversial topics such as legal abortion. Although framed in terms of rights, not as laws, the prestige of the Universal Declaration of Human Rights has underwritten this supposition, as also the work of Germain Grisez and his followers in developing the so-called "new" natural law, which is regarded as valuable on this supposition.

In the classical understanding, the natural law does not and cannot play such a role, any more than a reiteration of the Decalogue could play such a role. The fact of legal abortion would seem to prove the point.

Consider what has unquestionably been regarded as a natural law precept throughout the tradition, "Thou shalt not murder." We may take the precept to mean: any human being is enjoined from causing the death, deliberately or through negligence, of any other human being who is a nonaggressor. Everyone today accepts this precept and would say without hesitation that they accept it. Almost no one who supports legal abortion does so by rejecting this precept. But if we ask how it could be rationally tenable for someone to accept the natural law precept against murder while supporting legal abortion, we find it is quite possible to do so. Someone might reject that human beings constitute a uniform natural kind, believing that one human being can be more or less human than another—with unborn being less human than born. Or he might deny that there are essences—that is, unrealized powers that from the start define the kind of thing which an individual is—and thus he denies that what it is to be human may be entirely present in something so undeveloped as an embryo. Or perhaps he denies finality: he does not believe that natural processes of development have an inherent goal, such that, as Tertullian put it, "that which is to be a man is a man." Or perhaps he denies the distinction between substance and accident and entertains the possibility that the location of an unborn child, inside or outside the womb, might matter as to how he should treat it. Or he might not accept that there is a natural teleology of the sex act, such that its purpose is to conceive offspring: hence, he might believe that someone who engages in a sex act and becomes pregnant can intelligibly claim that she has become pregnant "against her will" and that, therefore, the unborn child can could be construed as an interloper, like J. J. Thomson's violinist, licitly separable from the mother on grounds similar to self-defense.

It may be granted that all of these positions involve confusions and commit someone to acting in ways that he wouldn't elsewhere. They serve self-interest and therefore appear to be forms of special pleading and rationalizations. But the confusions and rationalizations do not seem to pertain to the natural law aspect of the matter but rather in such notions as natural kinds, natural teleology, essences, substance, and purposes. Such notions find clarification in Platonic, Aristotelian, and Thomistic philosophy of logic, philosophy of nature, and metaphysics, not in natural law or a theory of natural law.

But what would be the purpose of a theory of natural law if not to underwrite a neutral meeting place for persuasion? One might wonder why a theory needs a purpose beyond its being true. Yet let's say that the upshot of the classical theory of natural law is similar to what one finds in C. S. Lewis's magnificent lectures *The Abolition of Man*. There, Lewis argues that what we find important about natural law is bound up with truths about human nature, society, and the natural world. These truths arguably stand or fall together, and they are grasped with the heart as much as the intellect. A theory of natural law should reveal those truths. The classical understanding of natural law reminds us, then, of how those truths are not grasped and passed on of their own accord; rather, they require, in our time also, a careful attitude of selection and curation, which seems possible only through institutions of education and culture which are explicitly dedicated to doing so. Countering the *Green Book* requires replacing it with an education, not pretending to correct it with a rational system.

The Claim That There Is a Natural Law

What is meant within the classical framework when one claims that there is a natural law?

Note first that law in the classical conception is internally related to other realities, such that it cannot be defined without also fixing those realities—in the way that, for comparison, to define *sibling* requires reference to parents with at least two offspring.

Consider for example a working syllabus for a university class. A syllabus serves as law for the class insofar as it prescribes which readings are to be done and when, and it proscribes absences from class. But there cannot be a working syllabus without a *class* for which it serves as the syllabus, an *instructor* who devises it and whose authority is binding, and a *subject matter* the mastery of which among the students serves as a common goal or good. Likewise, on the classical understanding, law implies a *community*, an *authority*, and a *common good* which it promotes, and it furthermore needs to be given or promulgated to those it binds—in something like the way an instructor hands out the syllabus to the class and goes over it with them.

Thus to give an account of a specifically *natural law* on the classical understanding would require giving at the same time an account of the *natural community* that it covers, the *natural authority* who issues it, the *natural common goal* that it advances, and its *natural* mode of *promulgation*. All of these must be identified, fixed, and explained.

But let us begin with its content nonetheless. In the classical understanding, it consists basically of articulable and naturally specifiable precepts that (1) enjoin piety to those responsible for our being, (2) forbid harm to others, (3) protect procreation, and (4) function as an outline or minimum of how we are to act toward one another, to be further filled in, in a person's particular facts and circumstances by free discretion. These three components were regarded as well-captured in a traditional saying of Roman law, that justice (*iustitia*)—or, better, fundamental lawfulness—consists in living virtuously, not harming anyone, and rendering to each his due.[1]

By a *precept*, I mean a statement that prescribes, proscribes, or permits an action or omission. We do not need excessive refinement here, but it helps to

---

1. *Honeste vivere; alterum non laedere; suum cuique tribuere.* Justinian, *Institutes*, 1.1.3

keep in mind that a precept always carries with it a scope in regard to how someone is enjoined: for example, "show hospitality, that is, *to strangers*," "do not harm another, that is, *human being*." A scope is implicit too in those who are enjoined. For instance, *those other than strangers* are to show hospitality to strangers.

To say that a precept is "articulable" is to say that we acknowledge it implicitly, we are in principle capable of articulating it explicitly, and we will recognize another's apt expression as articulating well what we might have said.

If a precept contains a general term, it is "specifiable," in the way that any general term can be broken into subclasses and come to be regarded as a genus embracing several species. Consider for example the general term *harm*. We can say, "Do no harm," which gives the genus, or we can begin to break down the genus into species. For properly natural law, all its features and relations need to be natural as well. Therefore, we are looking for, so to speak, naturally occurring or naturally recognizable species of harm. To harm is deliberately or through negligence to cause to suffer uncompensated loss against someone's will. What we lose are goods. A human being is naturally situated in a society with possessions and with persons related to him as his family or friends, enjoying a standing as decent and reliable (that is, he has a "good name"). Therefore, the natural species of harm include:

- harm to him in his life or person by murder or manslaughter,
- harm to him in his property by theft,
- harm to him in his relations, and
- harm to him in his standing by false accusation.

These species yield the second table of the Decalogue, assuming that adultery is an especially salient harm against our relations as it attacks the naturally occurring personal bond of marriage and saliently attacks procreation:

- Do not murder.
- Do not steal.
- Do not commit adultery.
- Do not bear false witness.

Likewise, "those responsible for our being" can be naturally specified into God or gods and parents. It is true that the virtue of *pietas* in the classical understanding was regarded as extending to one's city or country as well—consider Socrates in the *Crito*. But the city would not be suitable to differentiating a properly natural species of piety because people can change which city is theirs and in principle change or even abolish its constitution, effectively ending their city. Moreover, many human beings have lived in social arrangements not as complete as cities, such as tribes, or more extensive such as nation-states or empires.

So then this natural specification of *pietas* gives rise roughly to the first table of the Decalogue:

- worship the true God,
- keep the Sabbath, and
- honor your father and mother.

Here, "the Sabbath" stands in for due piety, and the proscriptions against idols and irreverence are understood as necessary for finding our way to the true God.

In the classical conception it is presumed that people not irrationally intuit or discern the existence of divine (immortal) beings, with a chief divine being among them, who are responsible for the blessings we enjoy. Indeed, widespread public atheism (which, although public, remains a minority position) began only in the twentieth century. One might follow Roman usage and refer to the chief deity recognized by a people or culture as the *numen supremum*, their "most august deity."[2] But I shall use the more common name in classical natural law literature, God.

The claim that there is a natural law is the claim that we are designed by nature to articulate these precepts and furthermore to regard ourselves as bound by them by nature. To say that we are naturally disposed to regard ourselves as bound by them by nature is to say that we typically take their observance as bound up with our being, with who we are, and that we take ourselves to be somehow undone if we violate them in serious ways. The

---

2. The Vatican II document, *Dignitatis Humanae,* when it wishes to use an expression for the common ground among all human beings in the right to religious liberty in recognition of the classical roots of this liberty, uses precisely this expression.

first table serves the role of supporting this claim upon us of natural law. But more on this later.

The Natural Setting of a Human Being

We need to pause and consider the natural setting of a human being according to the classical conception as well as the character of self-love.

Getting straight about the natural setting of a human being is important for seeing how natural law is teleological, as making possible human social life. Getting straight about self-love is important because, on the classical understanding, natural law functions mainly as a structure of side constraints on the pursuit of self-love properly understood. Therefore, one needs an account of self-love to see how this structure is conceived of as being filled in and to avoid the misunderstanding that natural law precepts work in the manner of motivations.

It is important to grasp that, on the classical understanding, to say that some kind of fundamental lawfulness is "natural" for human beings is to say not only that it is somehow discerned naturally and somehow has an authority by nature prior to human convention but also that it is part of the provision of nature for humankind. Natural law itself represents a kind of *philanthropia* of nature and of "nature's God" toward the human race.

Perhaps because they lived among animals, the ancients were deeply impressed by nature's lack of natural provision for an individual human being from birth. An ox, for instance, springs fully developed from its mother's belly upon birth and immediately starts walking about. It has a warm coat, sturdy hooves, natural sources of food, and shelter. Human beings lack all these things. On the other hand, the ancients noted, human beings are provided with intelligence.

Three conclusions apparently follow from such considerations. First, if we distinguish between lone animals (like hawks) and social animals dwelling in colonies or herds, human beings must be assigned to the latter. They are notably inept for surviving as individuals.

Second, human beings are meant by nature to use their intelligence corporately to meet their basic needs for food, clothing, footing, and shelter. In the classical world, this is what "the market" is, with its division of labor, trade, and the development of skills for supplying helpful tools—a natural institution for the corporate meeting of our basic needs. To say that "man is by nature a city-dwelling animal," as Aristotle puts it in his *Politics*,[3] is actually to say that human beings are meant by nature to dwell in a social group whose market has grown complete enough that it can meet basic human needs with relative ease—which is what a city is.

A market of such a degree of development will need to be protected, and disputes within the market will need to be adjudicated. A robust market also makes leisure possible, not only leisure for the whole city for a time for religious and harvest festivals but also permanent leisure for some citizens who can then be dedicated to the development of culture and knowledge.

Therefore, the natural setting of a human being, in the classical setting, is within a society that has a complete market, a defensive army, courts of law, a class devoted to the use of leisure, and a government sufficient to oversee the coordinated working of these parts. This is the basic form of life intended by nature for human beings. Such a description of the rudiments of a city on the classical conception gives the state of nature for human beings—not the wandering hunter-gatherer of Rousseau or Locke.

But this realization leads to a third conclusion. Clearly human beings would be well equipped to meet corporately their basic needs only if each person antecedently ruled out simply taking what he needed from another by force or stealth and instead was disposed "to truck, barter, and exchange" for it (in Adam Smith's famous phrase). And human beings would not be inclined to live as closely together as is needed to form a city if each regarded every other as a potential threat to his own life or his family. Therefore, it is clear that nature's equipment or provision for human beings, for corporately meeting their basic needs, would need to include not simply intelligence in the sense of craftiness but also intelligence exercised in relation to one another, some kind of fundamental lawfulness that makes it practically attainable to live in peace with one another. Obviously too this fundamental lawfulness would need to precede the formation of a government and its setting down of human law in a city.

The account of the natural setting of human beings on a classical conception therefore clarifies why human beings need to be equipped by nature with a fundamental lawfulness the content of which we have already seen.

---

3. *Politikon* in the context means "such as to live in a city, a *polis*."

The Nature of Genuine Self-Love

So much for the natural setting of human beings on the classical conception. But what in that conception motivates them? Why do they do everything they do? On the classical conception natural law functions as a set of side-constraints. It rules out theft, for instance, thereby opening up a space for trade. It rules out adultery and fornication, therefore opening up a space for marriage. It rules out impiety, therefore opening up a space for stable relations across generations and a common loyalty for the city. So before explaining how natural law acquires this status, we must say something about that upon which it is meant to be a side-constraint.

In the classical world, it was a truism that everyone without exception, and not by deliberate decision ("by nature," then), strives above all to attain happiness (*eudaimonia* in Greek, *beatitudo* in Latin). But happiness was regarded as initially a formal goal: the *sort of thing* it had to be was clear—it had to satisfy fully any longing, and upon reflection stand as someone's attaining what ultimately his life was for—but the possession or attainment of *what* precisely should truly count as happiness was regarded as a matter of lasting disagreement. This lasting disagreement about what materially counted as happiness was regarded as arising from human nature and the human condition. "The many," and all of us some of the time, would be disposed to take happiness to be a matter of attaining great wealth, power, fame, honor, or pleasures. But "the wise," and most of us in our better moments, discern that it involves virtue—first acquiring virtue, so as to become a good ("decent," "upright," "praiseworthy") human being, and then putting that virtue into practice.

As the practice of a life of virtue requires staying alive and is helped by material instruments ("wealth"), gives someone genuine strength of soul and leads to a robust network of friends ("power"), earns him a good reputation in their eyes ("fame" and "honor"), and carries with it a self-sufficiency of enjoyment and tranquility ("pleasure"), then it is clear (or so "the wise" conclude) that when "the many" take something like wealth actually *to be happiness* (a foolish idea, as even a little thought will show), then they are, not unaccountably, wresting away some aspect related to a life of virtue and exaggerating its importance, as if it were the whole, beyond reasonable bounds.[4]

---

4. Such is the line of thought in Aristotle's *Nicomachean Ethics* 1.8 and in that great work of synthesis of classical thought, Boethius, *Consolation of Philosophy*.

As Boethius's *Consolation* shows, a prominent idea in this line of thought is that a human being, in attaining *beatitudo*, is thereby imitating God, who enjoys untrammeled *beatitudo*, and is "possessing" him thereby, in the way that we possess something by imitating or "participating" in it. To succeed in living a life of virtue then, from this point of view, is to undergo a process of *theosis*, becoming like God in the way that we can.[5] That a virtuous life is one of *theosis* survives today prominently in the moral theology of the Eastern churches. The belief was by no means the exclusive possession of "the wise." Ordinary people accepted stories of the deification of heroes. They tended to construe glorious death in battle by young men as a sharing in the divine and therefore not at odds with these men having attained some extreme of *beatitudo*. They also were disposed to interpret the deepest natural urges as disposing to some kind of imitation of the divine—procreation for instance was easily construed as the corporate sharing in immortality by mortal animals, the only way a mortal animal can bodily attain anything like immortality.[6]

An important upshot of happiness as a kind of *imitatio*, which we can realize here and now and not in some distant future, is that it helps us to see why in the classical conception there was little temptation to instrumentalize action, perhaps by doing something fundamentally unlawful now in order ostensibly to "maximize" virtuous activity later on. Suppose the Thirty tell Socrates to arrest an innocent man, and he walks away instead of complying. By living virtuously he is attaining happiness as best he can: if the Thirty put him to death out of anger, no matter, as he has lived a good life and no one lives forever. (So Plato represents Socrates as reasoning, in fact, in the *Crito*.)[7] Besides, soldiers show how we must stay at our posts and accept death if necessary.

Another upshot is that, from within this project of living a life of virtue out of proper self-love, the following of the natural law gets endorsed,

---

5. The door is left open that upon death we can possess God in some fuller sense: Socrates, Plato, and Boethius clearly believed so.

6. Aristotle did not regard himself as saying something exoteric when he articulated such a view in *De Anima* or apparently in his work on household administration, the *Economics*.

7. The proposition that he should do something unjust and collaborate with the Thirty, to prolong his life, is the proposition that either he turn away from happiness, or, if he succeeds as he should in later seeking due punishment for his injustice, he should introduce shame, humiliation, and servitude into his life.

12 • Natural Law

additionally, as the fundamental way someone practices the cardinal virtue of justice.

I cannot review the doctrine of the cardinal virtues in its fullness on the classical understanding. But in outline it is the view that, for a human being to become good, each of his main centers of motivation needs to be rendered good. But this requires that a center of motivation become rational as best it can, by either becoming amenable to reason or itself exemplifying good reason. There are four such centers of motivation and therefore four main, or cardinal, virtues: practical reason, the virtue of which is prudence (*phronēsis, prudentia*); the will, the virtue of which is justice (*dikaiosunē, iustitia*); desire, the virtue of which is moderation (*sōphrosunē, temperantia*); and the boldness-fear complex, which we call "fight or flight," the virtue of which is courage (*andreia, fortitudo*). The relevant point here is that someone who has a correct understanding of his own good and who poses the question, "Why should I on reflection follow the natural law?" has a strong answer forthcoming: happiness requires that I become good and act virtuously; my being good requires my being so in all of my powers; to be just is through acts of will to observe reasonability in my relations with others; and the natural law sets down some basic side-constraints that must be followed if I am to observe reasonability in my relations with others.

The Promulgation of Natural Law in the Sense of Its Basis

We are now in a position to ask how human beings on the classical conception are led by nature to formulate the main precepts of the natural law and accept their authority.

We said that an account of natural law on the classical conception needs to give an account of the naturalness, so to speak, of the content of that law, of how a law having such a content is by some natural provision promulgated, of what natural community it binds and for what purpose, and of how naturally it has the appearance of being binding in virtue of being set down by its own, proper authority, presumably higher than any human authority.

Regarding its content, it has been claimed that on the classical conceptions it consists of basically two precepts, which are then differentiated into naturally more specific precepts: (1) show piety, namely to God and to parents, and (2) harm no one, either persons, possessions, relations, or standing. We have seen that its community is human beings in general, conceived of as placed within their natural setting, and it promotes their abiding together in peace, with a view toward their developing friendliness toward one another.

So next we need to consider how this law is naturally promulgated. To do so, we need to examine a series of related concepts: the *good*, the *due*, the strictly due or the *debitum*, the right (Greek, *dikaion*, Latin, *ius*), and then *law* as related to these. We shall conceive of a precept of natural law as a generalization of a claim of natural right, which in turn is based upon claims about the relevant goods in play.

The account of how the second table of the natural law is naturally promulgated is easier for us to grasp, so we will begin there, focusing on murder and theft rather than adultery, which brings in special considerations.

Nature on the classical understanding is a system of beings and processes working for ends and structures that are ordered as toward ends. To deny, then, that there are ends in the world—to deny teleology—is to deny nature and therefore to reject from the start any possibility of identifying a law *by nature*. In the classical understanding, an end, a goal, and a good all amount to the same thing, and they are all qualified coordinately: an apparent good is an apparent goal, a good by nature is a goal by nature, a highest good is a highest or ultimate goal, and so on. Therefore, to deny teleology is also to deny that there are any *goods* genuinely in the world, that is, goods apart from "as if" goods, which project upon or attribute to it in view of our purposes. But if one grants that there are ends in the world, then one at the same time grants that some things may additionally be due or not.

In illustration of these points let us begin with the simple example of an immature flowering plant growing in someone's backyard. Even to use the word *immature* is to suppose that it has a natural goal of growing to a certain height and then producing flowers and seeds. As these are natural goals, they are therefore natural goods for the plant. Let us next say that some thing or action is due to a thing if it contributes to its attaining or maintaining its goal. Daily sunlight and watering, then, are due to the plant because it attains its goal by them.

But these are not strictly due, so to speak, as the plant could in principle be placed in a dark room sometimes, watered once in a while, and

14 • Natural Law

still reach its goal. The reason is that regularities in nature take the form of propensities and have the character of being true "for the most part" (*hōs epi to polu*, in Aristotle's phrase). Let us say, then, that although daily sunlight and water are due to the plant, in the sense that as a rule they are to be provided, if the plant is to attain its goal, still, these things are not strictly due. On the other hand, that the plant not be chopped down, or incinerated with a blow torch, is strictly due. Let us say that if something is such that a thing cannot attain its goal *at all without it*, then that thing is strictly due. Likewise, if a thing cannot attain its goal *at all with it*, then its omission is strictly due. Note that the strictly due is clearer and more obvious than the merely due. It is perfectly plain that a chopped down plant will never attain maturity, while, as mentioned, there is considerable scope for overcast days and even brief droughts in its needed supply of sunlight and water. The strictly due we will also call a *debitum*. That a plant not be cut down is a *debitum* relative to the good of the plant; that on any day it be watered is something *merely due*.

Once we concede that something is due, we can express this fact in an impersonal rational precept, as in this case: "The plant is to be watered daily." That statement, which employs a passive gerundive, is the kind of expression that might be found in instructions for care of the plant. A *debitum* is also formulable using a gerundive: "The plant is not to be cut down." That it is strictly due rather than merely due is not clear merely from the expression, although one might wish to strengthen the expression and write something like, "Under no circumstances is the plant to be cut down" or even, perhaps, as in technical legal writing, "The plant shall not be cut down."

Note that there is *a reason* why it is good for a plant of a certain kind to be watered once daily. For example, gardeners know that a container plant generally needs to be watered each day. Suppose the backyard plant in our example is in a container, and that that is the reason underlying the precept, "The plant is to be watered daily." But this individual plant is to be watered in virtue of features that it shares with other plants of its kind. Therefore, we might also say, "This plant and others relevantly like it are to be watered daily," or "This plant like all container plants is to be watered daily." That is to say, any rational precept stating what is due will do so in virtue of some feature which can potentially be possessed by many individuals, and therefore any rational precept stating what is due implies a generalization having the character of a law. The precept implies what we called a scope.

For all of these precepts involving plants, we can add if we wish the qualification *naturally*, since they are all true of a plant in virtue of the nature of the plant, not as a direct result of any human decision. (That a container plant is in a container is the result of a human decision, but that a plant in a container needs daily water is not the result of a human decision.)

Plants are mainly passive. But animals are active, and therefore not simply *that something be done to them* but also *that they themselves do something* can contribute to their good. For example, it contributes to a predator's good if they hunt for food each day. A zookeeper might throw them meat, but it is better, and it certainly better contributes to their good, for the most part, if they hunt for their food. Thus, for such a predator, that it hunt each day is due to it given its nature, and a gerundive expression of the form "It is (naturally) due to this predator to hunt for food on a daily basis" is true.

Or suppose fancifully that our container plant were endowed with intelligent active power, and furthermore its nature was such that it was good for it that it intelligently take care of itself rather than be taken care of, that is, that its natural good or goal was that it become a plant which cared for itself. Then that it receive water daily would be naturally due to it, and that, out of deliberate intelligence, it watered itself daily would also be due to it.

Etymologically, the word *duty* means an action done with deliberate intelligence that is due to the agent as contributing to his good. Therefore, a plant like this would have the natural duty of watering itself on a daily basis. Similarly for such a plant it would be a *debitum*, that is, it would be a strict natural duty, that it not through deliberate intelligence cause itself to be chopped down or incinerated.

If there were a plant with the power to care for itself and whose natural good were that it care for itself, then anyone who wanted to take care of this plant and advance its good would need now to keep two things in mind: first, what passively is required for the plant to flourish, that it be watered daily, and, second, what actively is required for the plant to flourish, that it take care of itself by watering itself. To benefit the plant "against its will" would be against its active due, and to harm it, say, by cutting it down,

16 • Natural Law

would be against both its active and its passive due. Harm to the plant would necessarily be a matter of doing it harm "against its will."[8]

So then with these things having been set down, here is the general shape of the argument that needs to be pursued. Suppose it is the case that for any two persons who happen to engage with each other, that is, whose actions bear upon each other, it is good for them by nature that they act toward each other in a friendly way, that is, in a way appropriately respectful of the fact that each has self-mastery and a duty to care for himself. Then it is naturally due to them, each, to act friendlily to the other. Then it is naturally strictly due to them, each, that they not act unfriendlily. But for one person to cause deliberately or by negligence uncompensated loss in another against his will—that is, to harm him—would be unfriendly. Therefore, it is naturally strictly due to them, each, that they not harm each other. But, as we saw, the natural specification of goods and therefore of harm is as to person, property, relations, and standing. Therefore, it is naturally strictly due to them both that neither harm the other in person, property, relations, or standing.

The argument depends upon considering human beings as pairs with commutable goods at stake between them. It contrasts harms with voluntary exchanges, in which neither consents to suffer a loss to the gain of the other, except in exchange for a good received reciprocally from the other. That is to say, the argument depends upon a conception of what in the classical world was called right (*ius, dikaion*) as holding between them. Right can be conceived of as what retains peace and prepares for friendship between unrelated parties, who possess mastery over their actions and show self-love, in the exchange or not of goods between them. Natural law is simply the generalization of the scope of a claim of right to all human beings, because of the rational basis which underwrites a claim of right.

This is the basic schema for the promulgation of the natural law. If the derivation is obvious, given human nature, then natural law so understood is obvious by nature and its promulgation is natural.

---

8. Hence, when one person harms another, there are always two injuries: the loss, and the going against the other's will. The latter is the more important injury, as shown by the fact that the person injured may have been intending to give the taken good to the injurer as a gift: he would not deplore the mere loss of the good, but he would rightly deplore that his giving it as a gift had been taken away from him.

The Promulgation of the Natural Law in the Sense of Its Lawfulness

Therefore, we need to see how reasoning according to this schema is naturally obvious and obviously implies general laws. As a preliminary, we need to look first at how an analogue of the principle of noncontradiction works in the case of practical reason. In the classical understanding, all prohibitive law is regarded as imposing a side-constraint. It rules out a violation of a practical principle of noncontradiction, which would be the result if the prohibited action were done, on the grounds that doing that action would contradict the pursuit of some good to which one is already committed. So we must examine how laws that operate as side-constraints arise and when it would be appropriate to say that these laws are recognized by us and followed "by nature."

Remember, we are focusing on the second table. The precepts of the second table are regarded as side-constraints on action for someone engaged in the project of attaining happiness for himself and his own. For example, he may develop a business for trading with others, but in those trades he must take care not to defraud the other, which is a kind of theft. Avoiding fraud is a side-constraint on pursuing a living. Or in his living alongside others, one can expect that various strong emotions will unavoidably beset him, such as anger because of felt wrongs, or envy at someone's success. But he must learn to resolve these problems by control over his emotions and by prudential action (and perhaps when necessary recourse to some forum for justice) rather than by eliminating through murder the person he believes is the cause of them. Avoiding murder is most basically a side-constraint on living alongside others.

In the classical conception, reason exercised speculatively ranges over the whole universe: everything that is, is apt to be affirmed to be, and everything that is not is apt to be denied—that is, affirmed not to be. Similarly, reason exercised practically ranges over the whole universe. It is the same power as speculative reason, and therefore it has the same scope, although it considers each thing that is as a goal or good, to be affirmed that it be or come to be, in the respect in which it is. Practical reason, like speculative reason, has an unrestricted range. It is not of its nature restricted to the concerns of the reasoner; it is not originally egoistic. Everything that is good is apt to be affirmed as good, even if notionally, at least through an act of the will manifested in praise, and everything that is bad is apt to be resisted, even if notionally, at least through an act of the will of complaint or of praising its opposite.[9]

Classically, in speculative reason, it is regarded as universally true that nothing can both be and not be at the same time and in the same respect. This claim is thought to be true because of the nature of being and existence. Often it is referred to in this form as the principle of non-contradiction (PNC). Sometimes the claim is also given as "nothing is to be affirmed of the same thing at the same time and in the same respect," and sometimes this formulation too is called the PNC. But note that the second formulation actually governs our judgments and expressions. It is a principle or law that binds us in the manner of a side-constraint in the investigation of any truth. Strictly, it is a principle of practical reason, not of speculative reason, because affirmation, on this principle, is conceived of as a kind of endorsement of something as good because it is true. For clarity's sake, then, let's call this second principle the law of noncontradiction (LNC). Thus:

PNC: Nothing can both be and not be at the same time and in the same respect.
LNC: Nothing is to be affirmed and denied of the same thing at the same time and in the same respect.

There are four pertinent observations at the point about the LNC. First, it is a proscription that follows from a general description. The LNC tells us not to think or to express ourselves in certain ways, and, clearly, it follows and we rightly take it to follow from the PNC. Therefore, fundamental prescriptions may follow from fundamental descriptions. One might say: most fundamentally, from the nature of reality, it follows that we are bound to act in certain ways.

Second, the LNC functions in the manner of a side-constraint. That is, it does not tell us anything to think or to assert; neither does not tell us anything not to think or not to assert. It tells us, in our process of deciding

---

9. The Psalms are filled with such basic acts of affirmation of good and complaint about the bad. They reflect a basic fact about human nature and the human condition.

what to think or to assert, that we ought never to commit ourselves to judgments or affirmations that have the form of a contradiction. We might also understand the LNC as a proscription on a hypothesis: if one is judging or affirming P, then one is forbidden from judging or affirming not-P.

Third, the LNC admits of further specification for different domains that have more specific principles for the "beings" specific to that domain, such as geometry. For instance, one specification of the LNC suitable for geometry would be: nothing is to be affirmed to be larger than another and denied to be larger than that other at the same time and in the same respect. This specified form of the LNC would be just as obvious to us as the general form if it were obvious that the relation of "larger than" is asymmetrical.[10]

Fourth, the reason why the LNC follows from the PNC is a natural duty to care as regards judging and affirming the truth. The LNC follows from the PNC because if the PNC is true, then any combination of a judgment with its contradictory will contain at least one falsehood. To affirm a contradiction is inevitably to affirm a falsehood; not to care about whether one is affirming a contradiction is not to care about whether one is affirming a falsehood. But we have a duty to care about affirming truth because we have a natural love of truth. From the natural love of truth of each human being, it follows that truth and affirmation of truth are goods for us, from which there follows a natural duty to affirm truth. Therefore, one is strictly proscribed from affirming a contradiction; moreover, if one affirms a judgment, presumably on the grounds that it is true, then one is strictly proscribed from affirming its contradictory opposite, as it would be false on the condition that the first were true.[11]

We can now formulate for practical reason a principle and law similar to the PNC and the LNC. The principle would be that *nothing is good and*

---

10. Perhaps on the grounds that one thing is larger than another only if the latter stands to the former as part to whole, and nothing can be a part of itself—this seems to have been Aquinas's reasoning, see *ST* I-II, 94.2.

11. On the classical conception, the LNC gets a different justification from modern accounts. Modern accounts are formalistic and pragmatic. Contradictions are conceived of as being ruled out in formal systems, and the inference rules for formal systems are set up in such a way that from a contradiction any other proposition follows. Therefore, to derive a contradiction is to permit the derivation of all formulas in a formal system, in which case the formal system is incapable of modeling a restricted class of true propositions. But under the classical conception, which is very different, the affirmation of a falsehood is itself proscribed.

bad at the same time and in the same respect. Call this the practical PNC or P-PNC. Although it is an *is* or *descriptive* statement, since it considers things in relation to goals, it looks at them as it were practically. The corresponding law would be that *nothing is to be pursued and avoided at the same time and in the same respect.* Call this the practical law of noncontradiction or P-LNC. This law is obviously relevant to practice.

> P-PNC: Nothing is both good and bad at the same time and in the same respect.
>
> P-LNC: Nothing is to be both pursued and avoided at the same time and in the same respect.

The P-LNC does not say to pursue anyone's good or to wish anything in particular, or its contrary, to anyone, but only that, for example, on the assumption that good is being wished to someone, nothing opposed to that good is to be wished.

But it is naturally obvious that by nature it is good for each of two persons, who are in a position to engage with each other as respect to goods that are theirs, should live in such a way as to be at peace and to keep open the fostering of friendly relations. Therefore, it is due that each be treated in this way and so treat the other. Moreover, it is strictly due that neither offend nor be offended by the other in ways that would entirely rule out immediate peace and prospects of friendship. And each seeks and loves this mode of associating antecedently because of the social nature of human beings and the capacity of the will to see that this is good and will it as good. Therefore, to seek to gain at the other's loss without reciprocal compensation and against his will—that is, to harm him—would be to pursue what one is by nature committed to avoiding. As the naturally obvious species of harm are harms against someone's person, possessions, relations, and standing, then it is naturally obvious that harming someone in any of these ways is ruled out in the manner of a side constraint. But as this reasoning, as carried out in any particular case, is obviously generalizable in scope, given its basis, to anyone's engagement with any human being, then the precepts of the second table indicate what fundamental lawfulness consists of for us by nature.

The First Table

Aristotle and Cicero both held that it was obvious that human beings had a natural friendship for one another and were meant by nature to live cooperatively at peace. That truth alone would be sufficient to ground the idea that the paradigmatic mode of association among human beings who are "at arm's length" would be what traditionally was called "voluntary commutative exchange," that is, that neither one gains at the other's loss without reciprocal compensation freely agreed upon by each. We can see that this mode of association is good (and therefore *ius*) for any pair who engage each other, as well as for society generally; the will has universal scope; we are naturally inclined to will as good whatever is good—and these considerations alone are sufficient to hold that the subverting or destruction of this good by acts of harm, in any of the species of natural harm, would constitute a practical contradiction and therefore by nature is proscribed in the manner of a side-constraint.

However, to say this much is to leave out the strongest force of the natural law. Why for instance do those who violate it typically (not invariably), as was said, regard themselves as somehow "undone"? Why might a bad conscience plague them until they destroy themselves, like Anna in Tolstoy's novel? So we must consider other inclinations of the will, involving love of God and love of oneself, and their role in giving force to the precepts of natural law.

Here it is useful to bring in Aquinas's account of the natural movements of the human will, which I regard as faithful to the classical conception.[12] He distinguishes three. First, he says, the will is naturally moved to affirm as good whatever is good and wherever it is found—beautiful sunsets, creatures in the sea or air, fellow human beings, and so on. He calls this the will's movement by nature toward affirming good in general (*bonum in commune*). That the human will by nature would be disposed to pursue as good voluntary free exchanges simply because they are evidently good falls within this first natural movement. Such a movement and preference is real. It can and should be decisive when reasonable considerations so indicate, yet withal it is weak.

---

12. Aquinas, *ST* I-II, 10.1.

Second, he says, the will, recognizing that all visible goods are caused and dependent, traces them back as to their source and is naturally moved to affirm, love, and prefer that source as good. That source is God. The human will, then, has a natural movement to affirm as good what it conceives as the source of the goods we see and enjoy. This inclination lies at the basis of the first table and serves to reinforce the precepts of the second table.

Finally, he says, the will, after viewing goodness in general and its source, turns toward the power of the will itself and any power that helps us grasp reality and pursue the good. When it does so, it affirms as naturally good these powers, their objects, and the realization of their powers. This last natural movement of the will is what is otherwise known as "self-love." It is this third natural movement which makes it seem as if we hate ourselves if we violate the precepts of the second table.

So it is appropriate to say something briefly about the role of these other two natural movements of the will in natural law. They correspond, in the manner of natural analogues, to the traditional two commandments of charity: love of God and love of one's neighbor as oneself.

We saw that the by nature fundamental lawfulness in human beings, represented in the second table, should be interpreted teleologically in the classical understanding, and therefore, it should itself be regarded as a great benefit of nature. If there is a natural movement of the will to trace goods back to their source and affirm as good that source, then we are naturally moved to trace this fundamental lawfulness back to its source and affirm as good that source. This is what the first table effectively does. Remember what we said at the beginning, that any law must have four elements to count as a law at all: it must be a rational precept, be set down for a common good, be promulgated, and originate in someone with authority over and responsibility for the common good. We are now indicating how this fourth element is regarded as entering in, in the classical understanding of natural law. One might say, there can be no law without a lawgiver, and the second table cannot properly speaking be counted as law unless its provenance is recognized.

Sometimes laws are construed as performatives, since language suggestive of a performative is often included in the promulgation of a law, along the lines of, say, "Citizens are hereby notified that beginning January 1 of next year, . . ." To say that the promulgation of a law is a performative is to say that the law is made or made effective in its promulgation (even if it "comes into effect" at a later time). It accomplishes what it says. The first table can also be construed in this way as supplying performative language that pertains to the second table. It makes the second table effective precisely as natural law. The two tables wrote down precepts inherently articulable by us, as was said. To say that the first table works as a performative is to say that it is in inherent in an individual's articulation of a precept of natural law, precisely as law, that he regards it as both authoritative in its articulation and authoritative with an authority not deriving from himself or from any human being.[13]

The acknowledgement of a debt of piety typically reminds us of who we are and vivifies the duty to show honor, especially through obedience, to those responsible for who we are. The first table therefore reminds us of who we are and implies that the following of the law of the second table is not dispensable to who we are, while also vivifying the obligation to follow those precepts too because they are not of our own construction but set down by nature and nature's God.

Furthermore, through acknowledging the sources of our being, God, parents, and ancestors, we recognize a community to which we belong as "under" those sources, which is familial rather than arm's length. Fellow worshipers of God as the source of blessing and descendants of the same ancestors are meant to relate to one another in some fuller sense than according to the schema of voluntary commutative exchanges. Therefore, the first table too shows clearly the common good aimed at by the second table—namely, that by ruling out noxious harms the second table is meant to establish peace to provide the conditions for friendship under God. Its proximate end of peace is for the sake of the remote end of civil friendship.

What I am suggesting is that the first table's relationship to the second table admits of a teleological interpretation also: it plays the role of "completing" the aspect of law and claim of law of the second table, while showing the purpose of the second table.[14]

---

13. John Henry Newman's writing on conscience as the "voice of God" may be understood as a patient, phenomenological elaboration of this point. John Henry Newman, *An Essay in Aid of a Grammar of Assent* (London: Longmans, Green, 1903), 105-6.

14. For a fuller consideration of the teleological character of natural law, see Michael Pakaluk, "Two Conceptions of Natural Law," *Divinitas: Rivista Internazionale di Ricerca e di Critica Teologica*, LXII, Nova Series, numero unico (2019): 321–38.

Natural Law and "Other Selves"

We must touch briefly upon the role of self-love in natural law. We said that the duty to engage those who are "at arm's length" in the manner of a voluntary commutative exchange was obvious from the natural friendliness of any human being to any other. But Aristotle and Cicero also say that friendliness is a matter of regarding someone else as "another self." In the classical understanding, "love your neighbor as yourself" was thought somehow to generate the second table or at least to provide the best motive for following the second table. It was proverbial that "if men have friendship, they do not need justice." But how exactly would this work?

A parable helps illustrate the distinct motives at work. Suppose that two travelers through a desert region stop at the same oasis overnight and naturally enjoy food and conversation together in the evening. One of them eyes a fine necklace that the other one is carrying for trade and asks him what he would sell it for. After some haggling, the asking price, though fair, is more than the would-be buyer wishes to pay. So they do not reach a deal. Next morning, the one who wanted to buy it wakes up very early, looks for the necklace in the sleeping man's sachet, and takes it. He knows they are heading in opposite directions that day and that he will likely be far gone before the other discovers that the necklace is missing. That evening, he arrives at another oasis. At some point he inadvertently pulls out the necklace and notices that one man around the campfire is eyeing it with, it seems, a little too much interest. So he takes care to put it in a bag under his pillow. In the morning he is woken up by that other man trying to get into his bag. He pushes him away but to no avail: the other man grabs the necklace, then slugs him so hard that he is knocked out briefly. The other man gets away. When he regains consciousness, he goes to the manager of the oasis and angrily complains that someone stole his necklace and hires some men to go with weapons to get it back.

The parable is intended to illustrate St. Augustine's remark about natural law, that no matter how inveterate the thief, he still objects if someone steals something from him. In the parable, note the following.

- The institution of the oasis is premised on the presumption of friendliness. We are not surprised that the travelers show friendliness. The representation is thoroughly realistic.

- But it is not plausible to construe this natural friendliness as based on an implicit or hypothetical agreement, say, that both have hypothetically consented to the principle that each should seek only as much liberty as is consistent with the like liberty of the other. Rather, what is at work is a background consideration that if the one is to get something from the other, he should get it freely, through an agreement, by offering "equal" compensation.
- Again, we see that deception (theft) and coercion (robbery) are both at odds with this background consideration.
- Again, the thief's being able to relate in a friendly way with others in the new oasis on the second evening depends upon his hiding from the others that he is a thief. The trust and good name that he enjoys may be called his "standing." By nature we tend to extend it and expect it.
- Again, he is angry with the other who robs him rather than merely in pain and sorrow from the blow and loss. That is, he reacts as if to an injustice—he inevitably acts as though the other has violated a claim of *ius*.
- Finally, regarding the common good of the people in the parable as a whole, insofar as they violate the fundamental law "do not steal," they are all obviously worse off, as they pay large opportunity costs for the necessary deceptions, the impeded exchanges, and efforts of enforcement.

All of these remarks seem pertinent and true. But then we can also say the following, as regards self-love. Each of the travelers can additionally reason in this way.

It is my duty not to harm myself. Why? Because it is due to me to love myself, that is, through my deliberate actions to pursue and attain my good. But my good includes natural goods of self-preservation and forming a family. Therefore, it is strictly due to me not to harm myself in natural goods. But what I do through another, I do myself. Therefore, it is strictly due to me not to will that another harm me.[15] But the other is another self. Therefore, what is true of me is true of another like me.

---

15. I note in passing that formulations such as this seem puzzling—how could I will that someone take something from me against my will? That Aristotle devotes so many paragraphs to discussing

Therefore, it is strictly due to another that he not will that I harm him. But the other is another self. Therefore, what is true of another is true of me. Therefore, it is strictly due to me that I not will that I harm him.

The reasoning has this structure, at various points relying on the premise that the other is an "other self":

I love myself. → I cannot will that he harm me. → He is another self to me. → He loves himself (as I love myself). → He cannot will that I harm him. → He is another self to me. → I cannot will that I harm him.

The schema involves two distinct acts of reflection of oneself in another: first, taking one's own duty to oneself as a duty in him toward you, and, second, taking his duty toward you as a duty in yourself toward him. We measure his duty to ourselves in relation to our own interests, and then we measure our duty to him as the same as his duty to ourselves. The first is the easier to attain, indeed, we attain it inevitably, as the thief in the parable shows. The second is the more difficult, which is why "love your neighbor as yourself" is naturally reformulated as "do unto others as you would have them do unto you."[16]

---

the puzzle in his account of right (*dikaion*) shows that he was aware of this line of thought, indeed, he probably regarded it as automatic, intuitive, and obvious. Aristotle, *Ethica Nicomachea* 5, 9.11.

16. I have aimed to present the classical understanding of natural law in such a way as to show its power, appeal, and coherence. I have not presented the view through the exegesis of texts. For a careful reading of St. Thomas Aquinas showing the consistency of *ST* I-II, 94.2, with the view presented here, see Michael Pakaluk, "Cleaving the Natural Law at Its Joints," *The Thomist: A Speculative Quarterly Review* 88, no. 1 (January 2024): 41–76.

Biermann Response to Pakaluk

JOEL D. BIERMANN

Setting out to read an essay with the aim of crafting a response directs one's attention in a particular direction—on the hunt for items ripe for comment and perhaps debate. But sometimes, in spite of the best pragmatic intentions, the force of an essay actually takes over and the primary activity shifts from preparing a reaction to the simple delight of being taught. This was precisely my experience as I read Pakaluk's contribution to this volume. By the halfway point, I was simply along for the ride following wherever he led. And he was a competent leader providing a fascinating and illuminating journey, and one that in the end was more than a little humbling. But being a Lutheran and ardently committed to living as a theologian of the cross, I try not to be averse to the humbling when it happens.

At the very close of the essay (a footnote after the final period can't get much closer to the end), Pakaluk reveals his objective for the essay was not a review of texts but a presentation of the "power, appeal, and coherence" (p. 26n16) of the classical understanding of natural law. I, for one, am grateful for his approach and appreciated his steady and confident account of the necessary history and key thinkers that shaped the argument for natural law. Most of all, though, I was grateful for his skilled presentation of the actual foundations, interconnections, and then fascinating reenactment of the final full development of the classical argument for the natural law that occupied the last half of the essay. The final outcome was an exemplary tour de force of logic and argument building. While it might be fair to wonder about the overall significance of this outcome for the sake of the church's

28 • Natural Law

understanding and use of natural law—and I will wonder that, later—there is no question that the author achieved his stated goal of making a compelling summary case for a classical understanding of the importance of natural law.

It was in the first half of the essay, though, that I was gifted with some very helpful insights and presentations of simple truths that were somehow new to me—hence the humbling factor. Pakaluk's ready admission—that a classical understanding of natural law does not trace back to a unified ancient worldview but is in fact a select appropriation of ancient ideas by subsequent thinkers already committed by the tenets of their faith to truths about nature, human nature, and society—was a helpful reminder of the perennial complexity of the world and its thinkers. It is important to remember that pluralism is not a situation unique to our own era. This point is important in tempering what is too often an unthinking embrace of all things "ancient and Western" and thus naturally "classical" by Christians busily circling the wagons against the threats from culture wars. And it is good for us to recognize that the foundation for a belief in natural law is ultimately not ancient and medieval thinkers, no matter how brilliant they may have been, but the reality given to us in the fullness of God's revelation supremely manifest in Christ. Related to this point is the way that Pakaluk's essay leaves no doubt about the strong bonds of continuity that can be discerned between the natural law conclusions arrived at by ancient thinkers—even apart from faith in Christ—with those that are now widely accepted by today's Christians who subscribe to the truth of natural law. The paths taken diverge widely, but the conclusions reached are essentially the same. And from my perspective, the route provided by revelation and faith is far and away the less tortuous and taxing of the two.

Perhaps the greatest gift I personally gained from the essay was Pakaluk's discussion about piety. I may very well have missed it during the course of my education, but it had never occurred to me to consider the first table of the Decalogue in terms of the virtue of *pietas*, that is, the responsibility of humans to cultivate and express genuine gratitude, honor, respect, and deference for "those responsible for our being," in other words, those who have nurtured and cared for us, especially in our incapacity and helplessness. Understood this way, it is obvious that the fourth commandment to honor father and mother (yes, Lutherans share Rome's numbering of the Decalogue) should be considered as consistent with the other commandments usually grouped as the first table. Each of the first four commandments center on showing due appreciation and honor to those who have given and sustained our lives. We honor God and his name, keep the sabbath by delighting in the Creator and his creation through which he nurtures us, and we show respect to our parents who gave much to raise us. Even cultures not guided by biblical revelation recognize the validity and importance of these basic claims made on all human beings and consider those who violate them "to be somehow undone" (p. 7). Pakaluk even terms this obligation "a debt of piety" that is owed "to those responsible for who we are" (p. 23). This way of considering the first commandments of the Decalogue makes it clear that they are as firmly grounded in the natural or creational reality as those that deal with our more immediate human interactions and behaviors as enumerated in the second table.

Another perquisite of Pakaluk's essay is his assertion that the natural state of humans "is within a society that has a complete market, a defensive army, courts of law, a class devoted to the use of leisure, and a government sufficient to oversee the coordinated working of these parts" (p. 9). While I would overtly credit the Creator with this foundational arrangement, I can only applaud the essay's conclusion that this plan "is the basic form of life intended by nature for human beings" (p. 9). Indeed. It is clear that most people, even within the church, operate with assumptions about societal structure that are premised on the autonomous individual rather than on the individual within community. This taken for granted starting point of man as a splendid individual who seeks and creates society on his own terms profoundly impacts the way we understand ourselves, our relationships, and our responsibilities. To begin with the awareness of a complex and richly interconnected community as not merely a social construct generated by the needs of increasingly civilized individuals, as the world tells the story, but as an essential given of our human being could perhaps encourage those in the church to invest with a bit more zeal in their obligations to one another within both their ecclesial and civil communities. Like so many other aspects of natural law that are simply true whether we like it or not, we are made to be with one another.

The role of community, then, is to see that the truths of the natural law are brought to the forefront and carefully inculcated in all of her people.

30 • Natural Law

This work does not happen without deliberate effort. This is the final item on my list of benefits gained in the reading of this essay. Pakaluk reinforces, from the standpoint of the natural law, the critical work of the community in shaping her people to be the right kind of people, who know what it means to be human. This requires, we are reminded, "in our time also, a careful attitude of selection and curation, which seems possible only through institutions of education and culture which are explicitly dedicated to doing so" (p. 4). I would contend that though she certainly has an even more pressing responsibility boldly to proclaim the gospel of forgiveness in Christ, the church is also accountable and more than able to accomplish this vital work of formation. Through her own practices, the church can most certainly shape, habituate, educate, and so form her people to live as the humans God created them to be, which is, it should be clear, a way of being that is wholly in tune with the natural law wired into the creation itself. It is good for the church to remember that this work of formation is part of her task, and that if it is not exercised with some degree of intentionality, she will forfeit this role in the lives of her people, who will end up being formed by forces at odds with God's design and so will be shaped to be indistinguishable from those who surround them, those who live as if the only reality is the one they choose. The church must not forsake the critical responsibility of forming her people to live in tune with God's creational law.

As much as I am genuinely awed and humbled by the intellectual campaign that is the second half of the essay, when all is said and done, and the whole breadth of natural law—all that grows out of the basic precepts to practice piety and to cause no harm—has been established, my Lutheran self can't help but wonder what has actually been accomplished. At the risk of seeming unappreciative of the academic skill and rigor underlying the classical argument and perhaps even sounding a bit cynical, the truth is that the same conclusion can be reached simply by asserting that the Creator of the universe established ways for the universe to operate, made those ways known to his people intuitively and overtly (Sinai and the Sermon on the Mount, to mention two instances), and expects all humans to follow them. While it's good to know that a cogent and compelling argument can be built for the natural law apart from specific revelation, the actual benefit of such an argument is limited. As Pakaluk admits, those who violate the natural law usually do so for reasons other than a failure to understand the force of the natural law, and I would add that those inclined to follow that law, especially those committed to observing every detail of that law, almost always do so for other than intellectual reasons.

More interesting and perhaps troubling is the way that the entire classical argument is built from the premise of self-love. Without recourse to a Creator who continues to be engaged in his creation, this makes sense of course, but it does lead to some odd conclusions. One provocative example is what becomes, perhaps inadvertently, a rather muted denouncement of murder when it is concluded that "avoiding murder is most basically a side-constraint on living alongside others" (p. 17). Fair enough. But a tablet from the hand of God that says, "Thou shalt not murder," has just a tad more punch. Even more to the point, Christians live not by the maxim of self-interest but by self-denial as they follow the Lord, who graciously and freely gives them everything.

Honoring what we have learned from our namesake, Lutherans have a penchant—no, a focused commitment—to taking God at his word with or without supporting logic. Indeed, we are wholly disposed to endorse dogmatic truths that are wholly illogical. The dual truths of God's eternal election and complete human accountability stands as a poignant example, but so does the assertion that Christians are at once fully sinners and fully saints, and to be a bit more ecumenical, so does the truth that Jesus is fully human and fully God forever. There is much that Christians believe and teach that does not add up logically. Such is the way of faith. As is clear from the presentation of the classical view of natural law, when you don't have revelation and the resultant Spirit-worked faith to receive that truth, you have no choice but to build a grand argument of sublime logic and rationality. Christians have the great advantage of being able to engage in intellectual work not as a necessity or as a proof of our human worth but merely as a way of delighting in God's reality presented both in the revealed Word and in creation itself.

Littlejohn Response to Pakaluk

BRAD LITTLEJOHN

In his thorough exposition of "The Classical Understanding of Natural Law," Michael Pakaluk offers an account of Thomistic natural law theory that remains faithful to key historic principles while offering some distinctive emphases I've not encountered elsewhere.

Strengths

There is much to like about this exposition. For one thing, Pakaluk loses no time in dispelling the commonplace misconception of natural law theory (among both its advocates and critics) as seeking to offer a neutral common ground for morality in a secular age. Of course it is not *neutral*, he contends, for it rests upon both empirical descriptions and metaphysical conceptions of what is natural; it rests upon the fundamental idea that creatures have objective and knowable (at least in broad outlines) ends. It does not rest chiefly upon supernatural revelation (in the order of being, at least; although it may make great use of it in the order of knowing), but that does not mean that we should expect it to be uncontentious any more than most other areas of human knowledge are uncontentious. However, just because some matter of truth is regularly disputed (e.g., the causes of the Civil War) does not mean there *is* no truth of the matter or that all explanations are equally valid. The fact that a truth must be argued for should hardly be taken as a strike against it. So Pakaluk responds with serene unconcern to the worry that if natural law is not "neutral," it is therefore useless: "One might wonder why a theory needs a purpose beyond its being true" (p. 4).

For another, Pakaluk is clear that in speaking of the classical conception or the classical framework, he is not imagining some unanimous metaphysical and moral theory supposedly shared by Socrates, Plato, Aristotle, Cicero, and Seneca, a perfect pagan philosophical paradigm taken over unaltered by Christian thinkers. No, the classical framework represents a centuries-long process of picking and choosing of classical sources by Christian theologians, who examined and tested them against the touchstone of Scripture and synthesized them in relation to the Decalogue. Grace, here as elsewhere, corrected and perfected nature.

On both these points, as well as a number of others that space does not permit me to go into, Pakaluk succeeds in fortifying classical Thomistic natural law theory against many common misunderstandings or careless objections. This theory is not just philosophical but theological, and it emerges as the culmination of a long (and ongoing) conversation between reason and faith. Thus, its recovery and reassertion today will depend on a willingness to be forthright about its theological roots, even if particular arguments in particular contexts can gain traction by appeal to shared rational premises alone.

Weaknesses

Given this confession up front, however, Pakaluk's exposition proves startlingly thin on theological content as one reads on. Somewhat curiously, there is no mention of God at all throughout most of the discussion of the promulgation of natural law, although God is the only active subject of this promulgation. That's not to say that Pakaluk is wrong in what he says about the human intellect's reception of this promulgation, only that I would have expected an exposition of classical natural law theory to speak more explicitly of the nature of God as supreme Source and Lawgiver (knowable through natural theology) and then as Creator and Governor (knowable through revealed theology), and how these properties and activities of God generate and determine natural law. Moreover, Pakaluk seems to treat the second table of the Decalogue—our duties toward neighbor—as encapsulating the primary content of natural law, with the first table coming in only at the end "as supplying performative language which pertains to the second table . . . mak[ing] the second table effective precisely as natural law." While it is true that the first table grounds the second, one wonders why then it does not come first in Pakaluk's exposition. Moreover, the first table does more than simply provide a basis of obligation for the second: it outlines our duties toward God as our highest and greatest moral duties of all.

Most troublingly, Pakaluk seems to walk straight into common evangelical critiques of Roman Catholic natural law theory by the almost complete absence of Scripture from his account. We are left wondering whether the Decalogue is the only portion of Scripture relevant to any theory of natural law. Indeed, we are left wondering why we should need the Decalogue at all, given that Pakaluk's exposition says nothing about the fall and its effect on our rational faculties. The terms *fall*, *fallen*, and *sin* appear nowhere in the essay. Surely it is a crucial function of any natural law theory to explain not merely what we *ought* to do but also why we fail to do it, not merely what we *ought to know* about what we ought to do but also how readily we fall short of that knowledge and why. Evangelical skeptics of natural law often allege that it ignores the noetic effects of sin. This critique falls flat when lodged against Aquinas himself, who situates his whole discussion of natural law immediately following an account of the woeful effects of sin on humanity, clearly states that much of natural law can be "blotted out" by sin[1] and says that for this reason Scripture must restate much of natural law's moral teaching.[2] While I have little doubt that Pakaluk agrees with Thomas on all this, and I know that 10,000 words is a short space to expound an entire natural law theory, I would have expected at least some consideration of these themes in his chapter.

Another hesitation I have with Pakaluk's account concerns his recurrent language of natural law as providing "side constraints" on self-love. In thus framing things, I wonder whether Pakaluk is not trying to respond to frequent critiques of natural law theory, especially among antiperfectionist liberal thinkers, as far too morally maximalist, underwriting a nanny-state jurisprudence that is constantly trying to tell people what is good for them and force them to act accordingly. It really is the case that in the classical

---

1. Aquinas, *ST* I-II, 94.6.
2. Aquinas, *ST* I-II, 99.2.

framework, natural law is far more supple, flexible, and underdetermined than many imagine, leaving a large space of "permissive natural law"[3] that underwrites free human decision-making among myriad goods, many of them incommensurable. And it is also true that natural law theory presupposes the legitimacy of self-love—even as it often radically challenges our shortsighted ideas of what it means to "look after number one."

That said, to describe natural law as merely "side constraints on self-love" rings oddly, implying as it does that the proper *telos* of a human individual is merely seeking his own good, so long as he doesn't meddle with or undermine the good of others—in other words, something very like the liberal "harm principle." In fact, repeatedly throughout his essay, Pakaluk frames at least the second table precepts of natural law in terms very close to the harm principle: "Harm no one, either persons, possessions, relations, or standing" (p. 13). I am not sure how idiosyncratic Pakaluk may be in this framing vis-à-vis other Roman Catholic writers, but this is certainly very different from the way in which magisterial Protestant moral theology, as expressed in the catechetical tradition, saw the Decalogue. Although most of its precepts were framed in negative terms ("thou shalt not"), they were understood as encapsulating a set of corresponding positive duties. For instance, consider the striking language of the Westminster Larger Catechism on the Eighth Commandment (i.e., seventh in the Roman Catholic numbering):

> The duties required in the eighth commandment are, truth, faithfulness, and justice in contracts and commerce between man and man; rendering to everyone his due; restitution of goods unlawfully detained from the right owners thereof; giving and lending freely, according to our abilities, and the necessities of others; moderation of our judgments, wills, and affections concerning worldly goods; a provident care and study to get, keep, use, and dispose these things which are necessary and convenient for the sustentation of our nature, and suitable to our condition; a lawful calling, and diligence in it; frugality; avoiding unnecessary lawsuits and suretyship, or other like engagements; and an endeavor, by all just and

---

3. See the excellent study by Brian Tierney, *Liberty and Law: The Idea of Permissive Natural Law, 1100–1800* (Washington, DC: Catholic University of America Press, 2014).

36 • Natural Law

> lawful means, to procure, preserve, and further the wealth and outward estate of others, as well as our own.[4]

For the Reformers, the natural law was summed up in Jesus's two great commandments: love God and love your neighbor—both understood as positive duties and not negative "side-constraints" on self-love.

That said, there are certainly a number of important distinctions to be made between negative and positive duties. Negative prohibitions belonging to the natural law are always inviolable (at least, when properly defined), while positive commands are only binding *prima facie* and must be balanced against other obligations. This is true even with regard to the first table, where the positive duty to remember the Sabbath, by Jesus's own teaching, may need to give way to the positive duty to preserve life (thus we generally cancel church services when there is a blizzard). Thus Pakaluk helpfully distinguishes between the "strictly due or the *debitum*," which ordinarily attaches to negative prohibitions, and the "merely due" obligation which may attach to more positive duties (p. 13). Moreover, with regard to the second table, Pakaluk points out the added consideration that to do good to someone against their own will may be a form of harm. Thus Pakaluk's concept of "side constraints" begins to make more sense at least as a way of characterizing the absolutely nonnegotiable negative prohibitions of natural law, although I am not convinced it is the most helpful way of expounding natural law in general.

A Comment on the Two Tables

One other feature of Pakaluk's account warrants comment: his intriguing way of framing the division between the first and second tables of the Decalogue. Although the numbering of the commandments is famously disputed (with Catholics and Lutherans combining what the Reformed treat as commandments 1 and 2, and splitting what the Reformed treat as commandment 10), the distinction of the "two tables" has not usually depended on this question. Rather, on most treatments that I am familiar with, the two tables have been taken as corresponding to Christ's "two great

---

4. Westminster Larger Catechism, q. 141, https://www.apuritansmind.com/westminster-standards/larger-catechism.

commandments" with the first table (1–4 on the Reformed numbering; 1–3 on the Catholic) defining our duties toward God and the second (5–10 on the Reformed numbering; 4–10 on the Catholic) our duties toward neighbor. It has also sometimes been observed that the Sabbath command has a certain transitional character in this division, encompassing both duties of giving worship to God and giving rest to the neighbor (this latter being particularly highlighted in Deuteronomy 5:12–15).

However, Pakaluk follows a different principle of division (not unique to him but certainly less common in my experience): the second table concerns *general duties* (which are chiefly negative in nature) and the first table *special duties* (which are chiefly positive in nature). On this account, general duties are those duties of justice we owe to equals, and special duties are those duties of piety we owe to superiors, particularly those superiors on whom we depend as the source of our being. Using this principle of division, the fifth commandment (fourth in the Catholic numbering), "Honor thy father and thy mother" becomes part of the first table alongside duties to God. This way of framing the moral life certainly has advantages, highlighting as it does the virtue of piety (which is almost wholly neglected today) and clarifying the difference between reciprocal and nonreciprocal moral relations. However, it has the disadvantage—one I have already complained about—of decentering love of God as the source of all goodness from its proper position at the heart of the moral life.

On the whole, then, there is much in Pakaluk's exposition of the classical understanding of natural law that I would heartily commend and little that I would flatly disagree with. However, on the whole, I do not find his presentation of natural law theory to be the most rhetorically compelling or biblically faithful way of expounding this venerable doctrine.

Moschella Response to Pakaluk

MELISSA MOSCHELLA

Before commenting on Pakaluk's characterization of the nature and content of natural law, I would first like to briefly address his discussion of the purpose of natural law theory. Pakaluk is critical of the supposition that natural law "is a neutral meeting place for persons of goodwill that can serve as a starting point for rational persuasion as regards controversial topics such as abortion," and he suggests that new natural law theorists are among those who make this supposition. Whether or not this characterization of the new natural law view is true depends on what Pakaluk means by *neutral*. If he means neutral in the sense that the claims of natural law are not based on the tenets of revealed religion, then this characterization is true—though it would apply equally to his own approach to natural law. But if by neutral he means that natural law arguments about controversial issues are completely independent of metaphysical or anthropological claims or that natural law arguments will be equally persuasive to everyone regardless of their educational and cultural background, then this is not an accurate characterization of the new natural law account, as I hope that my main essay in this collection makes clear. To further clarify and illustrate this point in response to Pakaluk's discussion, allow me to say a few things here about new natural arguments regarding abortion and other controversial life issues.

In discussing abortion as well as the ethics of embryonic stem cell research and reproductive technologies, new natural law theorists address the biological question of when human life begins (which cannot be fully answered without certain metaphysical presuppositions about what it means to be a complete—even if immature—organism rather than a part of another organism) and the anthropological and metaphysical question of whether every human organism is a person, because these questions are—as Pakaluk rightly notes—central to the debate.[1] Thus, while new natural law theorists claim that the moral principle forbidding intentional killing is not derived from biological, metaphysical, or anthropological claims, we fully recognize the relevance of such facts for determining *whom* we are forbidden to kill—and, more broadly, *whose* good practical reason directs us to protect and promote.

It should also be noted that, despite Pakaluk's claim to the contrary, there are also specifically moral claims at issue in debates about abortion and other life issues. Many defenders of abortion and embryonic stem cell research (and euthanasia) defend these practices by implicitly or explicitly adopting a utilitarian moral theory, and the critique of utilitarianism both in general and as applied to these issues has been a constant theme in the work of new natural law theorists. Further, underlying most defenses of abortion is the voluntarist view that we can only acquire special obligations to others through implicit or explicit consent, and this too is a claim that new natural law theorists have argued against at length, while recognizing that to make headway on this issue we need a broader critique of the culture of expressive individualism that underlies this view. Obviously, as Pakaluk suggests, countering this individualist culture requires providing an education that goes beyond "correct[ing] it with a rational system" (p. 4). But we should avoid a false dichotomy here, for rational arguments that explain why this individualist culture is contrary to genuine human flourishing must be an integral part of any such educational effort.

Having made these clarifications with regard to the new natural law view regarding the role of natural law arguments in public debates on controversial issues, I would now like to comment on Pakaluk's characterization of the natural law and its content. While there is much that I agree with in Pakaluk's account, I will focus here on several aspects of his view that I find puzzling or problematic.

First, I find myself puzzled by Pakaluk's characterization of the natural law as a set of "side constraints on the pursuit of self-love properly

---

1. See, e.g., Patrick Lee and Robert George, *Body-Self Dualism in Contemporary Ethics and Politics* (New York: Cambridge University Press, 2008).

understood" (p. 40), which he later further specifies as "side-constraints which must be followed if I am to observe reasonability in my relations with others" (p. 12). For the reasons outlined in my own essay, I agree with Pakaluk's claim that proper self-love requires us to choose and act in morally upright ways—that is, to act virtuously. However, characterizing natural law as a side-constraint on the pursuit of self-love makes it seem like there is a potential conflict between what natural law commands and the pursuit of self-love properly understood. Yet if proper self-love directs us toward virtue, I do not see how there could be a genuine conflict.

Second, I have some questions about Pakaluk's account of the content of the natural law. Pakaluk claims that natural law "consists basically of articulable and naturally specifiable precepts that (1) enjoin piety to those responsible for our being, (2) forbid harm to others, (3) protect procreation, and (4) function as an outline or minimum of how we are to act toward one another, to be further filled in, in a person's particular facts and circumstances by free discretion" (p. 5). He then further specifies the first and second of these precepts, respectively, by specifying who is responsible for our being, and by specifying "the natural species of harm" as harms regarding one's person, property, relations, and standing or good name (p. 6). The result of this analysis is a set of precepts that mirror the precepts of the Decalogue, all of which can be understood as expressing requirements of justice.

This account of the content of natural law seems artificially restricted, for it is not clear on Pakaluk's account why the natural law is limited to these four categories of precepts (which he later reduces to the first two). Pakaluk does explain that he identifies the species of harm by identifying "naturally occurring or naturally recognizable species of harm" (p. 6). But since he does not define what he means by *natural*, this criterion is quite vague. I agree, of course, that the precepts of the Decalogue are all precepts of natural law (though, as should be obvious from my essay, my account of their derivation would be different from Pakaluk's). But I would not limit the content of the natural law to the precepts that Pakaluk outlines. Is it not natural for human beings to seek to know the truth (as Pakaluk recognizes) or to want to be persons of integrity whose emotions, judgments, and actions are in harmony with one another? If so, then it seems clear that one could harm someone by teaching him false things (thus harming him with respect to the good of knowledge) or by inducing him to act against his conscience (harming him with respect to the good of integrity). But these categories of harm do not seem to be included in Pakaluk's account. Further, it is not clear how positive duties to promote others' good fit in to this account.

These puzzles largely remain unanswered, and new puzzles arise after examining Pakaluk's more detailed account of natural law's derivation in the section on "The Promulgation of Natural Law in the Sense of Its Basis." Pakaluk begins this section by noting that we cannot know what is *due* to a being unless we know the end(s) or good(s) of that being. (As an aside, it is worth noting that the new natural law account agrees with this claim but thinks that the relevant ends/goods are identified in the first principles of *practical* reason, not by *derivation* from first-order, speculative knowledge about anthropology, biology, metaphysics, and so on. And the new natural law account also recognizes that speculative knowledge about what is possible for us is a prerequisite for practical reason's grasp of some of those possibilities as *good* or "to-be-pursued"). Pakaluk then asks us to consider a plant that needs to be watered daily and further to imagine that this plant has the capacity to intelligently care for itself in a way that is good for the plant. If such a plant existed, "then anyone who wanted to take care of this plant and advance its good would need now to keep two things in mind: first, what passively is required for the plant to flourish, that it be watered daily, and, second, what actively is required for the plant to flourish, that it take care of itself by watering itself. To benefit the plant 'against its will' would be against its active due, and to harm it, say, by cutting it down, would be against both its active and its passive due" (p. 16). Applying this general schema to human beings, he then reminds the reader of his prior division of human goods into the categories of person, property, relations, and standing, and concludes that it is "naturally strictly due" to each person that no one harm him with respect to these goods, defining harm as "caus[ing] deliberately or by negligence uncompensated loss in another against his will" (p. 16). While this explanation gives the reader a better sense of how Pakaluk thinks we determine what is due to someone, his limitation of human goods (and thus of species of harm) to person, property, relations, and standing remains unexplained.

With regard to positive obligations to promote others' good, Pakaluk does note in passing that each person ought to act "in a friendly way" toward the other—that is, in a way that is "appropriately respectful of the fact that each has self-mastery and a duty to care for himself" (p. 16). So it seems that his account does recognize positive obligations to promote another's good as part of the natural law but that he simply pays less attention to these positive obligations because they are not what the tradition calls "perfect" duties (or what Pakaluk seems to refer to as a "strict" duty). This interpretation seems to be in line with what Pakaluk says at the end of the following section, where he posits a general duty (but not a "strict" duty) to "live in such a way as to be at peace and as to keep open the fostering of friendly relations" (p. 20), and it is also in line with the presumption of natural friendliness referred to in the final two sections. Nonetheless, Pakaluk's account of the natural law seems to give short shrift to positive obligations and does not seem to offer much (if any) concrete guidance for how to think about those obligations.

Further, Pakaluk's definition of harm as *uncompensated* loss that is *against a person's will* also raises questions. What about a case in which someone agreed to be maimed by another person in exchange for compensation? (Perhaps the person really needs the money and is willing to suffer the injury to attain the compensation.) Or what if someone *wants* you to kill him because he is suffering and no longer thinks that life is worth living? While Pakaluk makes it clear that it would be wrong for a person to seek his own death (or injury) because this is contrary to the good of self-preservation, neither of these cases seems to count as *harm* according to his definition. Thus Pakaluk's definition of *harm*, along with his attempt to base the natural law (or at least its prohibitions) on the practical law of noncontradiction ("Nothing is to be both pursued and avoided at the same time and in the same respect," p. 20) seems to reduce natural law's prohibitions to cases of unfairness or violations of the Golden Rule. But I presume that Pakaluk thinks the natural law *does* prohibit violations of human goods even in cases—like those just mentioned—that do not necessarily involve any unfairness.

In sum, while there is much that I appreciate and agree with in Pakaluk's account, I find it puzzling in many respects and would welcome further clarification.

Leithart Response to Pakaluk

PETER J. LEITHART

I am grateful for many things in Michael Pakaluk's essay, but my gratitude is often tarnished by disappointment. He acknowledges the "tremendous diversity of thought" in the classical world (p. 1), but that only makes me the more disappointed when he fails to acknowledge the notable differences between Jewish, Christian, and Islamic appropriations of the classical tradition, as well as the diversity within each tradition. I am grateful he recognizes that Christian and Jewish thinkers identified and rejected "false, deceptive, and harmful" views inherited from the classical world, but I am disappointed he does not indicate whether we should expect to discover hitherto unidentified deceptive and harmful views in the classical inheritance. I affirm with Pakaluk that there is a moral obligation "to honor God, publicly as well as in private" (p. 4), but that only makes me the more disappointed he is not clearer about which God he means.

I am grateful for Pakaluk's admission that the natural law "does not and cannot" provide "a neutral meeting place for persons of goodwill" (p. 3).[1] His example is telling: though all may agree with "Thou shalt not murder," this does not produce universal condemnation of abortion because the commandment can only be elaborated and applied on the basis of anthropological and metaphysical premises that are not contained within the commandment itself. Natural law does not carry its own philosophy

---

1. Biermann makes a similar concession. Perhaps the discussion has moved past my objections to natural law.

44 • Natural Law

of nature or metaphysics; it does not include its own concept of teleology, essence, substance, purposes.

To my mind, this leaves natural law a diminished theory. Far from being a barricade against moral and political perversion, natural law seems to be susceptible to cultural and philosophical winds. Natural law is a set of side constraints, ruling out conduct that damages persons and society and thereby "opening up" space for productive life in family, society, and the city. The modesty of the theory is attractive. Yet the side constraint that prohibits adultery does not, as such, define *marriage*.[2] We must answer the question, "Side constraints to *what*?" on some other grounds. If natural law provides no more than side constraints, it seems possible to accept same-sex marriage so long as neither partner cheats.

While denying that the metaphysical frame is within the "natural law aspect of the matter," Pakaluk says natural law "is internally related to other realities" in such a way that we cannot define the natural law without attention to those other realities (p. 5). Specifically, natural law must be nested in an account of community, authority, the common good, and its mode of promulgation. From C. S. Lewis, he draws the conclusion that "what we find important about natural law is bound up with truths about human nature, society, and the natural world. These truths arguably stand or fall together" (p. 4). Later, he defines the classic understanding of nature as "a system of beings and processes working for ends and structures that are ordered as toward ends" (p. 13). A denial of ends entails a denial of nature itself and of the notion of goods. Natural law *does* require a basic theory of kinds, nature, ends, essences, and purposes. But if this essential apparatus does not arise from natural law itself, whence? And what happens when a culture (ours) renounces these essential truths?

I am left with the suspicion that Pakaluk distinguishes a specifically "natural law aspect" from its metaphysical surroundings to protect his claim that there is a universal natural law while at the same time conceding that the philosophical foundations of natural law are not universally acknowledged. His distinction begins to seem a rhetorical trick.

---

2. Along similar lines, the prominence Pakaluk gives to *harm* might give aid and comfort to the proliferating harm claims in our culture. Does his theory provide any way to identify misconceptions of harm? On the limits and dangers of John Stuart Mill's harm principle, see John Gray, *Liberalisms: Essays in Political Philosophy* (New York: Routledge, 2009), 220–21.

Pakaluk's essay confirmed my general hesitations about reasoning from nature. To say a plant is immature, he points out, is to imply it "has a natural goal of growing to a certain height and then producing flowers and seeds" (p. 13). Agreed. Then we ask, *How* tall? How many years of seed and fruit production? When does the tree reach its telos, and how can we tell? This matters because in Pakaluk's theory the tree's natural telos imposes *debitum*. How long is sunlight and watering due? Once it reaches its maximum height, is the debt paid in full? What if the tree was planted for the sake of its timber. Is it still the case that the plant's right not to be chopped down is "strictly due"?[3] Can a human being override the tree's natural right? It seems we cannot establish due and right merely by appealing to a natural teleological principle of growth. We must factor in external realities and intentions.

Pakaluk uses the plant example to show that dues and rights are not dependent on convention but are inherent in the nature of things. But human decisions cannot be excluded from consideration, and human decisions are and form conventions. What is natural is never neatly separable from what is human. Nature and culture are not cleanly distinct zones, either theoretically or practically. Pakaluk's theory assumes, it seems, isolated things maturing along their teleological trajectories without regard to other things.

My main complaint, predictably, is elsewhere: the lack of theological reflection in Pakaluk's theory. To be sure, he does not avoid theological questions. He provides a natural law argument for the first table of the Decalogue and insists that piety to God and parents is one of two basic precepts in the classical conceptions of natural law.

At least in the foundational structure of his argument, the theological content is thin. In Pakaluk's usage, *classical framework* does not refer to "some kind of basic philosophy" but instead to the "culling out and appropriation" of ancient Greek and Roman view nature, man, and society in the light of "Jewish, Christian, and Islamic beliefs" (p. 1). As noted above, that formula smooths over a great deal of diversity. Worse, it blurs the actual reception of classical thought. The American founders and leaders of the British Empire were shaped not by a Jewish or Islamic appropriation of ancient thought but by a specifically *Christian* appropriation. Can we defend the fruit of

---

3. His zoological illustration raises similar questions. It contributes to the good of a predator that it hunts each day and finds food. Is the food due? Is the freedom to hunt? But what, pray, is due to the prey?

46 • Natural Law

appropriation without mimicking the specific form of appropriation? Do Islamic appropriations of the classical inheritance yield a natural law theory compatible with Pakaluk's own?

Christianity makes a difference. Pursuit of happiness is, Pakaluk says, a "formal condition" universally recognized as the aim of human action. What happiness *is* has been disputed, and in the classical tradition that disagreement regarding ends is an ineradicable feature of human society. In simplified form, the classical tradition claims "the many" pursue tangible goods while "the wise" seek virtue. This certainly expresses the common sense of ancient political thought, but it is far from the common sense of Christian political and moral theology. Instead of reserving the virtue to an elite of sages, the Bible holds out the promise that women, slaves, and children will be conformed to Christ, suffer heroically, and share his glory. Menial activities are dignified as gifts of the Spirit, manual labor is lifted up, and the most despised members of the community are given abundant honor. Bizarrely, Pakaluk eases from an Aristotelian account of the appurtenances of virtue to a discussion of *theosis*. There is no smooth transition but an apocalyptic caesura, for, as he nearly admits and surely believes, beatitude is not reserved for an elite of spiritual athletes.

Further, nowhere does he explicitly acknowledge the role of sin, a factor that, as I show in my essay, plays a prominent role in Thomas's account of virtue and law.[4] That neglect gives Pakaluk's essay a breezy utopian air; natural law seems to be an ethics for Eden. I agree human beings are not "by nature at war with one another" (p. 2), yet there *are* wars. Consciences can be seared, as Thomas acknowledges; not every adulteress throws herself in front of a passing train. The natural form of association, he says, is a market, "a natural institution for the corporate meeting of our basic needs" (p. 9). But markets are abused and manipulated, and Torah demands just weights and measures and the prophets condemn market actors who defraud and abuse their fellows. Human beings "are meant by nature to dwell in a social group whose market has grown complete enough that it can meet basic human needs with relative ease" (p. 9). But there is a chasm between *meant to* and *do*. It would doubtless be a more peaceable world if everyone learned

---

4. This raises a question of sources: What natural law theorists come under the classical rubric? Pakaluk cites Thomas as a leading exponent of the classical view, and says he is "heavily indebted to Aquinas." But a comparison with my essay will make clear his sharp divergences from Thomas.

to "truck, barter, and exchange" instead of cheating and intimidating. But that's not the world we live in. Absent any reference to sin, it is not clear how classical theory accounts for the fact that the world is *not* peaceable? Perhaps Pakaluk would respond by emphasizing that he is describing human beings in their natural setting. Edenic ideals have their place in political and ethical reasoning, but he gives virtually no attention to how natural law operates in a world that is, by his standards, decidedly *un*natural?

Pakaluk refers repeatedly to the Decalogue but does not explicitly place it in its biblical setting: the Ten Words were spoken to Israel from Sinai by the God of the exodus, the God who has in the last days spoken in his Son. Failing to draw that conclusion, he gives no indication of the role this revelation might play in the life of virtue, piety, and justice. Nor does he anywhere mention the Spirit of Jesus, by whom, Christians believe, we are conformed to the character of Jesus and filled with the Spirit's virtues and fruits. Though Pakaluk is speaking of the Christian God, it is not at all clear that his theory requires anything particularly Christian. He says nothing about creation, the incarnation, Jesus, the Spirit, or the Trinity. His theory of virtue sounds Pelagian: men attain virtues when their motivation "become rational as best it can" (p. 12). Since sin is absent from his account, so too is grace.

All this leaves me with two practical questions. First, why do Christians want to construct natural law theory in this fashion rather than within the explicitly Christian framework Thomas uses? Despite Pakaluk's acknowledgement that natural law cannot provide a neutral basis for moral and political reasoning, the shape of his argument suggests he remains bewitched by this hope. Second, and to mark a final moment of gratitude, I am grateful Pakaluk recognizes that the *Green Book* cannot be replaced with a "rational system" but requires an education. But then I wonder: Why a pedagogy in natural law? Why not a pedagogy in Scripture, catechesis, or discipleship? Why would we want to—how *could* we—nurture virtue without reference to the supremely virtuous True Man?

Rejoinder

MICHAEL PAKALUK

Several of the responses to my essay seem to follow this line of thought: the natural law is the moral law; the moral law is the moral life; but how can Pakaluk or any Christian discuss the moral life without bringing in sin, salvation, grace, Scripture, and the centrality of God and his will?

Let me be clear. Had I understood myself as charged with the task of writing an essay on the theme, "the role of appeals to the natural law in Catholic moral life" or ". . . in Christian discipleship, from a Catholic point of view," I would have written a very different essay. I would have been sure to say, first of all, that a personal relationship with Christ—friendship with Christ—is the foundation of the moral life for a Catholic. I would have insisted that such a relationship can hardly be fostered except through daily meditation on the Scripture: "Ignorance of Scripture is ignorance of Christ" (St. Jerome);[1] "How I wish your bearing and conversation were such that, on seeing or hearing you, people would say: This man reads the life of Jesus Christ" (St. Josemaria Escriva).[2] I would have emphasized that I have written three books on the gospels precisely out of such a conviction.[3] I would have been sure to stress that a daily quiet time, or time of mental prayer (as Catholics call it), is also a practical necessity: "A Christian who neglects mental prayer needs no devil to carry him to

---

1. St. Jerome, *Commentary on Isaiah*, prol.: *PL* 24,17.

2. St. Josemaria Escriva, *The Way: Critical-Historical Edition*, ed. Pedro Rodriguez (New York: Scepter, 2010), n2.

3. *The Memoirs of St. Peter* (Washington, DC: Regnery, 2019); *Mary's Voice in the Gospel according to St. John* (Washington, DC: Regnery, 2022); *Be Good Bankers: The Economic Interpretation of Matthew's Gospel, with a Fresh Translation* (Southlake, TX: Gateway, 2025).

hell. He brings himself there with his own hands" (St. Teresa of Avila).[4] I would not have neglected to say that, to remain faithful to Christ, we need the illumination and assistance of God's grace, which comes to us in many ways but especially, Catholics believe, in the sacrament of the Lord's Supper: *sine Domenico non possumus*, "without the Lord's Supper we simply cannot carry on," as the martyrs of Abitinae exclaimed during the Diocletian persecution of 303–11 AD.[5] I would have been sure to emphasize that for a Christian, love of self means imitation of Christ, which implies conforming one's life to his, especially in turning one's life into a gift of self. And only after setting down such a context would I turn finally to the role of natural law.

However, that was not the sort of essay I understood myself to be writing. Rather, I aimed to give an intelligent, accessible, and plausible reconstruction of the way of looking at natural law that was common (although not universal) among classical philosophers. This classical conception was appropriated by early Christian thinkers and later given system and greater clarity by St. Thomas Aquinas. Such a reconstruction must omit Scripture since the major classical thinkers, who were pagan, did not enjoy the light of Scripture. It has to be "thin" in speaking about God because reason not assisted by grace arrives at only thin conceptions of God. It would have to give an account of self-love which extended only so far as including, or implying, the sacrifices and "gift of self" needed to live a life of virtue in supporting one's family and serving one's country. It might indeed have discussed sin: I might have explained how sin in classical sources was regarded as a "missing the mark" (Greek: *hamartia*), and I might have brought in the related notions of rash folly (*atē*) and presumption (*hubris*). But there was enough to cover already in simply discussing law, never mind violations of law, which is in any case a secondary task.

To what shall I liken my essay, then? I set before you a parable. Art historians say that the Jesus figure in Michelangelo's *Last Judgment in*

---

4. As quoted by St. Alphonsus Liguori in *The Great Means of Salvation and of Perfection*, ed. Eugene Grimm (Brooklyn: Redemptorist Fathers, 1927), 256. Liguori says that prayer is "morally necessary" for a Christian to attain heaven.

5. See Michael Pakaluk, "Making a Necessity of Virtue," *The Pilot*, November 2, 2007. http://www.thebostonpilot.com/article.php?ID=5415.

50 • Natural Law

the *Sistine Chapel*[6] is modeled on the Roman statue *The Belvedere Torso*.[7] Suppose, then, I were to write an essay explaining the features of the latter that made it so well suited to be used as a model for the former. It would be off point to complain that *The Belvedere Torso* is incomplete because it lacks arms, legs, and a head (it does), or that *The Belvedere Torso* was "utopian" or "Edenic" because the torsos of most human beings lack musculature and are sickly or obese (they are), or to object that the torso was not originally situated in a scene with saints amid spiritual combat (it wasn't). In much the same way, the ideal of human conduct prescribed by the natural law is far from complete. It tells of an ideal that no one ever reaches, and it must perforce be deficient, on account of its isolation from salvation history. And yet that ideal tells us a lot about the human nature that was assumed by Christ. To explain this ideal—to get it right—is highly valuable nonetheless.

But let me go back to that other essay I might have written but didn't: "the role of appeals to the natural law in Catholic moral life." After setting down the context as explained above, what else might I have said?—a very interesting question too.

In writing such an essay I would have said that the phrase *natural law* may refer to three different things for a Catholic. Natural law plays a different role depending upon which sense one means.

First, it might mean those fundamental commandments that mark out a "way" for us that leads to life. These commandments are so basic that their violation implies death, in the sense of separation from God and risk of eternal death. (That is why Catholics call such violations mortal sins, that is, sins which lead to death.) It is not that the observing of these commandments is the perfection of Christian life—far from it! Rather, these commandments are like safety ropes: they say, in effect, *do not wander off the way marked out by these ropes.*

The early Christian *Didache* ("Teaching") takes this very approach. At the start it announces the "way" or "path" of life (Greek: *hodos*): "There are two Ways, one of Life and one of Death; but there is a great difference

---

6. See the image at https://upload.wikimedia.org/wikipedia/commons/3/3f/Michelangelo%2C _Giudizio_Universale_03.jpg.

7. Compare the image at https://www.museivaticani.va/content/museivaticani/en/collezioni /musei/museo-pio-clementino/sala-delle-muse/torso-del-belvedere.html.

between the two Ways."[8] It then gives the two precepts of love of God and love of neighbor but interprets the latter as the Golden Rule in its negative formulation: "All things whatsoever thou wouldst not have done to thee, neither do thou to another." Then it specifies, to generate the second table, while also elaborating: "Thou shalt not kill. Thou shalt not commit adultery; thou shalt not corrupt boys; thou shalt not commit fornication. Thou shalt not steal. Thou shalt not use witchcraft; thou shalt not practice sorcery. Thou shalt not procure abortion, nor shalt thou kill the newborn child. Thou shalt not covet thy neighbor's goods. Thou shalt not forswear thyself (swear falsely). Thou shalt not bear false witness. Thou shalt not speak evil; thou shalt not bear malice."[9] It does this all the while clearly assuming that we don't wish to be killed ourselves, see someone else commit adultery with our spouse, and so on. That is, it explains love of neighbor as not harming one's neighbor, in relation to reasonable self-love.[10]

This language of a *way* is so fitting in speaking of the natural law that it turns up in many contexts. Psalm 1 is a good example. Or consider Rachel Saint and the missionaries who accompanied her in a second outreach to the Huaorani tribe in Ecuador: they would refer to the commandments against murder and theft as "God's good trail." Thus, when Minkayi, who had killed Jim Elliot and the four other missionaries, later converted to Christianity, he exclaimed, "Believing, I am now walking Jesus' trail to the sky."[11] A road is something that is already there. It is solid and marked in the earth. Not everything in the moral life has such a character—for example, finding just the right words to correct an erring brother (Matt 18:15)—but the natural law does.

It is "before" everyone too so that appeals to others based upon it have a force beyond one's own authority. In each town that Cortes and his band entered, in their march from Vera Cruz to Mexico City, "every day we saw sacrificed before us three, four, or five Indians whose hearts were offered to the idols."[12] The neatly stacked skulls in one town numbered

---

8. Philip Schaff, *The Oldest Church Manual Called the Teaching of the Twelve Apostles* (New York: Scribner's, 1885), 162.

9. Schaff, *The Oldest Church Manual*, 167–69.

10. "Love your neighbor," Jesus taught, "as you love yourself" (Mark 12:31). The *Good News Bible* paraphrases this verse correctly, just like this.

11. Janet and Geoff Benge, *Rachel Saint: A Star in the Jungle* (Seattle: YWAM, 2005), 170.

12. Bernal Diaz del Castillo, *The Discovery and Conquest of Mexico*, ed. Genaro Garcia, trans. A. P. Maudslay (New York: Farrar, Straus, & Cudahy, 1956).

100,000,[13] representing the sacrifices of almost a hundred years. Hardly any practice violative of the natural law could be said to have been more deeply entrenched. And yet when they explained to the Mexicans the teachings of "our holy religion" and declared that they had come to put an end to these kidnappings and murders, the Mexicans capitulated, allowing the Spaniards to expel the priests of Quetzalcoatl and clean out the temples—in a way that cannot be explained sufficiently by any military force, however great, that the Spaniards might have been supposed to project.[14]

The natural law as safety ropes that mark the way to life enters into Catholic moral instruction just as it did in the Sermon on the Mount. "You have heard that it was said to the people long ago" (Matt 5:21) (an unusual turn of phrase which seems designed not to bring in any merely human authority), "do not kill," or "do not commit adultery." But then, under each heading, our Lord proscribes actions which are similar to but milder than the obvious, gravely forbidden ones. *Do not kill*—the safety rope—but also *do not use abusive language*, and even *do not remain at odds with another* (5:23–24).[15] The natural law, then, in its first meaning, in the form of the Decalogue, provides a framework for explaining the virtues and refinement in charity.

Second, by the *natural law*, Catholics can mean prudential reasoning, illuminated by faith and assisted by grace, insofar as it reaches reliable precepts in any area of life, through reflection upon human nature and human social life, as these were intended by God in creation. It is in this sense, for example, that the teaching upheld by the Catholic Church, that artificial contraception is inherently wrong and never to be done whatever the consequences, is said to be a matter of natural law. That is to say, if one reflects soundly upon the nature of male-female complementarity and spousal love and the teleology of a procreative act, one should conclude that acts of artificial contraception are to be avoided. Moreover, such acts are deeply corrupting of married love, imply the replacement of God's wisdom by human craftiness, and carry with them manifold unintended consequences,

---

13. Diaz, *The Discovery and Conquest of Mexico*, 119.

14. Diaz, *The Discovery and Conquest of Mexico*, 103–5.

15. That wandering off "the way leading to life" leads to a seriously different ending is emphasized repeatedly by our Lord: you will be liable to hell fire (5:22); you will be thrown into prison until you pay the last penny (5:26).

which threaten the family, Christian culture, and human freedom.[16] Most obviously artificial contraception is inseparable from abortion and leads directly to it.[17]

Clearly there is a big difference between "do not commit adultery" and "do not use artificial contraception," even though both, by Catholics, are held to be matters of the natural law. The former enjoys an obviousness that is close to universal: societies or microcultures in which married persons agree flagrantly to commit adultery (such as the currently faddish "ethical nonmonogamy") are truly outliers. But the latter is genuinely difficult to see, a very clear case in our time of what St. Thomas called a difficult tracing out of a consequence within natural law, easily turned away from the correct conclusion by emotions, bad societal conventions, or from a bad natural condition.[18] We may surmise that in such matters ordinary folks will draw the sound conclusion only so long as those they take to be wiser do so. Thus, Protestants too universally rejected artificial contraception[19] until certain Protestant leaders began to change—at first, at the Lambeth Conference in 1930.[20]

It should be added here that *nature* in general is increasingly difficult to discern, as fewer human beings live an agrarian life with cycles and seasons, and they increasingly inhabit artificial worlds created on the internet. "Today we can illuminate our cities so brightly that the stars of the sky are no longer visible," Pope Benedict said in an Easter Vigil homily in 2012, "Is this not an image of the problems caused by our version of enlightenment?"[21] That is why many Catholics in discussing the natural law like to follow the example of our Lord and consider "what is natural" specifically through lens of the creation accounts in *Genesis*. What is "from the beginning" is also what is so by nature. Pope John Paul II was famous for using this method in his

---

16. See St. Pope Paul VI, *Humanae Vitae*, encyclical letter, July 25, 1968, https://www.vatican.va/content/paul-vi/en/encyclicals/documents/hf_p-vi_enc_25071968_humanae-vitae.html.

17. Michael Pakaluk, "The Link Between Contraception and Abortion," *First Things*, January 23, 2018, https://www.firstthings.com/web-exclusives/2018/01/the-link-between-contraception-and-abortion.

18. Aquinas, *ST* I, 94.4, co.

19. The 1873 federal law named after Anthony Comstock, a congregationalist, forbade "every article, instrument, substance, drug, medicine, or thing which is advertised or described in a manner calculated to lead another to use or apply it for preventing conception or producing abortion."

20. See Michael Pakaluk, "Lambeth, 90 Years Later," *The Catholic Thing*, September 1, 2020. https://www.thecatholicthing.org/2020/09/01/lambeth-90-years-later/.

21. See Michael Pakaluk, "Impoverished without Contemplation," *The Pilot*, August 5, 2016. http://www.thebostonpilot.com/article.php?ID=177126.

meditations on the "theology of the body."[22] The method does not have the philosophical "purity" of an approach that aims to appeal solely to reason, but for most people it proves to be more vivid and more convincing—not surprisingly, because the word of God has power.

Third and finally, by the *natural law* Catholics may mean simply the providential ordering of the world, especially insofar as it seems to express God's justice. Call this "the natural law as God's providence in the design and working of creation for a moral purpose." For example, if someone out of anger fails to pay attention to where he is walking and stubs his toe, this may be ascribed to the natural law. Certainly, the inner pain that someone feels in nursing a grudge is the working out of the natural law in this third sense.

When one thinks of the natural law in this way, as having a moral purpose, one thinks of what Bishop Butler and the philosophers of the Scottish Enlightenment referred to as "the human constitution." The structure of our psyches, the emotions we feel, and how things naturally go in transactions and among groups falls within God's moral providence. "There are two ways in which the subject of morals may be treated," Butler says, "One begins from inquiring into the abstract relations of things; the other from a matter of fact, namely, what the particular nature of man is, its several parts, their oeconomy or constitution, from whence it proceeds to determine what course of life it is, which is correspondent to this whole nature."[23] Butler was an Anglican divine, but the young John Henry Newman recognized the classical foundations of Butler's thought, just as the mature Newman, the Catholic convert, continued to affirm the harmony between Butler and Catholic teaching. Indeed, the best guide I know for this third way of construing natural law would be the corpus of Newman's *Parochial and Plain Sermons*, taken as a whole and considered in their complete effect.[24]

Grasping and admiring the natural law in this third sense we might want to exult in the words of the playwright Terence, as did St. Augustine, *homo sum; humani nihil a me alienum puto.*[25] And we might even want to make

---

22. John Paul II, *Man and Woman He Created Them: A Theology of the Body*, trans. Michael Waldstein (Boston: Pauline, 2006).

23. Joseph Butler, *Fifteen Sermons Preached at the Rolls Chapel*, 6th ed. (London: Rivington, 1792), 11.

24. John Henry Newman, *Parochial and Plain Sermons* (San Francisco: Ignatius, 2010). The sermons, in the public domain, are available online here: https://www.newmanreader.org/works/index.html.

25. "I am a man; I count nothing human as foreign to me."

the saint's conclusion our own: "Whole theaters would erupt in applause in unison at these words," Augustine said, "even though they were filled with dull and uneducated men. Which shows that the community of all human souls by nature touches the sympathy of every one of us, so that there is no one who will not feel himself to be the neighbor of any other."[26]

---

26. Augustine, letter 155 to Macedonius, *Corpus Scriptorum Ecclesiasticorum Latinorum* (*CSEL*) (Vienna: Tempsky, 1904), 44:445.

CHAPTER 2

A Lutheran Understanding of Natural Law

JOEL D. BIERMANN

Long ago when my children were young, our evening routine included books. Lewis, Tolkien, Twain, Dumas, Forester, and yes, all of Franklin W. Dixon. For the sheer joy of it, and for the inevitable formation linked to it, I read, and my children listened. Though, like a few others on my list, Kipling is sometimes viewed with suspicion, I also read some of his books too. *The Jungle Book* was a favorite. We all loved the stories, and I particularly appreciated the prominence accorded the "Law of the Jungle" that ordered life for all the characters in the stories and that Mowgli was compelled to learn through the hard pedagogy of Baloo, "the Teacher of the Law." The bear taught the young boy "the Wood and Water Laws; how to tell a rotten branch from a sound one; how to speak politely to the wild bees when he came upon a hive of them fifty feet above ground; what to say to Mang the Bat when he disturbed him in the branches at midday; and how to warn the water-snakes in the pools before he splashed down among them." The Law of the Jungle encompassed all of the material world and the relationships of those who dwelt in it. And yet it was still possible for that law to be resisted outright as Baloo warns: "Listen, Man-cub. . . . I have taught thee all the Law of the Jungle for all the people of the Jungle—except the Monkey-folk who live in the trees. They have no Law. They are outcasts. . . . Their way is not our way."[1] The

---

1. Rudyard Kipling, *The Jungle Book* (London: Puffin, 1984), 35, 40.

58 • Natural Law

universal contempt accorded the Bandar-log, the "Monkey-folk," served to confirm the depth and importance of the Law of the Jungle for those who lived in the jungle—even an orphaned man.

Given my evident admiration for the Law of the Jungle, it should come as no surprise that I recognize a tight correspondence between that law and the natural law. Fully cognizant of the surplus of often complex and often conflicting ideas about the right definition of natural law, I'm inclined to let the narrative description of the Law of the Jungle suffice for my own understanding of the natural law. It is simply the given, unchanging, "built-in" reality or truth that guides, norms, and shapes all of life for all creatures. Kipling's fiction has the great advantage of being submissive to its author's inclinations. A universal Law of the Jungle can be assumed without any threat of challenge being raised about the authority accorded certain characters to teach and enforce the law, the reason for the disdain of the law among an entire species, the possible eternal significance of the law, the legitimacy of a single moral code for all creatures, and perhaps most perplexing of all, the origin and foundation of the jungle's law. Such unsettling questions simply don't arise; the author sees to that. Fiction is easy. Real life is less so. In real life, questions get asked.

Few subjects, it seems, prompt more questions than the topic of natural law. Mercifully, I am tasked with answering only one: What is a Lutheran understanding of the natural law? While this question poses its own set of challenges, I will do my best to provide an answer faithful to my confession, an answer that in the end may not look so very different from the Law of the Jungle—well, perhaps minus the specificity related to bats and water-snakes. Since a Lutheran answer should presumably consider the work of Lutherans, beginning with a pair of proto-Lutherans seems a prudent course. Martin Luther and his younger colleague Philip Melanchthon meet the criteria.

The Doctrine of Melanchthon

While in most respects Melanchthon was Luther's junior, he preceded Luther in both the timing and extent of his reflection on natural law. This likely accounts for his reputation as an exemplar of a Lutheran endorsement of natural law. Beginning with his first efforts at articulating the Christian faith in his *Loci Communes*, Melanchthon fully affirms his commitment to natural law and even attempts to elaborate its content. Yet even as he makes his presentation, Philip hints at the difficulties inherent in the effort:

> Concerning natural laws, I have not yet seen anything worthily written whether by theologians or lawyers. For since they are designated "natural", their formulas ought [to] be collected by a method of human reasoning through a natural syllogism. That is precisely what I have not seen done by anyone, and I by no means know whether it can at all be done, since our human reason is so enslaved and blinded.[2]

In other words, Melanchthon observes that if the law is indeed "natural," then competent human reason should be able to establish and express the contents of that law. Yet it is precisely this feat, he notes, that had been accomplished by no one, a fact that still holds more than five hundred years later. Thus, even before embarking on his ambitious effort to express the truths of the natural law, the first Lutheran humanist diminishes and casts suspicion over the entire project. Indeed, rather than human logic or experience as the foundation for his teaching on natural law, Philip relies on Paul and his ultimate natural law "proof text": "For when Gentiles who do not have the Law do instinctively the things of the Law, these, not having the Law, are a law to themselves, in that they show the work of the Law written in their hearts, their conscience bearing witness and their thoughts alternately accusing or else defending them" (Rom 2:14–15 NASB).

Paul's declaration provides the basis for Melanchthon's concise definition of natural law that immediately follows: "So natural law is a common judgment to which all men alike assent, and therefore one which God has inscribed upon the soul of each man, adapted to form and shape character."[3] The Aristotelian overtones cannot be denied, a point acknowledged by Melanchthon, who goes on to offer a somewhat surprising assessment of the great Greek philosopher: "Now that this view may agree with Aristotelian philosophy, is not the point I labor. For what difference does it make to me what that wrangler has thought?" Thus, Melanchthon builds his case for

---

2. Philip Melanchthon, *The Loci Communes of Philip Melanchthon: With a Critical Introduction by the Translator*, trans. Charles Leander Hill (Boston: Meador, 1944), 111.

3. Melanchthon, *Loci.*, 112.

60 • Natural Law

natural law from the pages of Scripture and not the highest thoughts of men—a thoroughly Lutheran methodology, to be sure.

Melanchthon devotes another five pages exploring natural law as it was understood in the waning years of the medieval era he was helping to end. He then methodically unpacks "three orders of divine laws: some are moral, some judicial, others ceremonial."[4] Following the conventions of the time, he slots the Decalogue in the category of divine moral law that, like the natural law, was normative for all people in all places. After considering and denouncing at some length Rome's fallacious and pernicious teaching regarding evangelical counsels and monastic vows, Melanchthon lastly takes up the question of human laws. Over the course of more than thirty pages, these assorted categorizations of the law are explored in distinction from one another, each one comprehending some particular aspect of the law. With his trademark systematic precision and progression, Philip maps each distinction of the law along a scale from the most fundamental, comprehensive, and enduring tenets of the natural law to the most peculiar, idiosyncratic, and ephemeral local regulations.

Given his elaborate effort to subdivide and define the particulars of the law, it is critical to continue reading in the *Loci* to recognize that what Melanchthon finally considers most significant about the law is simply its power to convict sinners. "Just as the law is that by which the right is enjoined, and by which sin is made manifest," Melanchthon concludes, "so also the gospel is the promise of the grace or mercy of God and therefore the forgiveness of sin and the testimony of God's benevolence toward us."[5] In other words, while the law makes clear what humans are required to do, it inevitably and simply exposes and condemns humanity for its failure, indeed its inability, to do what is required. This convicting work of the law is critical because it paves the way for the declaration and delivery of the gospel. Melanchthon succinctly declares: "Indeed, in justifying sinners, God's first work is to reveal our sin."[6] This he does with the law.

For Melanchthon, the essential work in teaching the law is not teasing out a meticulous presentation of natural law for the sake of governing the

---

4. Melanchthon, *Loci.*, 118.
5. Melanchthon, *Loci.*, 145.
6. Melanchthon, *Loci.*, 162.

world or carefully distinguishing God's eternal moral law from mere Israel-specific ceremonial law; no, the important work is simply to present and then practice the law's power to convict and condemn sinners to prepare them to receive the comfort and joy of the gospel. What finally matters is always the proclamation of the gospel; ultimately, that is really all that matters. The centrality of the gospel is hardly surprising in any Lutheran argument. But for the sake of the present Lutheran exploration of natural law, what must not be overlooked in this gospel revelry is that at this critical point in the *Loci* Melanchthon makes no effort to specify which law he has in mind. In fact, it does not matter. When all is said and done, the law is just the law; it is God's will that reveals both what it means to be human and humans' failure to do it. Law is an all-encompassing term. All category distinctions are finally irrelevant because in whatever form it appears, whether a moral law not to kill a neighbor or a neighborhood ordinance limiting drivers to twenty miles per hour, the law's work of regulating human behavior and revealing human sin remains the same.

In other words, the law is not mapped on a continuum with a few heavyweight parts on one end that count enormously and some trifling parts at the other end of the spectrum that don't matter all that much. Too often, though, this is precisely how the distinctions are handled. Make sure that you don't kill your neighbor—but going seven miles per hour over the speed limit through the neighborhood is no big deal. Such thinking misses the point of the law altogether and abuses what should be understood as a merely didactic effort to offer distinctions merely for the sake of understanding or clarity. Obviously, any value gained in making distinctions within the law evaporates entirely when a three-year-old is cut down by a driver doing twenty-seven. The goal in thinking about the law is not to establish a set of rules one must follow to please God or create an ideal society; nor is it to divide and compartmentalize the law to determine a minimum threshold that can serve as a common moral foundation for all people, Christian or otherwise; nor is the idea to determine which laws actually matter and which ones can be bent or ignored altogether when inconvenient. The point of the law—in whatever distinction, form, or category one either discerns or creates—is to guide all people in their humanity and to show fallen humanity their need for the gospel. This is the argument that Melanchthon builds.

62 • Natural Law

Learning with Luther

Luther's teaching about natural law is similar but, true to form, offered with more polemic. Content to let Melanchthon provide a systematic presentation of the law in its various aspects, Luther's interest, as always, lies in the real situations unfolding in the lives of real people in the world around him. His zeal for God's truth and its impact on people's concrete lives drives Luther to craft strong, often seemingly contradictory, and even outrageous arguments designed to shock people into the joy and delight of living life God's way: the way of rightly distinguishing law and gospel. One of Luther's most direct treatments of the law came in 1525 in the thick of a series of seventy-seven sermons preached on Exodus. English readers know the work as his treatise "How Christians Should Regard Moses."[7] When reading Luther, context is essential. In 1525 the battle against Rome's works righteousness and papal authority continued, but a new set of problems emerged when enthusiasts like Thomas Müntzer and even his former colleague Andreas Karlstadt began pressing the reform spirit into teachings and actions that horrified Luther. He fought the threat with pen and paper.

At the outset of his sermon-become-treatise, Luther lays down clear definitions of law and gospel:

> The law commands and requires us to do certain things. The law is thus directed solely to our behavior and consists in making requirements. For God speaks through the law, saying, "Do this, avoid that, this is what I expect of you." The gospel, however, does not preach what we are to do or to avoid. It sets up no requirements but reverses the approach of the law, does the very opposite and says, "This what God has done for you; he has let his Son be made flesh for you, has let him be put to death for your sake."[8]

With a foundation in place, Luther quickly moves to the pressing objective of explaining how the particular law of Moses applies to the people of his

---

7. Jaroslav Pelikan and Helmut T. Lehmann, eds., *Luther's Works*, American ed., 56 vols. (St. Louis and Philadelphia: Concordia and Fortress, 1958–86), 35:161–74, "How Christians Should Regard Moses."

8. *Luther's Works*, 35:162.

day. His startling answer is that it does not apply: "We must therefore silence the mouths of those factious spirits who say, 'Thus says Moses,' etc. Here you simply reply: Moses has nothing to do with us."[9] Luther presses his case to the point of being absurdly scandalous. Arguing that since God did not actually bring Luther's readers, or gentiles in general, out of Egypt Luther concludes, "This text [Exodus 20:1] makes it clear that even the Ten Commandments do not pertain to us." When it comes to "Moses and all the commandments," he continues, "We will just skip that. We will regard Moses as a teacher, but we will not regard him as our lawgiver—unless he agrees with both the New Testament and the natural law."[10] The final concession is crucial.

As is so often the case with Luther, what initially seems outrageous is actually quite reasonable and internally consistent when rightly understood. Incensed by the legalism of those who would cast off the manmade requirements of Rome only to impose the Old Testament law of Moses, the Reformer makes the case that an individual is bound only by those laws specifically given to him. With one sweeping argument, Luther dismisses *all* Mosaic rules, commandments, regulations, and law. It all belongs only to the ancient people of Israel, not to sixteenth-century residents of Saxony, and not, for that matter, to anyone living in the twenty-first century, except perhaps for Orthodox Jews. For Luther, "The Gentiles are not obligated to obey Moses. Moses is the *Sachsenspiegel* for the Jews."[11] As a technical and precise term, the German noun is left untranslated. A translation might be "Saxon code of law." It refers specifically to "a thirteenth century compilation of the economic and social laws obtaining in and around Magdeburg and Halberstadt."[12] Luther's point is that each person must obey those laws that pertain to him and must not concern himself with particular laws given to another. The laws of Moses are for Israelites, the laws of the *Sachsenspiegel* are for late medieval Saxons, and the laws of Missouri are for twenty-first-century Missourians.

Of course, whether the peculiar laws in force in a particular time and place are from Moses, the *Sachsenspiegel*, or Missouri's legislature, they have

---

9. *Luther's Works*, 35:165.
10. *Luther's Works*, 35:165.
11. *Luther's Works*, 35:167.
12. *Luther's Works*, 35:167.

64 • Natural Law

much in common. That common ground is what Luther terms the natural law. Luther wastes no time arguing for the existence of the natural law and makes no effort to express its content. Like his contemporaries, he takes it for granted. It is the law that is simply part and parcel of the created world itself. It is not created or derived by any man. It is not agreed upon by committees or conventions. It is not established by consensus or common practice. It is rather the will of God that is built in to creation itself, hardwired into the very fabric of every created thing ordering, guiding, and facilitating the functioning of all of creation into a harmonious and unified design. Guided by this natural law, Luther reestablishes—for Saxons, Missourians, and all people anywhere in creation—the authority of the Decalogue he had only just dismissed. "Nature also has these laws," he writes. "Therefore it is natural to honor God, not steal, not commit adultery, not bear false witness, not murder; and what Moses commands is nothing new. For what God has given the Jews from heaven, he has also written in the hearts of all men."[13] It is not because a law appears in the work of Moses that it must be obeyed. But because it appears in the reality of nature, a reality established by God for all creatures, it must be obeyed. Luther summarizes it this way, "Thus we read Moses not because he applies to us, that we must obey him, but because he agrees with the natural law and is conceived better than the Gentiles would ever have been able to do."[14]

Luther navigates a course for his argument that may well seem circuitous and presumptuous, but it serves his purpose perfectly. By relativizing Moses, he quashes all the force of enthusiasts and legalists of every sort who would glean a higher and holier way of living from the pages of the Old Testament. Perceiving that the joy and comfort of the gospel hang in the balance, Luther spares no argument or weapon when fighting against such legalism. This accounts for his dismissal of the Decalogue as merely the word of Moses for Israel, followed shortly by its reinstitution as the best possible expression of God's will for his creation, or what he calls the natural law. No doubt twenty-first-century readers will be inclined, and mostly justified, to think that Luther is able to make such drastic arguments only because in his day the vast majority of people all agreed on the content of the natural law. He could take it for granted and get away with seeming to disparage whole portions of

13. *Luther's Works*, 35:168.
14. *Luther's Works*, 35:172–73.

the Bible. Those who reside in the long opaque shadow of the Enlightenment cannot indulge the same luxury. Invoking the guidance of nature filtered through human hearts is altogether perilous when those hearts have been carefully catechized to believe that every heart is a sacrosanct, autonomous, inviolable source of idiosyncratic truth, and that the unique personhood and individuality of each self-directed human is a sacred reality—indeed perhaps the only remaining sacred reality—that must be preserved and protected at all costs from any alienating imposition of outside authority or law.

It is worth noting that Luther's seemingly easy dismissal of the Decalogue during his 1525 battle with the new legalism of the enthusiasts would be reversed later that same decade when the battle he faced was a fresh appearance of licentiousness and antinomianism in parishes that professed to be Lutheran. After his participation in the Saxon visitation of 1528, Luther was moved to write his small and large catechisms. The rather infamous preface to the former is noteworthy in setting the stage for his renewed appropriation of the Decalogue in the catechisms:

> The deplorable, wretched deprivation that I recently encountered while I was a visitor has constrained and compelled me to prepare this catechism, or Christian instruction, in such a brief, plain, and simple version. Dear God, what misery I beheld! The ordinary person, especially in the villages, knows absolutely nothing about the Christian faith, and unfortunately many pastors are completely unskilled and incompetent teachers. Yet supposedly they all bear the name Christian, are baptized, and receive the holy sacrament, even though they do not know the Lord's Prayer, the Creed, or the Ten Commandments! As a result they live like simple cattle or irrational pigs and, despite the fact that the Gospel has returned, have mastered the fine art of misusing their freedom."[15]

Champion of the gospel that he was, Luther realized through firsthand experience that it was not so farfetched an idea that the free gift of the gospel could in some people foment a spirit of libertine indulgence of the flesh. Luther met the challenge with a robust elaboration of God's enduring law as articulated in the Decalogue. His extraordinary treatment of the Ten

---

15. Robert Kolb and Timothy Wengert, eds., *The Book of Concord* (Minneapolis: Fortress, 2000), 297, 347–48, SC preface.

66 • Natural Law

Commandments in both catechisms is incomparable and used extensively and fruitfully still to this day throughout the church that bears his name and well beyond that tradition. A careful exploration of either document is a worthy and rewarding undertaking that will yield rich dividends for pastoral care as well as quite practical insights into meeting the challenges of faithful living in ordinary life.

Changed Times—Changed Emphasis

Before leaving the sixteenth century for the twenty-first in our consideration of a Lutheran understanding of natural law, there remains another less familiar effort by Luther to combat recurrent forms of antinomianism that warrants particular attention. In his six antinomian disputations from 1537 to 1539, the well-seasoned and indisputably mature Luther offers some remarkably trenchant insights into the role of the law in the world and the relation between the law revealed by Moses and what Luther calls the natural law, that is the law of God grounded in the creation itself. Once again it is, at least in part, a problem in the church that prompts Luther to write. This time, though, the problem has sprouted and flourished within his own Lutheran camp. Some of Luther's most ardent followers were trying to surpass him in their insistence on a Christian life engulfed in the gospel alone, with no place left for the law. It was another round of the antinomian affliction. While Luther's no-holds-barred campaign against these confused Lutherans is fascinating in its own right, what is of present interest is Luther's handling of the law and his ardent defense of the Decalogue.

Faced with a different challenge in 1525, the Reformer had declared the Ten Commandments as only for Israel. A dozen years later he writes, "Only the Decalogue is eternal . . . because in the coming life things will be like what the Decalogue has been demanding here."[16] This new, expansive appreciation for the Decalogue becomes a recurrent theme throughout the disputations. Immediately after affirming the normative role of the Ten Commandments as God's will for the operation of his creation, Luther reasserts the law's accusatory function observing that it was actually the

---

16. Martin Luther, *Solus Decalogus est Aeternus: Martin Luther's Complete Antinomian Theses and Disputations*, English translation with the Latin text of the Weimar edition, ed. and trans. Holger Sonntag (Minneapolis: Cygnus Series of Lutheran Press, 2008), 129.

Decalogue that "brought Christ from heaven. For if there had not been the Decalogue that accused and condemned us, for what, I ask, would Christ have descended?"[17] These normative and accusatory functions of the law cohere neatly with Melanchthon's own summary treatment of the single law of God.

Luther then makes explicit a core understanding of the law that runs as a presupposition beneath his theology: "From the foundation of the world the Decalogue was inscribed in the minds of all men."[18] All nations, Luther insists (whether entirely accurately or not is beside the point!), operated with a sense of that law and so offered worship to what deity they could imagine, honored parents, and shunned vices. "But later," he continues:

> Since men finally arrived at a point where they cared neither for God nor for men, God was forced to renew those laws through Moses and, written by his own finger on tablets, to place them before our eyes so that we might be reminded of what we were before Adam's fall and of what we shall be in Christ one day. Thus Moses was merely something like an interpreter or illustrator of the laws written in the mind of all men wherever they might be under the sun in the world.[19]

This text is remarkable on many levels. First, Luther gives full-throated support to the idea that the Decalogue was not crafted at Sinai but was built into every part of the creation from the very beginning of the world. The Commandments simply spell out what had always been in place and had normed the lives of all people in all places—whether they knew it or not. Considered in this light, the law is seen in its full significance as nothing more and nothing less than God's will for the right functioning of his creation for all time. Yet the even more significant idea is that this will of God, this law inscribed into the very stuff of creation, including every human heart, and then spelled out in the Ten Commandments is the description of what God intended humans to be when he first created them and what they will be in the fullness of Christ's kingdom. In other words, the law *is* eternal. It is the plan, the order, the structure, the arrangement, the will of God for

---

17. Luther, *Solus Decalogus est Aeternus*, 129.
18. Luther, *Solus Decalogus est Aeternus*, 187.
19. Luther, *Solus Decalogus est Aeternus*, 189.

68 • Natural Law

his creation—a creation that was very good on the sixth day of the world and will be very good, indeed perfect, in Christ on the last day of the world.

In 1539, in his fifth disputation against the antinomians, Luther confirms the idea that the law is the foundation for all creation. He reiterates, "The law in general is not given and laid down for a certain people, but for all of humanity."[20] And then he continues by unfolding the history of the law and man's depraved failure to abide by that law so that "God was forced again to give us a limit, lest we forgot totally his law, so that we would at least remember who we were before and who we will be in the future."[21] The law, then, is not essentially or primarily God's attempt to curb sinful man or his merciful means of exposing sin and so fostering repentance. The law does both of those things, of course, but it actually precedes the appearance of sinful man. It exists not because of sin; it exists because the creation exists. And at the eschaton, when Christ returns to his creation visibly, and the entire creation is restored and remade into the fullness of God's perfect plan, the law, which is the will of God for his creation, will continue to be present as the order of the new creation.

Though he does not offer a systematic treatment of the law, Luther sheds much light on the present consideration of natural law. Like Melanchthon, Luther believes that this law is real and continues to play a vital role in directing the day-to-day lives of ordinary people going about their ordinary affairs. This natural law is not at odds with the Decalogue or, for that matter, with any other faithful expression of the law that God has hardwired into his creation. Even local laws, whether in ancient Israel, medieval Saxony, or twenty-first-century Missouri, may be—indeed *must* be—judged as good or bad according to the degree of their adherence to God's foundational, natural law as it is articulated and confirmed in the Decalogue. Finally, Luther also agrees with his younger Wittenberg colleague about the critical purpose of God's law as it is summarized in the Ten Commandments. "Thus the Ten Commandments," Luther offers, "are a mirror of our life, in which we can see wherein we are lacking, etc. . . . We read Moses for the sake of the promises about Christ."[22] The law makes clear the sinner's need for the gospel, and the law makes clear God's will for the way that humans are meant to live in his creation.

---

20. Luther, *Solus Decalogus est Aeternus*, 321.
21. Luther, *Solus Decalogus est Aeternus*, 321.
22. *Luther's Works*, 35:173.

While the teaching of Luther and Melanchthon carries significant weight for Lutheran confession, the definitive document is *The Book of Concord*. Though the law is a recurrent topic in this authoritative collection of confessional documents, natural law is mentioned only twice and in passing each time. In the *Apology of the Augsburg Confession*, Melanchthon begins his long defense of justification by grace through faith in Christ alone (as spelled out in article 4 of the *Augsburg Confession*) by discussing the law. His point here is simply to affirm the essential continuity between the law expressed in the Decalogue and the natural law written into the creation, but he is content to make the point in a parenthetical statement: "(because to some extent human reason naturally understands it [the law] since reason contains the same judgment divinely written on the mind)."[23] The second reference appears in article 5 of the Formula of Concord, which appeared a generation after Melanchthon's *Apology*. The *Formula* states, "For pagans had something of a knowledge of God from the law of nature, but at the same time they did not truly know him nor did they truly honor him."[24] Here it is the incapacity of the natural law to bring about the right worship of God that is the point, and so it is hardly a ringing endorsement of the importance of natural law. What is actually far more interesting is that same article's earlier definition of the law: "In its strict sense the law is a divine teaching in which the righteous, unchanging will of God revealed how human beings were created in their nature, thoughts, words, and deeds to be pleasing and acceptable to God."[25] The law's second function immediately follows: "This law also threatens those who transgress it with God's wrath and temporal and eternal punishments."[26] Again, the twofold purpose of the law is paramount. There is a steady consistency in the sixteenth-century Lutheran understanding of the law.

The Lutheran Position

The long preceding presentation of proto-Lutheran thinking on natural law is of more than merely historical or even parochial interest. From this

---

23. *The Book of Concord*, 121, Ap 4, 7.
24. *The Book of Concord*, 585, FC SD 5, 22.
25. *The Book of Concord*, 584, FC SD 5, 17.
26. *The Book of Concord*, 584, FC SD 5, 17.

foundation it is possible to venture an initial account of a Lutheran understanding of natural law. To begin, it should be stated pointedly, that what might be described as "natural law" does absolutely exist. Such is the case for the simple fact that nature exists and functions according to certain enduring laws. Starting from the givenness of a world created by God that operates according to his will significantly qualifies all efforts to distinguish meticulously between various sorts of laws, whether physical, moral, ceremonial, positivistic, or even local.

The law of gravity is not really so different from the law not to commit adultery. Both are part of the way God established the world to operate. Both are what we might call natural realities. So it is that life tends to work better when lived in tune with the limits established by each natural reality, and the violation of either the law related to gravity or adultery brings deleterious effects, whether that be a shattered marriage or a shattered skull.

Taking the next step from this starting point, the approach of the first Lutherans blunts any concerns about which laws really matter: in fact, they all matter. In other words, if one is living in sixteenth-century Saxony, one obeys all the ordinances and directives that guide life in that time and place. And if one is living in ancient Israel, then the laws regulating and guiding life in that time and place are normative for that person. Taken together, any given composite set of one locale's laws make clear what it means to be a human rightly living as God intended in the particularities of that specific circumstance or situation. That the peculiar manifestations or local laws in one place vary, or even vary widely, from those of another place is of little concern as long as the laws governing life in a given place are congruent with what God has clearly revealed about his will for the right functioning of human lives—hence the immeasurable importance and value of the Decalogue. A villager living in Papua New Guinea is living rightly when he follows all the international, national, regional, and local written and unwritten regulations, conventions, and even social niceties that lead him to be of good service to the creatures around him in his world, even if that way of life is markedly different than a life rightly lived by an urbanite living and working in downtown St. Louis. When different local accounts come into conflict as cultures interact and collide, the citizens of both places are obliged to work through the process of evaluating their local codes according to the standard of God's revealed will and in light of new insights perhaps gained by a different application of that will by another group of people. Thus, social mores, local statutes, and national law may shift and change without threatening the reality, validity, or authority of an unchanging law that is built into the structure of creation itself.

Finally, thinking about the natural law in terms of God's creation also means that those who are responsible for establishing and enforcing laws, whether in the home or the state, ultimately should be bound not by social convention or by human reason or by some assumed universal, common, human moral sense, but only by what God has made clear to be his will for his creatures, and whether or not it is recognized and embraced, that will has been spelled out for all people in the Decalogue. In other words, the reality of God's will is at work in the world, and it is accessible to any human interested in hearing and heeding it. So God's will for creation, his law, is wired into the universe as Moses teaches us and into our hearts as Paul teaches us. That hearts can be seared, corrupted, and deceived and that consequently governments in whatever form and level can be similarly at odds with God's will for his creation changes nothing about the reality and enduring authority of the law that permeates creation, what might fittingly be called natural law.

This approach to thinking about the natural law as but a name for the will of God for his creation lends support to what may well be a helpful alternate path between the ensconced rival positions of realists and nominalists. On the one hand are those who hold to the reality of transcendent universals that encompass all of life, and on the other are those who embrace the thoroughgoing relativism of robust nominalism. Among conservative-minded Christians, the position of nominalists is routinely disparaged as a threat to universal truth. Nominalism, after all, argues that "universals" are simply concepts of the human mind that were established merely for the sake of convenience and are not eternal ideals in which the things of this world participate in some derivative way, which, of course, is the classic view of Plato and later Aquinas.

Building on the Lutheran foundation, however, presents another option: God acts and establishes whatever he arbitrarily chooses based not on his unchanging nature or in accord with a natural law as if this preceded and superseded him. God simply does what God does for no other reason than that he chose it. He is God, bound by and to nothing. Nevertheless, the universal truths that result from his plans and actions related to creation are certainly not mere human constructs. They definitely exist outside the human mind, the result of God willing them for his creation and nothing more—and nothing less. This approach keeps the purpose of a "universal" in sharp focus: it does not limit, explain, or norm God but exists purely according to what God determined was good for the sake of a well-ordered creation. So it is that Lutherans are not interested in the various forms of realism or idealism found in Plato, Aquinas, or Calvinism and claim instead a sort of soft nominalism that allows God to exercise sovereign, absolute free reign over his creation as he chooses, bound only by his word and promises made to his creatures. This helps better explain what is and is not meant when Lutherans claim that the law is eternal.

Facing the Opposition

Lest the account provided to this point be guilty of even more naiveté than what is admittedly already amply suggested, the broad and frequently strident, to the point of virulent, attacks on the idea of natural law must be acknowledged. There have been Christians fiercely opposed to the natural law since the days of Karl Barth and his unrelenting attack on natural religion and, at least as he saw it, its concomitant ally natural law. No doubt, natural religion fully deserves every broadside it is dealt from any quarter. An ugly product of the Enlightenment, natural religion is the apogee of arrogant human hubris and alleged autonomy. But a tool bent to evil use is not thereby inherently evil. Such is the case with natural law. Still, it is not just the association with natural religion that damns natural law. There are other issues.

Probably the most compelling case against the idea of a natural law is the incredible lack of consensus and ambiguity that attend any assertion of a law that resides in all of nature, waiting at the ready for man to discover and follow. This charge was leveled with verve by a theologian now deemed inappropriate for proper use. Still, in the spirit of a natural law that exists whether or not one accepts its existence, I will follow the maxim that truth is truth regardless the voice that speaks it and make use of helpful insight and potent prose while implying no approval of the disgraced author who will be granted only the requisite credit entailed in a footnote. In 1964 when the robust rejection of natural law was yet in full force, this demolition of natural law appeared:

> The "law of nature" has been evoked in favor of both democracy and the divine right of kings, both primitive communism and capitalistic free enterprise. . . . *Nature* may be the struggle of the species for survival; it may be the existing social order in its interplay of hierarchies and power claims; or, on the other hand, it may be the *essence* of a person or thing that he is called to become. The word thus includes two different scales of variability; when *nature* is understood to mean a quasi-platonic *essence*, distinct from what things appear to do, we have the whole gamut of *ideals* which have not yet been actualized in experience: if, on the other hand, by *nature* we understand "things as they are" we must deal with the entire scale of empirical realities. The conviction, almost universally shared, that nature is a reliable source of knowable and binding ethical norms rests on failure to clarify either the content which it claims to have proved or the truth claims which it presupposes.[27]

More than half a century later, James K. A. Smith serves as another apt representative of the fervent disavowal of natural law, titling the fifth chapter of his book *Awaiting the King*, "Redeeming Christendom: Or, What's Wrong with Natural Law?" As the chapter unfolds, it becomes apparent that he believes there is plenty wrong with it, rejecting "the moral minimalism of a 'natural law' project as a sub-Christian expression of political theology."[28] In the spirit of Barth, Smith contends, "The shape of Christian political witness is not merely a nostalgic appeal to 'creation norms' or a minimalist appeal to 'natural law' that is accessible by 'natural reason'; rather, it is nourished by the Christological specificity of the gospel and the model of Christ the

---

27. John Howard Yoder, *The Christian Witness to the State* (Scottdale: Herald, 2002), 82 (italics in original). The untold damage done to individuals, to the church, and to the witness of God's truth by the great Mennonite theologian's personal sins stands as a stunning testimony to the extent of sin's reach into every life—even those who claim to follow Christ. It seems appropriate to wonder if this may not be an apt instance of one of Hauerwas's many axioms: "When Christians get their theology wrong they cannot help but get their lives and their accounts of the world wrong as well. Or rather, more accurately, Christians often get their theology wrong because they have gotten their lives wrong." Stanley Hauerwas, *With the Grain of the Universe: The Church's Witness and Natural Theology* (Grand Rapids: Baker, 2001), 215.

28. James K. A. Smith, *Awaiting the King: Reforming Public Theology* (Grand Rapids: Baker, 2017), 153.

74 • Natural Law

King and the relationship to his body."[29] As much as the criticisms of both men seem to negate any talk of natural law, it should be noted that I heartily agree with both assessments.

What must be recognized is that these criticisms take aim not at the idea of a natural law per se but rather at the errant application of the idea. I suspect that this is typical of the vast majority of natural law criticisms from Christians. The existence of a divine plan for the right functioning of the creation is not denied—indeed it seems to me that it would take a thoroughly atheistic argument to mount such an attack—rather it is the widespread and persistent attempts to make natural law do things it simply cannot do that is the actual problem. It is quite true that too many Christians, including Lutherans, assume that if there is a natural law, then that law can provide the common ground for Christians to dialogue and presumably influence unbelievers in the world. Or, more crudely, they invoke the natural law to claim rights for themselves or others assuming that everyone must simply agree with what is "clearly manifest in natural law" (such as, for example, the right to self-defense). Or they may understand natural law as a "good enough" minimum level of morality for the world and fail to witness to the world the fullness of God's will for his creation (for example, condemning homosexual activity while failing to insist on heterosexual chastity). These errant misuses of natural law are legitimate problems that merit stern rebuke and rejection, but these problems are not inherent in the idea of natural law.

No friend of natural law, Stanley Hauerwas devotes a significant portion of his classic text *The Peaceable Kingdom* to toppling the idea of natural law.[30] He makes a solid argument pointing out especially the damage done to the church when her theologians stopped doing the work of ethics in light of the revelation of Christ and instead attempted to base their ethical efforts on a common natural law. As he puts it, "Although moral theologians served an

---

29. Smith, *Awaiting the King*, 151. Smith's disdain for the notion of a natural law is so thorough-going and so typical that when I first read the book I reluctantly resigned myself to the fact that the very term *natural law* was irretrievably damaged, and it was necessary to enlist and champion another name for the reality it sought to describe. Given the title of the present chapter, it should be apparent that I have not maintained that erstwhile determination. Still, given the profound problems of ambiguity and negative associations with the term *natural law*, I have renewed my pledge and will offer an alternate label before this chapter's work is done.

30. Stanley Hauerwas, *The Peaceable Kingdom: A Primer in Christian Ethics* (Notre Dame: University of Notre Dame Press, 1983). The argument against natural law is spread throughout chapter 4: "On Beginning in the Middle: Nature, Reason, and the Task of Theological Ethics."

ecclesial function, their work was thought to be based primarily on 'natural law.'"[31] Hauerwas provides a summary list of seven "difficulties" encountered when attempting to use "natural law" as the "starting point for Christian ethics."[32] Those interested can read Hauerwas for a full accounting, but the bulk of the complaints rightly focus on the church's resultant failure to confess her unique truth centered in the life, death, and resurrection of Jesus Christ. After all, as Hauerwas writes, "The way of life taught by Christ is meant to be an ethic for all people."[33] This point is significant for this chapter because it supports the idea of a way of life for all humanity, which begins to have much in common with the idea of natural law I have presented. In fact, later in the book, Hauerwas admits, "Some kind of natural law assumptions, at least in a qualified form, are integral to Christian ethics."[34] Indeed. The entire argument of Hauerwas's Gifford Lectures, published under the title *With the Grain of the Universe*, makes precisely the sort of claim I am interested in making: there is a shape to the universe—a shape that points to Christ, is wholly embodied in Christ, and will be brought to perfect fulfillment at the return of Christ. That shape of the universe is identical to the will of God for his creation, what a Lutheran would call "God's law at work in creation," that is, the natural law.

Hauerwas is no Lutheran; in fact, he seems to delight in denying even the suggestion that he might be so identified (apparently there are limits to his checkered ecclesial identity). So for the sake of this chapter's task, it is time to hear from a couple significant Lutherans and let them point us to what I hope will be a final degree of clarity and certainty regarding a Lutheran view of natural law.

Two Lutheran Voices

Almost devotional in nature, Dietrich Bonhoeffer's *Creation and Fall* is a masterwork as it reflects on the first three chapters of Genesis. Pondering God's second and third day activity of distinguishing the waters above from the waters below the firmament and then the land from the seas,

---

31. Hauerwas, *The Peaceable Kingdom*, 51.
32. Hauerwas, *The Peaceable Kingdom*, 63.
33. Hauerwas, *The Peaceable Kingdom*, 58.
34. Hauerwas, *The Peaceable Kingdom*, 120.

76 • Natural Law

Bonhoeffer writes, "Unaffected by human life the fixed world stands before God, unchangeable and undisturbed. An eternal law binds it. This law is nothing but the command of the Word of God itself."[35] Remarkable in this passage is the grounding of the enduring, eternal law that holds and orders the earth itself wholly and simply in the command of the Word of God. No preexisting reality or universal law of nature constrains or directs the Creator. He creates the law *ex nihilo*. The law simply "is" because God has ordained it to be. And with the full authority of the Creator empowering it, this law norms and directs the fixed world of the earth itself, complete with all of the myriad physical laws and realities that continually shape its being and operation.

In his later, incomplete, imprisonment work that would become *Ethics*, Bonhoeffer fleshes out his theological thinking built around the twin foci of creation and Christ. These truths are not antithetical or even antagonistic but are bound together in a beautiful, unifying relationship. "The natural is the form of life," Bonhoeffer explains, "preserved by God for the fallen world and directed towards justification, redemption and renewal through Christ."[36] And, Bonhoeffer makes clear, the natural is "the form which embraces the entire human race."[37] Later, in the same chapter, "The Last Things and the Things Before the Last," Bonhoeffer emphasizes the givenness of the natural, that is, the things that are firmly established as part of the creation:

> What is natural cannot be determined by any arbitrary decision, and indeed whatever is set up in this arbitrary manner by an individual, a society or an institution will necessarily collapse and destroy itself in the encounter with the natural which is already established. Whoever does injury or violence to the natural will suffer for it.[38]

Removing any potential ambiguity regarding the source of authority of what he calls the natural, Bonhoeffer spells out his thinking explicitly: "Our view differs from the Enlightenment view in that it takes the natural to

---

35. Dietrich Bonhoeffer, *Creation and Fall* (New York: Simon & Schuster, 1959), 31.
36. Dietrich Bonhoeffer, *Ethics* (New York: Simon & Schuster, 1955), 145.
37. Bonhoeffer, *Ethics*, 145.
38. Bonhoeffer, *Ethics*, 146.

rest upon what is objectively given and not upon the subjective spontaneity of reason."[39] Bonhoeffer may not use the term *natural law*, but what he describes as the "established" and "objectively given," which then serves as the master over reason, is but another name for the same reality. God's will for his creation, his law for creation, founds and directs everything in the creation. Finally, in the opening sentences of the chapter "Christ, Reality, and Good," Bonhoeffer makes his delightfully disruptive declaration:

> Whoever wishes to take up the problem of a Christian ethic must be confronted at once with a demand which is quite without parallel. He must from the outset discard as irrelevant the two questions which alone impel him to concern himself with the problem of ethics, "How can I be good?" and "How can I do good?," and instead of these he must ask the utterly and totally different question "What is the will of God?"[40]

Given that the Christian ethic is in truth the one right way of life for all people, the centrality of knowing and doing the will of God becomes the dominant, indeed, the only concern. And as has been shown above, the will of God is rightly and straightforwardly understood as the design or plan for the creation that God implanted into the creation itself from the very beginning—a plan, incidentally, that also from the beginning included the redemption and consummation of the creation through the Spirit-driven work of Christ. Seen from this comprehensive perspective, the natural law is not a distant, impassive principle of nature that imposes a harsh reality on creatures without regard to their well-being, much less their joy. Nor is the natural law some rationally perceived bare-bones account of what people must do to placate other people or principles and so avoid punishment. No, the natural law is the specific plan, design, order, and will for the life of every human established by the tender, compassionate, personal, invested God who molded man from the mud and then breathed into him his own animating breath. The natural law is God's law that grounds all reality, holds the world together, guides every creature to flourish, and points to the consummation of creation in Christ. It is the law of God for creation. Such is the import of Bonhoeffer's insights.

---

39. Bonhoeffer, *Ethics*, 146.
40. Bonhoeffer, *Ethics*, 187.

78 • Natural Law

With an assertive reminder that the first article of the Creed comes first, Gustaf Wingren also highlighted the importance of creation and explored the implications of tackling the theological task centered on the divine action and continuing reality of the creation. The impact on an understanding of natural law is significant. Man's relationship with God, Wingren contends, is unlike any other interaction he has in all of the rest of his life. The Swedish theologian elaborates:

> God is Creator, and His relation to man is given in the simple fact that man lives. All of man's reactions to his own life are reactions within his relationship to God and this cannot be established by him through his acceptance of God, nor can it be broken by his denial of God. Rather it is established in birth, i.e. Creation, and although it may vary thereafter in content (it may display wrath or love, judgment or grace), it does not cease.[41]

This means that from conception, actually from even before conception, each person is in a relationship with God; this is the case simply because existence happens within God's creation, and so within and according to God's plan. God's will, his law for creation, thus surrounds and norms life for every creature. Indeed, Wingren observes, "The will of the Creator runs like an undercurrent beneath the stream of human works, and is not disturbed even when the surface is ruffled."[42] God's law, his will, is always there, always at work for all those in the world. "The law," contends Wingren, "is operative in the whole world, and is continually engaged in asserting its demands."[43] So it is that this singular law impacts each human being in two distinct ways:

> But while the Law exercises its positive function of compelling men to act, it also speaks of the man who *does* the Law. Here it speaks negatively, and its function is one of accusation. The first work of the Law, that of compulsion, is continually passing into the second work of the Law, that of accusation. It exercises both of these functions at the same time.[44]

---

41. Gustaf Wingren, *Creation and Law*, trans. Ross Mackenzie (Eugene: Wipf and Stock, 1961), 179.

42. Wingren, *Creation and Law*, 96.

43. Wingren, *Creation and Law*, 180

44. Wingren, *Creation and Law*, 181.

Wingren has now not only reinforced the universal impact of God's will built into the creation but has also reiterated the essential twofold function of the law in the lives of people living in a fallen world. The law both directs our living and rebukes our failure to live rightly. As a good Lutheran, Wingren then celebrates the gospel reality that aims at the restoration of creation through the salvific work of Christ who actually joins creation by becoming a part of creation in the incarnation. But such cheery and promising messages belong to the realm of gospel and so lie beyond our present preoccupation with the work of God's law that cajoles and condemns. The law that does this twofold work is none other than the natural law.

Summary and Conclusion: What Is and What Will Be

Other Lutherans can no doubt find much to criticize in this chapter and will be disappointed about my failure to include in my discussion one or another "absolutely essential thinker" on this topic, but it is time to draw this brief discussion to a close and offer four summary observations about "a Lutheran understanding of natural law," plus a final thought.

First, God's law for his creation should be understood as a singular reality binding on all people. The Creator has established a way for his creation to work, and that includes a way for humans to be rightly human within that creation. The sinful failure of humanity and the subsequent redemption accomplished by Christ has not negated God's will for his creation, but also fits within the plan and brings the creation to its completion. Thus, at the resurrection, freed at last from the old man, the saints "will perform the will of God by the power of the indwelling Spirit of God spontaneously, without coercion, unhindered, perfectly and completely, with sheer joy, and they will delight in his will eternally."[45] The will of God, the law, is eternal indeed.

Second, while there is one law of God for all people, there are in this broken world many kinds of people, and so there are a variety of users of the law. Those who by grace know Christ strive now, with the power of the Spirit, to live into the fullness of God's will as it is revealed in the Decalogue, and then revealed even more fully in the life of the one perfect, fully human, man who entirely accomplished God's will: Jesus Christ. The teaching, life,

---

45. *The Book of Concord*, 591, FC SD VI, 25.

80 • Natural Law

and example of Christ provide the pattern of life for all people. Certainly, those apart from Christ pay it little heed, yet the law in its fullness still compels, constrains, and judges them. Their own hearts and nearly every culture in the world bear testimony to at least some degree of the law that enfolds and binds them.

Third, since man is corrupted by sin, and the depths of evil at work in any human heart defy description, the reality of the natural law provides no functional foundation or concrete guidance when attempting to establish or adjudicate moral questions in the public arena. In the world, the church cannot assert natural law as if all people will naturally accede to its authority but instead merely witnesses to its reality.[46]

Fourth, while no unanimity on the content or application of the natural law in the fallen world is possible, the law is nevertheless very much present and at work in individuals, communities, and entire cultures. The natural law lays claim on all people, whether or not they admit it. Pastors and all who seek to guide people into God's truth should remember this reality and capitalize on it as they seek to apply the truth of God's will in individual lives and situations.

Finally, as promised, given the overwhelming negative connotations, shrill debates, and interminable confusions that cling to the term *natural law*, perhaps a new term is in order—one that can communicate all that should and should not be included in the discussion of God's will for his creation. As one less tainted, though probably also less elegant, I offer the term *creational law*. I suspect that few even in my own Lutheran orbit will be ready to sign-on and adopt it, but I'm willing to give it a try.

Like the law of the jungle, the will of God for his creation is just there. It needs no apology or defense. It needs no portfolio of empirical evidence or carefully reasoned explanation to account for its authority. The wise, through often painful lessons and long training, learn to respect and even love God's will and so prosper as they live in tune with it. The foolish dismiss it, violate it, and ridicule it and eventually, inexorably, pay the price for their willful rejection of God's creational law. But as long as fools remain—and

---

46. This point, among many others, was made convincingly in an insightful and important essay written by Reinhard Hütter before his catholic faith became fully Roman. See Hütter, "The Twofold Center of Lutheran Ethics," in *The Promise of Lutheran Ethics*, ed. Karen L. Bloomquist and John R. Stumme (Minneapolis, Fortress, 1998), 31–54.

until the last day when sin's reign will finally be ended forever, the fool certainly continues to reside in every human heart—the law that is built into every part of creation will perform its essential twofold purpose guiding the wise and condemning the fool. Hopelessly obscured, resisted, and denied by the continuing corruption of sin, unless defined and declared by direct revelation such as the Decalogue or the Sermon on the Mount and then embraced as such, God's law for creation cannot provide an indisputable ground for any positive law of any people or place; neither can it serve as a theoretical bare minimum of basic morality for all people; nor can it lead people into a deeper understanding of God's perfect grace and his eternal purposes—only the gospel can do that. Still, the law built into the creation itself can do what God intended it to do: it can norm the lives of the wise, and it can condemn the lives of fools. Such is the reality of the will of God for his creation, the enduring, eternal, creational law of God.

Pakaluk Response to Biermann

MICHAEL PAKALUK

Biermann's conception of the natural law as the will of God for creation, built into creation, is well expressed in the first verse of John's gospel, with its deliberate modification of the book of Genesis: "In the beginning was the *Logos*." *Logos* is a term deliberately taken from classical thought, meaning both word and reason. If everything that is, without exception (note John's careful language in verse 3), is created through, by, in, and for the *Logos*, then the creation must for us be incipiently expressible and rational, especially insofar as we ourselves have rational natures and are actors within it.

Along with Pope Benedict XVI in his famous Regensburg address, I take John's use of *logos* as signaling in revelation a special aptness between that revelation and the best strands Greek philosophy:[1] "The encounter between the Biblical message and Greek thought did not happen by chance. The vision of Saint Paul, who saw the roads to Asia barred and in a dream saw a Macedonian man plead with him: 'Come over to Macedonia and help us!' (cf. Acts 16:6–10)—this vision can be interpreted as a 'distillation' of the intrinsic necessity of a rapprochement between Biblical faith and Greek inquiry."[2]

If there is a logic of creation, or a "creation law," one would not be surprised to find that Christians such as Biermann would return to it and rediscover the notion of it—as it is true. But was such an understanding of

---

1. An aptness suggested long before, Benedict notes, by the "I am" of Exodus 3:16.
2. Pope Benedict XVI, "Faith, Reason, and the University: Memories and Reflections," September 12, 2006, https://www.vatican.va/content/benedict-xvi/en/speeches/2006/september/documents/hf_ben-xvi_spe_20060912_university-regensburg.html.

natural law salient for, or even present in, the thought of the Reformers of Wittenberg? If it was present, it was soon overwhelmed and as if shunted aside, because of three of their key positions: *sola scriptura*, human nature as corrupted with concupiscence, and a certain (praiseworthy) zeal to see that the gospel not be hidden beneath mere human learning.

This last is emphasized by Pope Benedict in his Regensburg lecture on "the three stages of dehellenization of theology." "Dehellenization," he says, "first emerges in connection with the postulates of the Reformation in the sixteenth century. Looking at the tradition of scholastic theology, the Reformers thought they were confronted with a faith system totally conditioned by philosophy, that is to say an articulation of the faith based on an alien system of thought. As a result, faith no longer appeared as a living historical Word but as one element of an overarching philosophical system."[3] Melanchthon's *Loci* shows such an attitude.

Indeed, Melanchthon's career and influence seem to illustrate this shunting aside. There even seems to be a divided person in Melanchthon, whereby the evangelical side of him pushed aside his classical humanist side. Luther was so fond of the *Loci* that he exclaimed it was worthy of being included in the canon of Sacred Scripture. But who would guess, from the skepticism about the natural law evinced by Melancthon in the *Loci*, that in other substantive treatises, such as his *Epitome of Moral Philosophy* and his *Commentary on the Ethics of Aristotle*, he would provide what he clearly regards as adequate deductions of the precepts of the Decalogue from what he calls *notitiae* implanted in us by God? (*Notitia* for him is a technical term that, he says, means the same as the Stoic notion of *prolepsis* as well as the Aristotelian notion of a *principium*. One might render it "implicit premise."). In one place he even refers to one of his deductions as a "syllogism."[4] But it is as if the assurance he would show in those (slightly later) philosophical works steps aside for the skepticism of the evangelical work, so as not to seem to eclipse the gospel.

Melanchthon, praised by Erasmus, wrote verses in Latin, and translated and commented upon dozens of classical texts.[5] In his humanistic and

---

3. Benedict XVI, "Faith, Reason, and the University."

4. Philipp Melanchthon, *Enarrationes Aliquot Librorum Ethicorum Aristotelis, Primi, Secundi, Tertii Et Quinti, Ad Intelligendum Aristotelem Utiles* (Mylius, 1546), 415, original from the Bavarian State Library, digitized June 29, 2016.

5. A. Pelzer Wagener, "Melanchthon: A German Humanist," *The Classical Weekly* 22, no. 20 (1929): 155–60. *JSTOR*, https://doi.org/10.2307/4389299.

84 • Natural Law

classical scholarship, he shows a deep appreciation for the admirability of action and virtues of the ancients, as well as the portraits of the virtues drawn by Cicero in *De Officiis* and Aristotle in his *Ethics*. He regarded human virtue as resplendent: "Practical principles are *notitiae* placed within minds by God, in order that we should show obedience to God; they serve to mark out good actions from base actions, and they govern morals. Indeed, when you hear that man is in the image of God, or that he is has a likeness to his creator, you should think especially of this light. . . . Whatever there is of splendor, whatever is praiseworthy, exists in us because God scatters rays of his own wisdom in us"—we become as if "mirrors of the wisdom of God."[6] This is his meaning when he says frequently that moral philosophy itself is a sharing in the wisdom of God.[7]

But because of *sola scriptura*, his treatment of moral philosophy insofar as it involves law becomes constricted to law to the neglect of virtue. Why? Christians in following Christ are bound to accept as regards natural law only what Scripture says about it. But Paul says that the gentiles are a law unto themselves insofar as they have a law written on their hearts (Rom 2:14–16). Therefore, for the purposes of Christian life, the natural law must be construed as no more than those principles that are somehow implanted in the human heart, together with any obvious consequences from those principles.[8] Note what such a conception does not include. It does not include the study of the *Logos* manifested in creation, to discover what the will of God is for creation. (Paul does not say, after all, that that is how the gentiles proceed; he says, or seems to say, that they start from lawlike premises implanted in their hearts, and that this is sufficient for "the law.") The rich tradition of the virtues and classical conceptions of human nature and society look to be irrelevant and are treated as irrelevant by Melanchthon in his various attempts at deductions of the natural law. Indeed, we see in Melanchthon how *sola scriptura* leads directly to "formalism" in ethics.

The other position of relevance, which I mentioned, is that corrupt

---

6. Melanchthon, *Enarrationes*, 406. All translations mine.

7. See for example *Epitome Philosophiae Moralis*, in Melanchthon, *Enarrationes*, 3.

8. "The law of nature consists of the *notitiae* of practical principles, and their conclusions, which are drawn out as necessary consequences from them. . . . And the summary of these is set down in the Decalogue." Melanchthon, *Enarrationes*, 406–7.

human nature is overcome by concupiscence.[9] If this is so, then studying human nature and human sociability is likely to be pointless. Indeed, Melanchthon says that any inquiry into *inclinationes* of human nature, of the sort that classical authors attempted, without the guidance of implanted *notitiae*, will end up countenancing bad things as good.[10]

These three positions of Wittenberg come together in the infamous case of Philip of Hesse.[11] I agree with those commentators who say that the Wittenberg authorities acted with much prudence in the context of their time and cannot be judged harshly. I simply want to draw attention to what materials they used in their deliberations and what else they might have made reference to but did not.

The case involved a nobleman who maintained that his propensity repeatedly to wander showed that his marriage was not playing the role for him of relief of concupiscence. Therefore, he believed (perhaps in conscience) as a matter of necessity that he should be granted a dispensation to take a second wife.

How did this case present itself to the authorities of Wittenberg? Sacred Scripture countenances multiple wives; therefore, applying *sola scriptura*, one cannot rule out the expedient of taking a second wife. Besides, the law implanted on the human heart, to which Scripture testifies, says solely not to commit adultery, which is precisely what Philip so earnestly wished to avoid through a second marriage.

The Wittenberg authorities also supposed that, because we are masses of concupiscence (the second position mentioned), marriage is in effect obligatory for us (as the Augsburg Confession asserts) for the relief of concupiscence. If a marriage is not playing that role, then might a Christian who remains exposed to sin, contrary to the will of God, plead some sort of necessity?

For all that, Philip showed himself a Christian of faith who accepted the forgiveness of sins promised by the gospel, and so he could not be counseled

---

9. "All men are full of evil lust and inclinations from their mothers' wombs." Article 2 of the Augsburg Confession, in Theodore G. Tappert, *The Book of Concord: The Confessions of the Evangelical Lutheran Church*, (Philadelphia: Fortress, 1959), 29. See also Philipp Melanchthon, *Apologia Confessionis Augustanae*, section 1.

10. Melanchthon, *Epitome Philosophiae Moralis*, in *Enarrationes*, 4–5.

11. See the excellent treatment in John Alfred Faulkner, "Luther and the Bigamous Marriage of Philip of Hesse," *The American Journal of Theology* 17, no. 2 (1913): 206–31, http://www.jstor.org/stable /3154607.

that his eternal salvation hinged on his remaining faithful to his first wife, who must continue to be his sole wife.

All of this is to say that the Wittenberg theologians nowhere in their deliberations gave thought to the logic of creation as regards marriage. They specifically do not reason from the purpose or ends of marriage. They do not appeal to creation law for marriage, nor could they really have done so if they were not to set themselves up as interpreters of the natural law, as the Romish church claimed to be.

How might such reasoning proceed? It might go as follows. One purpose of marriage is the procreation of children, and for rational creatures, procreation must include education up to adulthood and beyond. But such attention, on account of the sacrifices it demands given human nature, requires practically speaking an assurance of paternity. Therefore, most certainly polyandry would be forbidden. However, it would seem that polygamy cannot be practiced, practically speaking, given human nature, without also licensing polyandry. Therefore, polygamy too must be forbidden.

Again, if another purpose of marriage is conjugal fidelity, that is, the bond which consists of a reciprocal use and enjoyment in justice by each spouse of the body of the other through a complete gift of each to each, then a man who is already married to one woman cannot take another, as he would be attempting to take away what he had given.

Again, if another purpose of marriage is the fostering of a great bond of affection of friendship, and friendship requires equality, but equality is destroyed if one spouse takes a second spouse, then again, by the creation law of marriage, marriage itself would exclude one spouse's taking another spouse.[12]

All of this reasoning of the early church and more—a synthesis of classical and Christian wisdom, of philosophy and biblical thought—is found already in Thomas Aquinas's *Summa contra Gentiles* almost three centuries earlier than the *Loci*, and it is repeated beautifully in the *Catechism of the Council of Trent* in its commentary on the sixth commandment, published about forty years after.

But such construing of creation law seems off the radar screen to Luther and Melanchthon.

---

12. Melanchthon gives some slight attention to this idea in his *Epitome*, "Just as Eve was created from a rib, not from the head or from the feet, that equality might be signified, this joining together is ratified too by divine law, and by the law of nature." See *Enarrationes*, 206. Faulkner notes, "That any slight was done to either Christina or Margaret seemed never to occur to the parties in this famous history" (Faulkner, "Luther and the Bigamous Marriage of Philip of Hesse," 225).

Littlejohn Response to Biermann

BRAD LITTLEJOHN

Given the long neglect into which natural law had fallen in Protestant circles until the past generation, I must say I am delighted to be joined in this volume by a fellow Protestant making a positive case for natural law. That said, Biermann's case for natural law is so full of qualifications that many readers—including perhaps some of my fellow authors in this volume—might even wonder whether it should count as a *defense* of natural law at all in the traditional sense of the term. I would not go quite that far. Biermann, I think, can still be numbered among the natural lawyers, but there is no question that his version of natural law is quite an attenuated one. As a Protestant, I share many of his cautions about the limitations of natural law in a world full of sin and corruption, but I would still like to push back somewhat against what seems to me a hasty pessimism about natural law's utility.

Metaphysics and Epistemology

Every year when I teach my foundations class on "Natural Law and Scriptural Authority," I begin by explaining to the students that natural law can be viewed from either a metaphysical or epistemological standpoint. To affirm natural law as metaphysical reality is simply to affirm the reality of an objective moral order inscribed upon creation, to insist that human behavior, just as much as the growth of a tree or the flourishing of a salamander, is guided toward a God-given telos that is ignored only at our peril. If trees or

88 • Natural Law

salamanders are to thrive, they must obey the basic law of their being, and thankfully, they generally do. If human beings are to thrive, they must do so as well, and if they do not, they are not merely worse off because of it but also morally at fault. To hold to an epistemological theory of natural law, however, is to commit oneself further to the belief that this moral order is not merely naturally *present* but naturally *knowable*. This latter has proven much more controversial, especially with Protestants.

Although flirting with a soft nominalism that is likely to outrage many Thomist readers (and which I also have some questions about, though I will leave them aside for the sake of space), Biermann is keen to affirm the metaphysical reality of natural law in some sense. He declares for instance that "life tends to work better when lived in tune with the limits established by each natural reality, and the violation of either the law related to gravity or adultery brings its own deleterious effects, whether that be a shattered marriage, or a shattered skull" (p. 70). This claim he takes to be unthreatened by epistemological doubts about our access to natural law: "That hearts can be seared, corrupted, and deceived . . . changes nothing about the reality and enduring authority of the law that permeates all of creation, what might fittingly be called natural law" (p. 71). On this basis he represents himself as occupying similar ground as leading natural law skeptics such as Stanley Hauerwas and John Howard Yoder. He thus stresses that "the reality of the natural law provides no functional foundation or concrete guidance when attempting to establish or adjudicate moral questions in the public arena" (p. 80). Later he says, "God's law for creation cannot provide an indisputable ground for any positive law of any people or place; neither can it serve as a theoretical bare minimum of basic morality for all people" (p. 81).

What, then, is the natural law good for? In good Lutheran fashion, he emphasizes that the chief function of the natural law, like *any* kind of law, is to drive people toward the gospel. The natural law condemns us, showing us our failures and our guilt, revealing our inability to conform to its norms and achieve any kind of self-salvation. This is a healthy biblical emphasis. And yet not entirely biblical. For in the *locus classicus* on the natural law, Paul says that the "conflicting thoughts" of the gentiles guided by the natural law "accuse or even excuse them"—sometimes, apparently, they are aware of themselves as having done something *right*. Indeed, even if we focused purely on the law's negative role, one must have some *positive* knowledge of a norm to feel its condemnation for having failed to obey it.

Ultimately, the metaphysical and epistemological dimensions of natural law cannot be neatly separated. For if what separates humanity from the animals is (chiefly) our capacity for rationality, then surely the pursuit of that which is naturally good for us must be a *rational* pursuit, the conforming of our actions toward a rule grasped not merely by instinct but (at least in part) by knowledge. Put another way, what could it mean to say that the moral order for humanity is naturally present in us except to say it is naturally present *to our minds*? To be sure, any Christian must say that this natural knowledge is dimmed, obscured, and corrupted by sin. Indeed, there is no logical contradiction in affirming natural law as a reality for Adam but not for his offspring: it could be that whereas natural law provided Adam with a firm knowledge of God's will before the fall, afterward sin rendered this natural light useless. Such a statement preserves logical validity at grave theological cost, however, for human beings who are wholly incapable of exercising natural reason would no longer possess properly human nature at all and would be debased to the level of beasts.

Is Natural Law Useful?

Thankfully, I do not think that Biermann carries through his skepticism about our epistemological access to natural law quite that far. For instance, in the second of his concluding theses, he says, "Certainly, those apart from Christ pay it little heed, yet the law in its fullness still compels, constrains, and judges them. Their own hearts and nearly every culture in the world bear testimony to at least some degree of the law that enfolds and binds them" (p. 80). And in the fourth he concedes, "While no unanimity on the content or application of the natural law in the fallen world is possible, the law is nevertheless very much present and at work in individuals, communities, and entire cultures" (p. 80). But this is all quite vague. Should we really say that *no* unanimity is possible even on the first principles of human law? Most natural lawyers grant that as soon as we move from first principles to deductions and applications, fallen man twists the natural law to his own advantage, but this is often more by denying the *relevance*, not the *reality*, of key moral norms. For instance, the abortionist or the advocate of genocide

90 • Natural Law

does not deny that human life is a priceless good, but simply excludes many of his fellow men from the class of "human" on spurious empirical grounds.

Indeed, in denying that natural law can provide "an indisputable ground" for positive laws or a "common ground" for moral debate, Biermann seems to set the bar too high and thus scores easy points against a straw man. There are plenty of rationally indisputable truths that are nonetheless hotly disputed on a daily basis. Even in the hard sciences, petty jealousies may often stand in the way of scientific consensus for decades, as followers of one school or another refuse to concede the force of overwhelming arguments or even falsify evidence to maintain their position. Fallen man has a million mechanisms of self-deception, but they do not prevent us from being able to say in many fields that there really is a fact of the matter or an undeniable logical entailment that can provide grounds for action. We can appeal from Caesar drunk to Caesar sober, as it were, compelling stubborn sinners to concede truths that they would otherwise refuse to see. To a natural lawyer, the fact of persistent and pervasive moral disagreement, far from being an argument *against* natural law, is precisely why we need such a thing: as a mechanism to cut through obfuscations and sophistries and uncover basic moral intuitions that have been buried under a hundred self-justifications.

Reading the World with Spectacles

All that said, I want to reiterate that I share much of Biermann's Protestant caution against inflated claims for natural law. To say that the Decalogue is a restatement or summary of natural law, as Biermann notes, cuts both ways. On the one hand, it emphasizes that biblical law is not some arbitrary morality of divine fiat, but a reaffirmation of God's will given already in creation. On the other hand, it highlights that apparently natural revelation is not enough—we *need* the Decalogue (and the rest of Scripture) to tell us what natural law really looks like. That said, I want to bring in here Calvin's wonderful metaphor of Scripture as "spectacles" for correcting our fallen vision. For in this metaphor, what is it that we are meant to read, now that we can see rightly? Well, the *world*, of course—natural revelation. It is not as if, having failed to read the world rightly, we receive the Word instead and henceforth walk only by its light. Rather, having had natural law clarified for us by Scripture, believers are now able to make positive use of it far more than unbelievers can ever do.

This, then, is one more missing dimension of Biermann's account, which corresponds perhaps to a longstanding Reformed-Lutheran quarrel about the "third use of the law." Although the disagreement is (like most supposed Reformed-Lutheran arguments) generally overstated, it is the case that the Reformed have at least been much quicker and more emphatic in affirming that the law does not merely restrain sinners and, by its accusing voice, lead them to the gospel; it also serves as a positive guide for the regenerate as they seek to live out a life of gratitude and charity. Now, the Reformed have usually had in mind the revealed biblical law in this context and indeed have often been guilty of ignoring the natural law for instance in matters of church polity and discipline (unlike Luther!). But there is a third use of the natural law as well, helping guide Christian believers in what it means to live wisely within the world, particularly within the complexity of social and political life, where Scripture makes no claims to exhaustive guidance. For instance, a church might find the need to deploy natural law reasoning in determining just canons of evidence in church discipline proceedings. Or a group of churches, coming together to form a denomination, might use natural law to help them wisely structure their organs of communication and authority. Given the emphasis of Luther's two-kingdoms doctrine on the secular character of the visible church, such observations ought to be thoroughly at home in a Lutheran exposition of natural law.

If space permitted, I might also quibble a bit with Biermann's historical account, which displays a preference for paradox that was certainly a feature of Luther's thought, but not of all Lutherans. Absent, for instance, is the towering sixteenth-century Danish Lutheran theologian Niels Hemmingsen, whose "demonstrative" philosophical account of natural law would have struck a rather different note than those of Luther and Melanchthon cited in Biermann's essay.

In closing, I will simply note that while I am glad Biermann is willing to number himself among the champions of Protestant natural law, I hope that in future he will show more optimism and conviction. At the end of his essay, he expresses such pessimism over the "overwhelming negative connotations" of the term *natural law* that he proposes ditching it for a new one: *creational law*. While this term is theologically sound enough, I see no reason for such pessimism, coming as it does on the heels of a generation-long revival of natural law among Protestants that has largely succeeded in rescuing the term from pariah status. Like anything else in the hands of fallen men, *natural law* is far from perfect. But it is more than serviceable, if we know how and when to use it.

Moschella Response to Biermann

MELISSA MOSCHELLA

While there are many claims in Biermann's essay with which I agree, I will focus my comments on two aspects of Biermann's view which I find problematic: his failure to distinguish between the physical order and the moral order, and his denial of the importance of distinguishing between different types of law.

Biermann begins his discussion of natural law by reflecting on *The Jungle Book* and noting that he believes there is a "tight correspondence" between the Law of the Jungle and the natural law. What he means by this is that he conceives of the natural law as "the given, unchanging, 'built-in' reality or truth that guides, norms, and shapes all of life for all creatures" (p. 58). Later in his essay, he expands on this characterization of the natural law:

> It is the law that is simply part and parcel of the created world itself. It is not created or derived by any man. It is not agreed upon by committees or conventions. It is not established by consensus or common practice. It is rather the will of God that is built in to creation itself, hardwired into the very fabric of every created thing ordering, guiding, and facilitating the functioning of all of creation into a harmonious and unified design. (p. 64)

I believe that the law Biermann describes does indeed exist, but I would not call it *natural law* in the sense in which I use the term in my essay.

94 • Natural Law

Rather, I believe that what Biermann is describing corresponds roughly to what Aquinas calls the "eternal law," which is God's providential governance of the entire universe, "moving all things to their due end" in accordance with the Divine Wisdom.[1] Thus, while Biermann is describing an important reality, I believe that his account runs into problems because it conflates the natural law with the eternal law, failing to recognize important distinctions between the two.

On Aquinas's view (which I share), natural law differs from the eternal law in that it applies specifically to human beings *as rational creatures*. Aquinas defines natural law as the rational creature's participation in the eternal law.[2] As rational creatures, our mode of participation in the eternal law is categorically different from that of nonrational creatures. By contrast with other creatures, we are not passively or deterministically governed by God's providence but rather share in that providence through our capacity to "discern what is good and evil" through "the light of natural reason" and to freely direct ourselves toward what is good.[3] In other words, while all creatures are subject to God's governance (the eternal law), God enables us as rational creatures to participate in his governance by governing ourselves (and other creatures) in accord with the light of reason. Of course, we are also subject to the eternal law more broadly insofar as we are animals passively subject to the same physical, chemical, and biological laws as all other animals. But those laws—which we, like nonrational animals, follow by necessity—are not *moral* laws.

This distinction is crucial for a proper understanding of the natural law that can actually provide sound practical guidance. While our speculative knowledge of physical, chemical, and biological laws will often be relevant for discerning what is good and evil or right and wrong, knowledge of those laws is insufficient for such discernment. The mere fact, for instance, that many human beings have a natural tendency toward aggression and violence or a natural tendency to dominate others, as well as that such tendencies may be "built in" to our biology, does not mean that such tendencies are *good* or that we *ought* to act on them. This is why the new natural law account insists that it is important to recognize the distinction between

---

1. Thomas Aquinas, *Summa Theologiae* I-II, 93.1, corpus.
2. Aquinas, *Summa Theologiae* I-II, 91.2, corpus.
3. Aquinas, *Summa Theologiae* I-II, 91.2, corpus.

the physical or biological order, on the one hand, and the moral order, on the other hand. Without this distinction, we cannot explain why certain inclinations or behaviors that might be natural in the physical/biological sense are not natural in the moral sense. Moral norms direct us to our perfection *as rational agents* and are known through *practical* reason rather than *speculative* reason. What makes something natural in the moral sense is not that it occurs spontaneously or with predictable regularity or in accordance with some innate tendency but rather that it is *practically reasonable*, in line with practical reason's directives to respect and promote the genuine goods that constitute our flourishing.

While this is merely conjecture on my part, it seems to me that Biermann wants to collapse any distinction between the moral order and the physical/biological order because he wants to emphasize the objectivity of morality—a goal which I heartily share. Yet recognizing this distinction is fully compatible with Biermann's claim that the natural law is not something that human beings create but rather reflects a given objective order that we can discern. Indeed, recognizing this distinction is actually crucial for defending the objectivity of morality, for it is in fact obvious that physical and biological laws are very different from moral laws. Physical laws can, for instance, be proven empirically through observation and experimentation, but moral laws cannot be proven empirically. If we elide the distinction between different orders of knowledge and hold up the natural sciences as models of objective knowledge, this leads many people to deny the objectivity of morality. The solution is to recognize (along with Aristotle and Aquinas) that there are different types of knowledge and that the method for attaining knowledge, and even the meaning of objective truth, varies depending on the subject matter.

When I say, for instance, that the natural law norm forbidding rape is objectively true, what I mean is not that everyone necessarily abides by this norm but that rape is objectively contrary to integral human flourishing. No matter how many people engage in rape, it will still be objectively wrong. By contrast, if anything genuinely violated the law of gravity, then the law of gravity would be false. Both the natural law norm forbidding rape and the physical law of gravity are true, but each is a different *type* of truth because the first is a truth in the moral order and the second is a truth in the physical order. And the standard for truth in the moral order is not how we actually act (as it is in the physical order) but how we *should* act if our actions are to be fully reasonable—that is, to respect and promote integral human fulfillment.

Biermann claims correctly that people's failure to follow natural law in no way undermines its "reality and enduring authority" (p. 71). But if the natural law is just like the laws of physics, then it is not clear how this claim can be sustained. Indeed, Biermann himself notes that one common critique of natural law is that the term *nature* is used in apparently equivocal ways to refer both to "*ideals* which have not yet been actualized in experience," and to "the entire scale of empirical realities" (p. 73, quoting Yoder). To be able to defend the natural law cogently in the face of such critiques, Biermann needs to recognize the important differences between moral truths—truths that we refer to as natural law not because they are spontaneous or necessarily followed but because they are accessible to natural reason and point us toward our fulfillment as rational agents—and the sorts of truths about how the created order operates that are captured by scientific laws.

Recognizing that there are different types of law, as well as that the term *natural law* refers specifically to *moral* laws that we can discern through rational reflection about how to respect and promote human flourishing in all of its various fundamental dimensions, is also in tension with Biermann's desire to avoid "distinguish[ing] meticulously between various sorts of laws, whether physical, moral, ceremonial, positivistic, or even local" (p. 70). Biermann elaborates on this claim by offering the following argument:

> The law of gravity is not really so different from the law not to commit adultery. Both are part of the way God established the world to operate. Both are what we might call natural realities. So it is that life tends to work better when lived in tune with the limits established by each natural reality, and the violation of either the law related to gravity or adultery brings its own deleterious effects, whether that be a shattered marriage or a shattered skull. (p. 70)

If all that Biermann means here is that our moral deliberations need to take knowledge of physical causality into account insofar as physical causes can positively or negatively affect human flourishing, then his point is obviously true. But if what he means is that physical laws provide direct moral guidance in the way that moral laws do, then his claim is problematic.

Indeed, the laws of physics tell us nothing about the goodness or badness of shattered skulls or the rightness or wrongness of actions that might lead to a shattered skull. A shattered skull is bad not because it is a violation of the law of gravity—indeed, the skull's shattering is the result of the *operation* of the law of gravity, not its violation—but because it is contrary to the intrinsic good of human life. Further, the shattered skull may not be the result of any *moral* wrongdoing, for people can have good reasons for doing things—such as fixing a roof—that may make them susceptible to shattering their skulls. Clearly, respect for the good of human life means that one should avoid recklessly placing oneself or others in danger of shattering their skulls without a serious reason, but the law of gravity in itself provides no direct moral guidance. The implied normative judgment that Biermann makes about the badness of a shattered skull therefore depends not on his understanding of the law of gravity but on the basic principle of natural law directing us to preserve and promote the good of human life.

Further, while the law of gravity and the law against adultery can both be called "natural," they are natural in very different ways, and these differences matter. The law of gravity is natural because it describes the workings of the natural world. But the law against adultery is natural because it is accessible to natural reason and directs us to avoid an action that is always unreasonable because it is contrary to the basic human good of marriage and thus contrary to the fulfillment of our nature. Unlike the law of gravity, the law against adultery provides direct guidance for action because the law against adultery is a *moral* norm that flows from the basic moral requirement to act only in ways that are compatible with a will toward integral human fulfillment—the fulfillment of all human beings with respect to all of the basic goods.

Biermann's claim that we should avoid distinguishing between moral laws and positive laws of various sorts (including ceremonial laws) is also potentially problematic, depending on what he means. Again, if what he means is simply that positive laws are morally *relevant*, then it is obviously true. Indeed, positive laws provide more direct moral guidance than the laws of physics, for positive laws in principle direct us to the common good of our community, which we have a duty to promote. Nonetheless, it is crucial to recognize that the moral law (i.e., the natural law) has primacy over positive laws, for moral law provides the standard by which we judge

98 • Natural Law

positive laws. Biermann claims that "a villager living in Papua New Guinea is living rightly when he follows all the international, national, regional, and local written and unwritten regulations, conventions, and even social niceties that lead him to be of good service to the creatures around him in his world" (p. 70). But what if the local laws or conventions tell him to kill babies born with disabilities? What if they sanction and even encourage violent raids on neighboring villages? I am sure Biermann would want to say that such laws and conventions are unjust and therefore ought not to be followed. But this implies that the moral law has primacy over these other types of law, which means that distinguishing between types of law is crucially important for determining how we ought to act.

Leithart Response to Biermann

PETER J. LEITHART

I open my response to Joel Biermann's essay with a commendation of Luther and continue with a plea for clarification, a point of disagreement, and an attempt to press Biermann a few steps further. I conclude with a digression concerning an issue that, I suspect, lurks behind much natural law rhetoric.

However dictated by circumstance, Luther's sharply divergent statements on Torah are ultimately coherent and provide an accurate summary of the New Testament's stance toward the law. There is, on the one hand, a radical covenantal discontinuity between old and new, so radical that Paul can say, repeatedly, we're no longer "under law" (*hupo nomon*; Rom 6:14–15; 1 Cor 9:20–21; Gal 4:21; 5:18). There is, on the other hand, a total continuity of utility and profitability: every jot and tittle of Torah remains instructive (Matt 5:17–20; 2 Tim 3:16–17).

Biermann's voluntarist construction of natural law will, I suspect, attract some heat from other contributors to this volume. I limit myself to one observation: if Biermann were pressed, I suspect, and hope, he would retract or clarify the term *arbitrary*. Surely God's will is not whim, nor is it *wholly* unrestrained, but it is only unrestrained by anything outside of God.

Regarding revealed law, I have standard Reformed (and, I think, scriptural) objections to Biermann's treatment of law and gospel. "The law commands and requires us to do certain things," Luther writes. But the law also promises: mercy to thousands of generations, long life in the land, and many other blessings. "The gospel . . . does not preach what we are to do or to avoid," Luther says. But John and Jesus preach a gospel of repentance (Mark

100 • Natural Law

1:14–15), and the New Testament characterizes the proper response to the gospel as "obedience" (2 Thess 1:8; 1 Pet 4:17). Luther or Biermann may wish to whip out the scalpel and slice the second or fourth commandment into law portions and gospel portions, but that would rather confirm the claim that the law-gospel binary is imposed on Scripture rather than arising from it.

I agree with much of what Biermann wrote, largely because he shares many of my reservations about the tradition. Biermann recognizes the force of critiques of natural law and is honest about its limits, as when he admits that, because of sin, natural law "provides no functional foundation or concrete guidance when attempting to establish or adjudicate moral questions in the public arena" (p. 80). This is a remarkable concession from a defender of natural law because the capacity Biermann denies is precisely the capacity that commends natural law to many Christians.

This concession, among others, goes deeper than Biermann admits. He is entirely correct about the risks of seeking guidance from hearts "catechized to believe that every heart is a sacrosanct, autonomous, inviolable source of idiosyncratic truth" (p. 65). That raises the obvious practical question: What use then is natural law in the midst of our cultural confusions? However vigorous our efforts to demonstrate that natural law is "theonomous" (suited to human nature), will not many of our contemporaries view it as authoritarian heteronomy?[1]

But the epistemological issue raises more fundamental theoretical problems. In contrast to many natural law theorists, Biermann admits there are things we *can* not know. Is it coherent to talk about a natural law that can be catechized *out* of the human heart?[2] That appears to leave natural law an empty theory, a claim about created structures that may or may not be accessible to moral actors. Biermann's answer (and mine) is to point us to revealed law. All to the good, but the natural law theory that emerges from the far side of Biermann's qualifications and concessions is rather battered and bruised. I am not sure its head is still held high.

Now to the digression. I focus the remainder of my response on these sentences:

---

1. I use *theonomy* and *heteronomy* as Paul Tillich does; Tillich, *Systematic Theology: Three Volumes in One* (Chicago: University of Chicago Press, 1967) 1.83–94.

2. As I show in my main essay for this volume, Thomas claimed that the natural law is inexpungible but wisely and realistically limited inescapable knowledge to first principles: good ought to be done, and evil avoided. On specifics, there is no consensus.

Starting from the givenness of a world created by God that operates according to his will significantly qualifies all efforts to distinguish meticulously between various sorts of laws, whether physical, moral, ceremonial, positivistic, or even local. The law of gravity is not really so different from the law not to commit adultery. Both are part of the way God established the world to operate. Both are what we might call natural realities. So it is that life tends to work better when lived in tune with the limits established by each natural reality, and the violation of either the law related to gravity or adultery brings its own deleterious effects, whether that be a shattered marriage, or a shattered skull. (p. 70)

Biermann's analogy between natural moral and physical law is rooted in a theistic vision. The God who spoke the world into being and established the moral order of the world also spoke in many portions and ways to our fathers. If I press this analogy, perhaps beyond what Biermann intends, we might arrive at a personalist understanding of the physical and moral universe. Adultery does not "automatically" lead to marital disaster, but it does so because God actively brings sins on the heads of sinners. So too the sun does not rise "automatically" but, as Chesterton delightfully suggested, because the God of eternal youth never gets tired of saying, "Do it again." If this is the kind of analogy Biermann intends, I am largely with him.

But, for the sake of argument, suppose the argument works the other direction: instead of personalizing physical laws, the analogy depersonalizes moral law. This is worth exploring because at least some of the appeal of natural law theory in modern culture depends on an analogy of this sort, which seems to be rooted in several assumptions:

- Scientific truth is the gold standard of truthfulness. Science discovers truth about the world, disclosing the objective reality beyond subjective whim or interpretation or sensible appearance.
- What scientific investigation discovers has the character of law.
- Scientific laws are not the formulations of scientists but are universal regularities embedded in the world.

Based on these assumptions, a defender of natural law might say: natural law is to moral truth what scientific law is to truth about material reality.

102 • Natural Law

It is discoverable by investigation of the nature of things. We do not need revelation to come to sound moral conclusions any more than we need the Bible to explore quantum physics. The morality discovered has the character of law, and this moral law is embedded in cosmos, not a product of human projection of construction—just like the law of gravity.

To this, I briefly summarize several lines of critique. First, note the rhetorical charm of the comparison. Late modernity, and perhaps modernity as such, is an age of interminable moral disagreement in which all the traditional courts of appeal (e.g., an infallible ecclesial magisterium) have been neutered. For religious believers and many others, the situation is disquieting. What to do? Only the sciences appear to possess a consensus regarding truth, along with established methods for reaching consensus. If we can somehow link moral with scientific truth, moral reasoning can bask in the glow of scientific objectivity. Science once borrowed the category of "law" from politics and morals, and it is a coup to recover the term, now bolstered by its centuries-long association with modern science, in pursuit of moral and political truth.

Second, the analogy obviously does *not* work. Apart from artificially constructed gravity-free environments, it is a universal truth that every human being who jumps from a two-story building will fall. We can even predict the rate of fall and the energy of the impact. God's command "Do not commit adultery" is *not* the same kind of rule. It is *not* the case that every adulterer shatters his marriage. Adulterers go undetected, adultery can be forgiven and spouses reconciled, and some couples have polyamorous marriages that encourage adultery.

We can make the same point from the opposite direction: what scientists think counts as law depends on the kind of universe they think we live in. If physical reality is Aristotelian, it does not run by what moderns call "scientific law." Aristotle and Thomas were explicit that mathematical sciences (astronomy, optics, mechanics) are subordinate to physics, as "subalternate" sciences (Aristotle) or *scientiae mediae* (Thomas). The notion of scientific law in the modern sense emerges only with the mechanization of the world picture in the early modern period, that is, only after the physical world was evacuated of the "rich causal resources" of Aristotelian physics.[3]

---

3. Peter Harrison, "The Development of the Concept of Laws of Nature," in *Creation: Law and Probability*, ed. Fraser Watts (Farnham, UK: Ashgate, 2008), 13–36.

At the margins, it is now widely believed that natural phenomena do not obey natural law. Many cosmologists say the world emerged in a singularity in which mathematical laws and natural forces misbehave. At the quantum level too, laws break down: "The mathematical laws of the theory are completely deterministic, but the observable quantities are not deterministic: if something is not observable, it can be certain, but if it is observable it is not certain!"[4] Nature, it seems, will not give up her secrets, whether tortured or seduced: "Nature's secret is encrypted in randomness so complete that she herself could not solve it."[5]

Neither classical nor contemporary physics provide a suitable analogy with moral law. On a Cartesian-Newtonian definition of scientific law, calling both gravity and the commandment "Do not commit adultery" laws is an equivocation. In one realm, the law is operative regardless of the will of the parties involved; it cannot be violated without special conditions. In another realm, the law can be violated, not only without recognizable harm but, for some parties, considerable pleasure. If, on the other hand, the Cartesian-Newtonian concept of scientific law fails, then the actual workings of the world remain mysterious and the analogy between moral and scientific law is almost entirely verbal.

I return, inevitably, to theology. If the Bible and Christian theology are true, the scientific account of nature is, at best, radically incomplete. Nature is not autonomous, either in its origin or in its operation. The world is not a machine, but it comes and continues to be through the loving Word and life-giving Spirit of the eternal Father. There simply is no such thing as "pure nature" since what we call nature is always entangled with the God who is the source of nature.

The world's meaning—its scientific as well as its moral and political meaning—cannot be discovered within the world, but must be illumined through the revelation of God in Jesus Christ. I mean this quite literally: revelation solves metaphysical-scientific puzzles. For example, the ontological elevation of "person" in Christian theology has fundamental implications for science. No ancient thinker had the conceptual apparatus to distinguish between the incommunicable singularity of an individual thing and the

---

4. Peter Pesic, *Labyrinth: A Search for the Hidden Meaning of Science* (Cambridge, MA: MIT Press, 2000), 146.

5. Pesic, *Labyrinth*, 149.

104 • Natural Law

form it shares with other things of its kind, no way to explain that although Socrates is a man, he surpasses the definition of man because of his unique existence and history. Nor did they have the tools to explain how an effect can be more than an emanation of a cause but something genuinely novel. Though focused on Christology and Trinitarian theology, early Christian theologians introduced fresh metaphysical categories that helped explain how the world works.[6]

All this returns to my obsessive mantra: if we cannot understand the physical world without the light of revelation, the same is true, yet more obviously, of the moral order of the world.

---

6. See the splendid discussion in Michael Hanby, *No God, No Science? Theology, Cosmology, Biology* (Oxford: Wiley Blackwell, 2016).

Rejoinder

JOEL D. BIERMANN

It is customary, and arguably academic good manners, when afforded the opportunity of a final chance to put one's thoughts into writing that the moment be exploited to offer a word of thanks for the collaboration of the other authors and for the editors who extended the invitation to participate. In my case, however, it seems a word of gratitude is entirely insufficient. It would be far more appropriate and accurate for me to confess a sense of marked relief and even a note of surprise at the grace extended to me by the editors and other contributors to this volume. It was a genuine honor to be permitted to lend my feeble voice to such a learned and serious conversation and to be gifted such thoughtful and careful responses. I teach systematic theology at a denominational seminary. I spend my days preparing men and women for service in the church as pastors and deaconesses. I live in a world that is more the church than the academy. I am certainly not a philosopher and try not to pretend to be one—simply striving to be a faithful theologian provides me with all the intellectual and professional rigor I need. To put it bluntly, from the beginning, I have been somewhat dubious about my credentials for this project. But I have been trained to take calls out of the blue seriously, and so here I am writing one last piece in a book abounding in academic acumen, logical precision, nuanced argument, and genuine intellect by eminently qualified scholars of the first rate. I am grateful to have been granted a part in the discussion.

This final brief essay is intended to allow me to respond to the other essays with a last word, but I must confess no compulsion to say anything more than I've already said. Nevertheless, to fulfill all righteousness and in good spirit, I'll offer a few observations, most of a general nature, applicable

106 • Natural Law

to the entire project, addressing to varying degrees criticisms raised by my fellow contributors.

To begin, I will unconditionally affirm several concerns or charges that were rightly made about my original essay. I am at best an ambivalent supporter of what is commonly understood as natural law. This is not to say that I doubt the enduring, indeed eternal, existence of a law from God that is meant to direct the lives of all of his creatures, in particular the human creatures who bear his image. Given that rather basic definition, it still seems fitting to refer to this plan, design, or structure of the world as creational law. Such a term also serves to distinguish the sort of natural law I am willing to support from the sort of natural law assumed by the other contributors. As I tried to make clear in my initial essay, when the law from God, which is inherent in the fabric of the universe itself, is invoked in an effort to do serious political or social work, it is simply a bridge too far. Yes, this law is present in every human being. Yet given the fallen condition of these human beings, this is not saying very much. It is absolutely the case that I hold a decidedly pessimistic view of human nature in its present state corrupted by original sin. In this fatally compromised state, man and his rationality simply cannot be trusted to arrive at a right reading of the law that God has woven into his creation. And given his inherited perversity and obstinacy, man *can* be counted on to deny the very reality he knows to be true and rebelliously insist on exactly the opposite.

I am convinced that we are never going to get very far trying to leverage natural law in the realm of common grace. And while I'm certainly not one to consider pragmatic rationale as a viable line of argumentation in a theological discussion (pragmatic needs or exigencies can never establish or shape doctrinal truth), it seems that any argument for a practical usefulness of natural law would be bolstered with glowing examples of its successful implementation in the government or wider culture. But reflecting on the present realities at work in those realms, natural law seems all but impotent to shape any argument or even thinking. When has a natural law argument convincingly resolved a pressing social conflict in our lifetimes? In a world premised on rights, natural law has precious little measurable purchase on those not already committed to the idea of a divine lawgiver. And considering the persistent suspicion leveled at the very idea of natural law in so many corners of the church and world, perhaps seeking a better term for the reality of God's will at work in the world isn't an entirely bad idea.

I am certainly the odd man out (or is it pariah?) for holding to some form of nominalism and admitting it. In this regard, I readily profess my willingness to follow the lead of Luther. Whether the *via antiqua* or *moderna*, scholasticism was always suspect for Luther and was to be rejected outright when it departed from the church's *regula fidei* and imposed human reason or intellectual conclusions on theological reflection or teaching. Based on those criteria, it is necessary to forsake a great deal of both medieval ways of doing theology. Still, when it comes to God's utter distinction from his creation and his absolute freedom to act as he wills, I happily embrace the name of nominalism and wonder, with an affected naiveté, why it is treated like a dirty word—you call me nominalist like it's a bad thing. Perhaps it is true logically that without an analogical, essential connection from the Creator to his creation the very premise of natural law founders. But I am content to grant the wholly-other Creator's absolute dominion over his creation and willing to embrace the direction he provides implicitly and explicitly for the right operation of that creation whether it necessarily must reflect his own being or not. And maybe this points to the greatest divergence between my own overall position and that of my colleagues in this endeavor. I believe our most significant difference lies not in my willingness to embrace some degree of nominalism but in the markedly different level of confidence we invest in human reason.

Some forebears in my Lutheran orbit rightly accentuated the critical difference between a ministerial versus a magisterial use of reason. While it may come as a surprise, Lutherans are not inherently against reason. We are, however, exceedingly careful about the extent to which reason drives our theological work—or at least we should be careful. Our persistent skepticism in light of humanity's fallen nature is at its peak when it comes to the capacity and trustworthiness of human thinking. Reason is certainly essential for tasks as fundamental as basic grammar, the formulation of a doctrinal thought, and the construction of a coherent argument. But reason is worse than infallible—it is inflated with self-confident pride and inveterately prone to an overestimation of its own ability. Especially when doing the work of theology, then, reason must be kept on a very short leash and limited to the role of servant or minister and nothing more. It must never be allowed to assert itself as master or teacher. And reason must never be the arbiter of the truth, falsity, or usefulness of a doctrinal truth. Rationalism is sinful human hubris at its worst.

108 • Natural Law

Even more fundamentally, I question whether reason is actually the essential aspect that defines human being—a position likely to provoke significant opposition and angst for most readers. In the context of a faithful theology grounded in Scripture, what makes us human is not premised on our capacity for rational thought. What makes us human is living as God's stewards in the world in submission to his will for the right functioning of the creation. Reason is one of the tools we are given to fulfill that work, but it is not the essence of our humanity. Whether reasonable or not, we are contingent creatures who will be held to account for the conduct of our lives.

The position of peculiar Lutherans like myself who have made a promise to abide by the teaching of the entire *Book of Concord* is actually quite simple: God's revealed truth, normatively presented in the Bible and rightly articulated in the confessions is the final determining factor for all doctrine. Whether or not human reason agrees with a doctrinal declaration is immaterial. Neither human reason nor pragmatic necessity is ever able to establish, redirect, form, or blunt God's truth. In other words, we Lutherans aren't overly concerned about logically consistent, rationally satisfying, or intellectually compelling arguments about God and his revealed truth—with an emphasis on *revealed*. We strive to take God at his word without subjecting that word to the criteria of human explanation and evaluation on the basis of our reason. This is what Bonhoeffer is getting at when he declares that the task of ethics is simply hearing and following the will of God. We and our reason must be submissive to the will of God—not the other way around. It is not up to us to determine, establish, evaluate, or defend God's will given to us in his creation and in his Christ. Our task, then, is not a project of rule creation or clarification, self-improvement, or societal construction. Our goal is not a kingdom of God in this world or even individual human flourishing. Our goal is simply and relentlessly to be faithful creatures who follow Jesus—delivering his gospel to broken people and witnessing the reality of his new life in a world of pretense and futility. Along the way, warily using our reason as one of our many God-given tools, problems are confronted, challenges are embraced, grace is delivered, and both church and world are served.

One last issue raised by several of my conversation partners is the liability of the Lutheran penchant for reading all of doctrine and life through the paradigm of law and gospel. It is true that the distinction between law and gospel holds a particular attraction for Lutherans, especially those in my corner of Lutheranism. But while the distinction can and does often lead to a dualism that errantly advocates the gospel trumping the law—and in the process gutting any meaningful attempt to do the work of ethics—we are not all antinomian. Yes, the law convicts and reveals sin. The law does always accuse . . . but it does not only accuse.

The law teaches people what God expects of his creatures. This serves as a necessary guide for those who through the work of the gospel are in a right relationship with God—even as it also convicts them when they inevitably and routinely fall short; the *peccator* tenaciously hangs on in this life. And that same law, articulated in Scripture but present in the creation itself, constrains and motivates even those living apart from the gospel. So while I embrace the law's continuing accusatory function, I also celebrate its role in directing all human lives, Christian or otherwise. Which aspect of the law is dominant depends on the context. Before God, being accused of my inherent sinful failure and utter dependence on God's grace given in Christ alone is finally all that matters; before my fellow creatures, God's good guidance (and sometimes his undeniable compulsion) on how best to serve those around me is what counts the most. Either way, it is the same law at work. The law can be a carrot as well as a stick, of course. It condemns, but it also rewards. The gospel does not reward; it just forgives and restores. Jesus preached the gospel, but he also delivered the law which fosters the repentance that drives people to the gospel. Those who refuse to repent, who will not yield to God's lordship, will reap the reward of their obstinate disobedience. As even Asaph had to remember (Ps 73), the purported prosperity of sinners is never long-lived and quite likely more illusion than reality even in the thick of the proffered pleasure. Violation of God's law, in any and all of its forms, is never without consequence and the distinction between what is physically mandated and what is morally required may not make much difference in the final analysis.

Finally, one direct word to Michael Pakaluk seems in order as his willingness to delve into the thick of the Lutheran world for a bit was noted and appreciated. Melanchthon certainly counts as a legitimate Lutheran, and he was most certainly also a lover of the wisdom of the Greeks . . . well, at least of Aristotle. But Melanchthon also practiced a sharp distinction, taught by Luther, between the realms of spiritual and temporal realities. Aristotle was eminently useful in the latter but had no business in the former. Whether the Reformers missed a chance to employ the wisdom of Aristotle and natural law arguments in contending with the vexing problem of a lascivious lord is certainly an interesting question. Again, I appreciate Pakaluk's good spirit in engaging in Lutheran history—though his choice was not one that engenders much enthusiasm among Lutherans—it is hardly the finest moment in the history of Lutheran theology. While it is possible that too much focus on purely scriptural arguments blunted the response of the Reformers, I think Scripture itself could have provided ample support for a very different direction of spiritual counsel. In this case, and in most, I would contend, the wisdom gained by natural means in tune with creational law and that arrived at through attending to biblical sources are not fundamentally at odds. My suspicion is that the biggest problem in this instance had less to do with a failure to use the wisdom of creation; instead, it was a failure to champion the lofty view of marriage documented in places such as Genesis 2 and Ephesians 5, succumbing instead to merely logical maneuvers in an effort to appease a prince. Sadly, that course neither rebuked Philip nor protected the women he counted as his wives. Perhaps old sins, like the fear of man and dishonoring of women, were the real culprits in this miserable affair.

This brings me at last to the end of the essay and the end of the journey. I am grateful for having had the chance to ride along and hope I have helped in some small measure to push the conversation forward. Doing the work of theology is always a delight; doing it in the company of others so gifted is a peculiar degree of delight too seldom savored.

CHAPTER 3

Reformed Natural Law

BRAD LITTLEJOHN

As recently as a generation ago, an essay with this title would have been almost inconceivable. Chastened by long decades of Barthian influence within elite academic circles, and perhaps even longer decades of biblicism, pietism, and hyper-Protestantism within popular evangelical religion, the idea of natural law was driven underground within Reformed theology and ethics in the closing decades of the twentieth century. Indeed, even though more conservative Reformed thinkers and institutions had harsh words of criticism for both Barthian neo-orthodoxy and what they saw as the unsophisticated and ahistorical "me and my Bible"-ism of American evangelicalism, they had imbibed similar prejudices against natural law as representing "Roman Catholic scholasticism," "the myth of neutrality," or "autonomous reason."[1]

Whether in its Kuyperian neo-Calvinist variants or Van Tillian pre-suppositionalist variants, the dominant epistemology and ethics of most North American Reformed seminaries and denominational colleges focused on the idea of a "biblical (or Reformational) worldview," a comprehensive intellectual system built on exclusively biblical premises, within which alone a knower could have access to the contours of creational reality and a doer could deduce the principles of right moral action. Ironically, the philosophical premises undergirding this epistemology were themselves drawn more

---

1. For a good summary of the twentieth-century hostility to natural law in Reformed circles, see Stephen Grabill, *Rediscovering the Natural Law in Reformed Theological Ethics* (Grand Rapids: Eerdmans, 2006), ch. 1.

111

112 • Natural Law

often than not from the Enlightenment soil such thinkers most maligned (especially the idealism of Kant and Hegel), while the classical natural law tradition, nurtured within the deeply Christian medieval civilization, was dismissed as embodying a protosecular rationalism.[2]

The landscape has changed profoundly since the 1990s. Provoked by initiatives like Evangelicals and Catholics Together to give Roman Catholic thought a fair hearing and by historians like Richard Muller to pay closer attention to the contours of their own theological tradition, Reformed thinkers have rediscovered an appreciation for natural law as a crucial tool not merely for political engagement and moral reasoning but also for doing good theology and hermeneutics. Not only that, but they have come to terms with the fact that natural law was and always has been deeply embedded in the Reformed confessional tradition, with much of the twentieth century representing a curious case of theological amnesia. As Jennifer Herdt writes in the *Cambridge Companion to Natural Law Ethics*,

> We are now in a position to see this conception of a deeply ingrained Protestant hostility to natural law ethics as a short-lived aberration, extending from the end of World War I to the end of the century. In fact, the magisterial wing of the Protestant Reformation continued to employ the natural law tradition as a lingua franca for ethical reflection, even as that tradition was reinterpreted within new understandings of the Fall and of justification.[3]

Indeed, natural law was taken almost for granted by Reformed stalwarts on both sides of the Atlantic for four centuries following the Reformation as an aspect of general revelation. Far from being in tension with a Protestant commitment to *sola scriptura*, it was seen as a clear conclusion from scriptural teaching. As Presbyterian giant Charles Hodge wrote in his 1873 *Systematic Theology*, "That there is a binding revelation of the law, independently of any supernatural external revelation, is expressly taught in the Bible. Paul says of the heathen that they are a law unto themselves. They have the law

---

2. For a critique of some of the problems with "biblical worldview" thinking, see my essay, "On Naming the World: A Protestant Vision for Training in Wisdom," in *Reforming Classical Education: Toward a New Paradigm*, ed. Rhys Laverty and Mark Hamilton (Landrum, SC: Davenant, 2022), iii–xvii.

3. Jennifer Herdt, "Natural Law in Protestant Christianity," in *The Cambridge Companion to Natural Law Ethics*, ed. Tom Angier (Cambridge: Cambridge University Press, 2019), 155.

written on their hearts."[4] Moreover, it was also seen as part of the Reformed rejection of radical Protestantism's biblicist retreat from created reality: "natural morality and its fruits have very great values," insisted Herman Bavinck in his *Reformed Ethics*. "Not recognizing their value is narrow-minded, petty, and superficial Methodism and quietistic pietism—anything but Reformed."[5]

Even among those Reformed thinkers who resisted the anti-natural-law tide of the past century, however, there has been a tendency to insist upon the distinctiveness of a uniquely Reformed approach to natural law. Bavinck himself was an influential representative of this trend, frequently insisting that even when it came to foundational doctrines of creation and anthropology, Roman Catholicism was infected by corrupt premises that skewed its understanding of revelation and morality, so that a Reformed natural law must proceed on fundamentally different grounds. While such claims have some merit, they depend occasionally on polemical oversimplifications of Roman Catholicism that fail to reckon with the nuance and diversity of Roman Catholic theology both during the time of the Reformation and today. More often than not, the distinctives of Reformed natural law thinking (itself hardly a unitary phenomenon) are less categorical differences from other natural law traditions and more matters of preponderant emphasis and preferred terminology.

Accordingly, in my account here, I will seek as much as possible simple to offer a positive exposition of the central concepts, contours, and cautions of Reformed natural law thinking rather than going out of my way to draw contrasts and define my quarry by way of opposition to other natural law traditions. There will be ample opportunity for such contrasts to emerge in the responses and rejoinders.

A Few Definitions

Before proceeding further, it may be helpful to lay down a few definitions.

First, some might well know how broad the term *Reformed* is for purposes of this chapter. Quite broad indeed. I use the term to designate those

---

4. Charles Hodge, *Systematic Theology*, 3 vols., repr. (Grand Rapids: Eerdmans, 1940), 3:266.
5. Herman Bavinck, *Reformed Ethics*, vol. 1, *Created, Fallen, and Converted Humanity*, ed. John Bolt (Grand Rapids: Baker Academic, 2019), 233.

114 • Natural Law

families of Protestantism that (1) trace their descent from the *magisterial Reformation* (with its stress on catholic reform rather than restoration of the primitive church, and its conviction that grace perfects rather than replaces nature), (2) retain a commitment to the central doctrines articulated in the family of confessions that runs from Augsburg to Westminster, and (3) that do not feel bound by strict fidelity to the teachings of Luther, as summarized for instance in the 1577 Formula of Concord. *Reformed* is thus by definition "not Lutheran," although in my own (perhaps idiosyncratic) view this is more a matter of regrettable historical accidents and rivalries than of theological essentials, and so the boundaries between "Reformed natural law" and "Lutheran natural law" may prove rather porous.

Based on the definition above, it will appear that "Anglican natural law" is, at least for purposes of this analysis, subsumed into "Reformed natural law," a conflation that is certainly defensible if we restrict most of our attention to the sixteenth and seventeenth centuries, though Anglican thought began to develop in increasingly distinctive directions thereafter. The great English theologian and political philosopher Richard Hooker (1553–1600), who would have been surprised to be told that he was not Reformed, will accordingly make several notable appearances in this chapter.

Second, some working definition of *natural law* may be in order to get us started. Sometimes the term is used vaguely to refer to any sort of natural (or general) revelation, but clarity here requires greater precision. *Natural revelation* we may define as all those means whereby God reveals to humanity in general, without the aid of spoken or written word, (i) himself, (ii) his will for the created order, and (iii) his will for humans.

Natural theology then relates to (i) and names humanity's reflection, on the basis of natural revelation, on the existence and attributes of God. *Natural science* relates to (ii), constituting humanity's reflection, on the basis of natural revelation, on the nature of the created order. Finally, then, *natural law* relates to (iii) and designates humanity's reflection, on the basis of natural revelation, on the human moral order (which, as we shall soon see, must be triangulated in relation to both God and our fellow creatures).

The classic 1621 Reformed compendium *Synopsis Purioris Theologiae* thus offers a useful definition of natural law: "Natural law is the light and direction of sound reason in the intellect, informing man with common notions to distinguish right from wrong, and honorable from shameful—so that he may understand what he should do or shun."[6] This definition, it is crucial to note, commits us to the idea of natural law not merely as a *metaphysical* reality—that is, an objective moral order somehow wired into or inscribed upon creation—but also as an *epistemological* reality—that is, the presence of that moral order to and in the human mind. The former has been denied by few even of the most radical Reformed natural law skeptics, whereas the latter has seemed to many modern theologians to represent too much optimism about fallen humanity's rational capacities. I will have much more to say about the fall's effect on "sound reason in the intellect" below, but suffice to say here that if that effect is total, entirely eradicating sinful humankind's ability to "distinguish right from wrong, and honorable from shameful," then there remains no natural law in the traditional sense, however much one may believe as a matter of theological conviction that nature is governed by God's law.

We must also note the crucial role played by both halves of the phrase *natural law*, which brings together in a startling and stimulating fusion the ideas (so widely separated to the modern mind) of description and prescription, fact and value. On the one hand, natural law has an intimate connection to *nature*, to the way things *are*. Even the most blissfully amoral moderns, indeed, still speak of "laws of nature" in the sense of discernible regularities within the physical universe. Within the domain of living creatures, we might speak of it as a "law of nature" that each living thing seeks to protect itself, feed itself, and reproduce its kind, with each species defined by its distinctive way of doing so. A pine tree and a pelican must each do that which is natural to it and in so doing will achieve its fullest development and perfection—a fact that Aristotle described in terms of the primacy of the "final cause" or *telos*, and which has, through many variations of philosophical schools, been central to most natural law thinking over the centuries, Reformed and otherwise.

Human beings, like pelicans, have been created such that certain forms of behavior are *natural* to them, so that, by protecting themselves, feeding themselves, and reproducing themselves in those natural ways, they are more likely to survive and thrive. As the Leiden Synopsis observes, "Mankind seems to share with the other created living beings . . . those [behaviors] to which all creatures endowed with animate life and perception are inclined

---

6. William den Boer and Riemer Faber, eds., *Synopsis of a Purer Theology*, 2 vols. (Landrum, SC: Davenant, 2023), 182.

by natural instinct, in order to protect themselves and their offspring by innate affection and natural feeling. Traces of this kind are: guarding their own lives, propagating, nurturing, and cherishing their own offspring."[7] However, human beings differ from other creatures in two crucial respects: their possession of an intellect that strives after abstract truth and a will that strives after *the good* and shuns *the bad*—understood not simply, as a pelican might, as "good for me" and "bad for me," but "good as such" and "bad as such." Thus, the Leiden Synopsis notes, "Traces of the law that properly concern mankind are the ones to which his affections are directed by the bidding and guidance of reason (which the other creatures lack), in keeping with the norm of good and right that God has granted to him."[8]

Here, then, we come face-to-face with the *law* aspect of natural law, as something not merely descriptive but prescriptive, something that presents itself to our intellect as good and as right and indeed, if we are attending closely enough, as *binding*. Precisely because it is in the nature of humans to think in moral terms, human beings cannot rest, like other creatures, in the apprehension of food or sex or rest as naturally desirable, expedient, or beneficial. Sometimes, to be sure, this suffices for action—we see a dessert on the counter and, being hungry, we eat it. But if challenged to reflect upon why we did so, or whether we will do so again, we find ourselves grappling with moral categories, such as the awareness that perhaps the dessert was someone else's, and it was *wrong* of me (however pleasurable) to eat it. And unlike the mere generalizations arising from considerations of expediency, at least some moral intuitions present themselves as categorical and wrong *as such*; we experience, in short, the awareness of moral law. In so doing, of course, we find ourselves if not face-to-face with the idea of a *lawgiver*, at least dimly aware of such. Without this, the deliverances of natural law would devolve into the mere maxims of common sense.

I have spent a few paragraphs on developing this point because it lies at the heart of some of the key questions and debates within Reformed natural law reasoning: the realist-voluntarist debate, the problem of total depravity, and the question of common grace. Let us now turn to consider each of these in detail.

---

7. Leiden Synopsis, 183.
8. Leiden Synopsis, 183.

Natural Law, Created Order, and Divine Reason

Among more recent historians who routinely minimized the role of natural law in the Reformed tradition, it was sometimes conceded that the Reformers did indeed have a doctrine of natural law, but that it was a decidedly "voluntarist" one. Thus, for instance, A. J. Joyce, in one of many attempts to identify Richard Hooker as Thomistic rather than Reformed, says that "Hooker defined law as 'a rule or measure guiding an action to its appropriate end', rather than as a 'command coercively imposed by a sovereign', and upon this fundamental issue he parted company with the reformers."[9] Indeed, influenced by the intellectual historiography of Radical Orthodoxy and Catholic historians like Brad S. Gregory, many have framed the supposed battle between rationalism and voluntarism as *the* defining intellectual fault line of the sixteenth century, one on which the Protestant Reformers almost unanimously sided with the dangerous innovations of Scotus, Ockham, and the *via moderna* rather than that good old-time philosophy of Thomas Aquinas and the *via antiqua*.[10]

To readers unfamiliar with these fashionable debates, the distinction can be summarized as follows.

Rationalist or intellectualist theories of natural law, such as that propounded most famously by Thomas Aquinas, lay their stress on *nature* rather than *law*; for them, the natural law is simply *the way things are*, that which is objectively good given the nature of God and the nature of humans. It is determined by the intrinsic *telos* of human nature, with natural law describing the best way to achieve that telos. It is a product of the divine reason or intellect (hence the terms *rationalism* or *intellectualism*) that is then received and grasped by the human intellect as a participation in divine reason. Such doctrines of natural law are closely linked to metaphysical realism, with its

---

9. A. J. Joyce, *Richard Hooker and Anglican Moral Theology* (Oxford: Oxford University Press, 2012), 156, quoting Lee Gibbs, "Introduction to Book I," in *The Folger Library Edition of the Works of Richard Hooker*, vol. 6, *Of the Lawes of Ecclesiastical Politie, Books I–VIII: Introductions and Commentary*, ed. W. Speed Hill (Binghamton, NY: Medieval and Renaissance Texts and Studies, 1993), 88. See also Alexander S. Rosenthal, *Crown under Law: Richard Hooker, John Locke, and the Ascent of Modern Constitutionalism* (Plymouth, UK: Lexington Books, 2008), 61–72. See also the discussion in E. J. Hutchinson and Korey D. Maas's introduction to *On the Law of Nature: A Demonstrative Method*, by Niels Hemmingsen, trans. and ed. E. J. Hutchinson, Sources in Early Modern Economics, Ethics, and Law (Grand Rapids: CLP Academic, 2018), xviii–xxiii.

10. See for instance Brad S. Gregory, *The Unintended Reformation* (Cambridge, MA: Belknap, 2012), ch. 1.

118 • Natural Law

conviction that forms and essences (and thus *teloi*) are intrinsic to the nature of things and wholly objective.

Voluntarist theories of natural law, often attributed to Duns Scotus or William of Ockham, lay their stress on *law* rather than *nature*; for them, the natural law describes that which God has propounded and promulgated as his will for creation. It should be seen as contingent rather than necessary; God could, conceivably, have authorized a different morality for his human creatures, even after creating them. It is a product of the freely choosing divine will (hence *voluntarism*), which derives its force from his binding command and coercive enforcement of that command; moreover, since it is good *because commanded*, it can only be fully received by the human will responding to it in obedience, rather than merely intellectually grasping it. Such natural-law doctrines are often (though not necessarily) linked to metaphysical nominalism, with its teaching that created reality is irreducibly particular, with forms and patterns merely the impositions of mind or convention.[11]

If that summary sounds like an oversimplistic caricature, that's because it is—and yet I fear that it is rather more sophisticated and nuanced than the bulk of the scholarly literature that casually tosses around these terms. The fact of the matter, as we have already seen, is that any natural-law doctrine worth its salt must hold together fully in dynamic tension both the ideas of *nature* and *law*, both the faculties of *intellect* and *will*. As such, any natural law thinker worth their salt recognized that the natural morality had to be promulgated by divine command and that divine command had to be anchored in created structures. Both Thomas Aquinas and Duns Scotus agreed on as much, and within a few decades of the Reformation, scholastic theologians like Francisco Suarez were providing meticulously argued syntheses of the two poles within this (sometimes imaginary) debate, incorporating the essential insights of both in a way that preserved both the rational consistency of God (as Aquinas had stressed) and God's freedom and authority in relation to creation (as Scotus and Ockham had stressed). The Reformed, for their part, fell at various points along this spectrum but mostly clustered close to the modified Thomism represented by Suarez.

---

11. For a fuller account, see my essay, "'Vestiges of the Divine Light': Girolamo Zanchi, Richard Hooker, and a Reformed Thomistic Natural Law Theory," *Perichoresis* 20, no. 2 (June 2022): 43–62. See also Francis Oakley, *Natural Law, Laws of Nature, Natural Rights: Continuity and Discontinuity in the History of Ideas* (New York: Continuum, 2005), for a useful exposition of some of the relevant distinctions.

If it no longer seems surprising to speak of Reformed Thomism in this context, we have the pioneering labors of scholars like John Patrick Donnelly[12] and Richard Muller[13] to thank, along with a host of their students and appreciators, such as Stephen Grabill, Jordan Ballor, David Haines, Todd Rester, David VanDrunen, and many more. For purposes of this survey, the details of this debate can be safely set aside, but a couple points are worth highlighting.

Many of the Reformed speak of the natural law, as does Aquinas, as a "participation in the eternal law,"[14] that is, in God's own eternal knowing and willing of that which is good for his creatures. Richard Hooker and Franciscus Junius, simultaneously publishing classic treatises of theological jurisprudence on opposite sides of the English Channel in 1593, both expound the idea of the "eternal law"—"that order which God before all ages hath set down with himself, for himself to do all things by."[15] It is sometimes asserted that Calvinists cannot really hold to such a notion, since it would imperil their notion of a radically free, transcendent, and inscrutable divine decree, which must always be incomprehensible to human minds. To be sure, the Reformed tradition has been characterized by a strong emphasis on the truths declared in Romans 11:33–36 and a healthy skepticism of any theology or philosophy that would seem to confine the infinite divine mind within the narrow box of finite human reason. However, this problem was solved by means of a distinction between the first and second eternal law,[16] or between archetypal and ectypal law[17]—the first of which named the perfect but sometimes inscrutable righteousness of the divine will in its wholeness, and the second of which named the specification of that will for rational creatures, which we were created able to know and participate in.

---

12. John Patrick Donnelly, SJ, "Calvinist Thomism," *Viator* 7 (1976): 441–55.

13. See, e.g., Richard A. Muller, "Not Scotist: Understandings of Being, Univocity, and Analogy in Early-modern Reformed Thought," *Reformation and Renaissance Review* 14, no. 2 (2012): 127–50.

14. Thomas Aquinas, *ST* I-II, 91.2, *resp.*; cf. Franciscus Junius, *The Mosaic Polity*, trans. Todd Rester, ed. Andrew M. McGinnis, Sources in Early Modern Economics, Ethics, and Law (Grand Rapids: Christian's Library, 2015), 44–48; and Richard Hooker, *The Laws of Ecclesiastical Polity in Modern English*, ed. Bradford Littlejohn, Brian Marr, and Bradley Belschner (Leesburg, VA: Davenant, 2019), 1.5 (p. 62–63).

15. Hooker, *Laws*, 1.2.6 (p. 53).

16. Hooker, *Laws*, 1.3.1 (pp. 54–55).

17. Franciscus Junius, *A Treatise on True Theology, with The Life of Franciscus Junius*, ed. and trans. David C. Noe (Grand Rapids: Reformation Heritage, 2014), 116–18; cf. my essay, "Cutting through the Fog in the Channel: Hooker, Junius, and a Reformed Theology of Law," in *Richard Hooker and Reformed Orthodoxy*, ed. W. Bradford Littlejohn and Scott N. Kindred-Barnes (Gottingen: V&R, 2017), 234–49.

120 • Natural Law

Accordingly, the Reformed resist the idea (often attributed to voluntarism) that God's moral will expressed in the natural law could be essentially arbitrary. As the late seventeenth-century Reformed theologian Johann Heidegger wrote,

> The heads of natural law, especially those outstanding and universal, were not founded on God's sheer and indifferent decree as the result of His changeable *arbitrium*, but on His natural holiness. Love to God with the whole heart, in which neighbour love takes its rise, rests upon God's very nature, since He is the *summum bonum* and so lovable *per se*. . . . Could God will that He be not loved, neither would He be the *summum bonum* equally able to enjoin hatred of Himself; which is a dreadful thing and involves a contradiction. . . . From this it follows that the primaeval law of nature is quite unchangeable and indispensable.'"[18]

If the commands of the first table are unchangeably grounded in God's nature, those of the second table are likewise grounded in human nature as God created it. The early American theologian Samuel Willard wrote: "God, who is the Creator, is also the rightful Governour of his Creatures: and he in Wisdom governs them according to the Nature he put into them." The natural law "is the product of his infinite Wisdom, and was adapted for the Government of Man, being suited to his Nature; and was therefore *holy, just, and good*, Rom. 7.12."[19] These laws, wrote Charles Hodge, "are founded on the permanent relations of men in their present state of existence"— this side of glory, men will be mortal, reproduce, need property, and have imperfect knowledge, and hence the commands against murder, adultery, theft, and false witness will be "permanent so long as the relations which they contemplate continue." It is, argues Hodge, conceivable that God could have created humans differently, but given human nature as it is, these laws "founded on the nature of things . . . are now of universal and necessary obligation."[20]

---

18. Quoted in Heinrich Heppe, *Reformed Dogmatics*, rev. and ed. Ernst Bizer, trans. G. T. Thomson, repr. (Eugene, OR: Wipf and Stock, 2007), 291.

19. Samuel Willard, *A Compleat Body of Divinity in Two Hundred and Fifty Expository Lectures on the Assembly's Shorter Catechism* [. . .] (Boston: Green and Kneeland for Eliot and Henchman, 1726), 573.

20. Hodge, *Systematic Theology*, 3:267–68.

The Fall's Effect on Natural Law

What, then, of the fall? Even among those Protestant thinkers most hostile to natural law, few will categorically deny that there *is* such a thing; they will merely contend that, in the wake of the destruction wrought upon humanity in Adam's fall, the integrity of our nature has been destroyed, the light of reason extinguished, and natural law rendered inaccessible or useless. After all, doesn't the Reformed faith teach that we are totally depraved?

To be sure, it is not hard to find passages among Reformed thinkers that seem to suggest just the kind of moral and epistemological pessimism upon which modern critics of natural law insist. Calvin, for instance, writes, "Indeed, man's mind, because of its dullness, cannot hold to the right path, but wanders through various errors and stumbles repeatedly, as if it were groping in darkness, until it strays away and finally disappears. Thus it betrays how incapable it is of seeking and finding truth."[21] And one of his early successors in Geneva, Lambert Daneau, setting out to write a systematic treatise on Christian ethics, declared, "The reason and judgment of men, no matter how well meaning and well mannered, is blind when it comes to discerning and determining the upright and the immoral."[22]

And yet Calvin can write a few pages later, "If we regard the Spirit of God as the sole fountain of truth, we shall neither reject the truth itself, nor despise it wherever it shall appear, unless we wish to dishonor the Spirit of God. . . . What then? Shall we deny that the truth shone upon the ancient jurists who established civic order and discipline with such great equity?"[23] He even declares, in the context of discussing the *locus classicus* of Romans 2:14–15, "There is nothing more common than for a man to be sufficiently instructed in a right standard of conduct by natural law."[24] Daneau, similarly, no sooner finishes dismissing fallen reason as hopelessly blind than he begins favorably quoting from Aristotle's *Nicomachean Ethics*.

Examples of such jarring juxtapositions of negation and affirmation could easily be multiplied in almost any classic Reformed discussion of

---

21. John Calvin, *Institutes of the Christian Religion*, trans. Ford Lewis Battles, ed. John T. McNeill (Louisville: Westminster John Knox, 1960), 2.2.12 (1:271).

22. Lambert Daneau, *Ethices Christianae Libri Tres* (Geneva: Eustache Vignon, 1579) 1.1, unpublished translation by Timothy Griffith (used by permission).

23. Calvin, *Institutes*, 2.2.15 (1:273–74).

24. Calvin, *Institutes*, 2.2.22 (1:281).

natural knowledge under conditions of sin. The reader of such treatises can get a sense of whiplash as the authors toggle back and forth between ringing denunciations of fallen humanity's utter blindness and remarkably generous endorsements of the insight of pagan moral philosophers and the wisdom of pagan lawmakers. Is the Reformed tradition simply confused or wavering on the subject? I think not. Some of these contrasts can be explained as rhetorical devices of humanist rhetoric, but they also reflect a series of principled distinctions that, upon closer inspection, yield a carefully nuanced account of fallen reason's ability and inability to grasp and apply natural law.

First, Reformed thinkers, along with Aquinas, often distinguished between primary and secondary precepts of natural law, the first being much more general and abstract and the latter being specific and concrete enough to guide human action. For instance, the Leiden Synopsis observes, "Some of those notions are of a primary sort, and we call them practical principles; others, which are secondary, we call conclusions constructed from those principles with the help of reasoning." While originally "coupled together in delightful harmony," now after the fall we find that although

> the first, primary notions in his [mankind's] intellect remained unchanged, and they shine forth clearly; but the latter, secondary notions stagger with wretched hesitation whenever one goes from general things to particular ones, and they deviate from the sound rule of equity, as is shown by the examples of the very unfair laws and overly corrupt customs that are found in the histories of gentile peoples.[25]

Second, also following Aquinas, they recognized the powerful force of "vicious customs and corrupt habits"[26] to lead weak and impressionable humans astray to the point where, as Paul notes in Romans 1, even blatantly unnatural behaviors were condoned and celebrated. Richard Hooker describes this dynamic aptly: "Perverted and wicked customs—perhaps beginning with a few and spreading to the multitude, and then continuing for a long time—may be so strong that they smother the light of our natural understanding, because men refuse to make an effort to consider whether

---

25. Leiden Synopsis, 182.
26. Aquinas, *ST* I-II, 94.6, resp., https://www.newadvent.org/summa/2094.htm.

their customs are good or evil."[27] Since God created us to learn from experience, we rightly and naturally look to the behaviors of others in forming our own. So all it takes is one prominent sinner (acting by foolish reasoning or willful rebellion) to start an entire society down the road to moral blindness.

Third, applying the distinction between primary and secondary precepts, Reformed thinkers often stressed that there was an important difference between something being naturally *knowable* and naturally *known*. Although there may be certain universal moral intuitions, moral reasoning—like any kind of reasoning—involves hard work and sometimes rare intellectual skills. Emil Brunner offers a useful comparison: "It is true that there are mathematical truths that are accessible only to a comparative minority, but of whose rationality no one stands in any doubt. The question of the fundamental rationality of a truth must be strictly distinguished from its universal existence."[28] Thus it is that we can simultaneously celebrate the achievements of a Plato or a Cicero as evidence that many metaphysical and moral truths are still naturally knowable and yet deplore the moral turpitude of their societies as evidence of the noetic effects of sin. Peter Martyr Vermigli accordingly writes, with a close eye on Romans 1:19, "By stating 'It was manifest in them,' and not 'it was manifest in all,' Scripture distinguishes wise men and philosophers from the crude and ignorant masses."[29] Of course, in his view this simply condemns those philosophers for their arrogant failure to share what they had learned with the masses. Moreover, all Reformed thinkers, following Romans 1:20, were convinced that even the unlearned possessed enough sparks of natural conscience to render them "without excuse."[30]

Beyond all these fairly commonplace distinctions lay another even more fundamental one that was of great importance to Reformed thinkers. To think through it properly, we must return to the relationship between reason and will discussed above. Although originally united (in both God and in humans as his image-bearers), the fall threatened to tear them apart. Indeed, the putative split between God's reason and his will, between what

---

27. Hooker, *Laws*, 1.8.11 (p. 78).

28. Emil Brunner, *Revelation and Reason:* The Christian Doctrine of Faith and Knowledge, trans. Olive Wyon (Philadelphia: Westminster, 1946), 323.

29. Peter Martyr Vermigli, *Philosophical Works*, trans. and ed. Joseph C. McLelland, Peter Martyr Library, vol. 4 (Moscow, ID: Davenant, 2018), 19.

30. Cf. Willard, *Body of Divinity*, 577; Leiden Synopsis, 182.

is good for man and what God commands, has its source in the words of the serpent: "Did God really say . . . ?" In the first temptation, the serpent invites Eve to contrast what is obviously good, given the ends proper to human nature—a fruit "good for food," "a delight to the eyes," and useful "to make one wise" (Gen 3:6 NASB)—with God's seemingly irrational and arbitrary prohibition. Such an opposition of reason and will was of course imaginary, but by daring to see it in God, Adam and Eve made it a reality in themselves, God's image-bearers, dooming their offspring to the perpetual war within that Paul vividly described in Romans 7: "I do not do the good I want, but the evil I do not want is what I keep on doing" (Rom 7:19 ESV).

The Reformed agreed with Paul and the Augustinian tradition that the fall's most grievous effects were upon human will, disordering loves by warping all of them toward an idolatrous self-love until the sinner became *incurvatus in se* ("curved in upon himself"). However, they also recognized that this deformation of the will was not without its effect upon human reason: an effect that could be summed up as the tendency to perpetuate the delusion of the first temptation. Fallen humans retain their creaturely tendency, shared with all living things, to strive toward that which is "good for food"—corresponding to what Aristotle called the "nutritive soul," and what Aquinas (in a distinction followed by many Reformed thinkers) saw as the first level of natural law. He also retains the capacity of sense-perception, shared with animals, seeing that which is a "delight to the eyes" and pursuing it accordingly—Aristotle's "sensitive soul" and Aquinas's second level of natural law. Indeed, despite the corruptions of sin, we retain the uniquely human capacity to yearn after that which "makes one wise"—Aristotle's "rational soul" and Aquinas's third level of natural law. However, we no longer grasp these goods as part of God's will for us, but rather as means by which we might seek to displace him and become as gods ourselves.

In other words, fallen humans tend to tear apart natural law: we can still know (and do) what is *natural*, but we cannot see it as *law* because we do not want to; that would require acknowledging the Lawgiver. To be sure, even this knowledge of God is not wholly lost to us. As Calvin observes at the outset of the *Institutes*, "There is within the human mind, and indeed by natural instinct, an awareness of divinity." Indeed, he considers this "beyond controversy."[31] And we cannot contemplate God without becoming keenly aware of our moral failings before him.[32] But it is for this very reason that we try *not* to contemplate God, suppressing our natural knowledge of the Holy One and replacing it with "images resembling mortal man and birds and animals and creeping things" (Rom 1:23 ESV). After all, such humble creatures are no threats to our own quest for sovereignty; as long as we worship gods of our own creation, we can indulge the happy fantasy that we ourselves are gods. Even when the "glory of the immortal God" pierces the veil of our self-imposed blindness, as in Plato's beautiful image of the Sun shining outside the Cave of our self-imposed ignorance, and we build an altar to the "unknown God" (Acts 17:23), this God is conveniently reduced to mere Reason, no Will. Thus Aristotle's tantalizing glimmer of the divine majesty amounts to no more than an eternal Mind, toward which all else strives. This Mind issues no commands to us; instead, we obey the command of our own intellect, directing us to seek that which is good to eat, delights our eyes, and makes us wise.

For this reason the Reformed can both extol the wise discernment of pagan moralists and lawmakers in promoting civil justice, as Calvin does, and speak in stark terms of sin's destructive effect on natural law, as for instance Girolamo Zanchi does: "The law of nature was . . . thoroughly extinguished [*penitus extincta*], as respects . . . honest and just living together with our neighbor."[33] They have in mind much the same dialectic that preoccupied Augustine in book 19 of *City of God*, where he grants to ancient Rome a certain outward form of justice but also objects, "What kind of justice is it that takes a man away from the true God and subjects him to unclean demons?"[34] Love of neighbor that is not ordered to love of God as the lawgiver of nature is ultimately nothing more than a refined form of prudent self-love. Thus Emil Brunner observes,

---

31. Calvin, *Institutes*, 1.3.1 (1:43).

32. Calvin, *Institutes*, I.1.2 (1:38)

33. Girolamo Zanchi, *Hieron. Zanchii Tractationum Theologicarum Volumen de Statu Peccati et Legali* [. . .] (Neustadt: Wilhelm Harnisius, 1613): Post peccatum fuit haec lex naturae partim penitus extincta, ut quae respicit Deum, eiusque cultum, et quae proximum, honestumque et aequum cum illo convictum 246; cf. Girolamo Zanchi, *On the Law in General*, trans. Jeffrey J. Veenstra, with an introduction by Stephen J. Grabill, Sources in Early Modern Economics, Ethics, and Law (Grand Rapids: Christian's Library, 2012), 12, although there are key flaws in Veenstra's translation, as I have argued in my essay "Vestiges of the Divine Light."

34. St. Augustine, *The City of God Against the Pagans*, trans. Henry Bettenson (London: Penguin, 1984), 19.21 (p. 882).

126 • Natural Law

The more we are concerned with the concrete content of the law, the less plainly does this "darkening" appear, but the more we are concerned with the will which *gives* the law, that is, with the will of God, the more it is stressed. All men know what is commanded and forbidden; but the reason why this is so, and therefore the deepest and most peculiar meaning of the divine command, they do not know.[35]

Indeed, Brunner finds in the rebellious godlike striving of Genesis 3 a kind of hermeneutical key for making sense of the at-first bewildering spectrum of natural knowledge and ignorance. How is it that in some areas of knowledge pagan thought shines with dazzling brilliance, and in others unbelievers turn out to be as blind as bats?

The nearer anything lies to that center of existence where we are concerned with the whole, that is, with man's relation to God and the being of the person, the greater is the disturbance of rational knowledge by sin; the farther away anything lies from this center, the less is the disturbance felt, and the less difference is there between knowing as a believer or as an unbeliever.[36]

The more that a given object of knowledge requires to face up to the question of who is in charge—us or God—the more the sinful mind will find itself shrinking from a truth it cannot bear to admit. Then the science of botany, in which we contemplate creatures far lower than ourselves, is less tainted by sin than anthropology, in which we seek to know *ourselves* rightly. And anthropology, which considers human beings abstractly as mere objects, will be less tainted than ethics, which requires us to think about ourselves as subjects—and thus as either lords or servants. So the Reformed will concede that when it comes to the *content* of ethics—what makes rational sense for us to do given our natural ends and limitations— human beings may occasionally do well, but when it comes to the *meaning* of that ethics, as a set of constraining moral demands upon us emanating from God's law, it makes more sense to speak of natural ignorance than natural knowledge.

---

35. Brunner, *Revelation and Reason*, 70.
36. Brunner, *Revelation and Reason*, 383.

Common Grace and Natural Law

Reflecting with Augustine on the blinding effect of self-love, Reformed theologians have consistently marveled not that fallen humans know so little but that they should still seem to know so much. Why, after all, should a creature *incurvatus in se*, sucked into the whirlpool of its own self-regard, be capable of building pyramids or writing Hammurabi's Code rather than simply withering away like Narcissus? Over and over, they have been drawn to confess that even that which we call "natural knowledge" must be in some sense the effect of grace, a gift of God rather than something we can take pride in as our own. Just as God's *special revelation* in Scripture would be of no avail without God's work of *special grace* within the fallen mind and heart to enable us to respond, they reasoned, so even his *natural revelation* in the created order could be of no avail without some corresponding work of *common grace* to give us eyes to see it.

The term *common grace* became widespread in the twentieth century thanks to Abraham Kuyper, who wrote a three-volume treatise on the subject and made frequent use of the concept, but the idea can be found well back in the Reformed tradition. Indeed some, such as Girolamo Zanchi, state the idea in remarkably strong terms. Having noted the extent to which the fall destroyed our capacity to worship God rightly, he insists, "If we should ever see a sliver of this aspect of natural law again in a human being, we must believe that it was written in that person's soul a second time in its entirety by God himself."[37] Zanchi considers this idea of "re-inscription" the most plausible explanation for the fact that although all human beings are equally fallen, some individuals—and indeed some societies—evince a far healthier grasp of natural law than others. "If it came from nature," he argues "then it would exist equally in all people. . . . However, we see among different peoples that some are wiser, more devoted to justice and honesty, and more zealous for God."[38] After tracing this principle through a variety of different precepts of natural law as grasped by different cultures, he concludes, "It is clear that this law has been implanted and instilled more effectively in some and less effectively in others."[39]

---

37. Zanchi, *Law in General*, 12.
38. Zanchi, *Law in General*, 16
39. Zanchi, *Law in General*, 23.

128 • Natural Law

Many proponents of natural law might wonder whether on such an account the law in question is really "natural" at all. Instead, it sounds as if on Zanchi's account, fallen humanity is indeed stripped of all natural rational capacities whatsoever and then passively receives divine illumination so he can still function toward some rough approximation of human nature, with the quantity and quality of such illumination depending on divine whim. Thankfully, Zanchi nuances this account in important ways,[40] and most Reformed divines do not follow him in the metaphor of "re-inscription."[41] Indeed, Kuyper insists that common grace should be understood not so much as a form of positive knowledge but as a negative restraint on the destructive tendencies of sin.

> It tempers but does not extinguish. It tames nature but does not transform it. It reins in and restrains, but in such a way that when the bridle ceases to function, evil automatically gallops ahead once again. It prunes the wild shoots but does not heal the root. It leaves the inner driving force of the self to its own evil, but prevents the full effect of that evil. It is a restraining, detaining, impeding force that curbs and brings to a halt.[42]

The metaphor of a bridle goes back to Calvin's discussion of natural law.[43]

Even this, however, might leave the impression that natural law in the Reformed tradition remained something fundamentally *un*-natural, an intervention from outside, precisely because sin left nothing of human nature intact. Thus Kuyper emphasizes that although the product of divine initiative, "all working of common grace happens through powers that are present in the nature of man."[44] In common grace, God works in and through our good and natural created faculties to slow and restrain sin's corrupting power, which, left to itself, would soon reduce us to the level of beasts or devils.

---

40. See my "Vestiges of the Divine Light."

41. A key exception being Johannes Althusius in his 2017 *Dicaeologica* (Johannes Althusius, *On Law and Power*, trans. Jeffrey J. Veenstra [Grand Rapids: Christian's Library Press, 2013], 10: "Moreover, although those principles of nature are one and the same to all nations, still they differ in the level and means of their inscribing and urging. In fact, these principles are not equally inscribed on the hearts of all; in some, they are inscribed more eloquently, abundantly, and effectively . . . .").

42. Abraham Kuyper, *Common Grace: God's Gifts for a Fallen World*, ed. Jordan Ballor, trans. Nelson D. Kloosterman, 3 vols. (Bellingham, WA: Lexham, 2016–20), 1:302.

43. Calvin, *Institutes*, 2.2.3 (1:293); cf. C. Scott Pryor, "God's Bridle: John Calvin's Application of Natural Law," *Journal of Law and Religion* 22, no. 1 (2006): 225–54.

44. Kuyper, *Common Grace*, 2:74.

Although somewhat novel in its terminology, Kuyper's account is not that different from Richard Hooker's representative articulation of the relationship of natural law and human sin in 1593:

> Whatever I have said or will say about man's natural understanding, I want this to be clear: no faculty or power of either man or any creature can rightly perform any of its allotted functions without the perpetual aid and concurrence of Him that causes all things. Once God withdraws His support, the only possible result, as the Apostle says, is that men who have been blessed with the light of reason will walk "in the vanity of their mind, being darkened in their understanding, alienated from the life of God, because of the ignorance that is in them, because of the hardening of their heart" (Eph. 4:17–18).[45]

Supplements for Natural Law: Divine Law and Civil Law

Given their relative pessimism about natural law's efficacy in the intellect of fallen humans, the Reformed stressed the crucial role of both divine and human law in clarifying and specifying these now-obscured creational norms. First, God through Scripture offered an authoritative restatement of the natural law, comprehensive at the level of principle and specific enough to guide human action in obedience to the moral order of creation. Since, however, even Scripture leaves plenty of details to be discerned and applied by reason and wisdom to the ever-varied circumstances of human life, God also authorizes human authority to enact human laws that can act as contextually binding specifications of what the natural law prescribes in general. So, for instance, while "Thou shalt not steal" is universal, any number of legal arrangements concerning the distribution of property, rules of inheritance, and taxation policy—not to mention statutes prescribing the due penalties for theft—will depend upon human law.

On both of these fronts, of course, Reformed natural law follows largely in the footsteps of medieval antecedents, which likewise emphasized the complementarity of natural, divine, and human law, and the under-specification

---

45. Hooker, *Laws*, 1.8.11 (p. 79).

of the first.[46] However, the Protestant ecclesiology and theology of revelation did entail an important shift of emphasis. For within papalist theology, the obscurity and underspecification of natural law could be rectified by the authoritative interpretation of the magisterium (although this view was hotly contested by late medieval imperial theologians like William of Ockham and Marsilius of Padua). By firmly rejecting such a singular interpretative authority on earth, Protestant theologians were led to lay greater stress on the perspicacity of Scripture's presentation of the moral law and on the lofty office of local civil magistrates in adjudicating questions of natural law for their own communities. Of course, there was still ample room for tension between these twin appeals to the authority of divine and human law, which has proved a constant friction point within Reformed jurisprudence from the Reformation to the present day.

Divine Law

Although the whole of Scripture is "shot through with the laws of nature,"[47] the Reformed most commonly point to the Decalogue as the authoritative summary of the natural or moral law. Herman Witsius, for instance, declares, "It is further to be noted that this first-made law [the natural law] is the same substantially as that which has been expressed in the decalogue,"[48] and Samuel Willard concurs: "The *Ten Commands*, which are the Sum of the Law moral . . . were all in the Law of Nature."[49] Indeed, the idea of the Decalogue as a summary restatement of natural law is a basic commonplace of early Reformed thought. The Reformed were thus at pains to insist that the Ten Commandments did not create any new moral duties but simply declared anew those that were there from the very beginning: "Nothing else is contained in the 'tables of the covenant and the books of the Law, save what the law of nature once demanded of man in his integrity; at least so far as it is the substance of worship and the spring as it were of a more particular injunction.'"[50]

Among more modern theologians, it has become fashionable to question this equation, critiquing it as insufficiently attentive to the

---

46. See for instance Aquinas, *ST* I-II, 91.3–4.
47. Hooker, *Laws*, 1.12.1 (p. 99).
48. Quoted in Heppe, *Reformed Dogmatics*, 292.
49. Willard, *Body of Divinity*, 575.
50. Heppe, *Reformed Dogmatics*, 292, quoting Cocceius.

redemptive-historical context of the Decalogue as a covenantal code for the redeemed people of Israel. Those making this claim will stress the basic continuity between the Decalogue given in Exodus 20 and the specification of particular laws in the chapters that follow and may point to the Sabbath command in particular as a seeming anomaly within a document supposedly intended as a shorthand summary of universal morality. After all, not even the staunchest Christian Sabbatarian, unless a Seventh-day Adventist, follows the fourth commandment as written.

The early Reformed, however, were by no means oblivious to such considerations, distinguishing between the universal natural-law principle stated in the fourth commandment (the necessity of setting aside a day for rest and worship) and the particular specification of the seventh day, which was a matter of positive law belonging to the larger ceremonial code of the covenant people.[51] And Johannes Althusius, for one, warns against a strict one-to-one equation of Decalogue and natural law: "The Decalogue has been prescribed for all people *to the extent that it agrees with and explains the common law of nature for all peoples.*"[52] Indeed, as a tradition of Reformed Hebraism flourished in the seventeenth century, and Reformed writers closely studied rabbinical writings, some of them, such as the great English jurist John Selden, adopted the rabbinical preference for summarizing the natural law in terms of the "seven Noahide precepts." These, so named because they had supposedly been restated to Noah after the flood as a basic morality for humanity, were said to contain the following demands:

- Against idolatry
- Against blaspheming God's name
- Against murder
- Against sexual immorality
- Against theft
- For judicial courts and civil obedience
- Against eating limbs of a living animal[53]

---

51. See for instance Willard, *Body of Divinity*, 574.

52. Johannes Althusius, *Politica Methodice Digesta* (1603), trans. and ed. Frederick S. Carney (Indianapolis: Liberty Fund, 1995), 144 (emphasis added).

53. Ofir Haivry, *John Selden and the Western Political Tradition* (Cambridge: Cambridge University Press, 2017), 241.

Aside from the last (which might seem curious at first glance but may be taken as a synecdoche prohibiting cruelty to animals), we find that these line up closely with both the structure and content of the Decalogue, with only the fourth and tenth commandments lacking a clear correlate.[54] Even if one prefers this summary of natural law to the Decalogue, then it is clear that the natural law is summed up (as Jesus himself noted) in the two commands to love God and to love neighbor.

The earlier Reformed tradition of a Noahide natural law, then, has little in common with the recent endeavor of certain Reformed theologians to redefine natural law around a minimalist reading of the Noahic Covenant that involves merely human justice and brackets all religious questions.[55] The motivation for this novel departure from the tradition lies in the standard teaching of natural lawyers of all ages that it is the task of civil authority to enforce and promote the natural law by means of human laws—at least to the extent that circumstances and refractory human nature permit. If this is so, and if the natural law is summed up in the commands to love God and to love neighbor, then the first table of the Decalogue as well as the second provides a blueprint for civil laws—blasphemy may be forbidden as readily as adultery. This was indeed the standard Reformed understanding, but an eagerness to adapt to the assumptions of modern liberalism has driven recent revisionist efforts.

But let us not get ahead of ourselves. Before considering human law as such, we should attend to the classic distinction (characteristic of the Reformed although certainly not original to them) between the moral, ceremonial, and judicial laws of the Old Testament. Whereas the first binds all men as men, the second and third are more circumscribed. The ceremonial law might well be described as a contextually appropriate, divinely authorized specification of the forms under which God was to be worshiped and how Israel was to maintain her holiness before him. It thus encompassed such demands as those governing animal sacrifice as well as the dietary laws. The Reformed, following Galatians and Hebrews, understood all of these

---

54. Given that the Reformed standardly read the fifth commandment as a statement of the necessity for authority structures of all kinds in human society, this principle seems to be captured in the sixth Noahide precept.

55. See for instance David VanDrunen, *Divine Covenants and Moral Order: A Biblical Theology of Natural Law* (Grand Rapids: Eerdmans, 2014), ch. 2; Jonathan Leeman, *Political Church: The Local Assembly as Embassy of God's Rule* (Downers Grove, IL: IVP Academic, 2016), ch. 3.

laws as in some way symbolically anticipating the once-for-all sacrifice and sanctifying work of Christ, which, having irrevocably altered the context governing divine-human relations, rendered the ceremonial law obsolete. The Westminster Confession thus crisply affirms that "All . . . ceremonial laws are now abrogated under the New Testament."[56]

Similarly, the judicial law might be defined as a contextually appropriate, divinely authorized specification of how the broad demands of the moral law were to be implemented in the life of ancient Israel. As with the ceremonial laws, these too could be changed if the context changed, but unlike with the ceremonial law, redemptive history had not provided any categorical once-for-all change of context; murder, for instance, still needed to be punished after the coming of Christ just as before. However, changing historical circumstances will afford any number of contextual changes that will render certain laws more or less effective, even if the end aimed at is the same. As Hooker observes, "Laws are instruments by which to rule, and that instruments must always be designed not merely according to their general purpose, but also according to the particular context and matter upon which they are made to work. The end for which a law is made may be permanent, but the law may still need changing if the means it prescribes no longer serve that end."[57] Thus the Westminster Confession says of the judicial law, "To them [Israel] also, as a body politic, he gave sundry judicial laws, which expired together with the state of that people, not obliging any other, now, further than the general equity thereof may require."[58]

Of course, the moral/ceremonial/judicial framework should not be understood as a means of mixing and matching individual commands in Exodus, Leviticus, Numbers, and Deuteronomy, as if some verses set forth the moral law, some the ceremonial, and some the judicial. Occasionally things may be that clear-cut, but it is better understood as a hermeneutical tool for discerning three different aspects or layers of the law, all of which may be present in some measure within a particular Mosaic law.[59]

---

56. Westminster Confession of Faith 19.3.

57. Hooker, *Laws*, *III*.10.3 (p. 195).

58. Westminster Confession of Faith 19.4.

59. Consider for instance the law governing cities of refuge, or the law of the Jubilee, both of which clearly have both cultic *and* political dimensions, as well as encapsulating certain universal natural law norms. For a helpful exposition of how to properly handle the distinction, see Oliver O'Donovan, "Towards an Interpretation of Biblical Ethics," *Tyndale Bulletin* 27 (1976): 54–78.

Human Law

The subject of the judicial law brings us naturally to consideration of the topic of *positive human law*, a category that the Reformed take over seamlessly from the scholastic tradition. Johannes Althusius, for instance, sums up the need for human laws in terms reminiscent of Aquinas:

> The first reason is that not all men have sufficient natural capacity that they are able to draw from these general principles of common law the particular conclusions and laws suitable to the nature and condition of an activity and its circumstances. The second reason is that natural law is not so completely written on the hearts of men that it is sufficiently efficacious in restraining men from evil and impelling them to good.[60]

This twofold need of human law, both *specifying* natural law and *enforcing* it, gives rise to a distinction within the domain of human law, helpfully stated by Richard Hooker: "We must remember that all human laws written to order public societies must either establish some duty which all men had to obey before, or some duty which did not exist before. For distinction's sake, we may call the first sort *partly human* and the second sort *purely human*."[61] Both are derived from and dependent upon the natural law, but in different ways. For *partly human* laws, the demand of natural law is already clear and evident, such as in the prohibition on murder or theft. What is lacking is corrupt humanity's willingness to follow this demand consistently. Accordingly, human law in this case restates the moral demand and adds to it an appropriate and effective judicial penalty. With a *purely human* law, however, the relevant natural law demand remains too vague to guide action, or at least effectively coordinated social action. Human law steps in to fill the gap, supplying a precise action-guiding norm, such as the determination requiring all cars to drive on the right (or the left!) side of the road. Such a law is certainly congruent with natural law but can be described as "purely human" inasmuch as no one would be conscience bound to act accordingly until human law stepped in to specify our duty. To be sure, the distinction between *partly* and *purely* human is merely a heuristic. In practice, many laws

---

60. Althusius, *Politica*, 144.

61. Hooker, *Laws*, 1.10.10 (p. 88). This distinction corresponds closely to that in Aquinas between "conclusions" and "determinations" of natural law in *ST* I-II, 95.2.

fall somewhere on a spectrum between these two poles, such as a speed limit: natural law alone can tell you not to drive at an unsafe speed, but "unsafe" remains vague, and human law here both resolves the ambiguity and adds an enforcement mechanism.

Human law has ample space for discretion: while in principle magistrates were called to enforce the whole of the external dimension of the natural law (the tenth commandment constituted a standing reminder of an internal dimension of the natural law inaccessible to human law), in practice they had to limit themselves to what was feasible. Thus for instance Althusius, after enumerating the dangers of allowing false religion to proliferate in a commonwealth and the magistrate's right in principle to enforce the first table, concedes that this may not be possible "without peril to the commonwealth." "He shall therefore tolerate the practice of diverse religions as a skilled navigator bears with diverse and conflicting winds and clashing waves."[62] In this, Althusius was considerably more permissive than contemporary Roman teaching, which reproached Catholic princes who showed insufficient fervor in suppressing heresy; indeed, in the same year as the second edition of Althusius's *Politica* was published (1610), Henri IV of France was assassinated by a Catholic radical because of the toleration he showed to Protestants.

In general, the Reformed were keen to emphasize, against the accretions of Roman canon law and the interventions of papal bulls, the relative independence of civil magistrates in ordaining whatever laws local circumstances seemed to demand, guided always by the law of love. "Surely every nation is left free to make such laws as it foresees to be profitable for itself. Yet these must be in conformity to the perpetual rule of love, so that they indeed vary in form but have the same purpose,"[63] wrote Calvin. Although Calvin praised the office of magistracy as "the most sacred and by far the most honorable of all callings in the whole life of mortal men,"[64] he had no intention of rendering it unaccountable. The Reformed took as axiomatic the principle that "an unjust law is no law."[65] Just as the natural law functioned as the original source from which human lawmakers distilled their particular positive laws,

---

62. Althusius, *Politica*, 174.
63. Calvin, *Institutes*, 4.20.15 (2:1503).
64. Calvin, *Institutes*, 4.20.3 (2:1490).
65. Aquinas, *ST* I-II, 96.4.

136 • Natural Law

so also it remained a continual touchstone against which those laws could be tested and potentially found wanting. Opinions differed as to whether unjust laws could be opposed with mere passive resistance (disobeying and facing the consequences) or by open armed resistance and rebellion. Across the centuries, however, the Reformed sought to hold in dynamic tension the right of rulers to determine what the natural law required and the rights of citizens to judge these laws by reason or their own Bibles.[66]

Points of Tension

When it came to judging the commands of rulers by their Bibles, some of the Reformed were periodically drawn toward the idea of theonomy—that is, the doctrine that the judicial laws of the Old Testament were still binding upon Christian nations. Of course, as we have just seen, this doctrine was expressly denied by consensus Reformed teaching and even by a confession as Puritan in its ethos as the Westminster Confession of Faith.[67] Given the very high regard in which Protestants held the Bible, it was perhaps inevitable that, especially during times of political tension, more zealous Reformed writers might prefer to lean on the Old Testament's interpretation of natural law rather than that of their fallible prince. Thus for instance Elizabethan Puritan leader Thomas Cartwright adopted the Aristotelian dictum, "It is the virtue of a good law to leave as little as may be in the discretion of the judge,"[68] to contend that God provided the Mosaic judicial laws precisely to limit the discretion of Christian lawmakers. Modern-day theonomists just as Rousas John Rushdoony and Gary North have resurrected similar claims, with an influence far out of proportion to the small number of their followers.[69]

Although such explicitly theonomic claims have been confined to the Reformed fringe, there is no doubt that many Reformed, particularly among

---

66. See for instance the exposition in David P. Henreckson, *The Immortal Commonwealth: Covenant, Community, and Political Resistance in Early Reformed Thought*, Cambridge Studies in Law and Religion (Cambridge: Cambridge University Press, 2019).

67. See for instance Heinrich Bullinger, "Of the Magistrate," in Bradford Littlejohn and Jonathan Roberts, eds., *Reformation Theology: A Reader of Primary Sources with Introductions* (Moscow, ID: Davenant Press, 2017), 439–40.

68. Thomas Cartwright, *The Second Replie of Thomas Cartwright: Agaynst Master Doctor Whitgifts Second Answer Touching the Church Discipline* (Heidelberg: 1575), Appendix, i.21–22.

69. See, e.g., Rousas John Rushdoony, *The Institutes of Biblical Law* (Vallecito, CA: Ross House, 1982); Gary North, *Tools of Dominion: The Case Laws of Exodus* (Tyler, TX: Institute for Christian Economics, 1990).

English and Scottish Presbyterians and their American descendants, have tended to tie the natural law more closely to the text of Scripture and be wary of allowing civil law too long a leash. This same tendency, of course, is apparent in the "regulative principle of worship" common within such communities, which seeks to limit the corporate activities of the visible church within the constraints of divine positive law. On the other hand, Continental Reformed churches, along with Anglicans, have tended to be somewhat more relaxed about such matters and to allow greater discretion when it comes to the prudential application of natural law to civil law. In place of a narrowly applied "regulative principle," they felt free to apply natural law principles of order, decorum, and "fittingness" to the practice of corporate worship. Thus, for instance, the fierce clashes between the Puritans and Kings James I and Charles I in the early seventeenth century should be read as an intra-Reformed debate over the relative authority of magistrates and ministers in interpreting and applying the natural law.

Conclusion

Today in the twenty-first century, such debates over the meaning and application of natural law continue in Reformed communities. They might take the form, for instance, of debates over whether the civil magistrate has authority to apply the natural law principle "Thou shalt not kill" in the form of public health ordinances in a time of pandemic, even if these ordinances infringe upon ordinary rights and duties of religious worship. Or, less urgently but more broadly, they may take the form of debates between more and less libertarian Reformed thinkers over the extent to which the state should enact the natural law into specific human laws aimed at promoting the common good—with some emphasizing human depravity as a reason why such laws are needed, and others urging the same depravity as the reason why political authorities should not be trusted with such power. Far from suggesting that natural law is a flawed tool for moral and political deliberation, such debates attest to its enduring relevance and importance—not, to be sure, as the universal answer-machine that rootless moderns so yearn for, but as a summons to moral maturity.

In closing, let me suggest three key ways the Reformed natural law tradition retains its promise and relevance today. The reader may notice

138 • Natural Law

that in none of the three do I emphasize the natural law's value as a neutral "common ground" for moral and political reasoning in a pluralistic post-Christendom society. This is one role for natural law, and I do not wish to discount it entirely, but many have placed unrealistic hopes on just how much political common ground natural law can give us in a world that is in rebellion not merely against God but against nature.

First, natural law renders fallen humans "without excuse," as Paul teaches and the Reformed tradition has constantly emphasized. This may seem trivial, but it is not. We live in a world in which many basic precepts of human dignity and natural order are under assault. Too often, Christians' temptation has been to respond by retreating to the language of "biblical morality" or "a biblical worldview"—as if male-female marriage were simply a Christian faith-commitment that unbelievers could not possibly be expected to grasp or respect. Sin does have a powerful blinding effect, but the blindness is always (at first at least) self-imposed; it is a refusal to see. We must engage the moral chaos around us with the confidence that it is not merely a different religious value system but a *war against reality*. And we must engage individual sinners in the confidence that on some level of their being, *they know this*—they know themselves to be lawbreakers. As C. S. Lewis wrote, "Christianity is not the promulgation of a moral discovery. It is addressed only to penitents, only to those who admit their disobedience to the known moral law. It offers forgiveness for having broken, and supernatural help towards keeping, that law, and by so doing re-affirms it."[70]

Second, for those within the community of faith, natural law offers a rich and cosmic context for the truths and commands of Scripture that might otherwise seem isolated and arbitrary. Natural law is not something useful for unbelievers that is cast off as obsolete once we are led by the Spirit into the greater light of Scripture. Rather, as Calvin notes, Scripture is not merely something *that* we read but something *by which* we read—it provides the "spectacles"[71] through which the blurry world around us can come back into focus. But it does not do the reading for us—we must still do that. To use another metaphor offered by Al Wolters, fallen man is like a spelunker

---

70. Quoted in Justin Buckley Dyer and Micah J. Watson, *C. S. Lewis on Politics and the Natural Law* (Cambridge: Cambridge University Press, 2016), 45.

71. Calvin, *Institutes*, 1.6.1 (1:70).

lost in a cave, who can only guess at his surroundings by means of touch; the Bible is like a headlamp which brightly illumines it.[72] But we do not gain knowledge of the world by looking into the lamp; rather, we must point it at our surroundings and follow its beam with our eyes. Scripture is a "lamp to my feet and a light to my path" (Ps 119:105 ESV) by enabling us to *read the world rightly* and navigate it accordingly. With passions reordered by grace and thoughts corrected by Scripture, we as Christians are invited to study the world, soak in the riches of natural revelation, and reflect upon it with natural reason (sanctified, but still natural!) to discern God's will.

Finally, then, part of the enduring value of natural law is its role for moral deliberation *within the Christian community*. This may seem counterintuitive. We are accustomed to thinking of the natural law as something we use to talk with unbelievers. But amongst ourselves, the Bible is to function as the rule for our worship, our politics, and everything else—right? Such biblicism has been commonplace among American evangelicals over the past century, but it represents bad hermeneutics, bad ecclesiology, and bad ethics. Scripture, after all, does not present itself as a comprehensive rule book; its most extended body of law, the Mosaic judicial corpus, is by common Reformed consent addressed to a particular historical and political context, and the New Testament's rules for ordering church life are quite sparse. The church, while in certain respects a supernatural body, is also a temporal community that must organize its worship and set its budgets within the same constraints and according to the same canons of natural reason as other earthly communities. While we understandably yearn for a "thus saith the Lord" that can put an end to our arguments and uncertainties, the false certainty gained by such sloppy ethics and poor use of Scripture is simply a recipe for arrogant legalism and unending church splits. In fact, the very uncertainty of the natural law, as a framework of principles that demands careful prudence and sustained attention to circumstances, is a feature, not a bug. For it is only by living with and working within such uncertainty, it is only "by testing" that we can with prudence and humility learn to "discern what is the will of God, what is good and acceptable and perfect" (Rom 12:2 ESV).

---

72. Albert M. Wolters, *Creation Regained: Biblical Basics for a Reformational Worldview*, 2nd ed. (Grand Rapids: Eerdmans, 2005), 38.

Pakaluk Response
to Littlejohn

MICHAEL PAKALUK

I want to reply to Brad Littlejohn by considering what one might call the "phenomenology of a natural law" and tensions between this phenomenology and some of the distinctive holdings of the Reformed tradition, which I will draw from the Second Helvetic and Westminster Confessions.[1] These are:

- total depravity;
- double predestination;
- the common reprobation of men and demons;
- works as mere fruits;
- the assurance of the sufficiency of Christ's redemption as also the assurance of one's own salvation; and
- the prohibition against images.

That's a long list to deal with in a short span. Therefore, I will simply point to tensions.

Many of the tensions arise from how one answers this question: Is the natural law for the sake of the virtues, or are the virtues for the sake of keeping the law? In the classical conception of the natural law, as I explained, the purpose of our life is union with God, which is possible only if one becomes holy and good (Luke 1:75), which is possible only if one has the virtues, while

---

1. And the Westminster Catechisms.

Pakaluk Response to Littlejohn • 141

the moral law marks out necessary conditions for being good. (Someone who commits murder becomes "a criminal" or "an evildoer," and someone who fornicates becomes thereby "impure"; Matt 15:18–20; see 1 Cor 6:9–10.)

Suppose a young man "preserves the innocence of his childhood" until he gets to college. But there he falls in with accepted manners, starts sleeping around, and ends up living with his girlfriend. Later he converts, becomes a Christian, realizes he should follow the law of Christ as taught in the catechism, and separates from his girlfriend (who doesn't like his new direction anyway). How does he now conceive of his following of the commandment against adultery, as well as sex outside marriage? On the doctrine of total depravity, he was a wretch and now is found; his wretchedness is just the state of fallen man. But now he is a new creature. I agree, these claims are true—deeply true. And yet he may experience something else: namely, he may sense that, by following the natural law, he has "saved" something that he had enjoyed and took for granted as a child but had become wrecked. His wretchedness *was* to be wrecked. He had lost the childhood innocence given to him as a gift,[2] lost a certain clarity of vision and sensitivity (Matt 5:8), and had become selfish, prone to exploit others (1 Cor 6:12–13). He senses that, by following of the natural law, he has reclaimed and saved something that was deeply good about him but had been lost. The Lord has saved his created humanity. Yet the doctrine of total depravity[3] does not easily allow us to put things in this way; there is a tension at least.[4]

Another part of the phenomenology of the moral law is that someone striving to follow it is engaged in a battle, such that any serious abandonment of that law is not simply disobedience but also somehow is, and is felt to be, an act of treason, betrayal, and sedition. To murder or to commit adultery is not simply to fail in one's duty but also to aid the enemy. It is "to go over

---

2. Jesus was talking about any child in Matthew 18:3–5, obviously, not specifically the baptized children in Christian households.

3. "From this original corruption . . . we are utterly indisposed, disabled, and made opposite to all good, and wholly inclined to all evil." Westminster Confession, 6.4, in *The Creeds of Christendom*, ed. Philip Schaff, vol. 3 (New York: Harper, 1877), 615.

4. I would note here I was puzzled by Littlejohn's invocation of the phrase *incurvatus in se*, after Littlejohn had told us that by "Reformed" he meant the Reformation *sans* Luther—because that phrase was invented by Luther, in his *Romans* commentary. Luther asserts there that the notion is scriptural, yet the word *incurvatus* is nowhere found in the Vulgate. Augustine in *City of God*, book 16, uses rather the phrase *inclinatus ad se*, which has a very different meaning, namely, of departure from an *ordo amoris*. To be *inclined to oneself* is to have a *dis-order*, which can be corrected, by reordering. But to be *warped inwards toward* oneself is to have an *altered form*, which can only be superseded, never corrected, and that only by the imposition from without of a new relation to God in faith.

142 • Natural Law

to the other side." But posit the doctrine of double predestination.[5] Then reprobates are already on the side of the Enemy, foreordained to be so from all eternity. From the ultimate, divine point of view, reprobate men and the devils belong to exactly the same class. Thus, when a man abandons the moral law, this must be construed as revealing his allegiance all along (unless it is only an apparent, that is temporary, betrayal, among one of the elect). One may grant some slight scriptural support for the idea of revealed allegiance,[6] but still there is tension.[7]

Another tension arises from the contention, common to Lutheranism, that "works," including following the basic moral law, are properly construed no more as "fruits" of faith. The doctrine of predestination, especially supra-lapsarian predestination, insofar as it is meant to obliterate any traces of Pelagianism, also contributes to this next tension, as it makes God's choice from eternity (even if it remains a mystery) the sovereign consideration in human action. Fruits, after all, are gratuitous; a flowering plant may or may not bear a certain supply of fruit. It is not a necessary condition for a plant to be mature and leafy that it be bearing fruit.[8] Yet the phenomenology of the natural law is that keeping it is a necessary condition of salvation (Matt 5:17, 48): namely, "I will be lost if I am unfaithful" (or "go along with this command to murder an innocent," or "worship this false god," etc.). Indeed, the Westminster Catechism and all the catechisms of the Reformation speak of the Decalogue as setting down *duties*. But surely there is a tension between a duty and gratuitous fruit: we are bound to render the one, not the other.

To deal adequately with the antinomianism that constantly erupted in the Reformed movements, it is not enough to say that Luther opposed it firmly, as he himself pointed out, or that he, even, directed that children should memorize the Ten Commandments and repeat them daily. The question is: *Why* should it erupt? Should the Reformers have been surprised when it did? Had they explained correctly the seriousness of following the natural law?

---

5. "By the decree of God, for the manifestation of his glory, some men and angels are predestinated unto everlasting life, and others foreordained to everlasting death." Westminster Confession, 3.3.

6. For example, when Jesus calls Judas a devil, John 6:70–71. On the other hand, Peter surely saw his betrayal as a genuine betrayal.

7. As an aside I would note the deeply corrupting implication of the thought, "I suppose I never was one of the elect anyway. This is the kind of man (or woman) I am. I might as well give myself over to this sin fully."

8. While the blessed man's leaf never withers, he bears fruit simply "in due season," akin to his prospering (Ps 1).

This last point is compounded when one holds that one cannot have faith without being assured that one has faith and that faith is sufficient for salvation, so that assurance of one's faith in Christ is also assurance of one's own salvation.[9]

A final tension relates to the prohibition of the use of images in divine worship.[10] In the contributions to this volume, a frequent theme has been how the light of faith strengthens our natural power of grasping what the natural law is, and how the gift of grace strengthens the human will for following that law. These are important truths. But something else deserving of attention is that "part" of human nature, which has the natural role of supporting reason when it needs to master desire, which Plato referred to as *thumos*, and which C. S. Lewis in his first lecture in *Abolition of Man* calls the "chest" or the heart: "It may even be said that it is by this middle element that man is man: for by his intellect he is mere spirit and by his appetite mere animal."[11] This element is cultivated, so as to play its proper role, through literature and art.

Reformed divines have long sensed that this is so. According to a famous story, Karl Barth not simply held up the Bible but also sang a song, "Jesus Loves Me."[12] Long before that, in a remarkable passage in his *Systematic Theology*, Charles Hodge warned that speculative philosophy will threaten always to overcome and then suppress the gospel message (as he had seen firsthand in German universities), but then he explained that safety may be found in Christian hymns: "After all, apart from the Bible, the best antidote to all these false theories of the person and work of Christ, is such a book as Doctor Schaff's 'Christ in Song.' . . . We want no better theology and no better religion than are set forth in these hymns."[13]

---

9. Trent: "If any one shall say, That a Man is absolv'd from his Sins, and justified, in that he certainly believes himself to be absolv'd and justify'd; or that none is really justified, but he that believes himself to be so; and that by this Faith alone Absolution and Justification are wrought; let him be Accursed." Of Justification, Canon 14, in *The Canons and Decrees of the Council of Trent* (London: T.T., 1687), 29.

10. Among many authorities, see question 51 in the shorter Westminster Catechism.

11. C. S. Lewis, *The Abolition of Man* (Toronto: Macmillan, 1947), 34.

12. My pastor at the First Church Congregational in Cambridge, Alan Happe, of dear memory, used to say that he had witnessed Barth do this; the story is not a mere legend.

13. Hodge, *Systematic Theology* (New York: Scribner's, 1872), 2:590. Philip Schaff, ed., *Christ in Song: Hymns of Immanuel; Selected from All Ages, with Notes* (New York: Randolph, 1869). Ironically, the first hymn in that collection is Ambroses's *Veni redemptor ominium*, for Advent, dating from the late 300s. The editor, Schaff, explains that he has "smoothed down" its language. Indeed, he spiritualizes the third and fourth verses, which celebrate very earthily the perpetual virginity of Mary as seen in her

144 • Natural Law

But the same is true of pictorial art. The catacombs in Rome were discovered by Antonio Bosio in 1578, well after the deaths of Calvin and Zwingli, and just one year before the publication of volume 1 of Francis Turretin's *Institutio*. But now we know that from the earliest centuries Christians, in worship and under the gravest circumstances, used images to illustrate stories and themes from the gospel. Today the catacomb of Commodilla is famous, even, for its depictions of Christ as the supreme Lawgiver.

In comparison, consider a church in a small village in Scotland I saw once, bare and austere, with no ornamentation whatsoever. There was a simple inscription in Greek over its entryway: οὓς προέγνω, καὶ προώρισεν ("whom he foreknew, he also predestined"; Rom 8:29.). Compare that church with the architecture of St. Peter's in Rome, and with the religious art in the Vatican museums—art which was not "collected" so much as simply acquired when it was made, over the centuries, and conserved with a certain custodianship. Which of the two nourishes that distinctively human element that Lewis speaks of? Which inspires to magnanimity and greatness?

De-Hellenization in theology has effects that reach to the human heart also.

---

intact "barrier of chastity" (*claustrum pudoris*). Hodge had asserted (*Systematic Theology*, 3:265) that Mary's perpetual virginity was the first step in her "deification." Which faith then will such songs in their original language preserve, Romish or Reformed?

Biermann Response to Littlejohn

JOEL D. BIERMANN

There seems to be no shortage of advice offered to graduate students working their way along the long, lonely, and often contentious path toward a terminal degree and on into the academy. I received my share. But of all the unsolicited academic counsel I once received, the best was, "Take your friends where you can find them." The axiom gained force by the lived example of the one who gave it. I have since learned to embrace that bit of wisdom as an enduring guide and have routinely affirmed it and endorsed its adoption by my own students. Reading Littlejohn's article on Reformed natural law gave me the chance once again to practice the advice myself. It seems that I have found a friend—well, at least when it comes to the natural law.

This did not come as a complete surprise. In fact, I suspected as much and so singled out this essay to read first. For his part, Littlejohn also anticipated that the Lutheran and Reformed contributions to this volume would likely be mutually supportive as he suggested that "the boundaries between 'Reformed natural law' and 'Lutheran natural law' may prove rather porous" (p. 114). Indeed, the boundaries are altogether porous. And it might even help to consider the commonalities in our understandings not only in terms of boundaries delineating respective territories but in light of another analogy, that of a shared journey along the way toward the territory of right conception and practice of the natural law. If the project of this entire book is considered from the perspective of this imagery, there is no doubt that Littlejohn and I end comfortably situated very near one another in precisely

145

146 • Natural Law

the same territory—a nice stretch of tropical beach seems a worthy image. In fact, as we make our way to our respective chairs side by side on the sand, we can probably even share the same car and enjoy much of the same music en route. It is likely, though, that there would be some debate about which sites along the road were worthy of a full lingering stop. Littlejohn might be inclined to consider a list of historical museums and intellectual waypoints to be essential pauses in the journey. For my part, I'm one of those people who like to keep the car moving and am usually content with a photo snapped out of the window as we roll past the scenery on the way to the goal.

Relinquishing for the moment, albeit reluctantly, my beach and my Volkswagen, I was genuinely delighted with the final destination of Littlejohn's essay. His threefold summary conclusions about the natural law coincide precisely with my own understanding of that law. And he is exactly right to emphasize the importance of the natural law within the context of the church rather than as a vague minimalist moral code contrived to constrain the excesses of a faithless, licentious pagan world. My new Reformed friend—admittedly, a designation unilaterally asserted—dampens the familiar ardor that regularly attends the clichéd Reformed position of Christians transforming culture as H. Richard Niebuhr classically and normatively expressed it. Littlejohn is on target when he observes that such hopes are unrealistic "in a world that is in rebellion not merely against God but against nature" (p. 138). And while he rightly notes that God's natural law is not without value in the wider culture not "as the universal answer-machine that rootless moderns so yearn for, but as a summons to moral maturity" (p. 137), he emphasizes instead the important role this law should play in the life of the church and her people, or at least he rightly understands that this emphasis demands the top priority.

His first admonition—for the church to take seriously the idea that God's creational, moral law is relevant and binding for every single person in the world—is certainly one the church needs to heed. Succumbing to the adoration of pluralism and the concurrent suppression of universal truth that defines Western culture, the church has too frequently and too freely abandoned, at least functionally and practically, her conviction of the timeless and universal aspect of God's truth for all people. The prevalence of the tenets of Moralistic Therapeutic Deism continues unabated even in churches considered to be staunchly faithful. Christians need to believe and teach that God's reality applies equally to all of God's creation, regardless of what values any given person or people group might cherish. It is not insensitive to say this; it is, of course, the practice of genuine love. With such a commitment to the sweeping relevance of God's truth, it might even be possible for the church to act with confidence as she makes this truth known; though the venue for such bold declarations of God's sweeping truth will far more often be living rooms, breakrooms, boardrooms, and classrooms, where Christians engage their unbelieving neighbors in personal conversation, than in courtrooms, legislatures, or broadcast studios, where various efforts are made to foster or even compel compliance from a resistant, unbelieving, and self-obsessed populace.

Littlejohn is also correct when he asserts the role that the natural law can play for believers in helping them better understand, appreciate, and perhaps even to delight in the mysteries and wonders encountered in the world around them. Seeing the continuity of God's will at work in the whole of creation—even a creation shot through with sin—helps Christians better grasp the interconnected and comprehensive nature of God's truth. Consider the commandment against adultery. Rather than pursue the path of chastity for the sake of personal rectitude or out of sheer obedience to an ecclesial or domestic dictate (though in a pinch, and failing better and higher motivations, sheer obedience is certainly not something to be maligned), the Christian learns to see his pursuit of sexual purity as an essential aspect of God's purposes for the right functioning of marriage, families, communities, and all humanity. The broad, natural law realities that undergird and shape the right conduct of human sexuality and relationships offers a compelling context for understanding one's personal pursuit of the right way to live—the way that is in harmony with God's will built in to the very fabric of creation. The Christian life is not a series of daily checkoffs on a master list of established propriety or morality as defined by text or community. Rather, it is a life lived in harmony with the plan established by God for the right functioning of his world. No doubt, that plan does take shape in specific commands that can even be reduced to a list. But recognizing the natural law reinforces the overall continuity and beauty of God's comprehensive design, and the individual's part within that plan and nudges us away from the pursuit of to-do lists.

Since misery loves company—or framed more positively, and more in keeping with the spirit of friendship, a sorrow shared is a sorrow

148 • Natural Law

halved—I am fully sympathetic with Littlejohn's lament about the biblicism that runs rampant in so many corners of Christendom that are otherwise quite faithful to her Lord. Biblicism is certainly "bad hermeneutics, bad ecclesiology, and bad ethics" (p. 139), but I would add bad systematics and bad rationality to the list. There is some comfort in learning that battles against an overwrought piety of biblicism are being fought in other parts of Christ's church besides my own. Particularly helpful, and an angle I had not considered before, was the author's insight that it is most often not the Bible but rather God's natural law that rightly guides and governs the church's life together. Of course, it is not as if the Scripture and the natural law are at odds. They both have the same source, and the Bible's clear expression of God's will articulates the truths that resonate within the creation itself. But Littlejohn's trenchant point is that the Bible simply does not solve every quandary we are bound to face in living life together in the church. When Scripture is silent, believers are left to settle things with the tools available to every creature, as expressed in the natural or creational law which applies in the church as much as, or even more than, it does in the secular city's life where the natural law is so routinely denied and thwarted. The law built in to the world serves the church ably as it sorts through the inevitable questions that arise in the course of ecclesial life. That the implementation of a law on which every Christian should unhesitatingly agree nevertheless still always demands much careful reflection, discussion, and listening should certainly be esteemed as a great gift for God's gathered people who seek to live faithfully in the self-denying way of Christ. Practicing the truth of the natural law in our relationships within the church helps to concretize and hone a believer's ongoing striving to take up the cross and follow Jesus.

Littlejohn's essay reinforced many of my own convictions on a number of points, and it was good to have the vast common ground we share confirmed at so many places. We agree wholeheartedly on the "complementarity of natural, divine, and human law" (p. 129). We also agree that "the moral/ceremonial/judicial framework . . . is better understood as a hermeneutical tool for discerning three different aspects or layers of the law" (p. 133), rather than as a filter to sort out which laws still count, and which can now be safely ignored. And I have no argument when he asserts, "if the natural law is summed up in the commands to love God and to love neighbor, then the first table of the Decalogue as well as the second provides a blueprint for civil laws—blasphemy may be forbidden as readily as adultery" (p. 132). I am further grateful for the introduction to the thought of Johannes Althusius related to the problem of blasphemy and religious toleration. The seventeenth-century German Calvinist recognized the dangers of giving room for false religion in a commonwealth but was also aware of the problems created by a rising pluralism and so counseled skilled and nuanced religious toleration for the sake of the political realm. My own thinking on this matter has arrived at much the same place.

With all that we share in common, there are, of course, differences that remain between my new Reformed friend and me. Most of those differences stem from old and fundamental divides evident in our respective approaches and priorities in the process of doing theology. At the risk of appearing petty or belaboring the obvious, my Lutheran outlook—one that happily subscribes without reservation even to the Formula of Concord—is somewhat bewildered by the degree of interest in what is reasonable, or makes sense, or is intellectually compelling. One example among many is the discussion about the "twofold need of human law, both *specifying* natural law and *enforcing* it," which "gives rise to a distinction within the domain of human law" (p. 134). The discussion was intense, but it left me wondering what actually was gained by the intellectual expenditure. What was admitted as a "merely heuristic" distinction seemed to exemplify the different weight our respective traditions accord to the place of reason within the theological task. This emphasis on the importance of human reason appeared also in the discussion about the various appropriations of "common grace."

Granting the obvious fact that I am Lutheran and Littlejohn is Reformed, there is nothing surprising about my observation of the differences outlined above. While that disparity matters and generates significant concerns in other areas of doctrinal discussion, the far more important message of this response needs to be our overwhelming degree of agreement in virtually every area of discussion when it comes to our understandings of the natural law and its place in the life of the church. It is good to find a friend, and even better when he is so easily and readily found.

Moschella Response to Littlejohn

MELISSA MOSCHELLA

There are many parallels between the Reformed natural law tradition, as Littlejohn presents it, and the new natural law account. For instance, Littlejohn is careful to distinguish between laws of nature, understood as "discernible regularities within the physical universe" (p. 115), and the natural law, which is "something not merely descriptive but prescriptive" (p. 116). Similarly, the new natural law account distinguishes between the first order, or the order of nature (which is known through speculative reason, and is studied in disciplines like metaphysics and natural science), and the third order, or moral order (known through practical reason, and studied in moral philosophy). Littlejohn's account also seems to recognize that what makes something natural in the moral order is not that it happens with regularity or even that we spontaneously desire it at the subrational level, but that our intellect grasps it as good. In other words, what is natural in the moral order is determined by what is *reasonable*. What I want to probe further in my commentary on Littlejohn's account is the relationship between the reasonableness of natural law and its bindingness, or its character *as law*.

In discussing the bindingness of natural law, Littlejohn seems to assume two things: first, that in becoming aware of moral law, "we find ourselves, if not face-to-face with the idea of a *lawgiver*, at least dimly aware of such" (p. 116), and second, that the "law" aspect of natural law corresponds to the faculty of *will*, whereas the "nature" aspect of natural law corresponds to the faculty of *intellect*. These two assumptions seem to be inherently connected in his account. For if the source of law is *will*, then there cannot be a law without the command of a lawgiver. It therefore seems to me that the second of these assumptions is primary, and it is this assumption that I want to call into question. While I appreciate Littlejohn's avoidance of an oversimplistic dichotomy between rationalist and voluntarist accounts of natural law, I believe that his critique of that dichotomy fails to go far enough because it holds on to the premise that law is essentially a command, understood as an act of will.

Instead of thinking of law as essentially an act of will, however, why not think of it—as Aquinas did—as essentially an "ordinance of reason for the common good"?[1] On Aquinas's view, what makes law binding is not that it is commanded by the will of a superior (human or divine) but that following the law is necessary to achieve our end or good.[2] As Finnis puts it:

> Aquinas . . . treats obligation as the rational necessity of some means to (or way of realizing) an end or objective (i.e. a good) of a particular sort. What sort? Primarily . . . the good of a form of life which, by its full and reasonably integrated realization of the basic forms of human well-being, renders one a fitting subject for the friendship with the being whose friendship is a basic good that in its full realization embraces all aspects of human well-being, a friendship indispensable for every person.[3]

In other words, on the new natural law account and on Aquinas's account as Finnis understands it, the moral force or obligatoriness of natural law's directives comes from the necessary connection between those directives and our flourishing.

What Littlejohn proposes as the solution to overcoming the rationalist-voluntarist dichotomy—that "natural morality had to be promulgated by divine command and that divine command had to be anchored in created structures" (p. 118)—is essentially the solution offered by Francisco Suarez. But though Littlejohn says that Aquinas would agree with this solution, the claim is only compatible with Aquinas's view if *command* is understood to

---

1. Thomas Aquinas, *Summa Theologiae* (hereafter, *ST*) I-II, 90.4, corpus.
2. "Since a precept of law is binding, it is about something which must be done: and, that a thing must be done, arises from the necessity of some end." (*ST* I-II, 99.1, corpus)
3. John Finnis, *Natural Law and Natural Rights*, 2nd ed. (Oxford: Oxford University Press, 2011), 46.

152 • Natural Law

be an act of reason rather than an act of will.[4] Suarez's view on this point, however, is different from Aquinas's, and these differences have their roots in Suarez's rejection of a key element in Aquinas's moral psychology. I believe it is worth dwelling on these differences because of the significant influence that (according to Littlejohn's account) Suarez's thought has had on the Reformed natural law tradition.

Whereas for Suarez what ultimately moves an individual to act is a decision, an act of will, on Aquinas's view (which Suarez explicitly rejects), between the decision and the execution of that decision there is an intervening step that Aquinas calls *imperium* or "command."[5] *Imperium* is an act of intellect by which one represents one's plan of action to oneself—the end one seeks, understood to be good, and the means one has deemed appropriate for the attainment of that end.[6] This means that the psychosomatic execution of our action is not (as Suarez would have it) the result of a push from the will (one's own or another's) but rather the result of "a person's response to the attraction of (something considered to be) good."[7] Because *imperium* is "a representational 'act' of intelligence, there can (so to speak) shine through the *imperium* the attractiveness of the end or values at stake, and the adjudged appropriateness of the means elected; and it is *these* that account for one's carrying out this total action."[8]

How does Suarez's removal of *imperium* as an intervening step between decision and execution relate to his view that the binding force or obligatoriness of law comes from its being commanded? Just as Suarez views one's decision (an act of will) as what moves an individual to act, so too does Suarez see the decision or will of a superior as that which makes a certain type of conduct obligatory (whether that be the will of a ruler in the case of civil law, or the will of God in the case of natural law).[9] What drops out of view in both cases is the *good* that gives the act its intelligible point.

These differences between Aquinas's and Suarez's views of obligation may seem like philosophical hairsplitting, but they have important repercussions

---

4. "It belongs to law to command and forbid. But it belongs to reason to command. . . . Therefore law is something pertaining to reason." Aquinas, *ST* I-II, 90.1, sed contra.

5. Aquinas, *ST* I-II, 17; Finnis, *Natural Law and Natural Rights*, 338.

6. Finnis, *Natural Law and Natural Rights*, 339

7. Finnis, *Natural Law and Natural Rights*, 339.

8. Finnis, *Natural Law and Natural Rights*, 340.

9. Finnis, *Natural Law and Natural Rights*, 341.

for both political and moral philosophy. In political philosophy, Suarez's view separates legal obligation and moral obligation, reducing legal obligation in some instances to an obligation to do as the lawgiver stipulates *or* to accept the stipulated penalty.[10] The problem with this is that it disconnects legal obligation from our moral obligation to promote the common good, making legal obligation seem arbitrary and undermining the ability of citizens to judge that laws that are contrary to the common good fail precisely *as laws*. Suarez's view creates similar problems in moral philosophy, for by rooting obligation in God's command (understood as an act of will) rather than in the connection between the law's dictates and the good, it leaves the question of why we ought to obey God's will without a satisfactory answer.[11]

On Aquinas's view, by contrast, such problems are avoided entirely. While it is true that on Aquinas's view a law must be promulgated by someone who has authority over the community in question,[12] it is not the promulgation that gives the law its binding force. Rather, for both civil law and natural law, the law's binding force comes from its reasonableness, and—because reason directs us to the good—a law is reasonable insofar as it genuinely promotes the common good. Citizens are obligated to follow the civil law not because it is the command of a superior but because following the law is necessary if their actions are to be in line with the common good. They are obliged to follow the law, in other words, because and insofar as the law (by specifying the means by which they are to respect and promote the common good) gives them a conclusive reason to act that they can and should adopt as their own. In the central case, therefore, civil law should be understood as a "prescription of *reason*, by means of which rational and indeed conscientious and reasonable practical judgments about the needs of a complete community's common, public good, having been made and published by lawmakers, are understood and adopted by citizens as the *imperium* of their own autonomous, individual practical reason and will."[13] Laws that do not meet these requirements fail precisely *as laws* and therefore do not bind the citizens in conscience, although there might be a "collateral" obligation to follow them insofar

---

10. Finnis, *Natural Law and Natural Rights*, 329–30.
11. Finnis, *Natural Law and Natural Rights*, 342–43.
12. Aquinas, *ST* I-II, 90.4, corpus.
13. Finnis, *Aquinas* (New York: Oxford University Press, 1998), 258.

154 • Natural Law

as failure to do so could undermine a broader system of laws that does by and large serve the common good.[14]

Likewise, on Aquinas's view (which the new natural law account shares) one can know the natural law, and know it *as binding*, even if one does not recognize God as the ultimate source of that law.[15] The natural law is promulgated through reason,[16] and it is also reason that has the authority to govern our other faculties to direct us toward the good.[17] Of course, the very existence of a moral order—like the existence of intelligibility in the natural world more generally—in itself calls for further metaphysical explanation. It is possible to recognize (even without revelation) the existence of an intelligent and benevolent creator who is the ultimate source of the moral order and who is therefore the ultimate lawgiver. Littlejohn is thus in one sense correct to say that when we become aware of the natural law, "we find ourselves, if not face-to-face with the idea of a *lawgiver*, at least dimly aware of such" (p. 116)—but not because the idea of law essentially requires the command of a superior. And because on Aquinas's view law is understood not essentially as the command of a superior but as a prescription of reason directing us to the good, the question of why we should follow the law becomes moot, akin to asking why I should follow the road signs directing me to my desired destination.

This does not mean, however, that explicit recognition of God as lawgiver adds nothing to our sense of moral obligation. For once we recognize, with Aquinas, that the natural law is our participation in God's wisdom, in his benevolent governance of the whole universe, this greatly enhances the force and depth of natural law's principles. It does this not by way of the extrinsic push of a superior's command but by strengthening our sense of the intrinsic connection between those principles and genuine flourishing. For if we recognize the principles and precepts of natural law as guidelines from a wise and benevolent creator who is the source of our existence and nature, and who therefore knows better than we do how to promote our flourishing, this greatly deepens our sense of the natural law's reliability. Further, recognizing God as lawgiver helps us to see the natural law not as a

---

14. Finnis, *Natural Law and Natural Rights*, 361–62.
15. Stephen Brock, *The Light That Binds* (Eugene, OR: Pickwick, 2020), 190, 214, and 244ss.
16. Aquinas, *ST* I-II, 90.4, ad. 1.
17. Aquinas, *ST* I-II, 94.4, ad. 3.

set of impersonal rules but rather as a personal invitation to cooperate with God. And since harmony with God is (even without revelation) something that we can grasp as a human good that plays a special architectonic role in our overall flourishing, making the explicit connection between following the natural law and being in a harmonious relationship with God gives us a powerful overarching reason to act morally.

I have focused my response on what might appear to be a relatively minor point in Littlejohn's account because I believe that getting this foundational question right is essential to a sound understanding of natural law that always keeps firmly in view the connection between moral norms and human flourishing. Keeping this connection firmly in view is crucial for enabling us to respond to the "moral chaos around us" that Littlejohn refers to—not only to engage nonbelievers with confidence but also to strengthen believers who might otherwise succumb to the lie that "compassion" and "kindness" require us to abandon our defense of certain moral norms. Thus I hope that Littlejohn and other scholars in the Reformed tradition will take these comments not so much as a criticism but as a friendly invitation to reconsider the tradition's reliance on Suarez and to look to Aquinas (and to the new natural law theory, which claims to be a faithful development of Aquinas's natural law theory, correcting neo-Scholastic misinterpretations) to further refine an account of natural law that already has many merits.

Leithart Response to Littlejohn

PETER J. LEITHART

Brad Littlejohn opens his argument by carefully defining his key terms—Reformed, nature, law, and natural law. He does not define his terms of abuse, particularly "biblicist," with the same care. It appears to have something to do with sloppy, unsophisticated exegesis, an expectation that the Bible provides a comprehensive rulebook for life, and (in the subtext) generic yokelism. In this book, I am cast, as I often am, in the role of village fool and fundamentalist, a rube of biblicism. It is, admittedly, typecasting, because my biblicism is quite in earnest. I do not just play one on TV.

Funny thing is, I largely agree with what Littlejohn says about the relation of Bible and world toward the end of his essay. Reformed theologians love to cite Calvin's claim that Scripture is a set of spectacles that enables us to see the world rightly. *That* is what I mean by biblicism, and since Littlejohn appears to agree, I am happy to welcome him to our beleaguered but merry band. I wish Littlejohn had cited Calvin at several earlier points in his essay; it would have made things clearer and, to me, more congenial. He could have clarified his claim that nature is just "*the way things are*" (p. 117) by acknowledging we cannot clearly see what things are unless we are looking through Scripture's spectacles. He could have explained that, however many truths may be known naturally, natural man's vision is still shadowy until he sees with new eyes trained by Scripture. Littlejohn is well aware of sin's effects on the will and reason, but perhaps he could have explained earlier how our will and reason might be corrected.[1]

---

1. Throughout Littlejohn's essay, I had the uneasy sense he was operating with the same nature/supernatural duality that I have identified in other contributors. In his telling, special grace appears

Leithart Response to Littlejohn • 157

If the Bible is, as the Bible itself says, a lamp, then it seems a *necessary* part of our moral reasoning. If we set it aside, how can we know what might be lurking, unnoticed, in the shadows? I agree *we* must read the Bible. Of course.[2] I agree we see other things by the light of the lamp. But here the lamp image breaks down. Because the Bible is a book, we must look *at* the lamp to know how it dispels darkness. Exegesis is necessary if we want to use the lamp well.

To his credit, Littlejohn does engage in some exegesis, but his exegesis is almost entirely controlled by traditional Reformed readings of key passages. I fear he does not shine the lamp of Scripture on our tradition. To be sure, his assignment was to expound the Reformed understanding of natural law. As the resident biblicist, I am freer to inquire whether or not the Reformed readings are correct. I will discuss three passages. I do not pretend I can convince Littlejohn, or anyone else, in the brief space. I only want to demonstrate there are alternative readings that are far less friendly to natural law theory. Natural law, as Littlejohn presents it, is *not* a "clear conclusion from scriptural teaching" (p. 112).

In a discussion of Genesis 3, Littlejohn says the serpent is the source of the split between God's reason and will, "between what is good for man and what God commands" (p. 123–24). By challenging the command of God, "the serpent invites Eve to contrast what is obviously good . . . with God's seemingly irrational and arbitrary prohibition" (p. 124). I agree, but that misses the obvious. Everything in Eve's experience, everything she can discern about the nature of the tree's fruit, points to one moral conclusion: she *should* eat the fruit, because it looks delightful, because it is food, because it will make her wise (Gen 3:6). The only thing that stands in the way is Yahweh's nonarbitrary "Thou shalt not." But that means Eve cannot know what she should do at the tree apart from God's spoken word. She does not know what to do unless she shines the lamp of divine command. Here at least God's word *overrides* what nature appears to teach.

And if it happens in Eden, might it happen elsewhere? Might we often find ourselves in situations where "nature" appears to point in one direction

---

to be necessary for the attainment of eternal life, but *not* for natural life in this world—such things as moral action, rationality, and social and political order.

2. I am puzzled that Littlejohn does not here mention the work of the Spirit in guiding our reading. That does not relieve us of responsibility, but it does give us hope we can arrive at the truth of the text.

158 • Natural Law

but God commands otherwise? Based on Genesis 3, we ought not discount the possibility, and the only way to know for sure is to make Scripture integral to our moral reasoning. The dogmatic conclusion, which I discuss in my paper, is that special revelation, divine speech, is not a postlapsarian corrective but is inherent in man's original condition. Not only sinners but humans as such need the guidance of the word of God. It is natural for man to be on speaking terms with God.

Littlejohn alludes to and quotes Romans 2:14–15 several times, rightly identifying it as the biblical *locus classicus* for natural law theory. I do not think the passage supports the traditional conclusion. It is hard to see how Paul could praise gentile law-keeping a half-chapter after detailing the darkness of the idolatrous mind (Rom 1:18–32). How could he commend gentiles as a "law to themselves" shortly after portraying the horrors of gentile lawlessness?

In his discussion of Romans 2, Thomas Aquinas dismissed as Pelagian the idea that gentiles could obey God's commandments by their own natural powers. As an alternative, he proposes that Paul is speaking of converted gentiles, who have received the new covenant promise of the law written on their hearts (cf. Jer 31:33).[3] That fits the context. These verses are part of a polemic against Torah-breaking Jews, whose possession of Torah and temple does not protect them from the coming wrath. "You think you are righteous because you have Torah," Paul argues, "but look at these gentile believers, who keep Torah though they do not have Torah." In this reading, "by nature" does not modify the gentiles' doing ("nations . . . do by nature") but their having ("nations not having the law by nature").[4] Paul writes elsewhere that Jews and gentiles are such "by nature" (Rom 2:27; 11:24; Gal 2:15; 4:8).[5]

Finally, and more briefly, Romans 7. This passage has long been a bone of contention among Reformed theologians, who have debated whether the

---

3. The allusion is clear. Paul claims these gentiles have *to ergon tou nomou grapton en tais kardias*. In the Septuagint translation of Jeremiah 31:33, Yahweh promises *doso nomous mou . . . epi kardias auton grapso autous*. See Simon Gathercole, "A Law unto Themselves: The gentiles in Romans 2.14–15 Revisited," *JSNT* 85 (2002) 27–49.

4. That better fits the Greek word order: *ethne ta me nomon exonta* phusei *ta tou nomou poiosin*; woodenly translated, "the nations who have not the law by nature the things of the law do."

5. Some, Paul says, are "uncircumcised by nature" (Rom 2:27); but isn't *everyone*? See the more radical suggestion of Lloyd Gaston, who argues that what is on the gentiles' hearts is "what the law produces," that is, the curse and judgment that the law brings. Gaston, *Paul and the Torah* (Vancouver: University of British Columbia Press, 1987) 101–6.

I of moral lament is a regenerate or unregenerate man. That quite misses the function of this chapter in Romans. Paul's arguments have to do not with systematic questions about sin but with Israel, Torah, and the gentiles. Romans 7 is about the deadly effects that the Spiritual and good law has on people who live by flesh. The problem is not the law but its recipients, and the problem is solved, Paul goes on to say, by the gift of the Spirit. Spiritual humans—*only* Spiritual men and women—can receive the Spiritual Torah and live.

Littlejohn says biblicism is appealing (despite its "sloppy ethics" and "poor use of Scripture") because it promises an end to uncertainties. Natural law's very *un*certainty is its glory. If nothing else, the last few paragraphs have demonstrated that engagement with Scripture also leaves us "living with and working within . . . uncertainty" (p. 139).

Like many natural law theorists, Littlejohn's world is a fairly static one. Yes, things grow and develop toward natural ends, but it is not a world marked by the scars of catastrophe. Yet the real world is so scarred. That makes me wonder what role history plays in Littlejohn's understanding of natural law. I assume he would take the abject failure of twentieth-century utopianisms as material for natural law reflection. In the Soviet bloc, China, Myanmar, and countless other places, polities were established that ran against the grain of human nature, at great human cost. Such regimes are object lessons.

Once we introduce history into our reflections, I am thrown back—bumpkin that I am—onto questions about Scripture. Are the flood and Babel material for natural law reflection? What about the exodus, the covenant at Sinai, the conquest of Canaan, the Davidic dynasty, the ministry, death, and resurrection of Jesus? Even unbelievers like Tom Holland recognize Jesus' death as a critical event in the history of the world. It would seem imprudent to leave them out of consideration. But if natural law includes reflection on such episodes, it becomes hard for Littlejohn to maintain clear boundaries between natural law and special revelation—unless one includes supernatural events only after suitably naturalizing them.

As I point out in my primary essay, Scripture often appeals to history rather than nature to ground moral obligations and political institutions. Why must Israel release slaves in the seventh year? Because they are manumitted slaves called to enact perpetual exodus. Why ought they keep

160 • Natural Law

Sabbath? As a sign they have been delivered from Sabbath-denying Pharaoh. Why establish institutions and practices of care for orphans, widows, and strangers? Because they know what it is like to be strangers and because Yahweh their God has proven himself to be the Father of the orphaned Israel and the Husband of widowed Israel.

Littlejohn acknowledges that different cultures adhere to natural law in different degrees. But his explanation is ahistorical. It is far more plausible that Western culture is more humane, just, and merciful not because of some inexplicable variation in the intensity of natural law but because Western culture was formed by the church, the Bible, and the Christian liturgy. What we see in Western civilization is not a product of "common grace" but what I have called "middle grace," the cultural afterglow of the gospel. Western unbelievers are more in the light because they are heirs of the light of *special* grace and revelation.

I cheerfully concur with Littlejohn that natural law advocates have "placed unrealistic hopes on just how much political common ground natural law can give us in a world that is in rebellion not merely against God but against nature" (p. 138). It is just this incapacity that makes me "anti" natural law, because for many advocates, the whole point of the theory is to deliver the very thing Littlejohn says it cannot. Once he has made that admission, I ask (yet again) about the priorities of Christians' public witness. In the world Littlejohn describes, what is to be done? If men are in such darkness that they rebel against what they can see, how do we dispel the darkness? Littlejohn says he has a lamp. Perhaps we should switch it on.

Let me sharpen the point. What if the cultural chaos we face is, at bottom, demonic? Can natural law exorcise devils? Or might we give prayer, fasting, and suffering witness a shot? For Jesus did not say, "These kind come out only by a rigorous application of natural law."

Rejoinder

BRAD LITTLEJOHN

Let me begin by expressing my gratitude to each of my interlocutors for such a spirited and thoughtful discussion. In the process, I have gained greater insight not only into their own various approaches to the topic of natural law but also a fuller understanding and articulation of my own views. That is always the mark of a worthwhile conversation, and I hope that readers will benefit richly from the exchange.

This rejoinder presents a challenge, inasmuch as there were few if any common threads in the four responses I received to my chapter on "Reformed Natural Law." Thus I have no choice but to take each of my interlocutors in turn, responding piecemeal and all too briefly to different questions and concerns. That being the case, it may be best to begin with the least adversarial response and proceed in ascending order of polemical heat to the response that offered the most wide-ranging critique of my position.

I begin then with Michael Pakaluk's response to my essay, which took a curious approach. Rather than taking issue with anything I or the Reformed tradition actually *said* about natural law, Pakaluk essentially suggested that we couldn't possibly mean it because we were, well, Reformed. On his account, Reformed theology is committed to several propositions that stand in deep tension or outright contradiction to classical natural law theory, and thus whatever I, John Calvin, or Richard Hooker might *claim*, there cannot be a true Reformed natural law. I believe that I could with equal plausibility construct a case arguing that there can be no true Roman Catholic natural law because of the Catholic church's commitment to a magisterium whose supposedly divine teaching authority holds an effective epistemic trump card over conclusions derived from natural reasoning. Or else I might argue that

162 • Natural Law

the Roman doctrine of transubstantiation and accompanying sacramental system uses grace to destroy or replace rather than perfect nature and thus undermines a conception of normative natural ends. Such arguments, of course, would be dubious, for the simple reason that countless Roman Catholic thinkers through the centuries have held such doctrines together with a robust commitment to natural law, suggesting that they can in fact be reconciled. As an outsider to this tradition, it is unlikely that I understand its doctrines better than its leading exponents.

Respectfully, I would suggest that the same is likely true of Pakaluk's attempt to expose self-contradiction within the Reformed tradition. It does not seem to me that he has adequately understood or summarized the doctrines in question, and closer attention to their nuances would show them to be reconcilable with traditional natural law categories. For the sake of space, I will just briefly highlight two: total depravity and predestination.

The doctrine of total depravity, argues Pakaluk, does not allow someone saved in adulthood and brought back to righteous living to think that "by following the natural law, he has 'saved' something that he had enjoyed and took for granted as a child but had become wrecked" (p. 141). Yet the Second Helvetic Confession (which Pakaluk himself mentions as a source) makes clear that while all of man's faculties have been depraved, they have not been destroyed: "[Man's] understanding, indeed, was not taken from him, neither was he deprived of his will, and altogether changed into a stone or stock. Nevertheless, these things are so altered in man that they are not able to do that now which they could do before his fall. For his understanding is darkened, and his will, which before was free, is now become a servile will; for it serveth sin, not nilling, but willing."[1]

Similarly with predestination, Pakaluk worries that the Reformed teaching makes nonsense of our moral experience by consigning us from before birth either to God's side or the enemy's side so that the reprobate's sin cannot be understood as an act of treason against God. However, the Second Helvetic Confession explicitly warns against such a fatalistic interpretation

---

1. "Second Helvetic Confession," in Philip Schaff, ed., *The Creeds of Christendom*, vol. 3 (New York: Harper & Brothers, 1877), on *Christian Classics Ethereal Library*, chapter IX (https://ccel.org/ccel/schaff/creeds3/creeds3.v.ix.html). For more on this issue, see my essay, "'Vestiges of the Divine Light': Girolamo Zanchi, Richard Hooker, and a Reformed Thomistic Natural Law Theory." *Perichoresis* 20.2 (2022): 43-62.

of the doctrine,[2] which it seeks to safeguard as a mystery known only to God, which should in no way diminish our only creaturely experience of our moral agency. Indeed, on this doctrine, the Reformed teaching differs little from that of Aquinas,[3] so it is hardly plausible that predestination and natural law stand in contradiction.

Joel Biermann's engagement was gracious, so gracious that I felt a little sheepish about the critiques I had offered of his "Lutheran Natural Law" essay. It may be that even less separates our viewpoints than I had previously thought. Indeed, since penning my initial response I have found myself more inclined to agree with Biermann's suggestion that we favor the term *creational law* over the less theologically charged *natural law*.[4] I was particularly gratified by Biermann's enthusiastic agreement with a point I never tire of making, underemphasized as it often is in Protestant ecclesiology and ethics: that the number-one locus for us to fruitfully apply natural law reasoning is within the life of the church itself. I daresay that many if not most cases of scandal and abuse in our churches, and many if not most unpleasant denominational splits, could have been prevented if those involved, mindful of human frailty, had simply followed some of the principles of commonsense moral reasoning that God has written on our hearts.

I would push back on Biermann's appeal to irrationalism in his penultimate paragraph, where he confesses himself "somewhat bewildered by the degree of interest in what is reasonable, or makes sense, or is intellectually compelling" (p. 149). He questions the utility of even the most basic distinctions within the philosophy of law, such as the distinction between conclusions and determinations (or "partly human" and "purely human" laws). Although he represents this antipathy to reason as a Lutheran distinctive, I think that great Lutheran scholastics such as Niels Hemmingsen, Martin Chemnitz, and Johann Gerhard might disagree.

Readers worried about philosophical hairsplitting may question the utility of Moschella's response to my essay, but I for one appreciated her penetrating attention to one of the critically contested issues in the natural

---

2. See Second Helvetic Confession, chapter X.

3. See for instance the important essays in Jordan J. Ballor, Matthew T. Gaetano, and David Sytsma, eds., *Beyond Dordt and 'De Auxiliis': The Dynamics of Protestant and Catholic Soteriology in the Sixteenth and Seventeenth Centuries* (Leiden: Brill, 2019).

4. On this, see Oliver O'Donovan's incisive remarks in *The Disappearance of Ethics: The Gifford Lectures* (Grand Rapids: Eerdmans, 2024), 81.

law tradition. I had been keen to stress that for the Reformed, natural law requires a *Lawgiver*, and we must resist any temptation to allow natural law theory to slip into a free-floating theory of reasonableness that tempts us to think its principles would hold good, as Grotius infamously mused, "even if God did not exist." Moschella thus worries that on the critical question of "What gives the natural law its binding force *as law*?" I side with the semi-voluntarist account of Francisco Suarez (foregrounding the *divine will*) and not with the full-fledged rationalist framework offered by Thomas Aquinas (focused on the *divine reason*). I claim no expertise on either Aquinas or Suarez and so perhaps should not have dared venture even the very modest historical claim that "the Reformed, for their part, fell at various points along this spectrum [between Aquinas and Scotus] but mostly clustered close to the modified Thomism represented by Suarez" (p. 118). So I will leave it to others to decide exactly where my attempt to summarize the Reformed view falls in the history of philosophy, but let me try to restate the nub of the issue as clearly as possible, mindful that space permits only the barest outlines of a response to a very nuanced set of questions.

Simply put, Moschella, following John Finnis, insists that moral obligation is simply "the rational necessity of some means to . . . an end."[5] If there is only one road leading from my house to the grocery store, then of necessity, I must take that road—if, that is, I want to stay alive and feed my family (I am not known for my green thumb!). If I cannot rationally *not* will the good of staying alive, then as matter of rational and moral necessity, I must in fact take that road. Put this way, I don't really need to think in terms of the will of some lawgiver imposing that necessity on me—it is more like the law of noncontradiction. But of course, there *has* in fact been some lawgiver—namely God—who has thus established this connection between means and ends, creating the world in such a way that I must eat in order to live.

The question thus arises whether God *had* to do so, or whether he might conceivably have done otherwise. Moschella insists that the natural law arises simply as the product of God's own *imperium*, the "act of intellect by which one represents one's plan of action to oneself—the end one seeks, understood to be good, and the means one has deemed appropriate for the attainment

---

5. John Finnis, *Natural Law and Natural Rights*, 2nd ed. (Oxford: Oxford University Press, 2011), 46.

of that end" (p. 152). But I would stress that even for Aquinas, God's "plan of action" with regard to creation is contingent: God is not bound by his nature to create at all, or to create in one particular way rather than another. Aquinas is crystal-clear on this in his *Summa*: "God does not act from natural necessity, but . . . His will is the cause of all things; nor is that will naturally and from any necessity determined to those things. Whence in no way at all is the present course of events produced by God from any necessity, so that other things could not happen." Thus "the order placed in creation by divine wisdom . . . is not so adequate to the divine wisdom that the divine wisdom should be restricted to this present order of things." Since "the divine goodness is an end exceeding beyond all proportion things created, we must simply say that God can do other things than those He has done."[6]

God has thus in fact *willed* to create a world in which there are such creatures as human beings, a finite imprint of the infinite divine goodness, and in which those human beings need food in order to live. Why then must I drive to the grocery store? Because it is natural, yes, but we may with equal propriety answer, "Because God wills it." The natural law itself is characterized neither by radical contingency (as if it manifested simply a set of rules God handed down yesterday and may revoke tomorrow) nor by absolute rational necessity. It is rather characterized by *hypothetical necessity* from the ultimate standpoint, resting in God's decision to establish this particular order of things, even if from within that order, it possesses a strict rational necessity for us.

Now all of this matters to Moschella in part because of its ramifications for a theory of civil law, where she worries that Suarez's account and mine "disconnects legal obligation from our moral obligation to promote the common good, making legal obligation seem arbitrary" (p. 153). Not so. Again, let us start with the idea of law as a rational ordering of means to a good end. Sometimes there will be only one appropriate means, in which case there will be only one just law. But this is rare. More often there will be a multitude of possible means, some better suited to certain circumstances rather than others—just as for most people, there are in fact several different routes to be taken to the grocery store. Thus the scholastics spoke of the

---

6. Thomas Aquinas, *The Summa Theologiæ of St. Thomas Aquinas*, trans. Fathers of the English Dominican Province, 2nd ed. (1920; online edition 2017 by Kevin Knight), 1.25.5, https://www.new advent.org/summa/1025.htm#article5.

166 • Natural Law

category of "permissive natural law"[7] for the whole range of actions in which the natural law permitted many different morally appropriate courses of action. This category of permissive natural law explained why France and England might each have different laws governing inheritance or marriage, and neither law be deemed unjust. This diversity within law does not make legal obligation arbitrary or disconnected from the common good—it simply highlights that the common good is too rich and pluriform to be reduced to just one legal regime. What is it, then, that obliges citizens in England to conform to the property provisions of the common law rather than those of the Napoleonic code? It is not (at least on many particulars) because one is rationally ordered to the common good and the other is not, for both are ordinances of reason. Rather, it is simply the *will of the legislator* that supplies the binding force in such cases. In human law as well as divine, both *reason* and *will* join in order to make laws function as *laws*.

I end then with Leithart's spirited engagement, which represented the sharpest pushback. Indeed, I was taken aback by his response, given the extent of our agreement. I heartily agree that the Bible is "a *necessary* part of our moral reasoning" and that good "exegesis is necessary if we want to use the lamp well" (p. 157). Leithart represents his exegesis and mine as being in deep tension, but I'm not sure that I see it. On Genesis 3, he notes that the divine positive law *not* to eat from the tree stands in tension with the *prima facie* indications of natural law that the tree is good, and it was Eve's sin to allow the latter to override the former. That was, I had thought, precisely my own point, as I noted that it is the essence of sin to play natural and special revelation against one another rather than trusting in their harmony. Nor do I think that Leithart's brief observations about Romans 7 undercut my own passing reference to it as describing the conflict between our fleshly passions and "the law of [our] mind" that seeks to follow the mind of God.

Leithart alleges that I "allud[e] to and quote Romans 2:14–15 several times" (p. 158) and thus thinks that his alternative exegesis undercuts the biblical case for natural law. In fact, I can only find one mention of this text *en passant* in my essay, where I reference John Calvin's citation of it. The traditional exegesis of it plays no decisive role in my larger argument for natural law—unsurprisingly, since as Leithart notes, Aquinas himself

---

7. See Brian Tierney's essential study, *Liberty and Law: Studies on the Idea of Permissive Natural Law, 1100–1800* (Washington, DC: Catholic University of America Press, 2014).

built his theory of natural law on other bases. The fact is that the biblical testimony for the reality and utility of natural law is so comprehensive and pervasive that it does not hang on a single disputed proof text.[8]

I further agree with Leithart's emphasis on the role of history in the apprehension or corruption of natural law; in fact, in my essay I explicitly commend Richard Hooker's historicized account of the degrading effects of "perverted and wicked customs" in obscuring cultures' grasp of natural law over time, and so I am puzzled at his claim that "Littlejohn's world is a fairly static one" (p. 159). Leithart further suggests that it is "plausible that Western culture is more humane, just, and merciful not because of some inexplicable variation in the intensity of natural law but because Western culture was formed by the church, the Bible, and the Christian liturgy." I wholeheartedly agree and have praised historian Tom Holland's eloquent demonstration of this point in his book *Dominion*.[9] There is no doubt that much of the "common sense morality" we have till recently been able to take for granted is not the product of typical fallen human reasoning but of Christian civilization's gradual redirection of our perverted rational faculties toward their natural ends. Thus I (and I think the whole Reformed tradition) would agree that we are unlikely to save our societies from their current moral train wreck without a revival of faith.

Leithart poses some interesting questions about to what extent historical events should be understood as natural or supernatural revelation. The answer seems clear enough: any acts which represent God's miraculous intervention into the ordinary patterns of cause and effect he has inscribed on creation are *supernatural*, while any merely human actions in response are a form of *natural* revelation, inasmuch as they tell us about natural human faculties. To be sure, when Scripture narrates such human actions, we are treated to supernatural (and thereby infallible) testimony about otherwise merely natural events, providing us greater confidence than we could have from other sources of testimony.[10]

---

8. For a fine, highly-accessible survey of this biblical testimony, see David VanDrunen, *Natural Law: A Short Companion*, Essentials in Christian Ethics (Nashville: B&H Academic, 2023).

9. See my review, "The Ghost of Christian Past: On Tom Holland's *Dominion: How the Christian Revolution Remade the World*," *American Reformer*, July 28, 2022, https://americanreformer.org/2022/07/the-ghost-christian-past/.

10. See C. S. Lewis's *Miracles* (New York: HarperCollins, 2001) for an extremely lucid and useful treatment of the relevant concepts.

168 • Natural Law

Having signaled my considerable agreement with many substantive points in Leithart's response, I think his rhetorical framing misses the mark. Populism may be popular now, but theology is ill served by the trope of the "bumpkin" or "village fool" taking on ivory-tower elites. While teaching the priesthood of all believers, the Reformers also insisted on the importance of deep intellectual formation to fully grasp and faithfully transmit "the faith once delivered to the saints." If anything, I would argue that the shoe is on the other foot: a commitment to natural law is a helpful safeguard against the clerocratic elitism that may take hold if the world around us is taken to be a black box, illuminated only by the sophisticated biblical exegesis of trained theologians. After all, the brilliant exegesis and biblical theology that has been a hallmark of Leithart's own essential ministry to the church is hardly that of a village bumpkin but rather the product of decades of training and reflection. The ordinary believer need not await guidance from such exegetes before making everyday moral judgments but may consult the law written on his heart; that is the essential contention and significance of natural law theory.

CHAPTER 4

The "New" Natural Law

MELISSA MOSCHELLA

The "new" natural law theory (NNLT) is a development of the Aristotelian-Thomistic natural law tradition. While the characterization of the theory as "new" comes from critics who (mistakenly, in my view) see it as a break with the tradition, the label is now widely used by critics and proponents alike to refer to the account of natural law developed by Germain Grisez, John Finnis, and Joseph Boyle in the second half of the twentieth century. Like all theories within the Aristotelian-Thomistic tradition, NNLT is essentially *eudaimonistic*, meaning that it sees morality as fundamentally a matter of respecting and promoting human flourishing, understood as the fulfillment or perfection of human nature. NNLT has two basic, interrelated elements: the identification of basic human goods and the articulation of moral norms. (Virtue is also important in NNLT, but its importance is for the moral *life* rather than for the articulation of moral principles, as explained further below.) In brief, NNLT holds that practical reason's first principles identify and direct us toward certain basic goods—health, knowledge, friendship, and so on—that are constitutive of our flourishing insofar as they perfect the various dimensions of our nature. Moral norms flow from the *integral directiveness* of practical reason, requiring us to act in ways that respect *all* of practical reason's first principles and thus to respect all of the basic goods for all people. In what follows, I will unpack this extremely synthetic articulation of NNLT's key claims and then consider the implications of these claims for political philosophy. Though space limitations make it impossible to engage in detail with NNL's critics,

170 • Natural Law

I will present the NNL account with a view toward clarifying common misunderstandings, and allaying concerns frequently expressed by the theory's critics.[1] Because many of these concerns are based on the false impression that NNLT eschews metaphysics and anthropology, I will begin by briefly outlining NNLT's key metaphysical and anthropological presuppositions, as well as its understanding of the role of nature in natural law.

Metaphysical and Anthropological Presuppositions

Many have criticized NNLT for removing God from the foundation of natural law.[2] Yet NNL theorists recognize that the ultimate metaphysical ground of the natural law is God, without whom there would be no moral order, nor human beings governed by and capable of understanding that order, nor any beings at all. Indeed, the existence of a moral order, like the existence of all other forms of order, points to the existence of God as its source. While one can come to know the principles of natural law without knowing that God exists or that God is the source of those principles, recognizing God as the author of the natural law deepens our understanding of that law, its obligatoriness, and the point of following it.[3] Knowledge of the existence of God as the intelligent, personal, and benevolent uncaused cause of all that exists is accessible to human reason even without the aid of revelation.[4]

---

1. Readers interested in direct and detailed engagement with critics should pay careful attention to the footnotes and consult the works cited there.

2. See, e.g., Russell Hittinger, *A Critique of the New Natural Law Theory* (Notre Dame, IN: University of Notre Dame Press, 1987). One source of these criticisms may be NNL's rejection of divine command theories of moral obligation, or its related claim that explicit knowledge of God as the ultimate metaphysical source of natural law is not necessary for knowledge of practical reason's principles and their basic normative force (see, e.g., Steven J. Jensen, *Knowing the Natural Law: From Precepts and Inclinations to Deriving Oughts* [Washington, DC: Catholic University of America Press, 2015], 5, 153–58, see also nn21–22). Nonetheless, NNL theorists recognize that a full theoretical defense of natural law and its obligatoriness cannot be provided without recognizing God as its source. See n3 below.

3. Grisez writes: "When we understand [the directiveness of the principles of practical reason] as guidance provided by our Creator, our sense of its dependability deepens, and with that the normative force of the moral *ought* which it generates increases." Germain Grisez, "Natural Law and the Transcendent Source of Human Fulfillment," in *Reason, Morality and Law*, ed. John Keown and Robert George (Oxford: Oxford University Press, 2019), 449; see also John Finnis, *Aquinas* (Oxford: Oxford University Press, 1998), 10.4; Finnis, *Natural Law and Natural Rights*, 2nd ed. (Oxford: Oxford University Press, 2011), 406ss.

4. For further development of these points, including an account of how we can know (in principle) that God is a person without the aid of revelation, see Finnis, *Aquinas* 10.1–4; *Natural Law and Natural Rights*, ch. 13, plus corresponding notes in postscript. See also Germain Grisez, "Natural Law, God, Religion and Human Fulfillment," *The American Journal of Jurisprudence* 46 (2001): 3–36; Grisez, *Beyond the New Theism: A Philosophy of Religion* (South Bend, IN: University of Notre Dame Press, 1975).

Likewise accessible to reason is the intrinsic value of harmony with God (the basic human good of religion) and the special, architectonic importance of this good in the moral life, as discussed in greater detail below.[5]

The penultimate metaphysical ground of the natural law is human nature. This is true in at least three respects. First, and most generally, if our nature were different, human goods (which are perfections of our nature) would also be different.[6] For instance, if human beings reproduced asexually, marriage (a conjugal union ordered toward procreation) would not be a basic good, for such a union would not even be possible for us. Speculative knowledge of this possibility is a prerequisite for practical reason's grasp of that possibility as intrinsically worthy of pursuit (i.e., as "good"). (And the same can be said with regard to all of the other basic goods.) Second, if human beings lacked the capacity for free choice, moral norms would not apply to us, for moral norms govern free choices.[7] This is why NNL theorists have offered a robust philosophical defense of free choice.[8] Third, understanding that human beings are essentially *rational animals* whose bodies are essential and intrinsic to personal identity is also crucial for ethics. Indeed, as NNL theorists have argued at length, debates about issues such as euthanasia, abortion, sexual ethics and gender identity all turn on this anthropological truth.[9]

The above should make clear that—despite accusations by critics to the contrary—NNL theorists do not deny that speculative claims (about metaphysics, anthropology, etc.) are relevant to ethics or even in some respects prior to ethics.[10] Such accusations are often based on misunderstandings that

---

5. See Grisez, "Natural Law, God, Religion," and Moschella, "Beyond Equal Liberty," *Journal of Law and Religion* 32 (2017): 123–46.

6. Finnis, *Reason in Action* (Oxford: Oxford University Press, 2011), 5; Germain Grisez, *Abortion* (Washington, DC: Corpus, 1970), 313; Grisez, *The Way of the Lord Jesus*, vol. 1, *Christian Moral Principles* (Chicago: Franciscan, 1983), 124.

7. Grisez, *Christian Moral Principles*, 2.A, http://twotlj.org/G-1-2-A.html. For a detailed analysis of Aquinas's account of the interplay of reason and will in free choice, see Finnis, *Aquinas*, 3.3

8. Germain Grisez, Joseph Boyle, and Olaf Tollefsen, *Free Choice: A Self-Referential Argument* (Notre Dame, IN: University of Notre Dame Press, 1976).

9. Patrick Lee and Robert George, *Body-Self Dualism in Contemporary Ethics and Politics* (New York: Cambridge University Press, 2009); Melissa Moschella, "Trapped in the Wrong Body? Transgender Identity Claims, Body-Self Dualism, and the False Promise of Gender Reassignment Therapy," *Journal of Medicine and Philosophy* 46 (December 2021): 782–804; see also Christopher Tollefsen and Robert George, *Embryo: A Defense of Human Life* (New York: Doubleday, 2008), 3.

10. See, e.g., Jensen, *Knowing the Natural Law*; Steven A. Long, "Natural Law or Autonomous Practical Reason: Problems for the New Natural Law Theory," in *St. Thomas Aquinas and the Natural Law Tradition: Contemporary Perspectives*, ed. John Goyette et al. (Washington, DC: Catholic University of America Press, 2004): 165–93. See also n18, below.

172 • Natural Law

can be avoided if we think more carefully about what we mean by *human nature* and about the sense in which natural law is *natural*.

Natural Law, Nature, and the Four Orders

In what sense is natural law *natural*? Obviously, the naturalness of natural law cannot mean that our subrational emotions always spontaneously incline us to follow it, for natural law is a set of practical principles and related moral norms, and everyone who tries to live a morally upright life knows that acting in accordance with those principles and norms often requires resisting or moderating our spontaneous inclinations. Nonetheless, the natural law can be called natural in at least two senses: (1) It is (at least in principle) knowable by natural reason without the aid of supernatural revelation. (2) It directs us toward the fulfillment of our nature.

However, correctly interpreting what it means to say that natural law directs us toward the fulfillment of our nature requires further specification. For our nature is complex: we are animals, thinkers, moral agents, and makers.[11] The fulfillment of our nature in one respect may conflict with our fulfillment in another respect. Our fulfillment qua animal, for example, may be in conflict with our fulfillment qua moral agent, as when morality requires that one risk illness or even death in order to fulfill one's obligations. Similar conflicts might arise between our fulfillment qua thinker or qua maker and our fulfillment qua agent. For example, thinking through a philosophical argument or putting the finishing touches on a painting might not be compatible (at a particular time) with fulfilling one's duties as a parent. It seems, then, that the natural law (which is, after all, a *moral* law) directs us toward the fulfillment of our nature primarily qua moral agent (i.e., qua rational animals capable of shaping ourselves through deliberation and choice), even though, as will become clear shortly, our fulfillment qua animal, thinker, and maker cannot be entirely separated from our fulfillment qua agent, for human nature, though complex, is ultimately unified.

The preceding considerations rely upon Aquinas's distinction among what he calls the "four orders," which he explains as follows:

---

11. To be clear, these are all *aspects* of a single, unified human nature, aspects that can be analytically distinguished but are not metaphysically separate.

> Now order is related to reason in a fourfold way. There is one order that reason does not establish but only beholds, such is the order of things in nature. There is a second order that reason establishes in its own act of consideration, for example, when it arranges concepts among themselves. . . . There is a third order that reason in deliberating establishes in the operations of the will. There is a fourth order that reason in planning establishes in the external things which it causes, such as a chest and a house.[12]

This distinction is important because "according to the different modes of order that reason considers in particular, a differentiation of sciences arises."[13] Disciplines like metaphysics and the natural sciences that study "things that human reason considers but does not establish" belong to the first order, often referred to as the natural order.[14] Logic belongs to the second order, which might be called the logical or intentional order. The third, or moral order, is "the order of voluntary actions," which "pertains to the consideration of moral philosophy."[15] Finally, the fourth order, which might be called the technical order, encompasses "the mechanical arts" and, more broadly, the realm of artifacts and objective culture.[16] Knowledge in the first two orders is attained through the exercise of speculative reason, which aims at "consideration of the truth," while knowledge in the second two orders is practical and directed toward action.[17]

Moral philosophy, and thus natural law theory, is a third order inquiry, which means that its principles and norms are *practical*, known through *practical* reason (though informed by prior speculative knowledge).[18] As Aquinas

---

12. Thomas Aquinas, *Commentary on the Nicomachean Ethics*, trans. by C. I. Litzinger, 1.1, https://isidore.co/aquinas/english/Ethics.htm.

13. Aquinas, *Commentary on the Nicomachean Ethics*, 1.2.

14. Aquinas, *Commentary on the Nicomachean Ethics*, 1.2.

15. Aquinas, *Commentary on the Nicomachean Ethics*, 1.2.

16. Aquinas, *Commentary on the Nicomachean Ethics*, 1.2. See also Grisez's development of Thomas's account of the four orders in Germain Grisez, *Beyond the New Theism*, 230–40, 343–56.

17. Aquinas, *Summa Theologiae* I, 79.11, corpus.

18. Thus, NNL thinkers do not, as Long claims, deny the priority of speculative knowledge over practical knowledge, if this simply means that "practical knowledge presupposes and depends on a prior *speculum* or speculative truth." Stephen Long, "Fundamental Errors of the New Natural Law Theory," *National Catholic Bioethics Quarterly* (Spring 2013): 108. Nor do NNL thinkers hold that "practical reason depends in no way upon speculative reason," as Steven Jensen claims in *Knowing the Natural Law: From Precepts and Inclinations to Deriving Oughts* (Washington, DC: Catholic University of America Press, 2015), 14. Indeed, new natural law theorists *agree* with Jensen's claim—which he takes to be opposed to the NNL account—that the "*per se nota* character of the first precepts [of practical

174 • Natural Law

makes clear, practical reason has its own first principles, and these first principles are the first principles of natural law, identifying and directing us toward what is good (i.e., what fulfills or perfects us), and away from what is bad.[19] Further, while what is good for us will include our fulfillment in all of the orders (our fulfillment as animal, thinker, agent, and maker), moral normativity is third-order normativity and thus will ultimately direct us to our perfection as agents, which is the perfection of our will (and of our practical reasoning, which orders the will). As I will explain below, however, the perfection of our will is not unconnected to our perfection in other dimensions, for the perfection of our will requires respecting (and to the extent possible, promoting) the human good in all of its dimensions, not only for oneself but for all members of the human community.

By contrast, many critics of NNL theory treat moral philosophy (including natural law theory) as a first-order, speculative inquiry, attempting to derive moral norms from speculative (first order) knowledge of human nature.[20] NNL theorists hold that this is a mistake, both on the merits and as an interpretation of Aquinas, arguing that this approach is the result of reading Aquinas through a distorted neo-Scholastic lens.[21]

---

reason] does not make them independent from speculative knowledge. It only makes them independent from deductive syllogistic reasoning. It leaves open the possibility of other sorts of epistemological dependence" (Jensen, *Knowing the Natural Law*, 14). For the first principles of practical reason, though not *derived* from prior speculative knowledge, are intellectual *insights* into the relevant data of experience, including the data provided by prior speculative knowledge. See also n19 below.

19. Aquinas, *Summa Theologiae* I-II, 94.2. Grisez's work on natural law theory began with a commentary on this article: Germain Grisez, "The First Principle of Practical Reason: A Commentary on the *Summa Theologiae* 1-2, q.94, a.2," *Natural Law Forum* 10 (1965): 168–201, http://twotlj.org/EthicalTheory.html.

20. See, e.g., Stephen Long, "Fundamental Errors of the New Natural Law Theory"; Edward Feser, *Neo-Scholastic Essays* (South Bend, IN: St. Augustine's, 2015). For a critique of Feser's view and further explanation of the role of human nature (and speculative knowledge) in NNLT, see Melissa Moschella, "Sexual Ethics, Human Nature, and the 'New' and 'Old' Natural Law Theories," *National Catholic Bioethics Quarterly* 19 (Summer 2019): 251–78; "Sexual Ethics, Practical Reason, and the Magisterium: A Response to Irene Alexander," *The National Catholic Bioethics Quarterly* 22 (Spring 2022): 99–127.

21. NNL can thus be considered "new" insofar as it offers an account of Thomistic natural law theory that departs from the neo-Scholastic interpretation favored by the theory's critics. While NNL theorists believe their view is actually more faithful to Aquinas, most of their work has focused not on historical or exegetical arguments, but on developing a cogent account of natural law and defending that account on the merits. These historical and exegetical debates are beyond the scope of the current article. For more on these debates, see Finnis, *Aquinas*; Finnis, *Natural Law and Natural Rights*, ch. 2; Finnis, "Is and Ought in Aquinas," in *Reason in Action*, 144–55; Jean Porter, "Reason, Nature, and the End of Human Life: A Consideration of John Finnis's *Aquinas*," *The Journal of Religion* 80 (July 2000): 476–84; Patrick Lee, "Is Thomas's Natural Law Theory Naturalist?," *American Catholic Philosophical Quarterly* 71 (1997): 567–87; E. Christian Brugger, "St. Thomas's Natural Law Theory," *National Catholic Bioethics Quarterly* 19 (2019): 181–202.

Debates between "new" and "old" natural law theorists about issues like the relationship between facts and values or between human nature and morality—many of which are actually based on misunderstandings or semantic issues rather than on actual substantive disagreement[22]—ultimately come down to these distinctions (methodologically foundational for the NNL account) between the first and third orders, between speculative and practical reason and their respective roles in our understanding of human nature and of natural law. For, as already noted, NNL theorists recognize (along with their "old" natural law critics) that natural law is metaphysically grounded in human nature. However, NNL holds that knowledge of the ends of our nature in the morally relevant sense is grasped through *practical* reason, which, in deliberating from a first-person perspective about how to act, grasps the intrinsic and intelligible appeal of certain possibilities (e.g., being healthy, acquiring knowledge, developing a friendship), recognizing them as choiceworthy and to-be-pursued—that is, as good. Of course, prior speculative knowledge of these possibilities is a precondition for practical reason's grasp of their choiceworthiness. Upon subsequent reflection, these goods can then be identified speculatively as the perfections of various aspects of our nature.

By contrast, "old" natural law theorists hold that we determine what is good for us through first-order speculation about the ends of human nature considered from a third-person perspective.[23] The trouble with this approach (among other things) is that human nature considered as a first-order reality inclines toward many behaviors—violence, aggression, promiscuity—that are not actually good from a moral perspective.[24] Thus it is only through practical reason's identification of basic goods that we can determine which of the inclinations or possibilities of our nature are actually *ends* or *perfections* in the morally relevant sense. As Finnis explains (summarizing Aquinas's methodology), "One understands human nature by understanding human capacities, those capacities by understanding human acts, and those acts by

---

22. For a detailed analysis of Jensen's critique of NNL, distinguishing parts of the critique that are based on misunderstandings of the NNL view from genuine differences between the two positions, see R. J. Matava, "On *Knowing the Natural Law*: A Response to Steven Jensen," *The American Journal of Jurisprudence* 61 (2016): 237–57.

23. Feser, *Neo-Scholastic Essays*; Jensen, *Knowing the Natural Law*; Long, "Fundamental Errors of the New Natural Law Theory."

24. For more on this point, see Christopher Tollefsen, "Aquinas's Four Orders, Normativity, and Human Nature," *Journal of Value Inquiry* 52 (August 2018).

176 • Natural Law

understanding their objects."[25] And the objects of human acts, as will be explained further below, are basic human goods, grasped *as good* through the insights of *practical* reason (and then *subsequently* understood by speculative reason as perfective of our nature).

These points have been explained and defended at length elsewhere.[26] My aim in presenting them briefly here is to help prevent common misunderstandings by clarifying and making transparent the basic methodological premises of the NNL account, the central claims of which will be outlined in the following sections.

The First Principles of Practical Reason: Basic Human Goods

Ethics is about human acts. Human acts, in the paradigm sense, are acts done for a *reason*, aimed at some end understood to be good.[27] Not every human behavior is a human act. Sleepwalking, digesting, reflexive movements, and other nonvoluntary behaviors are not human acts. Even voluntary but purely habitual actions, like heading groggily to the bathroom upon waking, are not human acts insofar as they are performed without prior deliberation and choice. The first principles of ethics—and thus of natural law—will therefore also be the first principles of human action, the identification of the basic reasons, ends, or goods that get genuine human action (as opposed to mere human behavior) off the ground.

What are these first principles or basic reasons for action? Identifying them requires reflecting upon our own actions and the judgments we make about the actions of others. For example: Why am I writing this article? Perhaps I am doing it for the money (even though writing philosophy articles is not exactly a lucrative endeavor). But that is not a sufficient answer, because money's value is purely instrumental. What do I want the money *for*? Maybe I need it to pay the mortgage or cover the rising cost of groceries, and these things in turn are desirable because I need them for my health and survival. While I *could* identify additional reasons for

---

25. Finnis, *Aquinas*, 90.

26. See, e.g., Tollefsen, "Aquinas's Four Orders"; Moschella, "Sexual Ethics, Human Nature," and "Sexual Ethics, Practical Reason, and the Magisterium."

27. Aquinas, *Summa Theologiae* I-II, 1.1–3.

The "New" Natural Law • Melissa Moschella • 177

wanting to survive and remain healthy (to complete important work, for the sake of my family, to better serve God, etc.), my action would be intelligible—there would be a sufficient reason for it—even if health and survival were the ultimate ends of that action. Another way of putting this is to say that if you asked me why I was writing the article, and I told you that I was doing it to make money to preserve my life, you might think my horizons were somewhat limited, but you wouldn't find the account puzzling or unintelligible, nor would you question my sanity, as you would if I told you that I was just pressing random keys on the keyboard for its own sake. Thus we have identified one basic reason for action, or basic human good: life (including health).

What other reasons could I give for writing this article that would likewise suffice to make my action intelligible? Some possibilities include contributing to the understanding of natural law, developing my abilities as a scholar, maintaining good relations with my friends who are editing this volume, pleasing my husband, fulfilling a promise, or doing God's will. These possibilities correspond to the various other basic goods (in addition to life and health) identified by NNL theorists: knowledge and the appreciation of beauty, performative excellence (in work and play), friendship, marriage, integrity and authenticity (harmony between reason and emotion and between judgment and action, sometimes jointly referred to as practical reasonableness), and religion (harmony with God). Appeal to any instantiation of any of these goods is sufficient to make an action *intelligible*—that is, to provide a rational motivation for the act, and thus to make the act a genuine human act.[28] (It is not, however, sufficient to make an act *fully reasonable* [morally good], as will be explained below.)

To identify a list of basic goods is to identify the first principles of practical reason, which are the first principles of human action. Stated in its most general form by Aquinas, the first principle of practical reason is:

---

28. NNL theorists hold that this list is complete, meaning that any good sufficient in itself to provide an intelligible end for human action will turn out to be an instantiation of one or more of these basic categories of good, but should it turn out that there is something missing from the list, this could easily be accommodated. Indeed, the original list proposed by Grisez, Finnis, and Boyle did not include marriage. It was only later that they realized this good was not reducible to the goods of life-in-transmission and friendship, because the marital relationship is sui generis, uniting the spouses not only in mind and heart (as friendships do) but also in body (through the joining of the two complementary halves of the reproductive system in sexual intercourse), thus giving this union an inherent orientation to procreation (Finnis, *Natural Law and Natural Rights*, 447–48).

178 • Natural Law

"Good is to be done and pursued, and bad is to be avoided."[29] This general principle is specified by the concrete identification of what is intrinsically good for us and constitutive of our flourishing. Thus the fully specified set of first practical principles identifies each of the basic goods (life, knowledge, friendship, etc.) as to-be-pursued and their opposites (death, ignorance, social discord, etc.) as to-be-avoided.

This identification of basic goods can also, upon reflection, enable us to understand the ends of the various dimensions of our nature. Thus, for instance, life and health are perfections of our nature as rational *animals*; knowledge and aesthetic appreciation perfect us as *rational* animals; performative excellence in work and play perfects us in our unified rational-animal nature (i.e., in the use of our rational powers to direct and perfect our bodily powers); friendship perfects us as social beings; marriage perfects us as sexual beings; integrity and authenticity perfect us by harmonizing the various dimensions of our being; religion perfects us as beings whose rationality opens us to the transcendent.

In what respects are the basic goods *basic*? Epistemologically, the basic goods are basic in that they are first principles, and knowledge of them can therefore not be demonstrated or logically derived from anything else. Rather, their goodness is self-evident, known through an immediate insight of practical reason once a person has had the relevant experience (or acquired the relevant speculative knowledge of the good as a possibility). A young child, for instance, will have many experiences of being curious about something, asking a question, and receiving an adequate answer—that is, gaining knowledge. Upon reaching the age of reason, that child will grasp (though usually inarticulately) that attainment of knowledge is not merely emotionally pleasing (as the satisfaction of curiosity) but also intelligibly choiceworthy, and the child's motivation to pursue knowledge will then become not merely emotional but fully rational. Similar accounts can be given of how one comes to grasp the goodness of each of the basic goods. One's understanding of the various goods deepens as one's speculative knowledge of the goods improves (e.g., as one comes to a more accurate

---

29. Bonum est faciendum et prosequendum, et malum vitandum. Aquinas, *Summa Theologiae* I-II, 94.2, corpus.

The "New" Natural Law • Melissa Moschella • 179

understanding of what constitutes health, friendship, or marriage), and improved understanding of the good can also facilitate greater appreciation of its value or choiceworthiness. However, one's grasp of the good's *value* is not derived from speculative knowledge but is rather an immediate insight of practical reason (an insight *into* the data provided by experience or speculative knowledge).[30]

Second, the basic goods are basic insofar as they (and each of their instantiations) are irreducible to each other or to any more general category of good. This means that the goods[31] are incommensurable in their goodness[32] and thus that, for instance, choosing to visit a friend rather than read a book, or even choosing to visit one friend rather than another, means losing out on the distinct fulfillment one could have gained by making the other choice. It also means that no one good is, precisely as such, inherently better or higher than any other. This incommensurability of the basic goods is what makes free choice possible.[33] For if the goods were commensurable in their goodness, there would always be one option that offered all the goodness that the other options offer, plus more, and no other option would have any rational appeal (except insofar as one's calculations were mistaken or uncertain). For example, if goods were commensurable, one could in principle calculate that visiting a friend offers twenty units of goodness, while reading a book offers ten units of goodness. In such a case, there would be no real choice to make because there would be no reason at all to read the book rather than visit the friend. But because each of the goods offers a distinct, incommensurable benefit, there can be various options that each have a distinct intelligible appeal, and genuine choices are possible. Recognizing that the basic goods are incommensurable in value also helps to show why consequentialist moral

---

30. See notes 18–24 above, and corresponding text.

31. Every reference to the basic goods here should be understood to include each of their instantiations.

32. This does not mean that goods and their instantiations are incommensurable *in every respect*. Indeed, the moral norms outlined in the next section commensurate options for choice with reference to the requirements of full practical reasonableness. For examples of some of the ways in which the goods *are* commensurable, see Finnis, *Natural Law and Natural Rights*, 111.

33. Finnis argues that on Aquinas's account (which he believes to be true), the "very root" of freedom is "the fact that one's reason puts before one *more than one reason* for action, and more than one way of acting (option) that is good in some intelligible respect" (*Aquinas*, p.70). See also Joseph Boyle, "Free Choice, Incomparably Valuable Options, and Incommensurable Categories of Good," *American Journal of Jurisprudence* 47 (2002): 123–141.

180 • Natural Law

theories are fundamentally flawed, for consequentialist theories require us to act so as to produce the greatest net good, or at least to determine in certain circumstances whether one good "outweighs" another, but concepts like "the greatest net good" or the "greater good" are senseless if each of the goods offers a distinct and irreducible benefit.[34]

This discussion of the various basic goods as incommensurable might lead one to object: Does NNL not recognize any order or hierarchy among the goods? What about the concept of the highest good or final end that plays such a central role in the works of Aristotle and Aquinas? The answer (in brief) is that NNL does recognize hierarchies among the goods but argues that there is no single, objective hierarchy among the basic goods *just as such*, considered as basic reasons for action. However—as will become clear in the following section—moral norms and commitments do allow and even require the establishment of both objective and subjective hierarchies among the goods. In particular, NNL theorists have argued that the good of religion can and should play a uniquely architectonic role in the life of a person fully aware of its demands. Grisez, for instance, argues that we should commit ourselves to maintaining and promoting "harmony with God in an ongoing cooperative relationship" as the unifying overarching purpose of all of our actions, the ultimate end for which we pursue all other goods and with respect to which we structure and order that pursuit.[35] More will be said about this below.

Identification of the basic goods and recognition of their incommensurable value set the conditions for morally significant choice. In the face of a variety of options, and aware that time and energy are limited, *which* good and *whose* good should I choose to promote? The first principles of practical reason, considered independently, are insufficient to answer these questions. These principles provide us with first-level reasons for action, but to choose reasonably among these competing first-level reasons, we need moral norms—which are second-order reasons—to guide us.

---

34. For a more extended critique of consequentialism from an NNL perspective, see, e.g., Finnis, *Natural Law and Natural Rights*, 112–18.

35. Germain Grisez, "Natural Law, God, Religion and Human Fulfillment," *American Journal of Jurisprudence* 46 (2001): 3–28, at p.7). See also, Germain Grisez, Joseph Boyle and John Finnis, "Practical Principles, Moral Truth and Ultimate Ends," *American Journal of Jurisprudence* 32 (1987): 99–151, section XII; and Melissa Moschella, "Beyond Equal Liberty," *Journal of Law and Religion* 32 (March 2017): 123–146.

The First Principle of Morality and Intermediate Moral Norms

An act is intelligible—it is a genuinely human act—if it is chosen with the purpose of directly or indirectly instantiating a basic human good. But not every intelligible act is morally good. Torturing someone to obtain information vital to national security is intelligible—it is aimed at genuine goods and may even achieve those goods—but is nonetheless arguably immoral.[36] If all human acts—including immoral acts—are aimed at some good, what makes an action morally right or wrong?

The basic standard for morality is the *integral directiveness of practical reason*. In other words, moral actions are not merely rational or intelligible, but *fully reasonable*. Such acts are attentive to *all* of practical reason's first principles and thus respect *all* of the basic goods. And because practical reason directs us to protect and promote the basic goods not just for ourselves but for all who have the potential to participate in them and cooperate with us in pursuit of them—that is, for all human beings[37]—morally good acts will also be respectful of the goods of *all human persons*.

With these considerations in mind, the first principle of morality can be formulated as follows: *choose and act only in ways that are compatible with a will toward integral human fulfillment* (the fulfillment of all human beings, both individually and in community, with respect to all of the basic human goods).[38] Morally good choices, in other words, are choices in which our will (and through it our whole self) remains open to all of the basic forms of good, and to community with all human beings. Morally bad choices,

---

36. Christopher Tollefsen, *Biomedical Research and Beyond* (New York: Routledge, 2008), 93–100; and "Torture: What It Is and Why It Is Wrong," *The Public Discourse*, April 28, 2009, https://www.thepublicdiscourse.com/2009/04/233/.

37. "The direction the first practical principles give one's deliberation is towards goods one can share in along with others, and it has no rational stopping-place short of a universal *common good*: the fulfillment of all human persons" (Finnis, *Aquinas*, 132). For more on this point, see Patrick Lee and Robert George, "The Nature and Basis of Human Dignity," *Ratio Juris* 21 (June 2008): 173–93.

38. The notion of integral human fulfillment is equivalent to the notion of the common good of the entire human community, or the universal common good. Thus, the master moral principle could be rephrased as requiring that one's choices and actions be compatible with a will toward the universal common good. See Finnis, *Aquinas*, 114–15. The most basic principle of morality can also be expressed in religious terms as the command to love God and neighbor. John Finnis, Joseph Boyle Jr., and Germain Grisez, *Nuclear Deterrence, Morality and Realism* (New York: Oxford University Press, 1987), 284; Grisez, *Christian Moral Principles*, ch. 25, C.3.

182 • Natural Law

by contrast, involve closing our will to one or more basic goods and/or to community with one or more human persons.

A number of intermediate moral norms flow from this first moral principle. One way of spelling out these moral norms is to consider more concretely how one's choices and actions might fail to be compatible with a will toward integral human fulfillment. One way to fail in this regard is to choose in a way that sets one's will directly contrary to a basic human good. Correspondingly, there is an intermediate moral principle that forbids intentional damage or destruction of any basic human good. This moral norm is the source of most fully specified absolute moral prohibitions—for example, prohibitions on intentional killing, torture, slavery, lying, and rape—and also the source of absolute (inviolable and inalienable) human rights, which simply express those absolute moral prohibitions from the perspective of the beneficiary whose good is protected by them.[39]

It is important to note that this moral norm forbids only *intentional* harm to basic human goods, not harm accepted as an unintended side effect. This is not because *intending* harm is the only or worst way to act immorally but because intentional harm to basic goods is the only sort of harm that is *necessarily* incompatible with a will toward integral human fulfillment.[40] Harm accepted as a side effect *may* be incompatible with a will toward integral human fulfillment, but it need not be. This insight is captured by the "principle of double effect," according to which harms which it would be impermissible to intend may be permissible to accept as side effects, if there is a morally proportionate reason.[41] Another way of putting this is to

---

39. See Finnis, *Natural Law and Natural Rights*, ch. 8.

40. NNL theorists have a strict or narrow view of intention, according to which one's intention includes (only) one's end and all of the means one takes to be necessary to achieve that end, as reflected in the proposal that the agent adopts in choosing to act. This view has generated considerable criticism, particularly in its application to certain difficult cases. Given space limitations and the fact that this view of intention is logically separable from the more fundamental aspects of the theory, I will not enter into this debate here. For more on this issue, see, John Finnis, Germain Grisez, and Joseph Boyle, "'Direct' and 'Indirect': A Reply to Critics of Our Action Theory," *The Thomist* 65 (Jan 2001): 1044; Christopher Tollefsen, "Is a Purely First Person Account of Human Action Defensible?," *Ethical Theory and Moral Practice* 9 (2006): 441–60; Tollefsen, "Double Effect and Two Hard Cases," *American Catholic Philosophical Quarterly* 89 (2015): 407–20; Patrick Lee, "Distinguishing Between What Is Intended and Foreseen Side Effects," *American Journal of Jurisprudence* 62 (2017): 231–51.

41. For more on the principle of double effect, see Joseph Boyle, "Who is Entitled to Double Effect?," *The Journal of Medicine and Philosophy* 16 (1991): 475–94; Boyle, "Toward Understanding the Principle of Double Effect," *Ethics* 90 (1980): 527–38; Moschella, "Contextualizing, Clarifying and Defending the Doctrine of Double Effect," *Journal of Ethics and Social Philosophy* 26, no. 2 (Fall 2023): 297–324.

say that because willing and accepting are crucially different acts (the former sets one's whole self in the direction of the object of one's will, while the latter does not), moral norms governing the acceptance of side effects differ from (and are less absolute than) moral norms governing what one directly chooses or intends (as end or means).

What then are the moral norms that govern unintended harms—that determine whether or not the acceptance of harm as a side effect is morally proportionate? Answering this question requires considering how one's choices can be incompatible with a will toward integral human fulfillment without being *directly* contrary to such a will. This can occur in two primary ways: arbitrary prioritization of one person (or group's) good over another's and arbitrary prioritization of one good (or instantiation of a good) over another. I will consider each of these in turn.

Arbitrary prioritization of one person (or group's) good over another is incompatible with a will toward integral human fulfillment because integral human fulfillment includes the fulfillment of all members of the human community. Morality therefore requires that we choose and act with *fairness*. A helpful heuristic device for discerning the requirements of fairness is the Golden Rule—"Do to others what you would have them do to you" (Matt 7:12)—which requires that we imaginatively place ourselves in the other's shoes and consider how we would view the situation if the tables were turned. This helps to ensure that subrational factors, such as emotional attachments or aversions, do not distort one's choice, leading one to unreasonably discount the importance of a particular person's good in a way that would render one unfit for (closed to) community with that person (and thus closed in some respect to integral human fulfillment).[42] Some specific moral norms that follow from the Golden Rule include the requirement to keep one's promises and the prohibition on taking another's property. These norms, however, are not absolute because there are exceptional circumstances in which breaking a promise or taking another's property would not involve any unfairness, such as when the urgent need to take your child to the hospital requires that you cancel a lunch meeting or when you take a weapon away from a friend who is suicidal.

Not all prioritization of one person or group over another is unfair;

---

42. See the following section for a discussion of how application of the Golden Rule can help one to grow in virtue.

184 • Natural Law

indeed, some prioritization of one's own good and the good of those to whom one has special obligations is not only reasonable but morally required. (And remember that what makes something practically reasonable or morally required is always determined with reference to the basic goods, which are the basic reasons for action, considered integrally.) Some degree of self-preference is justified because once a person reaches maturity, she is the one most directly responsible for her own fulfillment, and in many cases the one most capable of concretely identifying and promoting that fulfillment.[43] Similarly, the goods of friendship and marriage (which includes family relationships) require a certain (though not absolute) prioritization of the well-being of one's friends and family members. For example, neglecting the care of one's own children to help destitute children in the developing world, like Mrs. Jellyby in Charles Dickens's *Bleak House*, is not morally praiseworthy but unfair to one's children, a failure to fulfill one's special obligations as a parent.[44]

The second norm governing unintended harms to basic goods is the norm prohibiting arbitrary prioritization of one good over another. I like to call this norm the "vocation principle," for what it requires, in the positive sense, is that one's choices about how to prioritize competing goods be made in light of one's overall vocational commitments and obligations. This implies that one should approach life with a vocational sense, attempting to discern one's talents and how those talents match up with the needs of one's communities as well as with the opportunities that present themselves, and making commitments (educational, professional, marital, etc.) in accordance with that discernment. Making a genuine contribution to human well-being in any of its basic dimensions requires a considerable investment of time, effort, education, and training, among other things, and thus a superficial or dilettantish flitting from one pursuit to another, eschewing commitments that might tie one down or foreclose other opportunities, is actually a failure to respond to practical reason's directiveness toward integral human fulfillment. Precisely for the sake of promoting the human good in meaningful ways, one must make commitments to prioritize one good or

---

43. This follows in part from the fact that many aspects of our fulfillment can only be participated in through free choices and also from the vocation principle, discussed below.

44. For a more in-depth discussion of special obligations and of parental obligations in particular, see Melissa Moschella, *To Whom Do Children Belong? Parental Rights, Civic Education and Children's Autonomy* (New York: Cambridge University Press, 2016).

goods over others. Such commitments (along with the obligations that they entail, together with other, nonchosen obligations) are precisely what justify such prioritization. For to prioritize one good over another without such justification (based on what is required to effectively promote the human good) is to unreasonably discount or ignore the goodness of some basic form of good, thus implicitly setting one's will contrary to integral human fulfillment, which includes fulfillment with respect to all of the basic goods.

Discussion of the importance of vocational commitments for the reasonable prioritization of competing goods would be incomplete without considering the need—if one is to respond fully to practical reason's integral directiveness—for an overarching purpose or commitment that can suitably integrate all of one's other commitments and structure one's life as a whole. Grisez argues that the only commitment that is suitable to unify one's whole life in this way is the commitment "to maintain and promote harmony with God in a cooperative relationship" by "[acting] always in accord with all the guidance God provides."[45] This includes a commitment to live in accordance with the requirements of practical reasonableness, which ultimately have God as their source. Beyond the avoidance of immorality, however, this commitment also requires a positive attempt to discern and follow the guidance God provides through one's "unique gifts and situation," which, "having their reality from the creator, are reasonably accepted as providential signs."[46] Such discernment provides guidance in choosing among morally acceptable options, such as the choice to become a doctor rather than a teacher or to marry rather than enter religious life. A person who consistently acts on the basis of God's providential guidance would live a life that is integrated in view of the single ultimate end of harmony with God;[47] doing so is a requirement of the natural law.[48]

---

45. Grisez, "Natural Law, God, Religion and Human Fulfillment," 7.

46. Grisez, "Natural Law, God, Religion and Human Fulfillment," 15–18.

47. Grisez, "Natural Law, God, Religion and Human Fulfillment," 18. For the Christian, this commitment takes on an even more definite shape as a commitment to cooperating with God in bringing about the kingdom of heaven. For, as Grisez, Boyle, and Finnis note, "Life on earth is no mere means to the kingdom but its embryonic stage" ("Practical Principles, Moral Truth and Ultimate Ends," 146). The kingdom is therefore the ultimate end toward which Christians should direct all of their actions, and which should unify their whole lives.

48. While this requirement of natural law is in principle accessible to natural reason, moral and theoretical obstacles often impede the attainment of the relevant speculative knowledge about God (as a personal, providential God who seeks our fulfillment and our cooperation in achieving that fulfillment) that is a prerequisite for recognizing that such an overarching religious commitment is possible, let alone required (Grisez, "Natural Law, God, Religion and Human Fulfillment,"

186 • Natural Law

The above analysis shows how the natural law can be both universal and unchanging in its principles and basic precepts, while nonetheless allowing for significant individual and cultural variation in particular applications.[49] The first principles of practical reason direct us toward a set of basic goods that are objectively fulfilling for all human beings. The integral guidance offered by those principles enables us to formulate an overarching moral principle requiring that we choose and act in ways that are compatible with a will toward integral human fulfillment. Analysis of this principle's implications leads to the identification of intermediate moral norms that in turn give rise to more specific rules. Morality's absolute prohibitions, which flow from the moral norm forbidding intentional harm to basic human goods, are both fully specified and universally binding. Yet while the identification and defense of absolute moral prohibitions is often the focus of moral philosophical debates, the above analysis should also make clear that they are only a small part of the moral guidance offered by natural law. For the

---

13–14). Christian revelation helps to overcome these obstacles and make the relevant knowledge of God more easily accessible (17–21). According to Aquinas, natural love of God "as the beginning and end of natural good" is, in principle, possible for human beings by their natural powers; supernatural love of God through charity, however, is possible only with the special help of divine grace (*Summa Theologiae* I-II, 109.3, ad. 1).

49. NNL theorists recognize, along with Jean Porter, that in many cases one will not be able to fully specify the requirements of natural law "apart from the traditions and practices of some specific community" and also that a full theoretical defense of moral norms "must rest on a more comprehensive philosophical, scientific or theological account which locates them in a wider context of reflection and explanation." Jean Porter, "Does the Natural Law Provide a Universally Valid Morality?," in *Intractable Disputes About The Natural Law*, ed. Lawrence S. Cunningham (Notre Dame, IN: University of Notre Dame Press, 2009), 91. Porter thus misunderstands the NNL account when she presents it as claiming that "practical norms can adequately (perhaps only) be analyzed in terms of the autonomous functioning of practical reason" (90). For NNL theorists have never claimed that natural law is based on "'pure practical reason' in a Kantian sense" or that practical reason functions *autonomously*, without any reliance on prior speculative knowledge (80; see nn15–22 above, and corresponding text). There is also no opposition between the NNL account and Porter's view that no rational defense of moral norms will be "rationally *compelling* to all well-disposed persons," for NNL theorists recognize that the theoretical presuppositions of natural law, as well as the specifications of natural law beyond the first principles, can be obscured by various factors, including miseducation or a corrupt culture, even though they are in principle knowable through reason alone. Whether or not the NNL view is compatible with Porter's claim that one cannot arrive at *any* fully determinate, universal moral norms without the help of Christian revelation depends on what exactly she means by this (91). If she means merely (as the above quotation suggests) that such fully determinate moral norms may not be rationally compelling to all well-disposed persons regardless of education and cultural context, this is a claim that NNL theorists can accept. If, on the other hand, she means that *in principle* one cannot arrive at any fully specific, universal moral norms through reason alone, then her view is at odds with NNLT. For NNLT holds that, at the very least, rational reflection can enable one to specify certain absolute moral prohibitions, binding always and everywhere—as Aristotle did in recognizing, for instance, that murder and adultery are always morally wrong (*Nicomachean Ethics* 1107a8–12). It is unclear, however, that Porter would deny this claim.

The "New" Natural Law • Melissa Moschella • 187

guidance natural law provides is fundamentally positive, directing us to promote human well-being in all of its various dimensions. Determining *which* aspects of human well-being to devote oneself to and *whose* well-being to prioritize make up the bulk of our morally relevant decisions. On these matters, natural law provides important guidance—like the Golden Rule and the vocation principle—but the application of this guidance will necessarily vary depending on individual and cultural circumstances. Precisely in this positive realm of the moral life—the realm where rules are insufficient to fully specify one's obligations—does the importance of virtue come to the fore. This will be explored further in the next section, particularly in the discussion of prudence.

Virtues: The Embodiment of Moral Principles

Another approach to fleshing out the requirements of natural law focuses on the internal obstacles that can fetter or obscure practical reason's directiveness, leading us to act in ways that are less than fully reasonable. These obstacles are primarily emotions that have not been fully integrated with reason. Attentiveness to the various ways these unintegrated emotions can lead us to act immorally yields a complementary set of intermediate moral principles that "exclude specific ways of acting unreasonably."[50] These principles, which Grisez refers to as "modes of responsibility,"[51] are embodied in virtues of character that correspond to them and are formed precisely by integrating the relevant emotions with reason through choices in line with the modes.

It is important to note that NNL theorists focus more on articulation of moral principles than on the discussion of virtues *not* because virtues are considered unimportant but because virtues cannot themselves be the basis for moral truth, which is grounded in the first principles of practical reason and the moral norms that flow from the integral directiveness of those principles.[52] Indeed, determining which character traits are virtuous or vicious

---

50. Grisez, *The Way of the Lord Jesus*, vol. 3, *Difficult Moral Questions*, appendix 1; http://twotlj .org/G-3-A-1.html.

51. Grisez, *The Way of the Lord Jesus*, appendix 1. Note that the term *modes of responsibility* can also be used for the intermediate moral principles discussed in the previous section, but I have reserved its use for this section to distinguish between the two complementary sets of principles.

52. Grisez, Boyle, and Finnis define moral truth as "the integrity of the directiveness of practical

188 • Natural Law

depends on whether those character traits incline one to act in accordance with moral truth.[53] Grisez's articulation of the modes of responsibility, which I outline nonexhaustively below,[54] thus serves as the basis for identifying certain character traits (which embody those modes) as virtues and others (which are opposed to them) as vices.

The ways unintegrated emotions can fetter or obscure practical reason's integral directiveness can be divided into three main categories:

1. Unintegrated emotions can lead us to act (or fail to act) for no real reason—that is, "just because I feel like it / don't feel like it." Such acts are rationalized with reference to some illusory good, often the illusory and short-lived inner harmony achieved by gratifying unmet desire.[55] The modes of responsibility that address this first danger are embodied in the cardinal virtues of temperance and fortitude.

2. Unintegrated emotions can lead us to act on the basis of unreasonable preference among persons or goods. The modes of responsibility corresponding to this second set of dangers are embodied in various aspects of the virtues of justice and prudence.

3. The sentient nature of emotional motivations can unreasonably narrow the range of goods that we attend to or are motivated to pursue,

---

knowledge." Thus, to act in accordance with moral truth is to act in accordance with the first principle of morality as articulated in the previous section, which also requires action in accordance with all of the intermediate moral norms (modes of responsibility) that flow from that first principle ("Practical Principles," 128).

53. Grisez, Boyle, and Finnis, "Practical Principles," 129.

54. My account does not directly follow the presentation of the modes of responsibility in Grisez's *Christian Moral Principles*, partially for the sake of brevity, and partially because I am synthesizing that account with Grisez's later attempt at a more systematic derivation of the modes in appendix 1 of *Difficult Moral Questions*, which offers a number of new insights and has not received the scholarly attention it merits.

55. In all of the instances when one acts on emotional motivation, the act can be rationalized with reference to the good of integrity or inner harmony, as acting on one's emotions will relieve the inner emotional tension and create a (short-lived) harmony between reason and emotion by subordinating reason to emotion. (Note that such rationalization is necessary if the act is to be a genuine human act, the object of a free choice, for every act aims at some good.) For example, "the vengeful person chooses, fettering reason by means of one of its own practical principles: that which directs toward the harmony of feelings with one another, and with judgments and choices" (Grisez, Boyle, and Finnis, "Practical Principles," 124). I refer to such rationalization as acting for a defective or illusory instantiation of a good (or acting for no "real" or "genuine" reason), insofar as lasting inner harmony requires governing emotion by reason, not the other way around, and because the inner harmony sought by subordinating reason to emotion is incompatible with moral truth. Further, because character traits—"which organize the various aspects of the complex human personality"—are judged on the basis of whether they are in line with moral truth, choices that organize one's personality in a way that subordinates reason to emotion are vicious choices that contribute to a vicious character.

The "New" Natural Law • Melissa Moschella • 189

thus distorting our judgment. Recognizing and overcoming these limits through various imaginative exercises (explained below) in order to rectify one's judgment, and acting in accordance with those rectified judgments, can help one to grow in the virtue of prudence.

In what follows, I will discuss each of these categories in turn, explaining the modes of responsibility that correspond to them and the virtues that embody those modes.

Unintegrated Emotions That Lead Us to Act (or Fail to Act) for No Real Reason[56]

We can group these emotions, and their corresponding modes of responsibility, into four sets. First, emotions such as hostility and anger can motivate one to seek to destroy one's own or others' good (rationalizing this with reference to some defective or illusory instantiation of a good). Such acts are clearly contrary to the integral directiveness of practical reason, and thus there is a mode of responsibility that forbids accepting or choosing harm to any intelligible human good out of hostility, anger, or other negative emotions.[57] By choosing not to act on such hostile emotions and to channel the energy of those emotions toward morally good objects, one organizes one's personality in line with moral truth and develops virtues such as meekness and patience.

Second, positive emotional desires, such as desires for pleasure and comfort, can lead us to act in ways that are unconnected to any genuine human good,[58] as when one seeks a high from drugs. Such acts, even when they are not directly harmful to some basic good (such as health), are, at the very least, a waste of time and energy that would be better spent in pursuit of genuine goods and undermine integrity by subordinating reason to emotion (which may lead to temporary inner harmony but will set the stage for greater disharmony in the long run).[59] Thus, there is another mode

---

56. Apart from the intelligible good of achieving inner harmony by relieving one's inner emotional tension. See n55. This clarification should be kept in mind throughout this section every time I speak of emotions leading us to act or fail to act in the absence of a reason (i.e., in isolation from a corresponding intelligible good or evil). Grisez, *Christian Moral Principles*, 8.H.1.

57. Grisez, *Christian Moral Principles* 8.G.

58. See n55.

59. See Lee and George, *Body-Self Dualism*, ch. 3.

190 • Natural Law

of responsibility forbidding the satisfaction of emotional desire in isolation from any intelligible good.[60] Virtues such as temperance and self-control are embodiments of this mode.

Third, just as emotional desires can lead us to act for no real reason, emotional aversions, such as repugnance or fear of pain, can lead us to refrain or desist from acting for no real reason, as when repugnance at the sight of blood prevents us from aiding someone who is injured. The mode of responsibility corresponding to this set of unintegrated emotions forbids acting (or deliberately refraining to act) on the basis of an emotional aversion that does not correspond to a genuine intelligible evil.[61] The virtue that embodies this mode is fortitude or courage.

Fourth, languor, apathy, or sluggishness can lead one to fail to act in pursuit of human goods, despite lacking any genuine reason to refrain from acting. Grisez articulates the mode of responsibility that corresponds to this danger as: "One should not be deterred by felt inertia from acting for intelligible goods."[62] This mode is embodied in virtues such as diligence and industriousness.

Unintegrated Emotions That Lead Us to Act on the Basis of Unreasonable Preferences among Persons or Goods

The aforementioned modes of responsibility all correspond to ways unintegrated emotions can motivate action (or inaction) in the absence of a corresponding intelligible good or evil (apart from relieving inner tension).[63] Yet emotions unintegrated with reason can also lead us to act immorally in cases that do involve intelligible goods (or evils).

One such case is when emotional attachments lead us to unreasonably prefer our own good and the good of those near and dear to us over the good of those to whom we have no such attachments. While some degree of preference for ourselves and those close to us is reasonable (as explained in the previous section), these emotional attachments, if not integrated with

---

60. Grisez, *Christian Moral Principles*, 8.C.1. Grisez also articulates a related mode of responsibility that forbids "sacrificing reality to appearance" by preferring "the conscious experience of enjoying a good" to a real or deeper participation in that good, such as when "a sick man who could have treatment which would really cure his condition prefers less effective treatment which offers a feeling of quick relief" (8.F.1–3).

61. Grisez, *Christian Moral Principles*, 8.D.1.

62. Grisez, *Christian Moral Principles*, 8.A.1.

63. See n55.

reason, will lead us to act unfairly. Grisez's articulation of this mode of responsibility is: "One should not, in response to different feelings toward different persons, willingly proceed with a preference for anyone unless the preference is required by intelligible goods themselves."[64] This formulation has the advantage of making it easy to see how the mode flows from the principles of practical reason in their integral directiveness. However, a more common formulation of this mode is the Golden Rule (discussed in the previous section), which has the advantage of suggesting a concrete method for following the mode by imaginatively putting oneself in another's shoes. Further, this exercise of imaginatively identifying oneself with another (and acting accordingly) is a way of educating one's feelings, extending one's sphere of emotional concern so that, even at the emotional level, one becomes more inclined to act fairly. Thus Grisez suggests that "regularly using the Golden Rule in moral judgments" can help one to "grow in the virtue of justice."[65]

Just as emotional attachments can lead to unreasonable preferences among persons, unintegrated emotional desires can lead to unreasonable preferences among goods, subordinating one good to another by deliberately harming one instance of a good in order to achieve another. The mode of responsibility that forbids acting on such desires is: "One should not be moved by a stronger desire for one instance of an intelligible good to act for it by choosing to destroy, damage or impede some other instance of an intelligible good."[66] Grisez calls the virtue corresponding to this mode "reverence," which could be considered part of the cardinal virtue of prudence, and the opposed vice "craftiness" or "amoral expediency."[67]

Positive Obligations, Prudence, and Expanding the Scope of Emotional Motivation

All of the modes of responsibility articulated above are negative norms that exclude choices and actions based on emotions unintegrated with reason. However, natural law is not just about avoiding immorality but is ultimately about the promotion of human flourishing. What guidance can natural

---

64. Grisez, *Christian Moral Principles*, 8.E.1.
65. Grisez, *Difficult Moral Questions*, appendix 1.
66. Grisez, *Christian Moral Principles*, 8.H.1.
67. Grisez, *Christian Moral Principles*, 8.H.4.

192 • Natural Law

law provide with regard to our positive obligations to promote the good? Determining this will require a more detailed consideration of the virtue of prudence, and in particular how to educate our feelings to expand the scope of our emotional motivations beyond the limitations of their sentient nature.

Before considering how these limitations on emotional motivation need to be overcome to develop the virtue of prudence, it is important to highlight that all of the principles of natural law discussed above are articulations of the requirements of prudence, for prudence is the perfection of practical reason. Further, "prudence presupposes experience and all the moral virtues . . . , and these are acquired by making and carrying out morally good choices."[68] This is because one's character (one's virtues and vices as a whole) is largely "the enduring structure of one's choices," which are self-determining and dispose one to further acts in line with them, unless and until a new contrary choice is made.[69] While the perfectly prudent person will easily and correctly judge what should be done, the development of prudence requires that one seek moral truth (which means determining which option is in line with all of the principles of natural law) and choose in accord with it. Thus, everything that has already been said about moral norms could be understood as an account of how to make prudent decisions and grow in the virtue of prudence.

However, attentiveness to the limits of emotional motivation and the danger of unintegrated emotion can provide additional practical insights regarding growth in prudence. What has already been said above about the dangers of unintegrated emotional motivations implies the need to seek counsel from prudent advisers and otherwise make ourselves accountable to others to avoid the common temptations to self-deception and rationalization.[70] In addition, although prudence is an intellectual virtue, the limitations of our emotional motivations (due to their sentient nature) can impede prudent judgment by leading us to be insufficiently attentive to certain goods or persons that might be affected by our actions. Even when we are aware of all the goods at stake, if that awareness lacks emotional resonance, we may lack the necessary emotional motivation to act accordingly. Thus, identifying the natural limits of our emotional motivations and considering

---

68. Grisez, *Difficult Moral Questions*, appendix 1.
69. Grisez, *Christian Moral Principles*, 7.H.6.
70. Grisez, *Living a Christian Life*, 5.A.1.

The "New" Natural Law • Melissa Moschella • 193

how to transcend those limits is crucial for the development of prudence. (Note that in speaking of the natural limits of emotional motivation, I use the term *natural* to refer to the first-order, animal aspect of human nature to which emotional motivation belongs.)

Grisez identifies these natural limits by considering the ways emotional motivation, because it "pertains to sentient nature," is not "naturally adequate to motivate us to act for intelligible goods and to avoid intelligible bads."[71] He argues that natural emotional motivation is inadequate in four ways. The first of these inadequacies—the lack of emotional concern for the good of others to whom we have no attachment—was discussed above, and application of the Golden Rule was suggested as a way to expand one's sphere of emotional concern, bringing into line with the requirements of practical reason. Second, natural emotional motivation is inclined toward sensible goods (or the sensible aspect of goods) but is inadequate with respect to the realization of goods that transcend the sensible realm. Third, natural emotional motivation is limited to imaginable goals based on prior experience and is thus inadequate given the need for creativity to promote the good and overcome evil. Fourth, natural emotional motivation is limited to transient goods, but the human good transcends time.[72]

Just as applying the Golden Rule by imaginatively putting oneself in another's place was suggested as one way to overcome the first inadequacy of our natural emotional motivations, other imaginative exercises can be used to help overcome the other three inadequacies.[73] Expanding our emotional motivation to transcend the sensible is necessary if we are to adequately appreciate "intellectual, moral, and cultural goods whose enjoyment presupposes various sorts of developed abilities—such as knowledge, moral virtue, and excellence in work and play." This requires expanding one's feelings "to respond to goods whose enjoyment presupposes developed abilities one lacks." The way to do this is to look to moral exemplars who *do* have these abilities and appropriate emotional motivation, so as "to share, at least imaginatively, in their excellent acts," to try to imitate them, and "to learn to feel as they do."[74]

---

71. Grisez, *Difficult Moral Questions*, appendix 1.

72. Grisez, *Difficult Moral Questions*, appendix 1.

73. Note that these exercises are presented as necessary but not sufficient for growth in prudence. See nn66–68 and corresponding text.

74. In particular, Grisez recommends that we learn from the example of Jesus and the saints, and also from upright people in our midst who can serve as concrete moral exemplars for living out

194 • Natural Law

Overcoming the third natural limit on emotional motivation—which "inclines people to persist in pursuing familiar goals in familiar ways and to be strongly attached to the ways and means, the projects and institutions that have served in fulfilling their commitments," even when they have ceased to serve their purpose or when new means, institutions, or projects would be more effective—requires "an imaginative exercise that will enable us to put into a larger but still concrete context the goals—and, indeed, all the imaginable aspects—of everything good we have done, are doing, and might yet do."[75] For nonbelievers, one way to do this is to imagine one's life from the perspective of one's deathbed or to consider how one will be judged by future generations. For Christians, Grisez suggests meditating on how our "lives in this world prepare material for the heavenly kingdom," which will include "all the good fruits of their human nature and effort . . . , unmarred by evil and completed, in the fullness of the kingdom."[76]

A similar imaginative exercise can help us to overcome the fourth natural limit on emotional motivation, its focus on transient, temporal goods. Overcoming this limitation is important particularly when fidelity to moral requirements demands considerable sacrifice; motivation to act morally in such circumstances will falter unless one "considers intelligible goods lasting and solidly real." Thus it is necessary to engage in "an imaginative exercise that sets those things apart and lifts them out of the flow of time," and for Christians, meditation on the heavenly kingdom is perhaps the most powerful way to do this.[77]

Growth in the virtue of prudence therefore requires (in addition to all of the other things mentioned above) frequent engagement in these imaginative exercises that expand one's emotional motivations beyond the limits of our animal nature (thus educating our emotions and integrating them more fully with reason) and also to engage in reflective analysis using these exercises when deliberating about how to act in cases where no options would run afoul of an absolute moral prohibition, in order to uncover unintegrated or unreasonably limited emotional motivations that might be distorting one's

---

aspects of one's vocation (such as marriage, or particular aspects of one's professional life) that are not directly exemplified in the life of Jesus or of most canonized saints. Grisez, *Difficult Moral Questions*, appendix 1.

75. Grisez, *Difficult Moral Questions*, appendix 1.
76. Grisez, *Difficult Moral Questions*, appendix 1.
77. Grisez, *Difficult Moral Questions*, appendix 1.

judgment. This sort of reflective analysis may lead one to recognize that some of the options one is considering are not fully reasonable (not fully responsive to the integral directiveness of practical reason but rather based on unintegrated or unreasonably limited emotional motivation that fetters one's reasoning).[78] Often, however, such a reflective analysis may nonetheless leave one with two or more morally acceptable options from which to choose. For the morally upright person who has an overarching commitment to living in harmony with God by living in accordance with all of the guidance God provides, making such a choice will be understood as a matter of prayerfully discerning which of these good deeds God is calling one to perform.[79]

Political Implications

While my focus in this essay has largely been on the ethical aspects of the new natural law theory, my overview of the theory would be incomplete if I did not at least briefly outline some of its political aspects. NNL's view of political community, the political common good, political authority, and related concepts all flow from the foundational principles outlined in the previous sections.

As already explained, natural law is fundamentally about respecting and promoting human flourishing. Human beings cannot flourish in isolation. We need families, religious communities, businesses, and associations of all sorts to meet the diverse needs of human beings, and to provide opportunities for participation in the full range of genuine human goods. These families and other communities have the responsibility and authority to direct their own internal affairs in the service of their own goods, yet are not self-sufficient for this purpose.

---

78. For concrete examples of this, see the cases discussed by Grisez in *Living a Christian Life*, 5.G.3–5.

79. Grisez, *Living a Christian Life*, 5.J. This discernment process, which involves returning to emotions "to determine how well possibilities otherwise judged good comport with the rest of one's individual personality," does not pertain strictly to the natural law, which guides action through rational reflection. From an explicitly Christian theological perspective, and drawing on the work of St. Ignatius Loyola, Grisez presents such discernment as comparing two sets of emotional motives, the set of emotions "related to faith and integrated with it," and the set of emotions "bearing on the possibilities between which one must discern," in order to determine which set of emotions harmonizes better with the emotions aroused by faith. (5.J.1). (It is important to note here that such discernment should occur only *after* one has concluded one's moral reflection and determined that more than one option is morally acceptable.)

196 • Natural Law

NNL theorists have pointed out four areas in which subpolitical communities lack self-sufficiency: (1) coordination between and among the various communities to ensure harmonious coexistence and provide public goods, (2) provision of defense against external threats, (3) adjudication of disputes and administration of justice, and (4) provision of resources to assure that dependents (children, the sick, the disabled, etc.) are fairly and adequately cared for.[80] I call all these needs "coordination problems," using this term to encompass all of the areas in which subpolitical communities require a coordinating authority in order to achieve their ends and facilitate human flourishing. To resolve these problems, an overarching community with corresponding coordinating authority is needed. That overarching community is called the political community, and that coordinating authority is called political authority.

The political community—in contrast with some subpolitical communities, such as the family or the church—is not aimed at *directly* securing the flourishing of its members but is instead a subsidiary community whose purpose is to *facilitate* the pursuit of flourishing by the community's members (individuals and subpolitical communities). The specifically political common good therefore consists in the conditions that enable the community's members to pursue their own flourishing. Political authority exists to serve the political common good, in large part by resolving the coordination problems mentioned above, and doing so in a just manner (in accord with the principles of natural law), both substantively and procedurally.

The substantive requirements of justice are captured by the moral norms outlined above, especially the norm forbidding intentional harm to basic human goods and the Golden Rule. While, as Aquinas notes, only the most serious and public transgressions of the natural law should be forbidden by the positive law,[81] all positive laws should be derived from the natural law,

---

80. This list is based primarily on the account offered by Christopher Tollefsen in "Pure Perfectionism and the Limits of Paternalism," in *Reason, Morality and Law: The Philosophy of John Finnis*, ed. John Keown and Robert George (Oxford: Oxford University Press, 2013), 208. Tollefsen broadly follows Finnis's more detailed account of the basis of political authority in *Natural Law and Natural Rights* but offers a clearer and more succinct outline of the reasons why political authority is needed and also explicitly identifies care for dependents who have no one else to care for them as one of the purposes of political community. See also Tollefsen, "Disability and Social Justice," in *Philosophical Reflections on Disability*, ed. D. C. Ralston and J. Ho (Dordrecht: Springer, 2010), 211–27.

81. Aquinas, *Summa Theologiae* II-II, 96.2.

either directly (such as laws against murder) or through the "determination" (*determinatio*) of the legislator (such as tax codes specifying a particular way to pool resources for public goods).[82] Respect for the authority of individuals and smaller communities to govern themselves in pursuit of their own goods—often referred to as the principle of subsidiarity—is a substantive requirement of justice, which flows from the very nature of the political community as inherently subsidiary and from the natural law requirement for individuals or communities to establish and follow a reasonable order of priorities among competing goods in line with their particular vocations and the corresponding authority that each individual or community has to do this.[83] Procedurally, justice requires the rule of law, for the clarity, stability, generality and impersonal character of law show respect for the rational agency of the community's members, help to facilitate their pursuit of flourishing, and embody fairness and reciprocity among citizens and between ruler and ruled.[84]

While there has been some disagreement on this point among NNL theorists, Finnis and others have argued that the political common good and political authority, which is justified only insofar as it serves that good, are inherently limited, subsidiary, and largely (though not entirely) instrumental. For they view political society's organs of governance as aimed at *indirectly* promoting the good of the individuals and communities that make up society,[85] and the specifically political common good as the *set of conditions* within which those individuals and communities can *freely pursue their own goods*. However, aspects of political society instantiate the basic human good of friendship and are therefore noninstrumental. The cooperation of political society's members in pursuit of the overarching common good of the political community (not just the more limited political common good

---

82. Aquinas, *Summa Theologiae* I-II, 95.2. For a more detailed discussion of the relationship between natural law and positive law, see Finnis, *Natural Law and Natural Rights*, 281ss.

83. Finnis, *Natural Law and Natural Rights*, 168–69.

84. For a more detailed account of the importance of the rule of law, see Finnis, *Natural Law and Natural Rights*, 10.4–5 (pp. 217–76); Robert George, "Reason, Freedom, and the Rule of Law," *Regent University Law Review* 15 (2002): 187–94; Moschella, "What a Pandemic Reveals about the Rule of Law," *Renovatio*, October 17, 2022, https://renovatio.zaytuna.edu/article/what-a-pandemic-reveals -about-the-rule-of-law.

85. Against this view, Robert George has argued that there is no reason in principle why political authority should not legislate with a view toward "making men moral," although he recognizes that in practice there will be many prudential reasons to avoid doing so. George, *Making Men Moral* (New York: Oxford University Press, 1993).

but the all-around good of the community's members) is a form of civic friendship, and the administration of justice (which can be understood as restoring the social harmony that has been damaged by unjust behavior) is also an instantiation of the good of friendship.[86]

Nonetheless, political society is subsidiary—that is, a society of societies that exists to *help* the subpolitical societies that compose it—and therefore political authority must respect the integrity and authority of those subpolitical societies. Political authority is also inherently limited because many human goods, such as friendship, integrity, and religion, can only be achieved by freely directing oneself toward them and because the capacity for self-constitution through one's choices and actions is itself a crucial condition for human flourishing.

NNL's emphasis on the limited and subsidiary nature of the specifically political common good should not, however, be misunderstood as denying the primacy of the common good over the individual good. For NNL's master moral principle requires that our actions be compatible with a will toward integral human fulfillment, which is equivalent to the universal common good of the whole human community. Yet NNL also recognizes that human beings are nested within various layers of community, each of which has its own common good, and each of which also has a responsibility to foster its own "sphere" of the universal common good.[87] NNL thus fully recognizes the priority of the common good and the moral obligation to favor and foster it, but also recognizes that there are many levels of human community with overlapping and sometimes conflicting common goods. Determining *which* of these common goods to prioritize in case of conflict will require an application of the moral principles outlined in the previous sections, and may often be a matter of vocational discernment that remains morally underdetermined.

---

86. John Finnis, "Reflections and Reponses," in *Reason, Morality and Law*, ed. John Keown and Robert George (Oxford: Oxford University Press, 2013), 514, 518–20.

87. Finnis argues that, for Aquinas, "pursuit of the 'all-inclusive' common good is stratified" into distinct spheres of responsibility—"individual practical reasonableness," "domestic practical reasonableness," and "political practical reasonableness"—and that the latter "neither absorbs the other two nor even includes, directly the whole of their content," for political jurisdiction only regards "promotion of the *public good*" (*Aquinas*, 236–37). It is therefore necessary to distinguish between the all-inclusive common good, "which is in a sense *the* common good of the political community," from the aspects of that common good—the more limited *political* common good or what Aquinas calls the public good—for which the state's rulers are directly responsible (*Aquinas*, 238).

Finally, it should be noted that while the NNL account of politics overlaps with a liberal account insofar as both support respect for individual liberty, limited government, and the rule of law, NNL theorists have sharply criticized liberalism's anthropological and moral presuppositions.[88] In contrast with most liberal accounts, the NNL account does not believe that the state should be neutral about the good or eschew perfectionism in all respects.[89] For, while NNL respects liberty as an important *instrumental* good, it does not believe there is any value in unreasonable choices just as such; while it might legally tolerate such bad choices to avoid greater harm, it certainly has no reason to promote or facilitate such choices. Further, NNL defends liberty and limited government precisely on perfectionist grounds—as instrumentally important for human flourishing and respectful of citizens as self-governing agents with authority to direct themselves (and the communities in their care) toward the good, not on the grounds of relativism or neutrality about the good. NNL therefore offers a morally substantive, balanced "third way" that avoids the extremes of antiperfectionist liberalism or libertarianism, on the one hand, and theological integralism, on the other hand.

Conclusion

NNL theorists have sought to develop the Aristotelian-Thomistic philosophical tradition on a wide variety of fronts, from metaphysics and philosophical anthropology to ethics and political philosophy. Their desire to place the natural law view in conversation with contemporary analytic approaches to moral and legal philosophy, as well as corresponding choices about how to present the view, have perhaps led some "traditional" Thomists accustomed to a different style and language to misunderstand the NNL view on a number of key points, including the metaphysical dependence of the natural law on God, the relationship between speculative and practical knowledge, and the importance of virtue for the moral life. My hope is that this essay will assist in clarifying these misunderstandings. Scholars working from an

---

88. See, e.g., George, *Making Men Moral*; Moschella, "Social Contract Theory and Moral Agency," in *Caring Professions and Globalization*, ed. Ana Marta Gonzalez and Craig Iffland (London: Palgrave MacMillan, 2014), 87–116.

89. Tollefsen, "Pure Perfectionism," 210.

200 • Natural Law

NNL perspective have also contributed to a number of debates on contemporary moral issues, including contraception,[90] marriage,[91] sexual ethics,[92] parental rights,[93] religious freedom,[94] nuclear deterrence,[95] war,[96] capital punishment,[97] torture,[98] embryonic stem cell research,[99] IVF,[100] abortion,[101]

90. Germain Grisez et al., "'Every Marital Act Ought to Be Open to New Life': Toward a Clearer Understanding," *Thomist* 52 (1988): 365–426; John Finnis, "On Retranslating *Humanae Vitae*," in *Religion and Public Reasons* (Oxford: Oxford University Press, 2011), 344–67.

91. Patrick Lee and Robert George, *Conjugal Union* (New York: Cambridge University Press, 2014); Sherif Girgis, Ryan Anderson, and Robert George, *What Is Marriage? Man and Woman: A Defense* (New York: Encounter, 2012); John Finnis, "Marriage: A Basic and Exigent Good," *The Monist* 91 (2008): 396–414; John Finnis, "The Good of Marriage and the Morality of Sexual Relations: Some Philosophical and Historical Observations," *American Journal of Jurisprudence* 42 (1997): 97–134; Patrick Lee, "Marriage, Procreation, and Same-Sex Unions," *The Monist* 91 (2008): 422–45.

92. Melissa Moschella, "Human Nature, Sexual Ethics and the 'New' and 'Old' Natural Law Theories"; Patrick Lee and Robert George, *Body-Self Dualism in Contemporary Ethics and Politics*, ch. 6.

93. Moschella, *To Whom Do Children Belong?*; Moschella, "Defending the Fundamental Rights of Parents: A Response to Recent Attacks," *Notre Dame Journal of Law, Ethics and Public Policy* 37, no. 2 (Spring 2023).

94. Moschella, "Beyond Equal Liberty;" Finnis, "Does Free Exercise of Religion Deserve Constitutional Mention?" *American Journal of Jurisprudence* 54 (2009): 41–66; Robert George with W. Saunders, "Dignitatis Humanae: The Freedom of the Church and the Responsibility of the State," in *Catholicism and Religious Freedom*, ed. Kenneth L. Grasso and Robert P. Hunt (Lanham, MD: Rowman & Littlefield, 2006), 1–17; Christopher Tollefsen, "Conscience, Religion and the State," *American Journal of Jurisprudence* 54 (2009).

95. Finnis, Boyle, Grisez, *Nuclear Deterrence, Morality and Realism*.

96. Finnis, Boyle, Grisez, *Nuclear Deterrence, Morality and Realism*; see also Joseph Boyle, "Traditional Just War Theory and Humanitarian Intervention," *Humanitarian Intervention: Nomos XLVII*, ed. M. Williams and T. Nardin (New York: New York University, 2006), 31–57; Joseph Boyle, "The Catholic Teaching on War and Peace: Its Application to American Foreign Policy After 9/11," *University of St. Thomas Law Review* 3, no. 3 (2005): 234–59; Joseph Boyle, "Just War Doctrine and the Military Response to Terrorism," *Journal of Political Philosophy*, 11, no. 2 (2003): 153–70; Joseph Boyle, "Just and Unjust Wars: Casuistry and the Boundaries of the Moral World," *Ethics and International Affairs* 11 (1997): 83–98; John Finnis, "The Ethics of War and Peace in the Catholic Natural Law Tradition," in *The Ethics of War and Peace*, ed. Terry Nardin (Princeton, NJ: Princeton University Press, 1996), 15–39.

97. E. Christian Brugger, *Capital Punishment and Roman Catholic Moral Tradition* (Notre Dame, IN: University of Notre Dame Press, 2003); E. Christian Brugger, "Rejecting the Death Penalty: Continuity and Change in Catholic Tradition," *Heythrop Journal* 49, no. 3 (2008), 388–404; E. Christian Brugger, "Catholic Moral Teaching and the Problem of Capital Punishment," *The Thomist* 68, no. 1 (2004): 41–67.

98. Patrick Lee, "Interrogational Torture," *American Journal of Jurisprudence* 51 (2006): 131–47; Tollefsen, *Biomedical Research and Beyond*, ch. 7.

99. Tollefsen and George, *Embryo*; Robert George, "Human Cloning and Embryo Research," *Theoretical Medicine and Bioethics* 25, no. 1 (2004): 3–20; Christopher Tollefsen, "Embryos, Individuals, and Persons: An Argument Against Embryo Creation and Research," *Journal of Applied Philosophy* 18, no. 1 (2001): 65–78.

100. Christopher Tollefsen, "In Vitro Fertilization Should Not Be an Option," in *Contemporary Debates in Bioethics*, ed. R. Arp and A. Caplan (New York: Wiley-Blackwell, 2013), 451–59; with response to Laura Purdy, 462–63; Finnis, "On Producing Human Embryos," in *Intention and Identity* (Oxford: Oxford University Press, 2011), 293–301, Moschella, "Rethinking the Moral Permissibility of Gamete Donation," *Theoretical Medicine and Bioethics* 35 (December 2014): 421–40.

101. Grisez, *Abortion: The Myths, the Realities, and the Arguments* (New York: Corpus, 1970); Patrick Lee, *Abortion and Unborn Human Life* (Washington, DC: Catholic University of America,

euthanasia,[102] end-of-life -decision-making,[103] economic ethics,[104] research ethics,[105] biomedical ethics,[106] and lying.[107] Whether or not one ends up agreeing with the NNL approach in whole or in part, NNL theory should be recognized as a rigorous and important contribution to the tradition that merits serious, open-minded study and consideration.

1996); Patrick Lee, "The Pro-Life Argument from Substantial Identity: A Defense," *Bioethics* 18 (2004): 249–63; Lee and George, *Body-Self Dualism*, ch. 4; Christopher Tollefsen, "Abortion and the Human Animal," *Christian Bioethics* 10 (2005): 105–16.

102. Grisez and Boyle, *Life and Death with Liberty and Justice: A Contribution to the Euthanasia Debate* (Notre Dame, IN: University of Notre Dame Press, 1979); Patrick Lee, "Personhood, Dignity, Suicide, and Euthanasia," *National Catholic Bioethics Quarterly* 1 (2001): 329–44; Lee and George, *Body-Self Dualism*, ch. 5.

103. Grisez, "Should Nutrition and Hydration Be Provided to Permanently Unconscious and Other Mentally Disabled Persons?," *Issues in Law and Medicine* 5 (1989): 165–79; Joseph Boyle, "Towards Ethical Guidelines for the Use of Artificial Nutrition and Hydration," in *Artificial Nutrition and Hydration: The New Catholic Debate*, ed. Christopher Tollefsen (Dordrecht: Springer, 2008), 111–21; Joseph Boyle, "Medical Ethics and Double Effect: The Case of Terminal Sedation," *Theoretical Medicine and Bioethics*, 25 (2004): 51–60.

104. Joseph Boyle, "Fairness in Holdings: A Natural Law Account of Property and Welfare Rights," *Social Philosophy and Policy* 18, no. 1 (2001): 206–26; Christopher Tollefsen, "Disability and Social Justice," in *Philosophical Perspectives on Disability*, ed. D. C Ralston and J. Ho (Dordrecht: Springer, 2009).

105. Tollefsen, *Biomedical Research and Beyond*.

106. Farr Curlin and Christopher Tollefsen, *The Way of Medicine* (Notre Dame, IN: University of Notre Dame Press, 2021); Moschella, "A Natural Law Account of Biomedical Ethics," in *Explorations in Ethics*, ed. David Kaspar (London: Palgrave MacMillan, 2020), 269–86; Joseph Boyle, "Personal Responsibility and Freedom in Health Care: A Natural Law Perspective," in *Persons and their Bodies: Rights, Responsibilities, Relationships*, ed. M. Cherry (Dordrecht: Kluwer Academic, 1999), 111–41; Joseph Boyle, "Catholic Social Justice and Health Care Entitlement Packages," *Christian Bioethics* 2 (1996): 280–92; Christopher Tollefsen, "Could Human Embryo Transfer Be *Malum In Se*?," in *The Ethics of Embryo Adoption and the Catholic Moral Tradition*, ed. S. Brakman and D. Weaver (Dordrecht: Springer, 2008), 85–101; Melissa Moschella, "Gestation Does Not Necessarily Imply Parenthood," *American Catholic Philosophical Quarterly* 92, no. 1 (Winter 2018): 21–48.

107. Christopher Tollefsen, *Lying and Christian Ethics* (New York: Cambridge University Press, 2014); Joseph Boyle, "The Absolute Prohibition of Lying and the Origins of the Casuistry of Mental Reservation: Augustinian Arguments and Thomistic Developments," *American Journal of Jurisprudence* 49 (1999): 43–65.

Pakaluk Response to Moschella

MICHAEL PAKALUK

I want to declare at the start, in view of Moschella's concluding paragraph, that I was trained as an analytic philosopher under W. V. Quine, Hilary Putnam, and others, but I am also a scholar of Aristotle and Aquinas. If I have difficulties with the NNL, they certainly do not spring from any unfamiliarity with that mode of philosophy which was my home—nor from any dislike, I might add, since I still enjoy reading J. L. Austin above just about anything else.[1] They spring, rather, from my appreciation of the distinctive genius of classical thought and a wish to do it justice.[2]

I once agreed with the NNL's strategy of seeking "conversation with contemporary analytic approaches to moral and legal philosophy," but now I reject it firmly. The chasm is too great and the need "on our side" too pressing. The reason for both the chasm and the need, in my view, in a word, is that what in the tradition has been meant by *natural law* cannot be affirmed or accounted for without an embrace of natural teleology[3]—from a third-person, not a first-person point of view. Of course, natural teleology has become increasingly problematic among ostensibly "educated" persons if one follows the historical line traced by Bacon, Descartes, Hume, and

---

1. Neophytes might begin with "Truth" in J. L. Austin, *Philosophical Papers*, 3d ed. (Oxford: Oxford University Press, 1979), 85–101.

2. That it fails from the start as an interpretation of St. Thomas has been argued by many but see Michael Pakaluk, "Cleaving the Natural Law at Its Joints," *The Thomist* 88, no. 1 (January 2024), 41–76. That it fails to accord, in any dimension, with the "old theory" of natural law, is argued for here: Michael Pakaluk, "On What a Theory of Natural Law Is Supposed to Be," *Revista Persona y Derecho* (Law Review of the University of Navarre) 82 (2020): 167–200.

3. We naturally presume that natural teleology admits of a providential interpretation.

Darwin. Yet if we lose a sense of it, then, humanly speaking, we have no hope. Christians still must recognize it perforce in marriage, family life, social cooperation, and the practice of the virtues. That's where one should begin then, but begin please with an accurate account! (The speculative project of justifying natural teleology in the physical and social sciences is something separate. "It belongs to a different inquiry," as Aristotle would say, and is not as pressing. Able philosophers and scientists are engaged in it.[4])

If the NNL's approach is justifiable at least in part as a strategy of persuasion, then one must ask how successful that strategy has been over the sixty or more years in which it has been applied. One may grant that it has been successful in an academic's narrow sense, in that it has given rise to a cohesive yet small "school" of thinkers who converse with one another, who control or influence venues for publication, and who have generated a suitable body of secondary literature: simply consider Moschella's footnotes. But whether any philosophers or theologians will continue to believe it after the immediate pupils of Grisez, Finnis, and George have passed away is yet to be seen.[5] Moreover, it would be difficult to defend that its mode of argument by appeal to basic goods and formal principles of practical reason has been successful in the public square. Even considered as an academic movement, it enjoys almost no standing in courses on moral philosophy: its main representation is in law schools. This is not an insignificant fact because the NNL is really a "type of ethical theory" rather than, directly, an account of fundamental law.[6] It is an ethical theory meant to provide a reasonable resolution of the "law and morality" debate and to shore up the idea that some kinds of actions are never to be done, whatever the consequences. But it is "virtue theory" and not the NNL that has established itself as some kind of alternative to deontology, consequentialism, and contractarianism in courses on moral philosophy.

---

4. For instance, Koons, Robert C., William M. R. Simpson, and Nicholas J. Teh, eds., *Neo-Aristotelian Perspectives on Contemporary Science* (New York: Routledge, Taylor and Francis, 2018).

5. It is not an easy thing for a view to continue to attract adherents after even a single generation. A colleague tells me that at a recent celebration of the fiftieth anniversary of *Theory of Justice*, the masterwork of my teacher, John Rawls, someone asked aloud in a large hall of Rawls scholars whether anyone still considered himself a Rawlsian—and apparently not a single hand went up. But it's not unreasonable to expect that the correct account of deeply ingrained and obvious principles of practical reason will find enthusiastic adherents across the ages. The "old theory" presumably remains alive.

6. As my former colleague of dear memory, Roger Scruton, once quipped to me: "It is neither law nor natural." Scruton by the way studied law at the Inns of Court and was called to the bar in 1978.

204 • Natural Law

The moral philosophy of NNL is not complex and consists fundamentally of two lists: a list of goods said to be basic on the grounds that chains of reasons for action, when rehearsed in the first person, may intelligibly end with them, and a list of formal principles ("Modes of Responsibility" according to Grisez,[7] "intermediate moral norms" for Moschella), which, it is claimed, our reasonable pursuit of these basic goods must observe without fail. The listed basic goods are conceived of as prior to the listed formal principles insofar as the latter are presented as constraining an agent already committed to the pursuit of the goods.

The chief liability of the theory, in my view, is that on its own terms its basic premises should be self-evident starting points for action. And yet both lists look to be arbitrary and incomplete, and the listed items appear contestable and dependent upon unstated implicit premises. None of the "modes of responsibility," in my view, has any sort of claim to self-evidence.

Feeling these difficulties, observers find it difficult to escape the inference that many of the NNL's commitments are based on the authority of those who are deemed to have held them (Aquinas, the tradition) rather than from the intrinsic, rationally compelling character of those commitments.

For example, as mentioned, the theory takes basic goods to be more basic than the formal principles. That is, it takes a stand on the old issue in moral philosophy of which is prior, the Good or the Right. It makes the Good prior—but why? An appeal to self-evidence does not settle the issue. Nor does the claim that the NNL is "eudaimonistic," that is, that it takes happiness to be the ultimate goal. Suppose our happiness consisted in following well a set of rules?[8] Then the Right would be prior to the Good after all. Then why is the NNL eudaimonistic anyway? Moschella says it is because it is within a certain tradition—but that is an appeal to the authority of a tradition.

Its list of basic goods reminds me of how experimental psychologists used to take data from studies of middle-class college students and generalize them to the entire human race. What about an alternative, bracing list of potential basic goods, such as that which Boethius grapples with in his *Consolation—power, fame, wealth, pleasure, networks of friends, glory,*

---

7. Germain Grisez, *The Way of the Lord Jesus*, vol. 3, ch. 8, summary, http://twotlj.org/G-1-8-S .html.

8. Rawls's theory has this basic structure.

reputation (distinction, honor)? These are goods that people pursue as basic in the real world.[9] I contend that any of these may, in a first-person rehearsal of reasons for action, be "intelligibly" given as the ultimate account of one's action.[10] What then?

Let's take the good that should be easiest to dismiss for Moschella: money or wealth. "Money's value is purely instrumental," Moschella says. "What do I want the money *for*?" (p. 176). Spoken like a professor in a university. I have met many people (males usually) who want as much money as possible, more than they expected to make, and more than others make. Suppose to Moschella's question one of these alpha males replied, "So that I am one of the wealthiest men in the world when I die." To be sure maybe he is, after all, equally interested in honor, besting others,[11] sheer power, or the ability to command the labor of others, or he simply wishes to avoid limiting his possibilities.[12] But *he* would wonder at you if you said you found his goal "not intelligible" or even lacking in "sanity" (Moschella's language). As I said, wealth is the easiest of the classical, deceptive ultimate goods to call into question.[13] What about the Nobel Prize? Or becoming President?

Moschella's exposition of the NNL seems to downplay that theory's insistence (prominent in Finnis) that *ought* statements cannot be inferred from *is* statements. But is a basic good one that we *ought* to follow? Then either one must infer that it *ought* to be followed from the fact that it *is* basic, or the claim that it is basic already contains the idea that it ought to be followed. The NNL must hold the latter. But how does a first person's rehearsal of his reasons for action, ending in his saying that he wants x, show that he ought to want x? At best it can show that he already wants it. And it could not possibly show (as the theory requires) that all of us ought to want x. I see no way out of these difficulties.

Space does not allow a consideration of whether laws or rights may

---

9. I omit nonclassical goods that became prominent in the romantic period, such as experiences of ecstasy and of being seduced and swept away.

10. Ultimate in the sense of stopping further questions.

11. And what good is that?

12. This last is usually assumed in discussions of liberalism to be an intelligible goal under a view of the self as autonomous.

13. I personally do not think they can be dismissed except through persistent dialectics, applied as does Lady Philosophy, in the manner of medicine for the soul, which then is followed by the exposition of a sound philosophical theory, which reveals these false goods as separated and partial representations a single, true ultimate good, God—that is, precisely as Boethius proceeds in the *Consolation*.

206 • Natural Law

plausibly be derived from this theory of morality; why those laws or rights would be commonly deemed self-evident, when the "modes of responsibility" commonly are not; or whether the laws immediately so derived would correspond to the Decalogue—as would be necessary if the NNL is to harmonize with the tradition.

Although admittedly there is a colorable claim that the basic goods of the NNL are self-evidently so, nothing like this can be claimed for its formal principles. Calling them "intermediate" does not solve the problem. Yet they do the lion's share of work in arriving at judgments concerning particular kinds of actions. For example, Grisez's very first mode of responsibility is, curiously, "*One should not be deterred by felt inertia from acting for intelligible goods.*" Mode 3: "*One should not choose to satisfy an emotional desire except as part of one's pursuit and/or attainment of an intelligible good other than the satisfaction of the desire itself.*"[14] What is obvious is that they are *ad hoc*.

Grisez cautions at the end of his exposition of the modes that "alternative world views tempt people to turn from [them]." He adds, "For Christians, their act of faith constitutes such an upright commitment; for those who have not heard the gospel, their basic commitment serves as an implicit act of faith." It seems bizarre and Pelagian to equate with the faith of a Christian someone's commitment to the modes. Let's all agree at least, whatever the merits of a "conversation with analytic approaches," that it is not some kind of implicit evangelization toward some sort of implicit "faith."[15]

---

14. Grisez, *The Way of the Lord Jesus*, 1.8, http://twotlj.org/G-1-V-1.html.
15. Grisez, *The Way of the Lord Jesus*, 1.8, summary, http://twotlj.org/G-1-8-S.html.

Biermann Response to Moschella

JOEL D. BIERMANN

Teaching at a denominational seminary, I spend the bulk of my time preparing men and women for service in the church as pastors and deaconesses. My classes in the department of systematic theology are about doctrine, the culture in which we live, and the interface between the two as God's truth is brought to bear on a world with no shortage of challenges for those who would follow Christ and seek to be faithful witnesses of his reality to their communities. Forays into philosophy are strategic and necessarily fleeting. All of which is to say that Moschella's essay on the "new" natural law (NNL) was a welcome diversion from the topics that ordinarily occupy my attention. In a situation not so different from that of my students who after a first encounter with a new author or argument are often left bewildered, I found myself stepping into the middle of an obviously very long and complex conversation about which I was essentially ignorant. It was clear at the outset, and made explicit in the conclusion, that this essay was aimed primarily at "'traditional' Thomists accustomed to a different style and language," who it seems have misunderstood "the NNL view on a number of key points," especially with regard to questions about the place and role of God (p. 199). The author's goal was straightforward: "My hope is that this essay will assist in clarifying these misunderstandings" (p. 199). Perhaps the essay succeeded in the objective, but from my vantage of one stepping into the conversation in midstream, I have my doubts. Not being a Thomist, and not in need of a new perspective on new natural law, I read as an interested outsider. And by the

208 • Natural Law

essay's end I was less bewildered than merely puzzled—a puzzlement that has only intensified and hardened after several days of further reflection.

Before delving into the questions that give shape and specificity to my unsettled but persistent puzzlement, I must voice my gratitude for Moschella's well-written and lucid essay. It brought a great deal of clarity to my grasp of several philosophical points and helped me sharpen my own convictions with regard to the relationship between living out the Christian confession on the one hand and philosophical practice and prowess on the other. In particular, three interrelated observations along these lines stand out for me. My first observation is that while I have perhaps lived too long in the isolated world of the church, I nevertheless find it remarkable that it is simply taken for granted and frequently repeated that "moral norms flow from the *integral directiveness* of practical reason" (p. 195). In my world, moral norms flow from the will of God, period. Of course, one could argue that the whole point of natural law is to make a case for morality without recourse to God, but to be frank, seeing that work actually done, especially by one as skillful at it as Moschella, makes me all the more skeptical of the premise.

My second observation is closely related to the first: for NNL the final goal for human beings (and the world?) is fundamentally and inarguably "the fulfillment or perfection of human nature" (p. 169). Again, this is fine as far as it goes—but that it goes no further than an anthropocentric argument can't help but strike me with my Lutheran commitments as problematic. In a typically Lutheran way, I would argue that the right goal for us and our world must be the restoration of the whole creation in the reality of the risen and glorified Christ. While we wait for that splendid unveiling on the last day, the objective of an individual's life is not fulfillment of the self—no matter how turned out toward his community his effort at self-fulfillment may lead him to be. Rather, the objective of human life is, counterintuitively, the death of self in service to the other. To be clear, I understand that without a personal and communicative God, human perfection is arguably, as Aristotle aptly illustrates, the only available *telos* a person can find. But one of the great joys of living as a Christian is precisely the revelry of not being enslaved to one's own rational rules and resources. There is a genuine delight, I must admit, in being able to confess the truth of doctrines that make no human sense at all.

A poignant example of good doctrine refusing to cohere with the demands of logic also happens to be my third observation; it's one that most people are likely to find disconcerting. Moschella's essay confirms the reasonable axiom that "if human beings lacked the capacity for free choice, moral norms would not apply to us, for moral norms govern free choices" (p. 171). Luther disagreed. The Reformer's all-out attack on free will is no secret, but it may come as a surprise to learn that there are Lutherans who continue to agree with him on this count; unsurprisingly, I'm in that number. That the notion and necessity of human free will is a forgone assumption even among Christians does not negate the doctrinal truth that the God who alone does the electing and choosing of his people does not grant to humans self-determining agency or freedom of choice as basic requirements for the exercise of genuine human agency. To follow Luther and to confess divine omnipotence, divine omniscience, and divine monergism with relish is to relegate human free will to a fiction or to an ego-soothing self-deception for those who can't quite let go of their own self-importance or need for a pretense of autonomy. It may gravely offend human definitions of justice for God to hold humans responsible and eternally accountable for choices they cannot make, but this is precisely the truth Lutherans confess. It's also worth noting that a robust ethical life is possible even without free choice. One does not need autonomous free will to receive the reality of human existence as both a gift of divine grace and a holy obligation to serve neighbors well.

All of these observations together illustrate my fundamental concern: it seems as if NNL is primarily, if not essentially, a philosophical pursuit that finds some aspects of Christian doctrine useful or perhaps even necessary— though is seems evident that any good theistic religion could provide the same required metaphysical underpinnings to ground the philosophical work. My own ecclesiological convictions run in the opposite direction and make me wonder why the only references to Jesus Christ in the entire essay are relegated to a handful of footnotes, all but one incidentally citing a book by Grisez with Jesus in the title, and the other invoking the same author who suggested Jesus as a worthy exemplar of moral living. If the task of God is to provide the obligatory metaphysics to ground the system, and the work of Jesus is reduced to one shining example of a perfected human life—achieved, no doubt, through the integral directiveness of practical reason—then it seems fair to wonder what is specifically Christian. In one

210 • Natural Law

sense, I suppose, this is an outrageous question since the essay clearly and admirably fulfills the task of outlining the relevant tenets of new natural law. And I am apprehensive about my own line of questioning appearing as merely querulous, ignorant, arrogant, or hopelessly naive and so flirting with the charge of fundamentalism. I do appreciate the philosophical proficiency, the intellectual dexterity, and the clarity of argument all evidenced in the essay. But in the context of my vocation, indeed my identity, within the church, I can't help but wonder about the point of it all.

The relationship between philosophy and theology is long and convoluted with a history marked by both remarkable flashes of brilliance and stunning failures—the particular assessment and categorization of the different personages, events, and ideas depending entirely on one's peculiar presuppositions and priorities, of course. But if the task of the church is to witness to the world the reality of God's work creating, redeeming, and finally restoring the world through Christ in the power of the Spirit, then philosophy must always be the servant and tool and never the master. It seems to me that this order has been subverted if not overturned by NNL. In Moschella's essay, the church plays a role that appears to be all but superfluous, enjoying the status of one possible instantiation of a community "that in many cases" is needed to "fully specify the requirements of natural law" (p. 187) according to which individuals pursue their fulfillment or perfection. In an extensive footnote on that same page, Moschella also pushes back against the accusation that NNL "is based on '"pure practical reason" in a Kantian sense,' or that practical reason functions *autonomously*, without any reliance on prior speculative knowledge" (p. 186n49). And since speculative knowledge appears to be synonymous with metaphysics, a space is now held open for God and even the Christian God if one is so inclined. Indeed, the author can even assert that for Christians, "the kingdom is therefore the ultimate end toward which Christians should direct all of their actions, and which should unify their whole lives" (p 185n47). Still, she concludes that "doing so is a requirement of the natural law" (p. 185). So the natural law is the frame into which Christianity fits and not the other way around.

As much as I sympathize with the essay's robust presentation of natural law's usefulness as a standard and guide for a moral life, I can't escape the impression that this is a moral system designed for people seeking a foundation that doesn't demand anything too overtly or inconveniently religious, much less Christian. It strikes me as similar to the way that some ardent proponents of "conservatism" instrumentalize religion as a necessary prop for their real goal: the promulgation of a life of conservatism for the sake of conservatism. But Christianity is not amenable to being trivialized into a tool for another agenda, and Jesus Christ is Savior and Lord, not just a worthy example or a moral visionary. The world's Lord is not available for use as needed; he is not to be coopted as a means toward the fulfillment of some other objective. Jesus is the Lord. He is the *telos*. He is the authority. He is the master of all. Jesus and his church are not merely one possible, or even the very best, means to "integral human fulfillment."

In a world still reeling and trying to find its way after Nietzsche's utter rout of the Enlightenment project—seeking to ferret out and establish the one foundational truth for all the world—it is good, and not surprising, that there are those ready to embrace the reality of normative truth. Faced with an existence emptied of meaning and devoid of purpose, there are people weary of their "freedom" and eager to find some solid foundation with an authoritative morality to orient, shape, and enrich their lives. And while it is reassuring to learn that the natural law tradition has fresh adherents, I can't help wondering who is actually buying what they are offering. With the admitted need of speculative and metaphysical first moves, the new natural law theory is no more successful at overcoming the nihilistic critique of foundational truth than is any other belief system and certainly couldn't substantiate any claim to universal application or authority—though, to her credit, Moschella doesn't even hint at such a venture. The thought that keeps pressing on me, then, is this: If NNL is compelled to assert some sort of metaphysical foundation to make the system work, then why not take a genuine leap of faith and instead of vague metaphysics, just go with the God who became incarnate and then rose from the dead? Though it may sound merely petulant, my concern is sincere and grounded in Christian confession. My issue is that, as far as I can tell, NNL gains nothing in particular against a nihilistic culture that levels all truth claims to merely claims. Given that harsh reality, why not just go all the way and make the Christian claim?

Littlejohn Response to Moschella

BRAD LITTLEJOHN

Melissa Moschella's excellent essay offers a compelling presentation and clarification of the new natural law theory that has dominated much Catholic philosophical ethics and public engagement over the past four decades. Along the way, she sets the record straight regarding many common misunderstandings and mischaracterizations of NNLT, making a persuasive case that it represents simply a clarification and sharpening of traditional Thomistic natural law thinking rather than a genuine innovation or Kantian distortion. Her essay showcases both many of the strongest features of NNLT as well as its intrinsic weaknesses.

I will briefly touch on each of these points—first drawing attention to Moschella's helpful clarifications of the essential claims of NNLT and the nature of practical reason, then highlighting features of her exposition that I found particularly helpful and useful, and closing by expressing some reservations about the limitations of this methodology.

Valuable Clarifications

Although NNLT is often accused of marginalizing both God and human nature in its effort to offer a pure, neutral, and formalistic account of moral reasoning, Moschella hotly denies both charges. "NNL theorists," she insists, "recognize that the ultimate metaphysical ground of the natural law is God, without whom there would be no moral order, nor human beings governed by and capable of understanding that order, nor any beings at all. Indeed, the existence of a moral order, like the existence of all other forms of order, points to the existence of God as its source" (p. 170). These natural law theorists simply insist—with traditional natural law theorists—that the basic principles of natural law can still be discerned by an atheist or polytheist, just as, for instance, celestial motions can be accurately observed and predicted by those with no grasp of the laws of gravity. Indeed, Moschella notes at a couple of points in her argument that friendship with God is in fact the highest aim of the moral life; the natural law is not simply about respecting fellow creatures or seeking temporal happiness.

Moschella also stresses that "the penultimate metaphysical ground of the natural law is human nature" (p. 171) so that careful attention to human nature is necessary for grasping the proper shape and application of natural law. Why then have NNL thinkers often been accused of detaching the natural law from human nature? Well simply because they deny, says Moschella, that we should "derive moral norms from speculative (first order) knowledge of human nature" (p. 174). We cannot begin with impartial third-person reflection on the conditions of human nature and then deductively arrive at the appropriate moral principles, for then these principles will always remain mere rules of expediency ("If you wish to enjoy long life, live at peace with all men") rather than obligatory moral norms. We must begin rather with the first-person grasp of these goods as *demanding* something of us and only then flesh out this intuition with theoretical reasoning or empirical observation about the conditions of human nature and the world we inhabit. "One's understanding of the various goods deepens as one's speculative knowledge of the goods improves. . . . However, one's grasp of the good's *value* is not derived from speculative knowledge, but is rather an immediate insight of practical reason."

All of this strikes me not only as essentially correct, but also as fairly traditional—thus I sympathize with Moschella's complaint that it is a slur to refer to "new natural law" as "new." C. S. Lewis makes more or less exactly the same points in *The Abolition of Man* (1943), as does James Wilson in his powerful account of the natural law in his *Lectures on Law* (1790).

I also particularly appreciated Moschella's careful distinction of NNL politics from that of liberalism. While stressing that it is not the task of human law to try and repress all vices, she notes that this claim (tolerate bad choices while still recognizing them to be evil) differs from contemporary

214 • Natural Law

liberalism's tendency to celebrate or promote maximal freedom of choice, blurring any distinction between good and evil. She also offers a particularly nuanced treatment of the way politics both does and does not seek the common good: in the main, it does so indirectly, by protecting space for "individuals and communities . . . [to] *freely pursue their own goods*" (p. 197). But it also directly fosters the good of civic friendship—a good not available in private life alone.

Strengths of NNLT

Moschella's nuanced and sometimes dense philosophical exposition also showcases the strengths of NNL as a moral theory, capable of doing justice at once to a wide range of moral duties that often seem in tension, if not outright conflict. Morality confronts us at once with claims that seem to have the force of universal and exceptionless norms and with myriad hard cases that seem to represent necessary exceptions to these norms. It challenges us at once to treat all human beings as equal, as ends rather than means, that cannot be instrumentalized or singled out for special treatment. At the same time, it asks us to recognize relationships of special duty and obligation that require us to distinguish between different individuals or groups and what we owe them. The two-edged-ness of our word *discrimination* highlights the dilemma: once it named an intellectual virtue (distinguishing between things really different), while today it is often seen as one of the worst evils (unfair or arbitrary differential treatment).

Moschella offers a set of careful destinations and distinctions to help lead us through these labyrinths. Her governing moral principle is that we must always will and act in such a way so as to respect *all* the "basic goods" for all people, but this is immediately qualified in key ways. First, the basic goods are *incommensurable*, meaning that they each present distinct demands upon us and cannot be reduced to one another. Pursuing the good of friendship will not automatically yield the goods of marriage, knowledge, or health as by-products—indeed, it will sometimes be in tension with them. Accordingly, our finitude means that we cannot actively promote all basic goods at once or give them equal attention even over a long life— much less promote the basic goods of all people. This means that we must strictly distinguish sins of *commission* and sins of *omission* (though Moschella does not use these terms): we are categorically prohibited from pursuing "intentional damage or destruction of any basic human good" (p. 182) but only conditionally commanded to positively promote a given basic good in a particular context. That said, Moschella stresses that even if it is negative prohibitions that have greater force, "the guidance natural law provides is fundamentally positive, directing us to promote human well-being in all of its various dimensions" (p. 187). (I prefer this framing to Pakaluk's more negative framing in his chapter.)

Moschella helpfully expounds "the vocation principle" here, which understands that individuals and indeed cultures are providentially gifted and called particularly to pursue certain goods (and the goods of certain people) more than others. What matters morally is simply that we never *arbitrarily* privilege one good over another or one person's goods over another person's. Of course, the adverb here is doing a lot of work, and there is liable to be very spirited moral debate as to which forms of prioritization are "arbitrary" and which are not. Why, for instance, is it licit to privilege the interests of those I have a close genetic connection to (my family) but not to privilege those I have a more distant genetic connection to (my "race")? I've no doubt that Moschella and her NNL compatriots have good answers to such questions, but the insistence that prioritization is fine so long as it is "nonarbitrary" can at first glance look like begging the question.

I do have a couple of other questions about the framework of "basic goods" that is so central to the NNL approach. One concerns their incommensurability, which seems to be in considerable tension with the more traditional Christian emphasis (particularly associated with Augustine) on the right ordering of loves. Whereas NNLT treats all the goods as having equal status and says none should never be subordinated to another, the Augustinian approach stressed that the task of the moral life is to rightly order one's loves of these goods, subordinating the lower to the higher and the higher to the highest: love of God. Moschella's "vocation principle" helps bridge this gap, as do some important remarks she offers on the need to integrate all goods under the highest good of friendship with God, but I was not wholly convinced by these qualifications. I also wonder about the claim that the list of basic goods is exhaustive and transcultural. I was struck, for instance, by the absence of "tradition" or something like it as

216 • Natural Law

a basic good—for many premodern cultures, it was a good that trumped many others. But I imagine that some tweaking of definitions might meet this objection.

Some Weaknesses of NNLT

In closing, I did have a couple of larger concerns with Moschella's essay. The first is largely rhetorical. While capable of great precision and explanatory power, NNLT tends to gain these attributes at the cost of accessibility. I suspect that most readers will agree that Moschella's essay is by far the densest of the contributions to this volume, demanding careful attention to many idiosyncratic and precisely defined terms. There is nothing wrong with jargon *per se*—it serves as a very useful shorthand by which specialists in a field can condense elaborate concepts and distinctions into individual words or phrases with stipulated meanings. But it does tend to be off-putting to outsiders. This matters less in fields like physics (where only specialists need to know what specialists are talking about) but considerably more in fields like ethics and politics. If NNL arguments are to shape public discourse, equip pastors, and inform laypeople, they will need the services of very gifted writers and communicators who can translate the jargon into clear and persuasive language.

The second may turn out to be rhetorical but seems more substantial. Even more than Pakaluk's essay, Moschella's contribution seems simply to accept the common Protestant caricature of Roman Catholicism: no Bible, no sin, no fall. While certainly mentioning God as an object of natural theology and natural law and referencing the role of "Christian revelation" in passing, Moschella makes no use of such revelation in expounding her theory of natural law. One wonders whether this is because she believes that the theory is philosophically complete in itself without the need of special revelation. Older natural lawyers could certainly agree that this is true *in theory* since Scripture makes no substantive addition to the moral principles of the law of nature. But they would deny that it is true *in practice* since our practical grasp of the law of nature is sufficiently clouded by sin that we would be fools not to make use of the "spectacles" (Calvin's term) that Scripture provides. One searches high and low in Moschella's essay for any discussion of sin or the fall or any acknowledgement that we have suffered damage not merely in our ability to *act on* the moral law (which is presupposed in her account of the virtues and vices) but also in our ability to discern and apply it rightly. In particular, when it comes to those thorny questions of vocation and what does and does not count as "arbitrary" privileging of one good over another, the moral teaching of Scripture might certainly come in handy.

Moschella might well reply that this is simply a methodological decision: she understood her task as one of expounding a philosophical theory, so that's what she did; if theology were called for, she could flesh out the same arguments with reference to special revelation as well. Perhaps so, but even if the audience in question were secular (which it is not for this book), I wonder about drawing such a neat distinction. Even unbelievers, after all, can understand that they are sinful and in need of some kind of divine help; they just don't know what that help is. Natural reason ought to be able to discern its need for supernatural revelation, and any discussion of natural law, then, ought not be afraid of suggesting that divine law may shed some much-needed light. This cannot but be "good news" to we who wander here in moral darkness and uncertainty, vexed by the labyrinth of incommensurable goods we are called to navigate.

Leithart Response to Moschella

PETER J. LEITHART

Melissa Moschella[1] tries to dispose of the "God objection" to the new natural law right at the outset. Far from expunging God from natural law, as Russell Hittinger and others have alleged,[2] new natural lawyers "recognize that the ultimate metaphysical ground of the natural law is God" (p. 170). He's the source of moral order and of human beings. Though belief in God isn't necessary to knowledge of the natural law, faith "deepens our understanding of that law, its obligatoriness, and the point of following it" (p. 170). Besides, religion is among the "basic human goods," and Germaine Grisez argues that friendship and harmony with God "should play a uniquely architectonic role" (p. 180) in the moral life.

Color me unconvinced. I am happy to acknowledge Grisez, John Finnis, Moschella herself, and other new natural law advocates as fellow worshipers of the triune God who created this world and redeemed it through his Son and Spirit. But the God of their theory is a more or less unspecified placeholder, and the religion that provides the scaffolding of the moral life is a generic piety. This has several consequences for their argument.

For starters, their theory operates outside of the narrative of creation, sin, and salvation through Christ and His Spirit that frames classic Christian expositions of the natural law, such as that of Aquinas. The God of new

---

1. In the nature of the case, my response zeroes in obsessively on areas of disagreement. So, an opening disclaimer: there is much in Moschella's essay I agree with, especially if it were resituated in an overtly Christian framework.

2. Hittinger, *Critique of the New Natural Law* (Notre Dame, IN: University of Notre Dame Press, 1988).

natural law is the Creator and sustainer of all that is, including the moral order of the universe. But it is not clear whether or not this God calls Abraham, releases his people from Egyptian slavery, elevates David to the throne of Israel, or intervenes in the world at all. Moschella says nothing about the God who saves. If, as she surely believes, the incarnation of the eternal Son is the crux of all human history, how can she ignore it when considering human nature, the norms and ends of the moral life, and the good of political order?

Moschella believes in supernatural revelation, but like other new natural lawyers, she puts it aside as she constructs her theory. We cannot factor in God's speech; we cannot even ask whether or not he speaks, for that would violate the methodological constraints of the theory. This seems imprudent at best. To repeat an argument from my main essay: If the living God has spoken, how can we afford to ignore his speech as we identify basic human goods and formulate moral norms? If he has spoken and we ignore it, are we not ignoring a (*the*) fundamental reality? For prudence's sake, if nothing else, it seems we should figure out whether he has spoken and what he has said. How can we follow Grisez's council to act "always in accordance with all the guidance God provides" without recourse to revelation? To put the question differently: Moschella acknowledges that God guides our moral choices through providential signs, but is not the fact that I have access to Scripture and the church a providential sign? If I am to read the signs, ought I not take note?[3]

All that may seem a theologian's typical (tired?) effort to assert the primacy of theology. Perhaps it is; I confess I honor theology as *regina scientiae* before whom all other sciences are useful and sometimes necessary *ancillae*. But my point is not simply methodological, nor simply a parry in the battle of the disciplines. My claim is a good bit stronger: insofar as it is detached from the biblical framework, natural law *is not true*. Let me offer a few details.

The Bible does speak of God's self-revelation in creation: "His invisible attributes, that is, His eternal power and divine nature, have been clearly perceived, being understood by what has been made" (Rom 1:20 NASB). That is *locus classicus* of natural law theories, but most versions of natural

---

3. In practice, Moschella's version of new natural law relies on theological insights, sometimes specifically Christian ones. She considers meekness as a virtue, for instance, and considers the circumstances of our lives not as surds but providential signs.

220 • Natural Law

law theory drastically *weaken* Paul's claim. He does *not* say creation reveals that some divinity or other exists. Rather, the God clearly revealed in creation is the God of heaven (v. 18–20), whose wrath is revealed against ungodliness and unrighteousness (v. 18), a specific God who jealously opposes anyone who exchanges his glory for the glory of idols (vv. 22–23). And what is revealed is not the placid existence of this God. He reveals *himself* as the creator God of justice and wrath who has declared unending war on rivals. He is very much an in-your-face God, a God inescapable because he confronts us in space and time as Lord. Natural law theory is un-Pauline not because it claims too much for natural revelation but because it claims far too little.[4]

Moschella is, of course, aware of the disorder of human nature. Though she does not use the word *sin*, she recognizes we act immorally and pursue evil ends. She knows we are inclined to "violence, aggression, promiscuity" (p. 175). My question is, How does natural law intend to overcome vice and immorality? In new natural law theory, victory over evil does not come by the passion of Jesus, divine grace, or the work of the Spirit. Virtue is within reach of every human being who pursues reason and subordinates emotion to rational ordering.[5] There is no absolute need for the communion of the church, prayer, reception of the sacraments, or the nourishment of the Word that is, Moses and Jesus agree, the bread by which we live.[6] Society too can reach its natural *telos* and be ordered according to natural law to its natural end without the presence of the church. I assume Moschella is not a Pelagian, but I cannot see how the theory she outlines is anything but.

Moschella and other new natural law advocates have a ready answer to these complaints. Their theory is rooted in an account of human action, and they deliberately exclude specific theological claims based on supernatural revelation. Moschella uses the word *grace* only once, in a quotation from

---

4. On the other hand, Paul's entire polemic is directed against those who deny and suppress what they know of God and His demands. Because sin darkens the mind and sears the conscience, fallen humanity does not acknowledge God or give Him thanks. Note that Paul does not, as some in the Christian tradition do, claim that we naturally know God as Creator but require supernatural grace to know Him as Redeemer. Rather, even our knowledge of the *Creator* is distorted until our hearts and minds are illumined by the grace of the Spirit.

5. We develop "meekness and patience," for instance, not by walking in step with the Spirit who produces these fruits (Gal 5), but "by choosing not to act on hostile emotions" and instead redirecting our emotions and organizing our moral life "in line with moral truth."

6. She acknowledges that prayer is a moral discipline for Christians, but does not make it integral to the moral life as such.

Thomas in footnote 48, where, she claims, Thomas distinguishes between natural love for God, which human beings are capable of achieving on the basis of natural powers, and supernatural charity, which requires the assistance of divine grace. New natural law does not speak of grace because it is focused on *natural* virtue.

But Moschella misrepresents the passage she cites.[7] Thomas does say that charity is a "higher" (*eminentius*) love than the love of nature since charity loves God as the "object of beatitude" and not merely as the "beginning and end of nature." As a result, he charmingly adds, charity adds "a certain quickness and joy" to natural love for God. But by "natural love for God" Thomas means the love man possessed in his state of integrity, before sin (*in statu naturae integrae*). In that condition, man was capable of doing "the good natural to him without the addition of any gratuitous gift" (*superadditione gratuiti doni*), though even in Eden Adam could not do good "without the help of God moving him." The distinction is *not* between man-guided-by-natural-reason and man-with-supernatural-grace; it is between man-before-sin and man-in-sin. Thomas's framework is not nature/supernature but the biblical frame of God, creation, sin, and redemption.

In his original state of integrity, man could do good by natural power. Alas, Thomas goes on (in the same article), we are no longer in that condition, and in our current corruption (*in statu naturae corruptae*)

> man falls short of this in the appetite of his rational will, which, unless it is cured by God's grace, follows its private good, on account of the corruption of nature. And hence we must say that in the state of perfect nature man did not need the gift of grace added to his natural endowments, in order to love God above all things naturally, although he needed God's help to move him to it; but in the state of corrupt nature man needs, even for this, the help of grace to heal his nature.

"Even for this" (*etiam ad hoc*) refers back to the capacity "to love God above all things naturally." Thomas says the opposite of what Moschella attributes to him: Given the fall, even "natural" love for God is possible only with the *auxilium gratiae* that heals nature.

---

7. Aquinas, *ST* I-II, 109.3.

222 • Natural Law

Thomas says nearly the same thing in the following article, now applied to the more general question: Can man without grace and by his own natural endowments fulfill the commandments of the law?[8] He distinguishes two ways of fulfilling the commandments. A man may do works of virtue, fulfilling the substance of the law. In the state of innocence (*in statu naturae integrae*), man was capable of this kind of moral living. Alas, once again, we are no longer in that state, and in our condition of corruption (*in statu naturae corruptae*) we cannot keep the law without healing grace. A man, alternatively, may keep the commandments not only in substance but in mode (*ad modum agendi*), that is, he may keep them out of *caritas*. Keeping the commandments charitably is impossible without grace, *even* for Adam in his state of integrity.

In short, Thomas nowhere sounds Pelagian because he is no Pelagian. He does *not* believe sinners can attain even natural religion or virtue without grace. He does not even believe sinless Adam could attain virtue without God's help.

It may seem unfair to focus so much attention on a single error of interpretation, and one buried in a footnote no less. But the error reveals broader problems with the new natural law theory as a whole. Moschella reads Thomas as proposing a two-tiered ethic of natural and supernatural virtue and religion, a framework capable of accommodating the claims of the new natural law. Thomas's *actual* framework, to repeat, is the biblical account of Edenic innocence, fall, and saving grace that leads to eternal bliss.[9] My "methodological" complaint arises again, but here the substantive stakes come clear. Outside the biblical context, certain natural law claims are simply *not true*. If Thomas is our guide—and here I believe he must be—we cannot say natural love for God or natural virtue is possible for fallen human beings through their natural powers alone. Surely Moschella does not want to suggest a double truth theory according to which something can be true philosophically (e.g., men can attain natural love for God without grace) but false theologically.[10]

---

8. Aquinas, *ST* I-II, 109.4.

9. For this reason, new natural law is less "a development of the Aristotelian-Thomistic natural law tradition" than a deviation from it. In fairness, it is not alone. Other forms of Thomism deviate from Thomas in just the same ways.

10. Though I do not think Moschella is an Averroist, the dualism of nature and the supernatural tends to bundle specific theological claims off into the realm of the supernatural, leaving philosophy to range free over nature, without having to worry about inquisitors or pesky theologians.

I am left to ponder, speculatively, the motivations behind new natural law. I suspect that it, like other forms of natural law theory, is intended to provide a theologically muted, if not neutral, account of moral and political life to appeal to unbelievers as well as varieties of believers. It is a consensus-building theory. If that is the case, it fails because it does not have a truthful account of the very people to whom it is designed to appeal. And if Thomas is right that in this corrupted world moral and political virtue cannot be reached without grace, moral renewal will not come except through the gospel that calls sinners to faith and repentance.

Rejoinder

MELISSA MOSCHELLA

If the living God has spoken, how can we afford to ignore his speech as we identify basic human goods and formulate moral norms?" (p. 219). So asks Leithart in his critique of my essay. Similar concerns are expressed by Biermann: "If NNL is compelled to assert some sort of metaphysical foundation to make the system work, then why not take a genuine leap of faith and instead of vague metaphysics, just go with the God who became incarnate and then rose from the dead?" (p. 211). Likewise, Littlejohn writes that my account "seems simply to accept the common Protestant caricature of Roman Catholicism: no Bible, no sin, no fall" (p. 216). To respond to these critiques, I will first clarify the nature and purpose of my essay and then offer a broader explanation of the relationship between new natural law theory and Christian revelation. Part 2 of my response will address Pakaluk's criticisms.

Response to Biermann, Littlejohn, and Leithart

The purpose of my essay was to explain a particular theory of natural law. And while there are various conceptions of natural law, I took it to be a basic point of commonality that natural law theories offer an account of ethics based on reason rather than divine revelation. In other words, I took myself to be engaged in a work of philosophical ethics, not theological ethics. That is why my essay makes no references to sacred Scripture or to any Christian beliefs that cannot be known through reason. This does not mean, however, that NNL theory discounts the importance of divine revelation or ignores the truths of revelation. No NNL theorist would say that one should ignore the wisdom of divine revelation when doing philosophy. Grisez and other NNL theorists have always been careful, however, to distinguish those truths that, though included in revelation, can in principle be known through reason alone—for example, the precepts of the Decalogue or the existence of a benevolent and provident Creator—from other truths—for example, the incarnation or the situation of humanity as fallen and redeemed—that cannot be known through reason alone. The latter are incorporated into Grisez's moral theology—which, as I explain in commenting on Leithart's essay, explicitly recognizes that natural law alone is an insufficient guide for the moral life—but for methodological reasons truths that can be known only through revelation (crucial though they are) are excluded from philosophical accounts of NNLT.

Those philosophical accounts do, however, point us toward Christian revelation in many ways, not least by highlighting the moral duty (knowable through reason) to seek the truth about God and to order one's life in line with that truth. As Finnis remarks, it is "peculiarly important" to know the truth about religious questions, in part because "one's life and actions are in fundamental disorder if they are not brought, as best one can, into some sort of harmony with whatever can be known or surmised" about God and his will for us.[1] That means that one has a duty to take seriously the claim that God has revealed himself to us in Jesus Christ, a claim that is supported by historical evidence of Jesus's life and teachings—including his implicit and explicit claims to be God, claims backed by signs and miracles, especially by his resurrection from the dead (which itself is well-supported historically). Thus, I agree with Leithart that "we should figure out whether [God] has spoken and what he has said" (p. 219), and the NNL account would consider this to be a serious moral obligation.

Further, on the NNL view morally upright choices must be in line with a will toward integral human fulfillment, thus maintaining openness to all human goods and to community with all human beings. Yet without revelation, integral human fulfillment remains an unachievable ideal, and the best we can hope for is that our actions will help to bring the world closer to that ideal in some respects. With Christian revelation, however, we can look forward to the kingdom of heaven (Luke 22:29–30; 2 Pet 3:13),

---

1. Finnis, *Natural Law and Natural Rights*, 89–90.

226 • Natural Law

which will both realize the ideal of integral human fulfillment—a perfect community in which we flourish in all dimensions of our being—and will also surpass that ideal with the supernatural gift of seeing God "face to face" (1 Cor 13:12).[2] This hope for the kingdom, as well as the assurance that "your labor in the Lord is not in vain" (1 Cor 15:58)—because we shall find the fruits of our good actions perfected in the kingdom[3]—can both powerfully strengthen our motivation to do what is good and also help us resist the temptation to attempt to promote the good through immoral means.

To respond to Biermann's critique that, on my view, "natural law is the frame into which Christianity fits and not the other way around" (p. 210), here I should clarify that for the Christian engaged in thinking philosophically about morality, the truths of the faith ought always to be kept in mind as a guide and a check. Any train of philosophical reasoning leading to conclusions that genuinely contradict a revealed truth *must* be faulty, for the truth cannot contradict itself. Further, as already noted, the NNL account recognizes that natural law alone is an inadequate guide for action because "our ultimate end is to share in fulfillment in the Lord Jesus, and we do not judge rightly what to do unless we judge in light of this end."[4] Nor, as Grisez explains, can we fully understand what we ought to do unless we take into account our human condition as fallen and redeemed.[5]

Of course, I realize that what I have said so far is insufficient to respond to the critiques of Biermann, Leithart and Littlejohn, for they all implicitly or explicitly claim that the methodological choice to engage in a work of strictly philosophical ethics is itself problematic for someone who believes, as I indeed do, that "the incarnation of the eternal Son is the crux of all human

---

2. For an overview of Christian teaching on the kingdom and an account of how this relates to NNLT, see Germain Grisez, "Natural Law and the Transcendent Source of Human Fulfilment," in *Reason, Morality and Law: The Philosophy of John Finnis*, ed. John Kweon and Robert P. George (Oxford: Oxford University Press, 2013), 443–56.

3. "After we have promoted on earth . . . the goods of human dignity, familial communion, and freedom—that is to say, all the good fruits of our nature and effort—then we shall find them once more, but cleansed of all dirt, lit up and transformed, when Christ gives back to the Father an eternal and universal kingdom" (Second Vatican Council, "Pastoral Constitution on the Church in the Modern World, *Gaudium et spes*, 7 October 1965," in *Vatican Council II: Conciliar and Post Conciliar Documents*, sec. 39).

4. Grisez, *Christian Moral Principles*, 7.A.

5. Grisez, *Christian Moral Principles*, 25.E.

history" (p. 219). Since Leithart presses this critique most forcefully, I will focus on his comments in my response. Leithart makes the provocative claim that "insofar as it is detached from the biblical framework, natural law *is not true*." This could mean (1) that we are entirely incapable of knowing moral truths apart from revelation, and/or (2) that we are entirely incapable of acting in a morally upright way without grace. The first of these claims seems obviously false, as pre-Christian and non-Christian thinkers have said many true things about morality (although there was also much that they missed or got wrong), and many basic moral norms are widely acknowledged (and followed) even by non-Christians. Further, Paul tells us that, even without supernatural revelation, people can know enough about God and morality to be "without excuse" for their "godlessness and wickedness" (Rom 1:18–20; see also Rom 2:14–16). This point also provides evidence against the second claim, which is the one Leithart emphasizes. For if human beings really were incapable of acting in a morally upright way without grace, then they would have an excuse for their moral failings.

This does not mean that I think the *fullness* of virtue is "within reach of every human being who pursues reason and subordinates emotion to rational ordering" (p. 220), nor even less that we can earn eternal salvation through our efforts alone, "for all have sinned and fall short of the glory of God" (Rom 3:23). But it does mean that human nature, unaided by grace, is capable of *some* virtuous actions.

The crux of my disagreement with Leithart here relates to a footnote in which I say that on Aquinas's view "natural love of God 'as the beginning and end of natural good' is, in principle, possible for human beings by their natural powers" (p. 186n48). Leithart points out that, in the passage I quoted, Aquinas is speaking of human beings prior to the fall, and that in the very same passage Aquinas argues that "in the state of corrupt nature man needs, even for this [i.e. natural love of God], the help of grace to heal his nature" (p. 221). (I was aware of this, which is why I added the qualifier "in principle" to my statement, though perhaps I should have been clearer about that.) Nonetheless, to make Aquinas's claim here consistent with other passages, I think it should be interpreted to mean that human beings after the fall cannot *consistently* love God naturally without the help of grace. In article 8 of the same question, Aquinas says that even without grace it *is* possible for human beings to avoid sin in individual acts, although it is

228 • Natural Law

not possible to do so consistently.[6] Yet as Angela Knobel argues, this claim is incompatible with interpreting article 3 to mean that human beings are entirely incapable of natural love of God without grace, for any act not ordered to love of God would be sinful on Aquinas's view.[7]

In addition to Leithart's claims about the natural law being "not true" apart from the Biblical framework, Leithart, Biermann, and Littlejohn also seem to question the value and legitimacy of natural law theory as I have defined it—that is, as a strictly philosophical inquiry seeking to explain and defend moral truths through reason-based arguments alone. As I have already responded to this concern in my commentary on Leithart's essay, here I will mainly summarize the points I made there. Natural law accounts of moral truths can be helpful in explaining our convictions to non-Christians and showing both Christians and non-Christians that Christian moral teaching is not a set of arbitrary restrictions but rather something that promotes genuine human flourishing. Natural law theory can thus lay the groundwork for a Christian humanism that presents Christianity as fulfilling (and surpassing) our otherwise-unattainable deepest human longings.[8] In these ways, natural law arguments can help equip Christians to give an account of our hope, as Peter exhorts us to be prepared to do (1 Peter 3:15). Further, learning how to think in a disciplined, reason-based way about morality is crucial because we need to understand the underlying rationale for Christian moral principles to be able to apply those principles correctly to complex questions about which the Bible does not provide direct answers.

---

6. Elsewhere, Aquinas states that even without grace it is possible "to abstain from bad actions in most cases," even though it will not be possible without grace to avoid mortal sin entirely (*ST* I-II, 49.2, ad.3).

7. Angela Knobel, *Aquinas and the Infused Moral Virtues* (Notre Dame, IN: University of Notre Dame Press, 2021), 42–43. Note that for Aquinas, "any genuinely good act . . . would necessarily have to be ordered to the creaturely love of God above all things" (42). It is also worth highlighting the Catholic belief God does not deny his grace to those who sincerely follow the truth as they understand it, but who lack faith in Christ due to no fault of their own. The Catholic Church bases this view on God's desire for all to be saved (1 Tim 2:4), arguing that a person who "seeks the truth and does the will of God in accordance with his understanding of it, can be saved," because if that person had known the full truth of Christian revelation, it can be supposed that he would have followed it, and thus would have made an act of faith and sought the sacrament of Baptism (*Catechism of the Catholic Church*, 1257). Thus, this view also affirms that Jesus Christ is the "one mediator between God and mankind" (1 Tim 2:5) and that all grace comes through Christ, for grace is granted based on a person's implicit faith in Christ and corresponding desire for baptism.

8. See Patrick Lee, "Germain Grisez's Christian Humanism," *American Journal of Jurisprudence* 46 (2001): 137–51.

Response to Pakaluk

Pakaluk argues that NNLT's basic premises are not in fact "self-evident starting points for action" as the theory claims that they are. He raises this objection both with regard to the theory's claims about basic human goods and with regard to the theory's articulation of "intermediate moral norms" (although NNLT actually does not hold that intermediate moral norms are self-evident). It is surprising that Pakaluk denies the self-evidence of practical reason's first principles—identifying the basic goods as to-be-pursued and their opposites as to-be-avoided—as this is clearly Aquinas's position in 94.2 of *Summa Theologiae*. Indeed, NNL's list of basic goods largely replicates Aquinas's list, with a few additions. Thus, Pakaluk's question—Why not embrace an alternative list of goods, such as power, fame, wealth, pleasure, and so on?—could equally be raised as a criticism of Aquinas. And like Aquinas—who elsewhere explains why such goods are not intrinsically valuable[9]—NNL theorists have dialectically defended the list of basic goods.

Pakaluk's critique on this point therefore seems to rest on a confusion about what is meant by *self-evident*. As Finnis clarifies, to say that a principle is self-evident simply means that it is "not *deduced* by syllogistic reasoning from some prior, more evident proposition."[10] It does *not* mean that everyone will agree with it, that those implicitly guided by it are necessarily aware of this fact, that those guided by it *could* accurately articulate it if they tried, that understanding it does not require prior knowledge or experience, or that it need not or cannot be defended dialectically.[11] NNL theorists have explained, for instance, why denying that knowledge is a basic good is performatively inconsistent, why denying that life is a basic good presupposes a false, dualist anthropology, and why pleasure and autonomy appear to be basic goods but are not.[12] They have also shown that the list is supported by anthropological studies (and thus can hardly be said "to take data from

---

9. *Summa Theologiae* I-II, 2.
10. Finnis, *Aquinas*, 88 (emphasis original).
11. Finnis, *Natural Law and Natural Rights*, 3.4.
12. See, e.g., Finnis, *Natural Law and Natural Rights*, ch. 3–4; Grisez, Boyle and Finnis, "Practical Principles, Moral Truth and Ultimate Ends," section 4; Finnis, Boyle and Grisez, *Nuclear Deterrence, Morality and Realism* (Oxford: Clarendon, 1987) (on life), 304–9; Lee and George, *Body-Self Dualism*, ch. 3 (on pleasure); George, *Making Men Moral* (Oxford: Clarendon, 1993), 173–77 (on autonomy).

230 • Natural Law

studies of middle-class college students and generalize them to the entire human race," as Pakaluk contends) (p. 204).[13]

Second, Pakaluk's reference to the is-ought problem shows that he does not understand that the list of basic goods is shorthand for the list of first practical principles, principles of the form: "*x* is good and is to-be-done-and-pursued, and its opposite is bad and to-be-avoided." The issue is not whether these principles state facts, for the word *fact* is ambiguous. The issue, rather, is whether these principles state first-order truths (speculative truths) or third-order truths (practical/moral truths). Thus, Pakaluk seems to miss the significance of my discussion of Aquinas's four orders and of the related claim that the first principles of practical reason in which basic goods are identified are the first principles *of the third (practical/moral) order*. There is not necessarily any problem in moving from *is* to *ought* just as such (for moral claims can be phrased as *is*-statements); rather, the problem is to attempt to derive third-order (ethical/moral) claims from *solely* first-order (speculative) premises.

Third, Pakaluk criticizes NNL's intermediate moral principles as "*ad hoc*" (p. 206). As already noted, Pakaluk mistakenly says that NNL claims these principles to be self-evident, although my essay explains that these principles flow from the more fundamental moral principle requiring us to act in a *fully reasonable* way, following the *integral directiveness of practical reason*. This basic moral standard indicates that we are to be attentive to *all* of the guidance provided to us by practical reason's first principles and thus to respect (and to the extent possible, promote) *all* the basic goods for all people, which means acting in ways that are compatible with a will toward integral human fulfillment. This overarching moral principle is, in effect, a principle directing us toward the universal common good, which is another way of expressing the concept of "integral human fulfillment." It is also equivalent to the command to love God and neighbor.

As I explain in my essay, intermediate moral principles are specifications of the master moral principle, and there is more than one way to articulate them. The fourth section of my essay, "The First Principle of Morality and Intermediate Moral Norms," articulates intermediate moral principles by considering the ways in which one's choices could fail to be in line with a will toward integral human fulfillment—that is, by intentionally seeking to

---

13. Finnis, *Natural Law and Natural Rights*, 4.1.

damage or destroy a basic human good, by arbitrarily prioritizing one good over another, or by arbitrarily prioritizing one person's good over another's. There is nothing *ad hoc* about this.

Nor is there anything *ad hoc* about the second approach to specifying intermediate moral norms, which I discuss in my section on "Virtues." At the beginning of that section, I explain that one can also articulate moral norms by considering how emotions unintegrated with reason fetter practical reason's directiveness, leading us to act in unreasonable ways. Grisez's account of intermediate moral principles (which he calls "modes of responsibility") in *Christian Moral Principles* follows this method. Grisez's articulation of the eight modes of responsibility is not perfectly systematic, but that does not make it *ad hoc*, for all the modes are cautioning us against specific ways emotional motivations can lead us astray. Further, my essay follows Grisez's later attempt to provide a more systematic account by categorizing the ways in which unintegrated emotions can fetter practical reason's integral directiveness. In criticizing the modes of responsibility as *ad hoc*, Pakaluk does not even mention my attempt to explain their rationale or present them systematically.

Finally, Pakaluk unfairly criticizes Grisez's view as "bizarre and Pelagian" (p. 206) after quoting (a portion of) Grisez's claim that "the upright person who has not already heard the gospel . . . implicitly makes an act of faith by the basic commitment to serve genuine goods and build up community."[14] It is strange to call this Pelagian, given that this remark is part of Grisez's answer to the question of how the modes of responsibility relate to integral human fulfillment, and that one of the first things Grisez says is that "integral human fulfillment will be realized by God's action; human persons can pursue it as a real goal only insofar as they cooperate with God by a life of faith in Jesus." Nor is there anything bizarre (at least for a Catholic) about the idea that those who have not heard the gospel but who sincerely seek the truth and order their lives in accordance with the truth as they understand it are implicitly seeking and following Christ, the Truth Incarnate. Coming to understand moral truth through rational reflection and trying to order one's life in accord with that truth can indeed often be a crucial factor leading a person of nominal faith or no faith at all toward genuine Christian conversion.

---

14. Grisez, *Christian Moral Principles*, 8.I.14.

CHAPTER 5

Anti–Natural Law

PETER J. LEITHART

I begin with an artist's sketch of the villain of my piece, accompanied by a flurry of supporting exhibits, which converge on the verdict: natural law, in its most popular modern formulations, contradicts fundamental Christian convictions.

Scattershot as my opening arguments may seem, I believe they are sound and persuasive. Yet they are admittedly superficial. So I follow the polemical flurry with a steadier and longer argument, in two parts. First, relying on Thomas Aquinas, I outline a theological account of "law"; second, I interrogate the concept of "nature." Regarding law, I conclude that the Bible has historically been,[1] and should continue to be, the framework for a Christian idea of law, moral or political. Regarding nature, I conclude we can never isolate nature cleanly enough to use it as an independent measure of human actions or institutions. My overall conclusion is that natural law, in its most popular modern formulations, is not a theory but a collection of fragments of a coherent theology.

The Villain: Atheological Natural Law

I am against *theories* of natural law that eliminate or bracket revealed Christian theology. Such theories claim to know the origin, shape, and end

---

1. A teaser: Jean Porter writes, "the scholastics approach the natural law within the parameters of a scripturally informed theology," grounding their belief in natural law in biblical texts and appealing to the Bible to establish moral rules. They "did not attempt to derive a system of natural law thinking out of purely natural data or rationally self-evident intuitions." Porter, *Nature as Reason: A Thomistic Theory of the Natural Law* (Grand Rapids: Eerdmans, 2005), 16, 29.

234 • Natural Law

of nature and human nature without reference to the Creator, the image of God, the Spirit, or Jesus. Since the sixteenth century, such theories have been predominant among both secular and Christian thinkers.[2]

Practically, I oppose the position John Habgood articulates in his Gifford Lectures: the belief that "rational thinking about morality, however much it might be buttressed within its Christian context, was nevertheless deemed to be possible within the natural law tradition without explicit reference to revelation."[3]

I submit that this is villainous. What is my evidence?

Exhibit I: Revelation Is Integral to the Human Condition

At a high level of abstraction, we must say: to be fully rational, moral reasoning must seek to take into account as many relevant factors as possible. Christians believe God has spoken to moral questions, and our Creator's spoken and written Word is the most relevant factor. Therefore, it is irrational to close our ears to his voice. As the late Benedict XVI never tired of saying, reason that forecloses the possibility of revelation is a shrunken, deflated reason.[4]

One response might be: Scripture says nothing about x or y and so is rightly ignored in discussions of x or y. I disagree. God has spoken in one

---

2. Early modern natural law theory is dogged by a fundamental ambiguity. On the one hand, writers like Grotius and Hobbes are theological writers. On the other hand, they derive moral and political norms from "the Principle of Reason only" (Hobbes). Later writers like Pufendorf dispense with the theological trappings. See Knud Haakonssen, *Natural Law and Moral Philosophy from Grotius to the Scottish Enlightenment* (Cambridge: Cambridge University Press, 1996), 15–62; Matthew Levering, *Biblical Natural Law: A Theocentric and Teleological Approach* (Oxford: Oxford University Press, 2012), 69–139.

Christian natural law theorists have likewise proposed atheological theories. Natural law, writes new natural law theorist John Finnis, can be "understood, assented to, applied, and reflectively analysed without adverting to the question of the existence of God." Finnis, *Natural Law and Natural Rights*, 2nd ed. (New York: Oxford University Press, 2011), 49. Part 2 of Finnis's book is an extended extrapolation of just such a theory. Nicholas Wolterstorff summarizes the new natural law as "a mode of ethical inquiry which is independent both of all comprehensive religions and philosophical perspectives, and of all concrete moral communities. In particular, they present it as independent of theology." Nicholas Wolterstoff, foreword to *Natural and Divine Law: Reclaiming the Tradition for Christian Ethics*, by Jean Porter (Grand Rapids: Eerdmans, 1999), 11. Eugene Rogers contrasts Finnis with Aquinas. Rogers, *Aquinas and the Supreme Court: Race, Gender, and the Failure of Natural Law in Thomas's Biblical Commentaries* (Oxford: Wiley-Blackwell, 2013), 64–69. For a deft summary of recent scholarship on Thomas Aquinas's theory, see Fergus Kerr, *After Aquinas: Versions of Thomism* (Oxford: Blackwell, 2002), 97–113.

3. Habgood, *The Concept of Nature* (London: Darton, Longman and Todd, 2002), 88.

4. Benedict XVI, "Faith, Reason and the University: Memories and Reflections," lecture delivered at Aula Magna of the University of Regensburg (2006), available at https://www.vatican.va/content/benedict-xvi/en/speeches/2006/september/documents/hf_ben-xvi_spe_20060912_university-regensburg.html.

way or another to every moral question. Even if I were to agree, however, we can know Scripture says nothing about *x* or *y* only if we first consult Scripture. But in that case, our moral reasoning would have to reckon with revelation.

There is, further, an epistemological question. Human beings are fallen, and sin affects moral reasoning and action. God gives idolaters over to darkened minds (Rom 1:18–32), and repeated, unrepented sin leaves scar tissue on the conscience (1 Tim 4:2). As Thomas Aquinas recognizes (see below), revelation is a necessary corrective to fallen moral reasoning. If we want to reason well, we must attend to God's Word.

Even in Eden, man needed God's verbal instructions to live rightly. In succumbing to the serpent's temptation, Eve reasoned as Habgood suggests, without reference to God's command. She was right: the fruit of the tree of knowledge was indeed good for food, a delight to the eyes, and desirable to make her wise (Gen 3:6, 22). To avoid sin, Eve needed to allow God's "Do not eat" to override what she learned from nature.

We are created for communion with God, and this necessarily includes verbal communication. By nature, we are recipients of God's promises and commands; we are of the species *homo orans*. Verbal revelation is integral to human flourishing, not an extrinsic imposition.

Exhibit 2: Events, Not Nature, Ground Revealed Ethics

In the Bible, moral demands are often grounded in contingent events of history rather than in the general and fixed structures of created life. Sabbath keeping is imitation of Yahweh's rest at creation (itself an *event*; Exod 20:8–11) and his gift of rest in the exodus (Deut 5:12–15). Israel keeps and gives Sabbath because they have been delivered from Egyptian bondage to Sinai's rest. Israelites free slaves after a six-year term because Yahweh freed *them*. Israel shows kindness to strangers and aliens because they know the anguish of alienation (Exod 22:21; 23:9). Other commands are grounded in the character of the particular God who revealed himself in word and act. The Decalogue comes from Yahweh, the God of Israel and exodus. The prohibition of venerating images is supported by a reminder of Yahweh's jealousy—certainly not a universal divine attribute (Exod 20:4–6). Israel cares for orphans and widows in imitation of Yahweh, Father of the fatherless and husband of widows (Deut 10:17–19).

236 • Natural Law

The ethic of the New Testament likewise centers on *imitatio Jesu* (Matt 4:19; 8:22) and *imitatio Patri* (Matt 5:43–48). While Paul appeals to nature (1 Cor 11:14), his exhortations are more often grounded in the resurrection of Jesus. Crucified and buried with Christ in baptism, we are to consider ourselves dead to sin and to walk in newness of life, offering the members of our bodies as instruments of justice (Rom 6:1–14).

As True Man, Jesus is the way of human flourishing. Following him and obeying his commandments, we live a life that suits the sort of creatures we are and become the creatures we are meant to be. The source, justification, and model for full human life is found not in creation but in new creation.

Exhibit 3: For This Reason, the Decalogue Is Not a Transcription of Natural Law

According to Thomas Aquinas, some principles of natural law are self-evident to everyone. Others, such as the laws of the Decalogue, can be derived with little reflection. Only the wise are capable of giving detailed specifications.[5]

Thomas can sustain this opinion only by ignoring specifics. The God before whom there are no others is a specific God, Yahweh, the God of exodus. If we eliminate the specificity, the first word turns into its opposite, a generic demand to "worship *something*." Israel bears the name of Yahweh, and Yahweh promises long life in the land. The "second table" is implicitly grounded in the revealed truth that man is the image of God.[6]

Some claim the Decalogue is too general to serve as a moral guide. The real problem is that it is too specific to be derived from "minimal reflection" on human nature without reference to revelation.

Exhibit 4: A Natural Moral Consensus Is Thin at Best

Natural law theorists often claim there is something close to a universal moral consensus. Every society has rules governing sexuality and marriage, moral expectations concerning the raising of children, prohibition against killing humans and sometimes animals, protections for property, and so on.[7]

---

5. Aquinas, *ST* I-II, 100.3.

6. See Peter J. Leithart, *The Ten Commandments: A Guide to the Perfect Law of Liberty* (Bellingham, WA: Lexham, 2020).

7. Lewis, *Abolition of Man* (San Francisco: HarperOne, 2015).

The argument from consensus can serve different ends. C. S. Lewis makes the universality of the moral consensus the *basis* of moral authority: thus and such ought to be done because all human societies do them. For Germain Grisez and John Finnis, the universality of basic goods such as life, play, aesthetic experience, sociality, and religion is proof these goods are self-evidently good.[8]

But the consensus collapses when we inquire after specifics.[9] All cultures prohibit murder, but some approve infanticide.[10] Every culture regulates sexual activity, but the balance of pleasure and procreation, the toleration for extramarital and homosexual intercourse, the norms governing husbands, wives, and divorce, differ widely. In some cultures, honor, shame, and loyalty justify killing as retribution for an insult (see Gen 4:19–24). "Religion" is all but universal, but for a Christian, religion is certainly *not* a self-evident good, unless we specify "*true* religion." We are not reasoning Christianly if we reason away the possibility of idolatry. At a more abstract level, individuals and cultures differ regarding the relation of means and ends, and whether a good end (disclosing crucial information) justifies otherwise immoral means (torture).[11]

A thicker consensus requires more-than-natural ingredients. A dense *Christian* consensus cannot arise without Scripture.

Here ends the flurry. On to my longer, steadier argument in which I examine the two faces of the villain—law and nature.

Law in Biblical Perspective

Thomas Aquinas never wrote a treatise on natural law—not in the *Summa Theologiae*, not in the *Summa contra Gentiles*, not anywhere. In the *prima secundae* of the *Summa Theologiae*, he wrote a treatise on *law* that covers eternal, natural, human, and the twofold Old-New divine law. Six pages

---

8. Habgood, *Concept of Nature*, 97.

9. This paragraph summarizes Alasdair MacIntyre, "Intractable Moral Disagreements," in Lawrence S. Cunningham, ed., *Intractable Disputes about the Natural Law: Alasdair MacIntyre and Critics* (Notre Dame: University of Notre Dame Press, 2009) 8–10.

10. Aristotle, *Politics* 1335b–1336a; *The Twelve Tables*, IV.1. Obviously, this is not ancient history, as the modern history of abortion testifies.

11. This paragraph draws on Alastair MacIntyre, "Intractable Moral Disagreements," in *Intractable Disputes about the Natural Law: Alastair MacIntyre and Critics*, ed. Lawrence S. Cunningham (Notre Dame: University of Notre Dame Press, 2009), 1–52.

238 • Natural Law

are devoted to natural law. Thomas wrote one hundred and fifty pages on human and divine law, and that is nothing compared to the massive treatise on virtue that precedes his discussion of law.[12]

Counting words and pages is superficial, but it is a hint that Thomas saw natural law as a component of a larger concept of law. This concept is thoroughly theological and dependent on revelation, in at least two ways. First, the foundational form of law, the law from which all law is derived,[13] is the *lex aeterna*, which Thomas describes in explicitly theistic and even Trinitarian terms. Second, Thomas's treatise is structured by a biblical narrative of law that includes an account of the limits and failures of natural law and a defense of the necessity of divine law. Whatever their strengths and weaknesses on their own terms, atheological accounts of natural law can hardly claim to be Thomistic.[14]

Law, Thomas says, is "nought else than an ordinance of reason for the common good made by the authority who has care of the community and promulgated."[15] It is an exterior guide or directive (*regula*) that provokes and guides action toward particular goods. Law is also a standard of measure by which we determine whether an action is the kind that conduces to appropriate ends.

Though it might initially appear flat, this is a remarkably rich and supple concept of law. It includes what we normally mean by law: written statutes issues by a political authority. Even at this basic level, Thomas's conception holds some surprises. The recipients of law are subject to it, but Thomas insists law exists in a manner within the subject insofar as he is directed by law.[16] Tax law is an external statute that impels millions of citizens to embark on a complex series of actions to meet the deadline for

---

12. Rogers, *Aquinas and the Supreme Court*, 9.

13. Aquinas, *ST* I-II, 93.3.

14. My summary of Thomas has been influenced by Fulvio di Blasi, *God and the Natural Law: A Rereading of Thomas Aquinas* (South Bend: St. Augustine's, 2006); Rogers, *Aquinas and the Supreme Court*; Levering, *Biblical Natural Law*; Andrew Willard Jones, *Before Church and State: A Study of Social Order in the Sacramental Kingdom of St. Louis IX* (Steubenville, OH: Emmaeus Academic, 2017) ch. 14. Contra Anthony Lisska, I do not think Thomas's theory can be reduced to a purely philosophical account; *Aquinas's Theory of Natural Law: An Analytic Reconstruction* (Oxford: Oxford University Press, 1996).

15. Aquinas, *ST* I-II, 90.4; 91.1. I rely, in the main, on the translations of Thomas Gilby, *St. Thomas Aquinas Summa Theologiae*, vol. 28, *Law and Political Theory* (Cambridge: Cambridge University Press, 1966); and David Bourke and Arthur Littledale, *St. Thomas Aquinas, Summa Theologiae*, vol. 29, *The Old Law* (Cambridge: Cambridge University Press, 1969).

16. Aquinas, *ST* I-II, 90.1.

filing, but their actions indicate the external law has been internalized as an inclination, often a desperate one, toward a certain goal. The internalized principle of action is also, in Thomas's terminology, *law*, albeit in a derived sense. In their obedience to law, subjects become something of a law unto themselves.

Thomas's definition of law also covers directives we do not normally think of as "law." No one orders me to protect my existence, yet Thomas includes this basic impulse under *lex natura*,[17] because this inclination comes from outside (God) and impels me to act for the good of my own self-preservation. In part, the flexibility of Thomas's definition is exegetically rooted, an effort to make sense of Paul's references to a "law of sin" (Rom 7:23–25)[18] and a "law of the Spirit of life" (Rom 8:2 ESV). For Thomas, both concupiscence and grace have a quasi-legal quality.

Providence too is a sort of law. God is sovereign over the community of the universe, ruling by his divine reason.[19] The ruling idea of things (*ratio gubernationis rerum*) is in God, and this ruling idea has the nature of law. Since God does not exist in time, the *ratio gubernationis* must be eternal. Insofar as God is Creator, exemplars of all things exist in his mind; insofar as he is governor of the universe, exemplars of ordered action exist within his mind.[20] As he actively exerts this eternal law, he harmonizes creation according to a score that moves all things toward their ultimate end in God.

Law, Thomas argues, must be promulgated, and that principle holds also for eternal law. To explain how this is the case, Thomas turns to Trinitarian theology. A spoken word expresses what it signifies; a mental word expresses a thought. So in God, the Word expresses whatever is in the Father's knowledge, including the eternal law. Though *eternal law* is not a name for the second person, yet it is "appropriated" to the Son because of the analogy between exemplar and word.[21] The promulgation of eternal law is thus God's eternal utterance of the Word, his generation of the Son, who, according to the principle of appropriation, is "himself the eternal law."[22]

---

17. Aquinas, *ST* I-II, 91.6.
18. Cf. Aquinas, *ST* I-II, 91.6.
19. Aquinas, *ST* I-II, 91.1.
20. Aquinas, *ST* I-II, 93.1. Thomas's conception is close to what Reformed theology means by the "divine decree."
21. Aquinas, *ST* I-II, 93.1.
22. Aquinas, *ST* I-II, 93.4.

240 • Natural Law

As noted above, all law is derived from eternal law.[23] *Derived* does not mean "deduced." Eternal law is the governing idea of the sovereign Lord of the universe. All other rulers of the universe are subordinate to his government, and therefore all laws that share in right reason derive from eternal law. Thomas's argument seems to be this: God governs every act and motion of every creature, so they reach their fulfillment in him. Some men issue laws to direct other men to act toward the good. Insofar as human law aims at the achievement of the human good, it seeks the same end as eternal law and in this sense is "derived" from it. Even the law of concupiscence derives in a sense from eternal law. When men turn from God, he justly turns them over to another law, the law of lust. Because it is a penalty in accord with God's justice, concupiscence is tributary to eternal law.[24] Though God does not directly move men toward lust, those who are ruled by concupiscence are included within the scope of his just government of all things.

All things participate in some fashion in eternal law, as each thing is moved toward its proper end by the impression of eternal law upon and within it. Rational creatures, however, share more nobly in the eternal law, participating in providence by their own providing.[25] This is fundamentally what Thomas means by natural law: God providentially directs us toward our end in him, and we rationally and voluntarily share in that direction. Natural law is human beings' capacity knowingly to keep in step with the way the Lord directs us to himself. Thus natural law is promulgated because God instills (*inseruit*) it in our minds;[26] its light nothing but an impression of divine light.[27]

Thomas claims that the impression of eternal law, human participation in eternal law, provides self-evident principles for practical reason, parallel to the self-evident principles of theoretical reason. What has become known as the "first principle of practical reason" is this: good should be done, and evil avoided; all other precepts are founded on this.[28] Reason recognizes things man naturally inclines to as goods, and recognizes the contraries as bad. Man, for instance, shares the inclination to self-preservation with

---

23. Aquinas, *ST* I-II, 93.3.
24. Aquinas, *ST* I-II, 93.3.
25. *Et ipsa fit providentiae particeps, sibi ipsi et aliis providens*; Aquinas, *ST* I-II, 91.2.
26. Aquinas, *ST* I-II, 90.4
27. Aquinas, *ST* I-II, 91.2.
28. Aquinas, *ST* I-II, 94.2.

all creatures. In common with animals, male and female humans have a tendency to couple, produce and bring up offspring, and such like. Because man is rational, he has ends that surpass the ends of all other creatures. Thus, we have inclinations to seek the truth about God and to live in society.[29] The light of natural reason from God enables us to discern good and evil, and this capacity for discernment is our sharing of eternal law.[30]

A few things should be noticed about this account of natural law. First, when Thomas speaks of animal and human inclinations, he uses very general language. Sex and the raising of offspring are "said to be of the natural law" (*dicuntur ea esse de lege naturalia*). Seeking the truth about God and living in society "pertain to the natural law" (*ad legem naturalem pertinent*). The sense appears to be that areas of human experience come within the scope of natural law. Thomas's fundamental thesis about the relation of eternal and natural law is in the background. God providentially directs all creatures, including men, toward their fulfillment in him. Human beings uniquely participate in achieving those ends; that rational participation is the natural law. Sex is one zone of human life in which man should rationally direct his actions toward his end in God. Life in society is another, and, clearly, the pursuit of knowledge of God is another. Natural law pertains to other human activities, which Thomas marks with an open-ended *et similia*.[31] Note: *How* we shape our sex lives, our raising of children, our life in society, or any other realm of human life toward our end in God, Thomas does not say.

Second, the new natural law has made much of Thomas's treatment of human inclinations. These, it is argued, lend texture to the first principle of practical reason. An inclination to x is a sign that x is a basic good; x should therefore be pursued and anything that inhibits this pursuit must be evil. Jean Porter demurs. By setting Thomas's argument in the context of medieval debates, she concludes Thomas did not mean the inclinations to be "construed as natural law precepts."[32] Natural law in the strict sense is not a set of moral rules, but consists of our participation in eternal law and foundational principles of practical reason. When Thomas speaks of moral precepts, he normally appeals to revealed law.

---

29. Aquinas, *ST* I-II, 94.2.
30. Aquinas, *ST* I-II, 91.2.
31. Aquinas, *ST* I-II, 90.4.
32. Porter, "Does the Natural Law Provide a Universally Valid Morality?" in Cunningham, *Intractable Disputes about the Natural Law*, 63–73.

242 • Natural Law

Finally, for Thomas, eternal law qualifies as law only because it is promulgated by a sovereign, and natural law is law only because it is rational participation in eternal law. Natural law is "always specified by a lawgiver . . . whether human or divine."[33] Remove the sovereign, and you entirely undercut the basis for calling natural law *law*. Thomas would not recognize atheological accounts as accounts of law at all.[34]

As soon as Thomas introduces natural law, moreover, he begins to enumerate its limitations. Theoretical reason has no difficulty moving from self-evident axioms (e.g., noncontradiction) to conclusions. Practical reason does not have the same inevitability. The further we move from the general principles of natural law to specifics, the less certain our conclusions become: "The more we get down to particular cases the more we can be mistaken."[35] In the realm of theoretical reason, "truth is the same for everybody, both as to principles and to conclusion." With regard to practical reason, the actions demanded are not the same for everyone. Particular decisions vary, though all derive from common principles. As a result, "there is no general unanimity about what is right or true."[36] Practical reason admits of many exceptions, so that "the more you descend into the detail the more it appears how the general rule admits of exception." In making moral judgments, we must always hedge our conclusions "with cautions and qualifications."[37]

Some exceptions are divine exceptions. Thomas asks whether the natural law is changeable,[38] and he answers no. But it is an intriguing no. Things can be added to natural law (e.g., private property), but this does not amount to a change. When he considers "subtractions" from natural law, he distinguishes. First principles are "altogether unalterable," but secondary principles that are

---

33. Porter, "Does Natural Law," 88. In Porter's view, the divergence among natural lawyers is between those who think norms can be determined and analyzed by "the autonomous functioning of practical reason" and others who insist that norms must be founded on "a more comprehensive philosophical, scientific, or theological account" (90). For her, as for Thomas, "the natural law as we Christians understand and formulate it will inevitably involve some degree of theological specification" (91). Though Porter has since qualified her position, I agree with her earlier conclusion that "we cannot make theoretical sense, or practical use, of the natural law in purely rational or philosophical terms, without taking the contingencies introduced by theological considerations into account" (90). Only theology and the Bible justify using natural law in a *prescriptive* fashion.

34. Di Blasi, *God and the Natural Law*, 83–84, 175–77.

35. Aquinas, *ST* I-II, 94.4.

36. Aquinas, *ST* I-II, 94.4.

37. Aquinas, *ST* I-II, 94.4.

38. Aquinas, *ST* I-II, 94.5.

immediately derived from first principles may be changed on rare occasions. Thus God can overrule the normal application of natural law without violating natural law. God commanded Abraham to kill Isaac, but this is consistent with natural law because God can inflict death on anyone without injustice because all are guilty. God commanded Hosea to take Gomer the prostitute as his wife, but this is not adultery or fornication because God commanded it. Israel plundered Egypt, but this was not theft because God is "owner of the universe" and can dispose of his property however he wishes. Thomas concludes the argument by declaring, "Whatever God commands is just."[39] Just as whatever God does in the world is, by definition, natural, so too whatever he commands must be according to natural law.[40]

Given the limits of practical reason, natural law is not sufficient to guide either morals or political society. As theoretical reason is aware of general principles but does not apprehend all truth, so practical reason naturally grasps general principles without knowing what individual directives follow from it. Even in the best circumstances, natural law needs to be supplemented by human law.[41]

But we do not live in the best of circumstances. We live east of Eden, which means natural law has been weakened, damaged, destroyed, confined.[42] God sowed the light of reason in man at creation, but almost immediately the devil "oversowed" (*superseminavit*) a different law, the law of concupiscence. Man rebelled against God, so God gave man over to the rebellion of his flesh, which makes it impossible for postfall human beings to do what the law requires. Thomas goes so far as to say the law of nature was "destroyed" by the law of concupiscence (*lex naturae per legem concupiscenientiae destruit erat*).[43]

In his commentary on Romans 1, Thomas uses other imagery to describe the dimming of the divine light. God clearly displays his power and divine nature in the visible things of creation. In sin, men detain (*detinent*) the truth in injustice. True knowledge of God leads to good, but it is bound (*ligature*)

---

39. Aquinas, *ST* I-II, 94.5.

40. These arguments make many uneasy, but the category of "obedience to God's will" is fundamental to Thomas's ethics. Not every reference to God's will is a symptom of creeping voluntarism. See di Blasi, *God and the Natural Law*, 77–86, 132–35.

41. Aquinas, *ST* I-II, 91.3.

42. N.B.: Thomas's words, not Calvin's.

43. Thomas Aquinas, *Collationes in decem praeceptis*, trans. Joseph B. Collins and Joseph Kennedy (New York: Wagner, 1939). Available at https://isidore.co/aquinas/TenCommandments.htm.

244 • Natural Law

and held captive (*quasi captivate detenta*) by the love of injustice.[44] Wise men among the gentiles know the truth about God; they possess true knowledge by the inner light within and by the radiance of God's self-revelation in creation, but this knowledge renders them inexcusable for their idolatry and ingratitude. Paul's intention is to show these men cannot plead ignorance. They are not guilty because they are ignorant but ignorant because of their guilt.[45]

As a result, even the wisest are "deprived of the light of wisdom." Turning from God as if turning from the sun, they are plunged into spiritual darkness. They become fools. Because they sin against the glory of God, exchanging God for bestial images, God gives them over to bestial desires. Sinners live under cruel masters, as Israel did in Egypt. Though they have the truth, and though they know the truth, they exchange true knowledge for "false dogmas with their perverse reasoning."[46] Their interior sense, given by God to judge behavior, becomes reprobate. In all this, God is perfectly just. Those who sinned against their knowledge of God by refusing to worship him or by pretending they do not know him are controlled by perverse senses. They are filled with sin, that is, their affections are "totally dedicated to sinning," their sexual lusts a clear indication of their disordered appetites.[47]

Once man is delivered to the law of lust, he is no longer straight-forwardly under the law of nature. A discharged soldier is no longer under martial law but comes under a different law, perhaps regulations pertaining to manual laborers. So too when man turns from God, he is given over to the law of concupiscence. Sensuality so overcomes some individuals that they fall and deviate from reason (*a ratione recesserit . . . deviatio a lege rationis*) and become like beasts. Reason loses its vigor, as man is led by sensual impulses.[48] As reason is darkened, so the desire to do good is blocked by a variety of factors—by passion, by bad custom, by the habit of an entire nation. More than once, Thomas cites the example of the Germans, who, according to Julius Caesar, do not regard robbery as wicked.[49] Natural law, Thomas insists, cannot be removed from the human heart, but this denial

---

44. Thomas Aquinas, *Super ad Romanos* 1, 6.111–12, available at https://aquinas.cc/la/en/~Rom .C1.L6.n111.

45. Aquinas, *Super ad Romanos* 1, 7.126.

46. Aquinas, *Super ad Romanos* 1, 7.137–38.

47. Aquinas, *Super ad Romanos* 1, 8.154–56, 158.

48. Aquinas, *ST* I-II, 91.6.

49. Aquinas, *ST* I-II, 94.4.

applies only to the most general principles and their immediate conclusions. Secondary principles can be effaced by wrong persuasions, perverse customs, corrupt habits (those Germans again!).[50] So much more the specific precepts of natural law.

Thomas cites Romans 2:14 as the *sed contra* when he first introduces natural law.[51] Is there a natural law? Yes, because Paul says so. But Romans 2:14 does not contradict what has been said above about the weakness and corruption of natural law in a world of sin. In the *Summa*, Thomas glosses Romans 2:14 with, "Although they have no written law yet they have the natural law, whereby each understands and is aware for himself of what is good and what is bad." This is perfectly compatible with Thomas's interpretation of Romans 1. In his commentary on Romans, Thomas closely follows Paul in saying men know God, even as they defy him. To say men naturally know what is good and evil does not mean that this knowledge remains unimpaired.

There seems to be a sleight of hand. Paul says the gentiles "do," but Thomas shifts to "know." But his exegesis of Romans 2:14 in the Romans commentary does not depend on that shift. Thomas is puzzled by Paul's claim that gentiles do by nature what the law requires. The apostle seems to favor the Pelagians, who taught that man can observe God's commandment by their own natural powers. Paul cannot be a Pelagian. Thomas offers two possible readings. First, Paul might be speaking of converted gentiles (*gentilibus ad fides conversis*). On this reading, *by nature* does not refer to human nature as such but to human nature transformed by grace (*per naturam gratia reformatam*). Such gentiles do keep the precepts of the law, but only by the grace of Christ (*qui auxilio gratiae Christi coeperant*). Second, Paul might be referring to the light of reason that shines in every man made in God's image. Even on this interpretation, Thomas insists Paul must imply the working of grace, which alone moves the affections toward obedience.[52] On neither interpretation does Thomas leave open the possibility that natural law is sufficient to enable sinners without revelation or grace to obey God.

Once Thomas has introduced the fall and sin into his account of law, he has placed it within the biblical narrative of *exitus et reditus*. Natural

---

50. Aquinas, *ST* I-II, 94.6.
51. Aquinas, *ST* I-II, 91.2.
52. Aquinas, *Super ad Romanos* 2, 3.216.

246 • Natural Law

law does not stand on its own in Thomas's theology but is included in the history of creation, fall, redemption, and consummation. And that means that Thomas's natural law theory is inseparable from his theology of divine law, which comes to Israel as Old Law and to the world as New Law.

Even if Adam had never sinned, divine law would be necessary. As noted above, only the most general principles of the natural law are ineradicable. People come to diverse conclusions concerning particulars, and to know what is right without doubt we need a divine law that is not subject to error (*quod non potent error*).[53] Besides, Thomas adds, something beyond natural law is needed to direct men toward their ultimate end. If men were destined for a merely natural end, they would not need any guide but natural law. As things actually stand, men are created for the end of eternal happiness, and therefore human beings need a divinely given law that surpasses natural law.[54]

We can draw the same inference by another route: rational creatures cannot attain their last end without knowing this end. Since this end is supernatural, it must be revealed.[55] This final end, further, does not cancel more immediate ends. Rather, the ultimate end encompasses penultimate ends. Knowledge of the ultimate end is essential not only for salvation, but for good human desires and actions as such: "All a man's desires are on account of his love for the ultimate end. . . . Secondary objects of desire do not attract except as subordinate to the supreme good, which is the final end."[56] Since man has been destined to a final end in God, and since he can know this final end only by revelation, and since all other goods are desired and pursued with reference to this final end, divine law is necessary to human existence as such. Divine law is not extrinsic but integral to human flourishing.

---

53. Aquinas, *ST* I-II, 91.4.

54. Aquinas, *ST* I-II, 91.4. Some infer from statements such as these that, in actual fact, natural law suffices to direct men toward their immanent end, but we need a transcendent divine law to bring us to our supernatural end. Whatever Thomas says elsewhere (and see below), here he does not suggest that man has a natural end *and also* a supernatural end. The clause that mentions a natural end is entirely conditional, a hypothetical (*si quidem homo ordinaretur . . .*): *If* man were destined for a merely natural finality, he would need nothing beyond natural law. *But in fact*, he is destined for eternal happiness in God, and so needs divine law. Divine law is intrinsic to human existence as such, not merely to fallen human existence.

55. Aquinas, *ST* I, 1.1.

56. Aquinas, *ST* I-II, 1.6. Translation of Thomas Gilby in *St. Thomas Aquinas, Summa theologiae*, vol. 16, *Purpose and Happiness* (Cambridge: Cambridge University Press, 1969).

Written divine law is all the more necessary because of the corruption and decay of the natural law. It clarifies and reignites the light of reason; it liberates our participation in the natural law.[57] Scripture is necessary to draw men out of the path of vice toward the works of virtue.[58] Divine law does not override human nature but rather fulfills it. Eternal law impresses itself on man to direct him toward the good; natural law is human participation in eternal law; since natural law fails, divine law has to enter in to achieve the end set by eternal and natural law.

Divine law comes in two phases, as Old and New. The difference is not a difference in kind or purpose, but in maturity. The Old Law was a tutor to the "schoolboy" Israel, while the New Law is revealed to men who have reached "the condition of an adult who is no longer subject to a tutor.[59] The Old was insufficient to guide man to his final end. It restrained the hand, not the desire.[60] The Old law was earthly, temporal, and material, while the New is more exalted, offering heavenly and eternal promises. While the Old Law impelled men to act out of fear, the New depends on the love of God shed into our hearts.[61]

The law of love is now the standard and measure of good actions. To be good, an action must be in concord with the rule of divine love (*regula divinae dilectionis*). The New Law does not consist primarily in additions to the canon, but it is the internal "law of love," the Spirit who impels men toward their final end. Love is external because it comes from God, but like all law, it becomes an internal principle of action and life. The divine law of love draws us into union with God since "what is loved is within the lover." It impels us toward deification, since love transforms the lover into what is loved. We act virtuously when we act through charity. Only those indwelt by the love of God conform to the standard of divine love. Only those who have received the grace of Christ know and do good and act virtuously.[62]

---

57. Aquinas, *ST* I-II, 94.5.

58. Aquinas, *Collationes in decem praeceptis*.

59. Aquinas, *ST* I-II, 91.5.

60. Aquinas, *Collationes in decem praeceptis*.

61. Aquinas, *ST* I-II, 91.5. Thomas's contrasts of Old and New are infelicitous, traditional though they are. The Old Law directed Israel toward communion with Yahweh, not merely toward earthly and temporal blessings. Conversely, the New offers earthly and temporal promises (the blessing of Abraham to the nations) as well as the promise of eternal life. "Love God" is an Old imperative (Deut 6:5); "Fear God" is a precept of New Law (1 Pet 2:17).

62. Aquinas, *Collationes in decem praeceptis*.

248 • Natural Law

The biblical framework of Thomas's treatise on law explains why his treatment of natural law seems superficial to many. He does not need to draw detailed ethical precepts from nature because the precepts are readily available in Scripture.[63] Yet natural law is not left behind. As a participation in eternal law, natural law impels us toward the end intended by God. That end is happiness, union with God that transforms us into Godlikeness. But natural law cannot achieve what it aims at, and never could. We fulfill the natural law, the law of our being, the law that fulfills our humanity, only by receiving the grace of the New Law, only when the law of the Spirit of life delivers us from the law of sin and death. The only truly natural man is the Christian, and the only truly natural regime is the church, the people among whom the natural law is fulfilled as the law of the Spirit, the community under the reign of the New Law. Other societies achieve peace and justice only as they receive the gifts of the graced community.[64] For Thomas, natural law sets the trajectory, but human beings cannot remain on that trajectory or reach their destination by natural law alone.

This also explains why Thomas characteristically appeals to natural law when explaining how divine law is harmonious with creation and human nature.[65] His lengthy treatment of fornication in the *Summa contra Gentiles* is not a demonstration of the evil of fornication. Thomas knows fornication is evil because God forbids it. His argument elaborates the divine law by exploring the purposes of sex and demonstrating that God's prohibition of fornication, like all revealed law, is good for man—good, that is, for man to attain his final good of union with God, good for man to be fully human.[66] Obedience to divine commands is how human beings rationally participate in eternal law and so reach their supernatural end.

I am not hiding behind Thomas. I have given detailed attention to his theology of law because I agree with its basic contours: God is revealed in creation, and his purposes are evident in creation. Even now, after the fall, he is clearly seen and known from creation. Yet even in innocence, man needed something more than creation's revelation in order to grow to full

---

63. Di Blasi, *God and the Natural Law*, 188–89.

64. Jones, *Beyond Church and State*, 418, 428–29.

65. Di Blasi writes, Thomas "always" deals with natural law "not extensively and systematically, with a view to extracting ethical norms from it directly, but rather, in a residual and general way, with a view to showing the natural foundations of divine Law" (*God and the Natural Law*, 188).

66. *Summa contra Gentiles* 3.122. See di Blasi, *God and the Natural Law*, 208–21.

Godlikeness. After the fall, God subjected men to another law, the law of the flesh, and so, in spite of their knowledge, men actively defy God and his commands. As men persist in idolatrous rebellion, God gives them over to darkness, ignorance, perversion, disobedience, and moral chaos. Divine law restores man's knowledge of God and his commands, and men recover moral light only by the grace of the Spirit of the risen Jesus.

Atheological natural law theories naturally offer atheological theories of law. These may be more or less coherent on their own terms. They most assuredly cannot be Christian. Nor are theories that propose an atheological account of nature. So I argue in the next section.

Nature, Culture, Grace

Nature and its cognates are notoriously elastic words.[67] Yet there is a persistent and recognizable core. The Greek *phusis* is derived from *pheuein*, which means "inhabit" or "grow." It can refer to a thing's origin, its process of growth, or its completed form; commonly, *phusis* encompasses the entire sequence of a thing's coming-to-be.[68] Thus it refers to the quality or character of something, what something is like.[69] *Natura*, with etymological links to *natus* and *nasci*, has a similar range of meaning. Up to the nineteenth century, its derivatives were virtually equivalent to "description."[70] The Greeks were responsible for extending the concept to include the totality of what exists, though later thinkers demoted nature by identifying realities beyond *phusis*—forms for Plato, the Unmoved Mover for Aristotle.[71] *Nature* can mean "everything," or essence, or a principle that determines movement and growth, or the original, or a norm or ideal.[72]

Given the variability of the concept, it is not surprising that there is no single tradition of natural law.[73] Nor is it surprising that the meaning of *nature*

---

67. The variability of the term was not lost on Aristotle (*Metaphysics* 1014b–1015a). See R. G. Collingwood, *Idea of Nature* (New York: Oxford University Press, 1945), 80–82. See also the delightful opening paragraph of Habgood's *Concept of Nature* (1), where the author uses variations of *nature* in five different senses.

68. Gerard Naddaf, *The Greek Concept of Nature* (New York: SUNY Press, 2005).

69. C. S. Lewis, *Studies in Words*, 2nd ed. (Cambridge: Cambridge University Press, 2013), 34.

70. Lewis, *Studies in Words*, 24.

71. Lewis, *Studies in Words*, 25.

72. David G. Ritchie, *Natural Rights* (1903; New York: Allen & Unwin, 1952), 71–77.

73. A. P. d'Entrèves, *Natural Law: An Historical Survey* (New York: Harper Torchbooks, 1951), 9.

250 • Natural Law

becomes confused. Natural-as-original shades into natural-as-ideal, as when Aristotle rejects certain forms of wealth-creation as unnatural simply because they appear at a later, more complex phase in the history of the *polis*. Money making is unnatural (not ideal) because it is unnatural (not original).[74] Modern political and ethical debates are often struggles over conflicting understandings of nature. In Adam Smith and other early political economists, the market is treated as a natural institution, coordinating man's characteristic habits of "trucking and bartering" and seeking advantage through efficiencies. Romantics condemned the dark mills of industrialized Europe as unnatural and Satanic.[75] France's revolutionaries denounced the *ancien regime* for its violations of natural *equalité* and *liberté*, while their opponents insisted that the old order must be perfectly natural because it was so very old.[76] Some follow nature's example of frugality; others, regarding her as a strumpet and a spendthrift, imitate her example of excess.[77] Until the early modern period, Western thinkers considered nature an instrument of God or a maidservant of the Creator. With the mechanization of nature, God became an engineer, then an absentee engineer, and finally a retired engineer.[78]

Nature has always been an oppositional concept, taking its meaning in part from the various correlative terms with which it has been paired. Ancient thinkers typically contrasted nature with human practices. Sophists set *physis* over against *nomos* to argue that every human convention or institution "stifles what exists by nature."[79] As C. S. Lewis observed, this opposition is intuitive.[80] I readily distinguish my mowed (though not manicured) yard from the acres of unimproved forest that surround it. Nature is "the given," the thing we start with before we modify it.

This rough-and-ready distinction does not hold up under scrutiny. The forest around my home is what it is because of a human decision *not* to build

---

74. Ritchie, *Natural Rights*, 28, referring to *Politics* I.8–11.

75. Phil Macnaghten and John Urry, *Contested Natures* (New York: SAGE, 1998), 10–13; Raymond Williams, "Ideas of Nature," in *Problems in Materialism and Culture* (London: Verso, 1980), 67–85.

76. D'Entrèves, *Natural Law*, 48–63.

77. Pierre Hadot, *Veil of Isis: An Essay on the History of the Idea of Nature*, trans. Michael Chase (Cambridge, MA: Belknap, 2006), 190–200.

78. Hadot, *Veil of Isis*, 134–35.

79. Spaemann, "What Is Nature?," *The Robert Spaemann Reader*, trans. D. C. Schindler (Oxford: Oxford University Press, 2015), 22–23. John Walter Beardslee argues that the Sophist distinction has been overstated; they opposed *phusis* and *nomos* more for rhetorical than philosophical reasons. Greeks in general never abandoned the idea that all *nomoi* were founded on *phusis*. See John Walter Beardslee Jr., *The Use of Phusis in Fifth-Century Greek Literature* (Chicago: University of Chicago Press, 1918), 68–81.

80. Lewis, *Studies in Words*, 45.

a subdivision, just as the nature in national parks is the product of a human decision to refrain from certain kinds of development and intervention. Both the forest and the national park are owned, embedded in complex conventions of property law. I have driven and hiked in Yellowstone. Rutted roads of Alabama red mud snake through our forest, and we hear the sounds of four-wheelers, dirt bikes, and gunfire on a typical weekend afternoon. Untouched wilderness it ain't.

A simple point, but one with profound implications for understanding the concept of *nature* in "natural law." To use nature as a standard to measure human actions and institutions, we need to be able to make clean distinctions between nature and artifice. That is precisely what we cannot do, whether we consider nature as everything, as a principle of movement and action, or as human nature.

Nature understood as the totality of creation has never been free of artifice. From the beginning (so Genesis tells us), man lived in a hybrid world of cultivated creation. Yahweh planted an enclosed garden (Gen 2:8, 15) and placed man there with instructions to serve and guard it and a warning not to eat from the tree at the center of the garden (Gen 2:15–17). Before God created a woman, the man was already engaged in a quasi-scientific task of assigning names to, perhaps classifying, cattle, beasts, and birds (Gen 2:19–20). At his first encounter with Eve, Adam breaks into poetry (Gen 2:23). Can we distill "nature" from this artificial world of garden, gardening, observation of animals, naming, marriage, and poetry?

At a more abstracted level, Christian theology is fundamentally at odds with the idea of a purely natural nature. Creation is an artefact of divine art, constructed by the Creator who speaks what is not into being.[81] Every created thing exhibits the glory of the Creator who is concurrently active in every action and motion of every creature. As Aquinas put it, "God's glory or brilliance is the principle of every nature and form,"[82] and again, "God operates in every operator."[83] We never encounter a world independent of

---

81. On the revolutionary impact of this insight on Western thought, see the controversial essays of Michael Beresford Foster, "The Christian Doctrine of Creation and the Rise of Modern Natural Science," *Mind* 43 (1934): 446–68; Foster, "Christian Theology and Modern Science of Nature," *Mind* 44 (1935): 439–66. Voltaire recognized nature's misnaming; "I am called nature, yet I am all art" (quoted in Hadot, *Veil of Isis*, 127).

82. Aquinas, *Super ad Romanos* 1, 7.135.

83. *Deus in quolibet operante operator.* Aquinas, *ST* I, 105.5.

divine influence. Our every encounter with creation is an encounter with the Creator. Just as there is no theology proper that is not also a theology of God-and-world, so too there is no philosophy of nature that is not, at least implicitly, theological—certainly, no *Christian* philosophy of nature.[84]

Nor do we ever encounter *human* nature in the raw. *Nomos* is always already fused with human *physis*. In the beginning, humanity lived in neither a savage Hobbesian anarchy nor a more peaceable Lockean state of nature.[85] From his first moment, Adam lived in a created environment shaped by "supernatural" artifice, subject from the first to extranatural commands. No sooner was Adam formed from dust and placed in Eden than he was organizing the world by constructed linguistic conventions.

"Language belongs," John Milbank has written, "within our primary artisanal interaction with the external world." Because this interaction "is always both receptive and externally constructive," it is "impossible to disentangle the two components." We cannot peel off the linguistic layer of our contact with reality to get at a pre-linguistic natural encounter. Thus we cannot access an a-linguistic nature in order to test our language by it. What is true of language is true of culture generally: It does not simply intervene between me and the world but is a condition of knowing the world at all. Thus, Milbank argues, the "world is how we take it, yet what we take and modify is always the real world and always involves us in real relations to that world."[86] As a result, "we always arrive too late to disentangle what we have received from what we have constructed or what we have constructed from what we have stumbled upon." We have genuine contact with reality, but that contact is linguistically, which is to say, culturally mediated. We cannot measure *nomos* by *phusis*. We are entirely surrounded by nomistic modifications of nature and are thus

---

84. See Michael Hanby's *No God, No Science? Theology, Cosmology, Biology* (Oxford: Wiley-Blackwell, 2013).

85. One might offer a linguistic meta-critique of social contract theory: Neither Hobbes nor Locke actually posited a state of *pure* nature, since in both cases people have to *talk* with one another in order to form a social contract. Language, and hence social and cultural order, must already exist.

86. Milbank, "Only Theology Saves Metaphysics," 14–15, https://www.scribd.com/document/19773672/John-Milbank-Only-Theology-Saves-Metaphysics-On-the-Modalities-of-Terror. Milbank adds, "Trees are seen and are at once seen as shelter; they are buildings before buildings, while wooden buildings allow us to see both trees anew, and shelter anew, and then to observe the trees now more for themselves and for the other relations in which they stand. . . . Water observed is already water drunk and traversed and channelled, while fountains show us new and symbolic aspects of this liquid foundation for our lives" (15).

left to measure some nature-culture hybrids by reference to other nature-culture hybrids.

Milbank is sounding an Aristotelian note. In contrast to the Sophists, Aristotle considered nature and human practices to be complementary rather than contradictory. Nature consists of all that man has not made, but it is possible for man to make things only because "nature itself exists as pre-formed material."[87] Human action does not suppress nature but modifies and at times perfects it. Thus, though nature is what man has not made, man-made artifacts may also be natural, insofar as the maker gives form and structure to natural realities.[88] A statue is not a product of nature, but skilled sculptors work with the natural properties of stone.

In his ethical theory, Aristotle distinguishes "mere nature" as the raw material of human excellence from enhanced "ethical nature." A man attains excellence through habituation and pedagogy within a society with laws and customs and modes of education. In society, *phusis* and *nomos* intertwine to form a complex unity.[89] Political justice, Aristotle argues, is "one part natural, the other legal." He rejects the notion that "since what is natural is unchangeable and has the same force everywhere," law and justice should likewise be everywhere the same. To be sure, "fire burns here and in Persia," but "among us, while there is such a thing as what is natural, everything is nevertheless changeable."[90] Not for nothing does Aristotle declare in the *Politics* that "man is by nature a *political* animal,"[91] not merely gregarious and social but an animal naturally suited to the artificial world of the *polis*. *Poleis* may be better or worse, but we arrive at that judgment by comparing them to one another, not by testing them against an inaccessible apolitical nature.

The complications of attempting to measure *nomos* by *phusis* are evident in debates about slavery. Aristotle notoriously claimed certain men are natural slaves, though he recognized not all who are legally slaves are naturally so. During the medieval period, theologians taught that slavery and private property were not part of man's original condition but defended them as things "added" to natural law. Modern thinkers condemn slavery as

---

87. Milbank, "Only Theology Saves Metaphysics," 14–15.

88. Spaemann, "What Is Nature?," 23.

89. Thomas C. Lockwood, "*Phusis* and *Nomos* in Aristotle's Ethics," *The Society for Ancient Greek Philosophy Newsletter* (2005): 23–35.

90. Aristotle, *Nicomachean Ethics*, 5.7, trans. C. D. C. Reeve (Indianapolis: Hackett, 2014).

91. Aristotle, *Politics* 1.2.

254 • Natural Law

an unnatural institution, incompatible with man's fundamental equality.[92] Aristotle and the medievals are realistic in recognizing the inescapable knottiness of nature and convention. Enlightenment theorists claim access to a nature stripped of all accretions of history, but that raises an epistemological puzzle: If man is everywhere in chains, how do we know he is born free?

This modern concept of *pure nature* is the fruit of centuries of theological development, which has been the subject of intense debate for a century. Thomas has been at the center of the fray, and the battle has focused on whether or not man was created with a natural desire for the beatific vision. According to Henri de Lubac and others of the *nouvelle theologie*, Thomas taught Adam was created with a *single* finality, happiness in union with God.[93] Thomas sometimes writes of *pura naturalia*, but this is a sheer hypothetical designed to clarify the concept of nature. Thomas distinguishes man's natural capacities from his orientation to God, but he teaches they were given simultaneously as a complex gift given with the breath of God.[94] As he puts it in the *Summa contra Gentiles*, man is *naturally* ordained toward God as toward an end (*homo naturaliter ordinatur in Deum sicut in finem*).[95]

Later Thomists departed radically from their putative master's teaching. *Natura pura* came to be seen as the original state of humanity. On this model, humans have a double finality, one natural, which can be achieved by natural resources without grace or revelation, and one supernatural, which requires supernatural grace and guidance.[96] Contrary to Thomas, later scholastics conclude it is *not* natural to surpass nature.[97] Salvation is no

---

92. D'entrèves, *Natural Law*, 43–44.

93. De Lubac, *The Mystery of the Supernatural*, trans. Rosemary Sheed (New York: Herder and Herder, 1967); de Lubac, *Augustinianism and Modern Theology*, trans. Lancelot Sheppard (New York: Herder and Herder, 1969). See also John Milbank, *The Suspended Middle: Henri de Lubac and the Renewed Split in Modern Catholic Theology*, 2nd ed. (Grand Rapids: Eerdmans, 2014).

94. Jean-Pierre Torrell, "Nature and Grace in Thomas Aquinas," in *Surnaturel: A Controversy at the Heart of Twentieth-Century Thomistic Thought*, ed. Serge-Thomas Bonino, trans. Robert Williams (Ava Maria, FL: Sapientia, 2009), 155–88.

95. Aquinas, Summa contra Gentiles 3.129.

96. As Jacob Schmutz shows, this was preceded by shifts in the theology of causation and the understanding of *influentia*; "The Medieval Doctrine of Causality and the Theology of Pure Nature," in Bonino, *Surnaturel*, 203–50.

97. Some later scholastics argue that if man has a natural desire that points beyond a natural fulfillment, salvation becomes a right rather than a gift. If God gives man a natural inclination to fulfillment in Him, God owes it to everyone to fulfill that desire. Otherwise, the natural inclination to God becomes vain, and it is axiomatic that nature does nothing in vain. To ensure that grace remains grace, theologians claimed man is created in a state of "pure nature," and that the inclination to

longer the fulfillment of humans, but an *un*natural and extrinsic addition to human nature.

For late scholastics, nature refers to what all human beings can do and achieve simply by being human—manual skills, mathematical equations, perception, and reason, including moral and political reason. Human doing and making, the entire realm of culture and artifice, is bundled under the rubric of nature and then sharply distinguished from supernatural virtues and knowledge. Eventually, as Francis Schaeffer used to say, nature "gobbles up" nature, and because nature encloses all that is naturally human, nature gobbles up *everything*. Secularism, the culture of the immanent frame, arises from the misty depths of medieval debates about nature and grace.

The late-scholastic paradigm leaves space for a secular standard of "pure human nature," stripped of cultural accretions, the effects of sin, and the operation of grace. But on Christian premises, no such nature exists. To think Christianly about human nature, we must run it through the same biblical grid as we used above when examining law. Adam's original inclinations are not simply identical to the inclinations of fallen Adam, nor are the impulses of fallen nature identical to the impulses of redeemed nature. Both as fallen and as redeemed, man is subjected to an external law—the law of sin and death or the law of the Spirit of life. Fallen and redeemed humanity is moved by different principles.

Through all this, we may acknowledge man's original inclinations remain operative—instincts to self-preservation, to sexual union, to reproduction, to knowledge and worship, *et similia*. But they are "oversown" by sinful inclinations. We can isolate the original inclinations, and the moral principles and social institutions consistent with those inclinations, only with the aid of revelation. Jesus could say of divorce, "In the beginning, it was not so," because he had access to a written record of the beginning (Matt 19:3–9). As with law, so with human nature: we need the Bible to grasp it.

Once redeemed, human nature is no longer quite "natural." For the New Testament writers, certain human practices and actions—the fruits of the Spirit—are *not* the product of nature but of the superhuman power of grace. At the same time, graced human existence is the fulfillment, not the

---

fulfillment in God is added to nature. Salvation no longer fulfills created human beings but becomes "purely accidental" (Spaemann, "What Is Nature?," 27–28).

256 • Natural Law

cancellation, of created human nature. Here is the paradox of grace: to reach the end for which he was created, man must have the capacity to reach an end beyond his capacity.[98]

Conclusion

Atheological accounts of nature, law, and natural law contradict basic Christian convictions. Perhaps there is salvation for natural law. If the *law* of natural law is nested within a biblical narrative of creation, sin, and grace, if the *nature* of natural law is recognized as a graced gift from the world's Creator and Lord, I might be agreeable to dropping the "Anti-" from my title. Not till then. When natural law is uprooted from its biblical-theological framework, Christians must regard it as a heap of theoretical fragments that retains its semblance of coherence only by surreptitious borrowings from divine law.[99]

---

98. Spaemann, "What Is Nature?," 26. John Milbank has observed a homology between the nature-culture duality and the nature-grace duality. In both cases, we are dealing with something above and beyond the given that is simultaneously essential to the realization of what is given. The paradox of nature and grace echoes the paradox of nature and culture.

99. Famously, Alastair MacIntyre, *After Virtue*, 3rd ed. (Notre Dame: University of Notre Dame Press, 2007), 2: "What we possess, if this view is true, are the fragments of a conceptual scheme, parts which now lack those contexts from which their significance derived. We possess indeed simulacra of morality, we continue to use many of the key expressions. But we have—very largely, if not entirely—lost our comprehension, both theoretical and practical, or morality."

Pakaluk Response to Leithart

MICHAEL PAKALUK

Peter Leithart has given so expert a review of natural law within the thought of St. Thomas Aquinas that it nearly represents a sound Thomistic and indeed Catholic view of natural law. I say "nearly" because there are two ways I, as a Thomist and Catholic myself, would wish to see it supplemented or revised.

First, it seems to me not quite correct to regard our grasp of natural law, as Leithart apparently does, solely as dependent upon biblical revelation. Rather, the dependence goes both ways. Just as faith and reason depend on each other like two wings,[1] so also do natural law and revelation. To give some examples:

- "Events" have the importance that they do in the Christian life in part because of the natural law: it is through our antecedent grasp of the natural law that Christians understand that, in response to our Lord's freeing us from the slavery of sin, we owe to him, in justice, the obedience of service (see 1 Cor 6:20).
- Revelation makes a claim on us as Christians in part because of the natural law: it is because we accept by natural law that lying is forbidden and because we understand others to accept it that we are antecedently prepared to accept as truthful testimony about the life of the Lord and the early church (see 2 Pet 1:16–21).

---

1. "Faith and reason are like two wings on which the human spirit rises to the contemplation of truth." Pope John Paul II, *Fides et Ratio*, encyclical letter, September 14, 1998, https://www.vatican.va/content/john-paul-ii/en/encyclicals/documents/hf_jp-ii_enc_14091998_fides-et-ratio.html.

258 • Natural Law

- In general, it is because we have an antecedent grasp of natural law that we see that the claims of Judaism and Christianity are on their face distinctive, because the God of Jews and Christians is the God both of the numinous and of righteousness (see Luke 5:8). (This is the argument of C. S. Lewis in *Mere Christianity*.[2])

In these and other ways our acceptance of revelation presupposes an antecedent grasp of the natural law.

It is not as though once one becomes a Christian this antecedent grasp becomes unimportant. How can a Christian show to nonbelievers what the will of God is "what is good, acceptable, and perfect" (Rom 12:1–2), unless there is a domain of good, acceptable, and perfect action accessible to nonbelievers? The apostles could tell pagan converts, simply, to abstain from fornication (*porneia*), confident that the recipients of their instruction knew what they were talking about; by the same token they thought it unnecessary to tell them to abstain from murder (Acts 15).

Second, although difficulties abound, admittedly, in the attempts of Christians to distinguish between what they believe is binding upon them because of the natural law on its own and what is binding (perhaps additionally) because of revelation, the effort is nonetheless important and surely can be successful.

Again, some examples help:

- Christians need to distinguish between (1) cases where the commands of human authorities are legitimate but at odds with what, as Christians, they believe they ought to do, and (2) cases where the commands of human authorities simply lack authority, because they contradict the natural law. For example, if a commander in the field commands his unit to attack on Sunday, his decision is merely *at odds with* the Christian duty to worship the Lord on a Sunday, while if he commands a soldier to shoot a civilian, his command simply lacks force. It is *ultra vires*. In the first case Christians need to seek accommodation if possible; in the second they must disobey the command, always.

---

2. C. S. Lewis, *Mere Christianity* (New York: Macmillan, 1952).

- Christians likewise need to distinguish between (1) ideals that are admirable but that one should not reasonably expect a society to be practically able to live by, and (2) ideals that represent a kind of stable state of equilibrium for a society, reasonably attainable especially for a Christian society whose members are assisted by grace. Identifying the natural law helps us to distinguish the two. Refraining from alcohol can be admirable, but it is no violation of the natural law to drink alcohol: prohibition was not practically sustainable. But living a life in which one remains chaste before marriage and within marriage, in contrast, does seem an attainable condition for a society in general—just like a general rejection of theft or murder. Practices that are practically necessary not to break the natural law seem to fall within the second class. We need to identify the natural law to identify the class.

In cases like these, Christians are asked to pick out actions or practices in relation to some distinct and isolable standard. Christians exercise a kind of custodianship over all things human, because Our Lord took on human nature and lived within natural institutions such as the family and the market.

So against Leithart I wish to assert that natural law is not something solely dependent on revelation. But with Leithart I wish to say that it doesn't follow that a "theory" of natural law can express or capture how Christians proceed when they identify something as conforming or not to the natural law. In my view one grasps the natural law through acquiring, rather, *wisdom* about human nature and human sociality, not a theory. And acquiring this wisdom and acting on it, in practice, given fallen human nature, will require a lot of study, and not simply the illumination we receive from revelation but also active grace and the guidance of the Holy Spirit.

What is a theory of natural law anyway? If by *theory* we mean simply a systematic treatment, then no one could object. But in an academic culture in which, since the time of C. D. Broad at least,[3] moral philosophy is taught through the comparison of various theories, a theory for us must mean a quasi-axiomatic system or model by which one can supposedly generate "correct" rules of action and "correct" judgments about right or wrong in

---

3. C. D. Broad, *Five Types of Ethical Theory* (New York: Harcourt, Brace, 1936).

260 • Natural Law

particular circumstances. As Leithart suggests, the search for a theory like that is an Enlightenment project. One might add that the project is typically based on a bad analogy between scientific theorizing and practical reason. It aims to satisfy our craving to attain agreement through shared methods (the *calculemus* of Leibniz—compare Charles Taylor[4]), misplaced in practical matters, as Leithart so deftly points out. The project also seems to suppose, wrongly, that there is some viewpoint we can assume outside of human nature, as if one could put on hold or didn't need to presuppose that lying and murder were excluded.

Catholics got pushed into offering "theories" of natural law by two pressures. The first pressure was the felt need to defend traditional Christian teaching against artificial contraception, believed to be based on the natural law, against challenges to that teaching from theologians stemming from the moral "theory" of proportionalism. But "only a theory defeats a theory"—or so might someone suppose. Thus, it seemed an alternative "theory" was needed.

The second pressure came from the need to defend laws fostering "morality" within secularized societies where courts would enforce the separation of church and state. It was felt that it had to be shown that legislation Christians in particular favored—against artificial contraception, against abortion, against sodomy, in favor of marriage as between a man and a woman—was favored not on the basis of revelation (since then the legislation would violate the separation of church and state) but on the basis of, let's say, reasoning such that any reasonable person would be bound to accept.

However, such "theories" of natural law, as the historical record shows, have proved ineffective for both purposes.

I will bring in the example of my seven-year old son, Finnan, to illustrate in conclusion another kind of investigation into natural law. He is being homeschooled. For the subject of religion, he is currently memorizing the Ten Commandments. The other day, after he recited them for me, I asked him about the commandment against killing. "Finnan," I said, "did you learn that it was wrong to kill when you learned the commandment, or did you already know that it was wrong to kill before you learned it?" He looked at me with a mixture of incredulity and contempt, and spoke out in a loud

---

4. Charles Taylor, "The Diversity of Goods," in *Utilitarianism and Beyond*, ed. A. Sen and B. Williams (Cambridge: Cambridge University Press, 1982), 129–44.

voice, sarcastically, "Like it's not *obvious* that you shouldn't kill people." I will make several observations on this case.

First, it was Finnan's contribution not mine to emphasize the obviousness of the commandment. He apparently believed that such obviousness precluded doubt. It's not clear that he would have conceded that anything else could be more obvious. But it seems that nothing less obvious can corroborate or support the more obvious. (Whitehead and Russell's famous proof in *Principia Mathematica* stretching over hundreds of pages that 1+1=2 hardly corroborated that truth.)

Second, note how Finnan restated the obvious, not "I shouldn't kill," but "You shouldn't kill people." That is, no one should kill anyone. Here was a seven-year-old boy of his own accord stating a law which he regarded everyone everywhere as being bound by—including kings, presidents, and dictators. His assertion would strike us as ridiculously presumptuous if we did not share exactly the same conviction.

Third, his restatement implicitly contained reference to a community— call it, the entire human race. Yes, with Leithart we must assign to Finnan's good Christian upbringing his free, spontaneous, strong, and intuitive extension of the commandment to every human being, including the unborn child.[5]

Fourth, Finnan also implicitly affirmed an authority, if a law must have an authority. It was not on my authority (I had never taught it or set it down), or his own, or the authority of any local or national politician, or religious leader, or even of the Bible—as he had not yet studied the Ten Commandments—that he came to know this law. Yes, admittedly, with Leithart we agree that it took some education to lead Finnan to affirm, truthfully, that its authority is God—and yet only a little bit, since who else's could it be?

Fifth, we could if we wish look at Finnan's assertion in the manner of philosophers and ask for reasons and explanations. What explains how he asserted it so boldly? Does the formulation of the law as a proscription have anything to do with its obviousness? For what purpose did he come to see the truth of the commandment as obvious?[6] How did his understanding come

---

5. See Michael Pakaluk, "The Light of the Truth of the Gospels for the Common Good," Proceedings of the XIII Plenary Session of the Pontifical Academy of St. Thomas Aquinas, Credere, amare e vivere la verità, 21–23 June 2013 (Vatican City: Libreria Editrice Vaticana, 2014), 183–93.

6. See Michael Pakaluk, "Two Conceptions of Natural Law," *Divinitas, rivista internazionale di ricerca e di critica teologica*, 2021, 319–36.

262 • Natural Law

to be in the condition that once the law was presented to him he assented to it as something he already knew? Can we give a rational reconstruction of the steps? He did so through what Newman calls "implicit reason." Can we give a kind of accounting of the steps, rendering them as "explicit reason"?[7] Yes, indeed, we can investigate this matter also, so long as we understand that our findings speak to only an aspect of the reality, that they cannot claim greater assurance than the law itself, and so long as we do not presume that such a reconstruction could play any practical role in persuading anyone in any important matter where something significant was at stake.

---

7. John Henry Newman, "Sermon XIII, Implicit and Explicit Reason," in *Oxford University Sermons* (London: Longmans, Green, and Company, 1909).

Biermann Response to Leithart

JOEL D. BIERMANN

Though I'm not quite certain of the reason, I determined to follow a deliberate approach in responding to the other four essays in this project: read one essay, write my response, and then move to the next until all four had been completed. With only titles to guide me, I settled on a plan of attack. Guessing rightly that there was likely to be much agreement with my Reformed colleague, Littlejohn's essay served as a good warm-up. It seemed reasonable to turn next to Pakaluk's classical approach to natural law followed by the new take on the topic by Moschella. That left Leithart's for last, of course. For my purposes, this turned out to be quite a fortuitous sequencing. Still, I should be clear that reading this essay last was hardly simply by default; this essay was always, obviously, going to be last. After all, given my own commitments, Leithart's title seemed to suggest a significant likelihood of disagreement between the two of us, so I elected to save the biggest battle for last. It turns out, though, that one does not need even a cover to lead to a mistaken judgment; clearly one should also not make the mistake of judging an essay by its title. Though we would need to iron out some of our verbiage and come to agreement on our labels, from what I can tell, my basic position on the law that undergirds the creation aligns quite nicely with that of Leithart. What he calls divine law I would suggest calling creational law and could even be content to label natural law—though I have no particular objections to his preferred verbiage. Everything certainly hangs on the definitions used. Nevertheless I am confident we are aiming at the same truth or concept, whatever label we put on it.

263

264 • Natural Law

It would be premature, though, to celebrate the happy circumstance of hostilities ended before they had even begun. And those who undertook the task of reading this volume in the hopes of perhaps glimpsing just a bit of a dustup may yet get their money's worth. There is a battle to be engaged, and an enormously significant one at that, but it is certainly not the one I had expected. More on that in a bit. First, I need to offer some elaboration on the battle that wasn't.

While Leithart insists on the presence of a villain and offers proof of the same, the fact is that none of the essays in this volume actually stake a position that entirely "eliminate[s] or bracket[s] revealed Christian theology"(p. 233). No doubt, the author's admission may be less than robust and utterly lacking in enthusiasm, but even the new natural law position explicitly granted that without a grounding in metaphysical reality the entire project would collapse. Still, I am well aware that a mere metaphysical grounding or even an appeal to God is a far cry from Christian confession. And it is true that after granting the need for some form of metaphysical foundation, both the classical and the new natural law arguments set off on their respective pursuits without an overt need for either the Bible or Jesus. And yet neither venture was an anti-Christian or even antirevelation project but precisely the gambit of seeking, for good or ill, to make a case for the law and law-keeping that could be palatable for even an unbeliever and so potentially a bridge of some sort for some good purpose or another. If this is, though, as I suspect, the atheological natural law that Leithart considers to be the villain of his essay, then I can confidently and cheerfully declare that in my case at least, his fear of such an un-Christian form of natural law does not apply. Not all who argue for natural law are seeking to craft an ethics without recourse to God, revelation, or Jesus. Leithart seems to know this as he grants at the close of his essay that he is ready to retract his anti-natural-law stance if the natural law that is advocated is kept firmly rooted in "its biblical-theological framework" (p. 256). While I can't speak for the other essays, I know that I can conceive of no other viable form of natural law besides one grounded in the work of the Creator and consistently made known to creatures through both his general revelation in the creation and his specific revelation in Christ.

So the argument evaporates and the battle I expected fails to materialize. Leithart's divine law is simply the will of God wired into the universe—what

I name creational or natural law. On this seemingly central and critical topic, we are not disagreeing. That so much of the essay is devoted to an exploration of Aquinas's natural law thinking and then a fulsome and forthright understanding of *nature* could be construed as somewhat overwrought for the conclusions ultimately reached: what Thomas termed *natural law* can have no meaning apart from the *lex aeterna* grounded in divine law, and the term *natural* is hopelessly fuzzy and cannot possibly refer to a realm or a way of operating apart from the creating God. While I readily concur with both conclusions, it is difficult to imagine anyone who *faithfully* confesses Christ as the incarnate Son of God; the architect of creation; the only way, truth, and life; and the only means of salvation advocating for a different position (note the emphasis on *faithfully*). Still, it is interesting that what I had assumed would be the area of contention between us, the question of the existence and importance of natural law, turns out to be a nonissue. But far more importantly, it also turns out not to be the most pressing issue in the essay. To my considerable surprise and without warning, another far more urgent disagreement emerged as the essay unfolded. Perhaps it was not by design; it could be that the pressing matter of making a case for God's prominent place within any discussion of law skewed the presentation; or it might have been merely an oversight or an unfortunate articulation; but whatever the reason, the argument of Leithart's essay actually undercuts and negates the gospel itself.

I recognize that this is a rather serious claim, and it is certainly not made lightly. The evidence, however, is there. Since such vital things should not be merely assumed and so left unsaid, and since, to my own shame, I recognize that I failed to do this in my own essay, let me begin with an explicit and immoderate declaration of the gospel. The gospel at the very heart of Christian faith and confession is that sinners and the fallen world are made right with God and so saved from his wrath and hell not by any human work or activity but solely and wholly by grace through faith in Jesus Christ alone. What sinful men could not do, the Son of God, incarnate in Jesus of Nazareth, did perfectly. By his obedient life, sacrificial death, and triumphant, vindicating resurrection, he redeemed and restored the creation to a right relationship with God the Father, and on the last day that same risen Lord of creation will return in glory to bring God's people and the creation itself into the fullness of his eternal, eschatological kingdom. That is the gospel. Any declaration, discussion, or practice of the law in any form can have no greater or more important task than making clear to human beings their abject inability to fulfill the law, thus revealing, painfully, crushingly, and unflinchingly, each person's utterly desperate need for what only God can give: the gospel of Jesus. The law is never the means of salvation. The law can never be the end or goal of Christian theology. And Jesus cannot be made into a new Moses.

My acute concern with the essay begins as the discussion of Thomas and advocacy of the New Law draws to a close. There, Leithart writes, "We fulfill the natural law, the law of our being, the law that fulfills our humanity, only by receiving the grace of the New Law, only when the law of the Spirit of Life delivers us from the law of sin and death" (p. 248). Once more, everything hangs on the definitions one employs. If the New Law in mind is a law that is not law at all, a law that has nothing to do with human performance, a law that is actually the gospel of God's favor on account of Christ, then all is well. But if *New Law* means a fresh, Spirit-infused, Jesus-inspired, reinvigorated, grace-fueled, keeping of the law impossible in any "natural" way but now made possible solely by the working of God, then there is a significant problem. Though it operates with much evangelical Christian verbiage, such a position amounts to salvation through works and is the antithesis of the gospel. My predisposition to read the essay's New Law declaration using the former definition was thwarted by the sentence itself, which begins, "We fulfill . . ." This is precisely the problem. *We* do not fulfill anything—not even with a fresh dose of grace. What is at issue, then, is nothing less than the fundamental battle of the Reformation itself—the battle between a view of justification as forensic or declarative (grace as the *favor Dei propter Christum*) on the one hand and, on the other, a sanative understanding of justification in which doses of grace are granted to people who then use them to become people worthy of God's favor and salvation. It is a fundamental issue of the distinction between law and gospel.

That the essay tracks with a classic, Roman, sanative view of justification is given yet more credence when Leithart asserts, "Yet even in innocence, man needed something more than creation's revelation in order to grow to full Godlikeness" (pp. 248–49). In fact, Adam was not on a growth trajectory aimed at achieving a higher status. Created in God's image, Adam simply lived according to God's plan as the dependent recipient of God's grace and favor. He lived, as all God's people do, not on the basis of his own performance but only by faith. The essay further obscures the gospel when it argues, "Fallen and redeemed humanity is moved by different principles" (p. 255). That is, what distinguishes Christians from unbelievers is simply a matter of which law is at work directing a given life, whether "the law of sin and death or the law of the Spirit of Life" (p. 255). The essay's argument culminates with the declaration: "Here is the paradox of grace: to reach the end for which he was created, man must have the capacity to reach an end beyond his capacity" (p. 256). To this, the gospel-drunk Lutheran that I am can only say, "No. Absolutely not." Man has no such "capacity to reach." He never has. Human beings, much less sinful and broken human beings, can only plead for mercy and then delight to be bathed in the sweet gospel grace of Christ's declaration of forgiveness and righteousness.

While I am not inclined to urge violation of any of the commandments in the Decalogue, it seems necessary in this case that I embrace my dubious heritage that so concerned the Angelic Doctor. Perhaps his fears were well founded, if not prescient, as yet another thieving German seeks to steal the glory from man and his unceasing and pretentious attempts to scale the heights of divinity along the path of his own moral progress and spiritual growth. Man cannot console his pride and salve his dignity by striving to climb heavenward toward divinity—even if that climb is fueled by divine grace, inspired by the Spirit, and exemplified by Christ. This is still nothing but the way of the law, and whether old or new, it remains the law. This thieving German wants nothing less than to steal the thunder of the law and give the glory only to Jesus—and not just Jesus as the perfect exemplar, encourager, or motivator but Jesus as the perfect and only savior. As much as creatures need the law of God that shapes and guides his extraordinary creation and the way of his people within that creation . . . they need the gospel infinitely more. And if it pleased God to make his law great and glorious, how very much greater and more glorious has he made the gospel of his Son? In the end, it is not the salvation of natural law that is at stake but the salvation of sinful human beings. The law must always, finally, give way to the gospel.

Littlejohn Response to Leithart

BRAD LITTLEJOHN

When it comes to Peter Leithart's rousing essay "Anti–Natural Law," I am tempted to pen the briefest of responses: "If that's what natural law meant, I'd be against it as well. But thankfully it does not, and never has—at least in the mainstream of the Christian tradition."

Fighting a Straw Man?

For very long sections of his essay, I found myself nodding along in agreement. In particular, although Aquinas specialists might find bones to pick here and there, I found his entire lengthy exposition of Aquinas on law to be lucid, faithful, and more or less the theology of law I myself would hope to promote. Certainly, the Reformed tradition as I read it would have few quarrels with this exposition or with many other claims in Leithart's essay. The Reformed too "believe God has spoken to moral questions, and our Creator's spoken and written word is the most relevant factor" (p. 234). The Reformed too confess, "If we want to reason well, we must attend to God's word" (p. 235). A Reformed natural law theory concurs with Leithart that a natural law theory must place God at the center, for if you "remove the Sovereign . . . you entirely undercut the basis for calling natural law *law*" (p. 242). And the Reformed of course have no problem emphasizing the many problems of total depravity that Leithart highlights.

Indeed, I am inclined to say that very few strands of the Christian tradition, at least until quite recently, could be said to propound the "atheological accounts of nature, law, and natural law" against which Leithart ranges himself. However, I will let the other contributors to this volume speak for themselves and confine myself to emphasizing that a Reformed natural law account, at least, bears little resemblance to the straw man that Leithart seeks to tear down.

This, I hope, is clear enough from my own main chapter in this volume, in which I quote extensively from sixteenth and seventeenth century Reformed theologians on the inextricability of theology and law, the relationship between natural and divine law, and just what reason can and cannot achieve in the wake of sin. However, since Leithart at least in passing takes a historical swipe at Protestant natural law, a few more citations might be helpful. Near the outset of his essay, he names his nemesis as the idea that we can "know the origin, shape, and end of nature and human nature without reference to the Creator, the image of God, the Spirit, or Jesus" (p. 234). He then says, "Since the sixteenth century, such theories have been predominant among both secular and Christian thinkers" (p. 234). The sixteenth century, of course, happens to be the period of the Protestant Reformation, suggesting that Leithart intends to tar much of Protestant natural law theory with this brush.

Although this is a vast, complex, and fiercely contested historical terrain, and we cannot conclusively adjudicate such a claim here, I do at least want to cast some doubt on it by citing as counterexamples two Protestant natural lawyers who are comparatively late (1670s and 1780s respectively) and comparatively secular in their methodology. One of these, Samuel Pufendorf, Leithart accuses of "dispens[ing] with the theological trappings" (p. 234n2) of natural law altogether. In fact, however, after noting how many principles of natural law can be rational deduced as advantageous for survival, Pufendorf declares emphatically, "Now though these *Rules* do plainly contain in themselves that which is for the general *Good;* yet that the same may obtain the Force of *Laws,* it must necessarily be presuppos'd, that there is a God, who governs all Things by his Providence, and that He has enjoyn'd us Mortals, to observe these *Dictates* of our Reason as *Laws.*"[1] He goes on to ground his account of natural law in Romans 2:14–15 before turning to the first heading of natural law, our duties toward God. The

---

1. Samuel Pufendorf, *The Whole Duty of Man according to the Law of Nature,* ed. Ian Hunter and David Saunders (Indianapolis: Liberty Fund, 2003), 56.

270 • Natural Law

God in question he then clearly distinguishes from Spinoza's pantheistic God of the philosophers and describes in terms familiar to the tradition of classical theism.

More than a century of Enlightenment later, the founding-era Supreme Court justice James Wilson began his *Lectures on Law* with a thorough treatment of natural law. Reviewing the various possible foundations for natural law, he concludes quickly that all law must find its basis in the eternal law of God: "His infinite power enforces his laws, and carries them into full and effectual execution. His infinite wisdom knows and chooses the fittest means for accomplishing the ends which he proposes. His infinite goodness proposes such ends only as promote our felicity."[2] This eternal law becomes binding for us as natural law not simply as the abstract "nature of things"[3] but as the ordained *will* of God: "Having thus stated the question—what is the efficient cause of moral obligation?—I give it this answer—the will of God. This is the supreme law."[4] But how do we go about to understand and know this will? Surely as a product of the late Enlightenment, Wilson will answer that pure reason alone is more than sufficient for the task, and we may safely set the Bible aside as an accommodation to weaker minds. Not at all:

> How shall we, in particular instances, learn the dictates of our duty, and make, with accuracy, the proper distinction between right and wrong; in other words, how shall we, in particular cases, discover the will of God? We discover it by our conscience, by our reason, and by the Holy Scriptures. The law of nature and the law of revelation are both divine: they flow, though in different channels, from the same adorable source. It is, indeed, preposterous to separate them from each other. The object of both is—to discover the will of God—and both are necessary for the accomplishment of that end.[5]

In offering these citations, I by no means intend to suggest that these two thinkers, or others of their eras, were above reproach, or are the best guides

---

2. James Wilson, *Lectures on Law*, in *Collected Works of James Wilson*, ed. Kermit L. Hall and Mark David Hall, 2 vols. (Indianapolis: Liberty Fund, 2007), 1:503.

3. Wilson, *Lectures on Law*, 1:505.

4. Wilson, *Lectures on Law*, 1:508.

5. Wilson, *Lectures on Law*, 1:509.

Littlejohn Response to Leithart • 271

to follow in retrieving and reconstructing a fully Christian natural law theory. Both are in different degrees open to the charge of putting too much confidence in reason and showing too little interest in Scripture. I do not necessarily ask that Leithart embrace them as paragons of Christian moral and political theory. But I do argue that it is unfair to suggest that they—or most thinkers of the venerable tradition they represent—promoted an atheological account of natural law. For them, natural law found both its first origin and its final end in God. Moreover, it is false to suggest that for such thinkers, natural law had no need of revelation, as we see Wilson explicitly declaring our need for Holy Scripture.

Some Metaphysical Disagreements

My primary disagreement with Leithart then might be merely historical: while we both agree that natural law should not be "atheological," he thinks it quite often has been, especially since the sixteenth century; I am much more doubtful. That said, I think there are probably also a few important differences of substance on what a proper natural law theory should look like.

Some of these differences are rooted in questions of theology proper, where I would take my stand with the tradition of classical theism, while Leithart's doctrine of God contains echoes of Robert Jenson and other modern theologians who prefer to historicize the divine essence. Consider Leithart's claims that the God whom we are called to imitate is a specific kind of God, a jealous God ("certainly not a universal divine attribute"; p. 235). On traditional Christian natural law theory, God represents the necessary pinnacle of being itself, containing in himself all possible perfections, such that the creatures he creates in his image cannot but imitate this goodness and be drawn toward it. For Leithart, all of this seems merely contingent. There are many possible gods, but Yahweh is the only one who happens to exist, and since he has created us, he can prescribe the rules for our behavior.

Of course, inasmuch as Leithart grants that these rules are rooted in our nature, natural law would seem to remain as an objective creaturely reality, but Leithart still stresses that "moral demands are often grounded in contingent events of history rather than in the general and fixed structures of created life" (p. 235). And later in the essay he even casts doubt that there are such "fixed structures of created life," when he seeks to break down the

272 • Natural Law

boundary between nature and artifice, saying, "The forest around my home is what it is because of a human decision *not* to build a subdivision, just as the nature in national parks is the product of a human decision to refrain from certain kinds of development and intervention" (p. 251). There is a truth here; the human decision not to interfere is still a human decision. But we cannot allow this truth to distort the reality of natural ends, natural kinds, and natural processes. As Oliver O'Donovan warns in *Resurrection and Moral Order*, according to such thinking, "All ordering becomes deliberative ordering, and scientific observation, failing as it does to report the given teleological order within nature, becomes the servant of techne. Of course, man continues to eat vegetables; but he no longer knows that he does so because vegetables are food, and comes to imagine that he has devised a use for them as food."[6]

At points such as these, I am led to suspect that Leithart and I are divided not merely by historical judgments about how theological early modern natural law theory was and wasn't but by fundamental metaphysical commitments.

Slippery Language and the "Sufficiency" of Natural Law

Aside from these points, however, there are many points in this essay where I am simply not sure how much we may agree; the language seems too slippery. For instance, he insists that "to be fully rational, moral reasoning must seek to take into account as many relevant factors as possible" (p. 234), including special revelation. This is true, but a lot of emphasis falls on the word *fully*. By this standard, very few of our judgments in life about anything can be said to be *fully* rational, but that does not mean we cannot give some kind of rational account of them. So moral reasoning based on natural revelation can still be valid, if imperfect and incomplete. When a little further on Leithart tweaks his language to "If we want to reason well, we must attend to God's Word" (p. 235), I again find myself inclined to agree, depending on exactly what we mean by *well* and what

---

6. Oliver O'Donovan, *Resurrection and Moral Order: An Outline for Evangelical Ethics* (Grand Rapids: Eerdmans, 1986), 52.

it means to *listen*; I do not need to have a proof text in mind before every moral judgment I make.

Leithart again allows weasel words to do a lot of work for him when he says "God has spoken [in Scripture] *in one way or another* to every moral question" (p. 234–35, emphasis mine). Perhaps, but on many moral questions, Scripture does little more than clarify general intuitions, leaving us to use our God-given reason to fill in the blanks. And when Leithart says later that "given the limits of practical reason, natural law is not sufficient to guide either morals or political society" (p. 243), everything depends on what we mean by *sufficient*. Calvin, after all, said, "Nothing, indeed is more common, than for man to be sufficiently instructed in a right course of conduct by natural law,"[7] and particularly stressed the sufficiency of such principles for "civil order and honesty."[8] I can agree with both Leithart and Calvin here depending on just what we might mean by *sufficient*.

Examples of such ambiguity could be multiplied. At the end of the day, I find myself enthusiastically agreeing with Leithart that natural law is deeply clouded by sin and thus its chief utility is *alongside* Scripture, within the redeemed community rather than out in the secular public square. And yet I see nothing wrong with saying that while distorted, flawed, and incomplete, fallen man's rational faculties continue to serve him in good stead as a restraint on the worst impulses of his disordered appetites and a tool for devising fitting civil laws. As I said in my response to Biermann's essay, natural law does not have to be perfect to be useful. By all means let us acknowledge its source, the Creator, but in doing so, let us give him thanks for leaving us this natural gift alongside his many supernatural gifts.

---

7. John Calvin, *Institutes of the Christian Religion*, trans. Ford Lewis Battles, ed. John T. McNeill (Louisville: Westminster John Knox, 1960), 1:281.

8. Calvin, *Institutes*, 1:272.

Moschella Response to Leithart

MELISSA MOSCHELLA

The first thing to notice about Leithart's essay is that it does not deny the existence of natural law understood as a set of objective practical principles and moral norms that can in principle be known and defended by reason. Instead, Leithart's critique of natural law seems to focus on two points: (1) knowing the content of natural law apart from revelation is extremely difficult in practice (perhaps even impossible beyond the most basic principles), and (2) this knowledge is so incomplete and inadequate by contrast with the moral guidance provided by revelation that it is fruitless and wrongheaded for Christians to try to develop and employ natural law arguments rather than making arguments from within an explicitly biblical-theological framework. I will briefly respond to each of these points in turn.

Leithart presents several arguments for why it is difficult to know natural law apart from revelation. One of his arguments is that "to use nature as a standard to measure human actions and institutions, we need to be able to make clean distinctions between nature and artifice," which is something that he thinks we cannot do (p. 251). While this critique might undermine theories of natural law that claim that we derive knowledge of what is good and bad or right and wrong from speculative knowledge of human nature, this critique leaves the new natural law theory completely untouched. As I explained in my essay, we know what is good for us—and therefore identify the ends of our nature *as rational agents*—by reflecting on our practical reasoning. In other words, the standard for what counts as *natural* in the morally relevant sense is what is *reasonable*, not what we happen to be inclined to by our subrational inclinations. (Leithart seems to misunderstand the new natural law on this point when he claims that "an inclination to x is a sign that x is a basic good" (p. 241). This is not an accurate description of the new natural law unless *inclination* is used to mean "*rational* inclination"—that is, practical reason's grasp that x is not a mere possibility but an *opportunity* that is to-be-pursued, or it is intrinsically choiceworthy.)

Another argument Leithart makes for the difficulty of knowing natural law without revelation is that because our natural inclinations are "oversown" by sinful inclinations, "we can isolate the original inclinations, and the moral principles and social institutions consistent with those inclinations, only with the aid of revelation. Jesus could say of divorce, 'In the beginning, it was not so,' because he had access to a written record of the beginning" (p. 255). Again, however, the new natural account does not hold that we determine what is good and right with reference to some original human condition. Rather, the account holds that even though the principles of natural law can be obscured by disordered subrational inclinations (which, from a theological perspective, are ultimately explained by the fall), it is nonetheless possible to grasp and defend many moral truths through reason—as many pre-Christian and non-Christian thinkers have done. Indeed, the natural law account explained in my essay offers reason-based principles for distinguishing between good and bad and right and wrong, and this account has been used to make arguments and draw practical conclusions about a wide range of moral issues.

Leithart might say that new natural law thinkers are only able to make these arguments through "surreptitious borrowings from divine law" (p. 256). But while my essay articulates many moral principles that correspond to divine law, none of the arguments I make involves an appeal to revelation. Truths of revelation can certainly provide a helpful guide and check to reasoning via natural law (just as the answers in the back of the math book can help a student to see if she has reasoned through the problem correctly), but if all the premises of an argument are based on reason, then the argument is based on reason, and its soundness is independent of the data of revelation—regardless of whether the author knew the conclusion from revelation in advance (just as the soundness of a student's mathematical problem solving is independent of whether or not she consulted the answer

276 • Natural Law

at the back to see if she was on the right track). Further, many of the topics about which new natural law thinkers have written are topics that revelation does not directly address. Revelation says nothing, for instance, about in vitro fertilization. So how could the writings of new natural law thinkers on this topic—or other topics that revelation does not directly address—be borrowing from divine law?

None of this should be taken to imply that new natural lawyers believe reason can tell us *everything* that we need to know about morality or downplay the importance of revelation in any way. Indeed, Germain Grisez, the founder of this approach to natural law thinking, wrote a three-volume work called *The Way of the Lord Jesus*—hardly an "atheological" book! Nonetheless, in the first volume of that work, *Christian Moral Principles*, he offers a detailed, reason-based account of the principles of natural law and affirms that all of these moral truths "can in principle be known without faith."[1] And while Grisez recognizes that "in the actual order of things natural law does not stand apart from the law of Christ," because they are "two agreeing streams from the same divine font," he still maintains that "natural law and divine law can be distinguished from each other."[2] Grisez's account thus seems to both avoid the problems that Leithart claims are inherent in "atheological" accounts of natural law, without denying the possibility or value of knowing, articulating and defending moral truths on the basis of reason alone. I would be interested to hear what (if anything) Leithart finds problematic in this approach.

Perhaps Leithart's response will be to emphasize the second point of his critique as I characterized it at the outset—namely, that natural law on its own is inadequate. Before responding to this aspect of Leithart's critique, I should first emphasize that the new natural law view does not deny natural law's inadequacy. Grisez explicitly states that natural law must be supplemented by faith because "our ultimate end is to share in fulfillment in the Lord Jesus, and we do not judge rightly what to do unless we judge in light of this end."[3] Grisez explains that while Christian teaching neither negates nor replaces natural law, it nonetheless specifies it in light of what revelation tells us about the human condition as fallen and redeemed, and also proposes

---

1. Germain Grisez, *Christian Moral Principles*, 25.E, https://twotlj.org/G-1-25-E.html.
2. Grisez, *Christian Moral Principles*, 7.B.
3. Grisez, *Christian Moral Principles*, 7.A.

options for choice that "either cannot be conceived without faith or would lack sufficient appeal to be considered in the absence of Christian hope" (and specifically the promise of fulfillment in the kingdom).[4] For example, Grisez argues that because we know that we live in a fallen world in which many will fail to fulfill their duties toward others, Christians must be merciful and generous in their service to others, going beyond what is strictly owed as a matter of justice to make up for the injustice of others and alleviate its negative consequences for the vulnerable.[5] Further, without the assurance that "your labor in the Lord is not in vain" (1 Cor 15:58), because we are promised that the good deeds we do on earth will ultimately bear fruit in the kingdom of God,[6] it can often be difficult to have sufficient moral motivation to pursue the good energetically when the earthly fruits of our efforts seem very uncertain.

Given what I have just acknowledged regarding the shortcomings of natural law in isolation from Christian revelation, why do I not agree with Leithart's claim that engaging in moral reasoning without explicit reference to revelation is "villainous" or—to put the point more softly in a way that seems to capture the spirit of his argument—simply a waste of time that could be better spent teaching people the gospel? This question, as well as Leithart's critique in general, invites explicit consideration of the purposes of developing and articulating a natural law account of ethics (understood as an account of ethics articulated and defended based on reason alone). Here I will articulate several of these purposes, though I certainly do not consider my list exhaustive.

First, we live in a world in which many people do not believe in Christianity. We need to be able to give an account of our moral convictions to our non-Christian family members, friends, colleagues, neighbors, fellow citizens, and so on. While there are times when it will be fruitful to do that by making explicit reference to our Christian beliefs, there are many instances in which appeals to Christian revelation will alienate people, make

---

4. Grisez, *Christian Moral Principles*, 25.E.

5. Grisez, *Christian Moral Principles*, 26.H.

6. "After we have promoted on earth . . . the goods of human dignity, familial communion, and freedom—that is to say, all the good fruits of our nature and effort—then we shall find them once more, but cleansed of all dirt, lit up and transformed, when Christ gives back to the Father an eternal and universal kingdom" (Second Vatican Council, "Pastoral Constitution on the Church in the Modern World, *Gaudium et spes*, 7 October 1965," in *Vatican Council II: Conciliar and Post Conciliar Documents*, sec. 39).

278 • Natural Law

them stop listening, or simply be less persuasive than a reason-based account. This is true in both private contexts and in the public square. Further, since moral obstacles are not infrequently a reason why people reject Christianity, giving people reason-based arguments for moral truths, which can show how moral norms protect and promote human flourishing rather than being (as many falsely suppose) arbitrary restrictions imposed on us by a God who does not want us to enjoy life, can sometimes be the first step in leading people toward Christianity (or at least removing a barrier to conversion). Indeed, I know of many cases in which people were drawn to the Christian faith precisely because they became convinced (through reason-based arguments) that Christian moral teaching is true.

Second, Christians also need to understand that the gospel is not contrary to human flourishing and that the divine law is not an arbitrary imposition. The serpent tempted Eve to disobey God by insinuating that following God's command was contrary to human flourishing, leading her to doubt God's goodness and trustworthiness, to view God as a rival rather than as the very source of life, freedom, and fulfillment. As Benedict XVI put it, this Genesis narrative describes "not only the history of the beginning but the history of all times," for "we all carry within us a drop of the poison of that way of thinking."[7] And while only grace can fully remedy this poisonous mistrust of God's goodness, it is also important to shore up that trust through reasoned arguments that show the connection between God's law and our flourishing. Natural law theory serves this crucial function. And once the convergence between reason and faith has strengthened our trust in God's law, this in turn makes it easier for us to trust and obey those aspects of Christ's teaching that are more difficult to understand through reason alone. As a philosophy professor, I have heard time and again from students that learning the philosophical (natural law) arguments for the moral truths that they already believed by faith greatly increased their confidence in those truths and in the trustworthiness of the church's teaching more generally. This has also been my own personal experience.

Third, life is full of difficult and complex moral decisions for which the gospel does not provide direct answers. In order to know, for instance, how to respond to novel biotechnologies or how to navigate daily life in a

---

7. Benedict XVI, Homily, December 8, 2005, https://www.vatican.va/content/benedict-xvi/en/homilies/2005/documents/hf_ben-xvi_hom_20051208_anniv-vat-council.html.

society in which cooperation with evil is unavoidable, we need a rational understanding of the basic principles that underlie Christian moral teaching to then apply those principles to the specific circumstances of our lives today. In other words, Christians, especially Christian leaders and those with a responsibility to advise and teach others, need to know how to engage in sound, reason-based moral deliberation, which means that they need to learn natural law theory. Obviously, Christians should take the data of revelation into account in their deliberations, for that data will help to specify the natural law in the ways mentioned above. But revelation does not replace natural law; we still need to do the hard work of thinking things through rigorously and methodically, using the God-given resources of both reason and revelation.

In sum, Leithart's account seems to be overly pessimistic about our capacity to know, articulate, and defend moral truths on the basis of reason and to ignore the crucial need for natural law reasoning not only as a tool for evangelization but also as a source of moral clarity and conviction within the Christian community.

Rejoinder

PETER J. LEITHART

Rather than respond to the other contributor's critiques of my original paper, I use my final essay to return to the concept of nature. Common ideas of nature, both modern and ancient, fall under the same criticism I lodged against natural law theory: they either ignore theology, bracket theology, or incorporate theological errors, which is to say, falsehoods. Only a theological account of nature can support the natural law theories the contributors to this book wish for. But a theological account of nature must be an account of creation, which means, unavoidably, also an account of the Creator. The God question cannot be bracketed, and no generic God will do. There is only one living Creator who speaks the eternal Word by the breath of his Spirit. Once we begin talking about nature as the creation of that Creator, we are no longer confining ourselves to nature but have introduced metaphysical and moral truth known only by revelation.

Early modern concepts of nature are heretical, reducing the Creator to the status of a divine cogwheel. If the universe is a great machine, a nature-based ethics can reason along two paths. First, since no *ought* can be derived from what *is*, since no moral order is built into reality, the moral life is subjective, primarily, for example, a matter of good will. That is, one line of modern ethics traces from Newton through Hume to Kant. Second, and more chillingly, if the universe is a giant machine, human beings are themselves no more than little machines to be programmed and used by other, more powerful machines. There is, in short, a line from reductionist Newtonian nature to social engineering, whether liberal or totalitarian.

After Darwin, teleology of a sort reenters the natural world, now guided not by a principle of *physis* or by a benevolent God but by the sovereign rule of Lady Natural Selection.[1] Nature, especially every animate product of nature, pursues survival. Since nature is quasi-purposeful, natural law reenters, initially in a Social Darwinist register. Still today, evolutionary thinkers claim that nature provides moral guidance for human beings and societies. Homosexual relations are perfectly natural because dolphins and giraffes do it. The dominance of human males is not natural because many female animals are as nasty as any male.[2]

No contributor to this volume holds a mechanical or Darwinian view of nature. The problem is, many of our contemporaries *do*. Before they will be persuaded by classical natural law arguments against gay marriage or in favor of traditional sex roles, they must become Aristotelians or Thomists. True, my anti-natural-law position also requires a new outlook on nature, but the creationist position is of a piece with the self-revelation of the triune God in creation, redemption, and Scripture. I wonder, not for the first time, about the value of urging any conversion other than conversion to Jesus: Why try to make our unbelieving neighbors Aristotelians when we can seek to make them Christians?

Besides, Aristotle's principle of *physis* cannot be imported wholesale and unaltered into a Christian framework. As Oliver O'Donovan has recently noted, antiquity offered what to Christians seems a "genial" idea of nature as *physis*, which means essentially "birth."[3] *Physis* is determined by origin and is the "energy of life itself directed toward growth." Within this frame, ethical action is "conscious conformity to emergence and development of life."[4] During some periods of Christian history, *physis* and creation seemed to interlock tightly, but with the rise of the scientific world picture, and the resulting shifts in moral theology, theologians have rightly devoted more attention to distinguishing nature from creation. To discern the moral import of nature, "we need an authority beyond nature" that can assure us of life's ultimate triumph over death.[5] But then we are in the realm of theology, and, O'Donovan insists, we will need to revise our ideas of nature to accord

---

1. Darwinists deny natural selection implies teleology, but the frequent recourse to the language of purpose, from Darwin on, belies their denial. See Michael Hanby, *No God, No Science? Theology, Cosmology, Biology* (Oxford: Wiley Blackwell, 2013), 211–16.

2. See Lucy Cooke, *Bitch: On the Female of the Species* (New York: Basic, 2023).

3. Oliver O'Donovan, *The Disappearance of Ethics: The Gifford Lectures* (Grand Rapids: Eerdmans, 2024), 78.

4. O'Donovan, *Disappearance*, 78.

5. O'Donovan, *Disappearance*, 80–81.

282 • Natural Law

with the "logic of creation."[6] In sum, modern culture and thought require a rigorously Christian approach to the natural world.

Ancient *physis* is, further, not as genial as it appears. Alasdair MacIntyre issues a stark challenge in now-classic *After Virtue*: today, we face a moral choice between Aristotle and Nietzsche, between antique virtue and nihilism. "There is no third alternative," he ominously concludes.[7] What if, on the contrary, there is a hidden continuity between Aristotle and Nietzsche? What if Aristotle is not a solution but part of the problem? What if the antithesis is not Aristotle versus Nietzsche but Christ versus both Aristotle and Nietzsche?

We may note, first, the ambiguity of Aristotelian "nature." Aristotle never harmonizes the *physis* of the *Physics* with his various appeals to the *physis* in the *Ethics* and *Politics*.[8] Even within the *Physics*, *physis* does not have a consistent meaning. It is, on the one hand, "the cause of what is the same always or for the most part," the opposite of *tuche*, "chance."[9] It is an internal principle of development that continuously drives things of the same *physis* toward "a certain end . . . provided there is no impediment." Acorns and oaks and all that.[10] Here the natural is what is usual, and the unnatural is what emerges when something knocks a substance off course. Yet, on the other hand, *physis* also refers to the full realization of a thing. Only in this latter sense can nature function as a norm: A fully-grown oak is *para physin*, while an oak is *kata physin* if its growth is somehow stunted.[11] Here the natural is the ideal, even if it is *un*usual.

That is not necessarily incoherent, but it creates incoherences when Aristotle applies it to political order. Nature, according to the *Politics*, justifies slavery and the subordination of women and also prohibits

---

6. O'Donovan, *Disappearance*, 81. O'Donovan admits that earlier theologians did not see the need to distinguish between nature and creation. The demand is placed on us by the actual historical circumstances we find ourselves in.

7. MacIntyre, *After Virtue: A Study in Moral Theory*, 3rd ed. (Notre Dame: University of Notre Dame Press, 2007), 118.

8. The following argument summarizes Julia Annas, "Aristotle on Human Nature and Political Virtue," *Review of Metaphysics* 49, no. 4 (1996): 731–53.

9. Aristotle, *Eudemian Ethics* 1247a33–34, trans. Brad Inwood (Cambridge: Cambridge University Press, 2013).

10. Aristotle, *Physics* 199b15–18, trans. C. D. C. Reeve (Indianapolis: Hacket, 2018).

11. This double use is built into the word *physis* itself. See Gerard Naffaf, *The Greek Concept of Nature* (Albany: SUNY Press, 2006), who argues that it covers the whole process of birth, growth, and completion, though one or the other dimension of this process might be highlighted in particular contexts.

certain uses of money. In the first two examples, *physis* overlaps with "the usual." Slaves and women are naturally subordinate because that is the way societies are normally organized. But the "natural" use of money is the opposite, natural not because it is common but because it is ideal.[12] Similar tensions appear in book 7 of the *Politics*, when Aristotle explains why Greeks have developed superior political institutions. Unlike northern Europeans, who are naturally spirited but lack intelligence, or Asians, who are intelligent but indolent, Greeks have the right natural balance of *thumos* and *phronesis*.[13] That argument runs aground when Aristotle tries to explain why some Greeks are justly members of a superior leisured class who devote themselves to excellence (*arete*) while others are part of the banausic masses whose productive labor supports the leisure of the leisured. Aristotle never explicitly claims workers and farmers lack the natural endowment to achieve virtue or that they have a different nature from the aristocracy.[14] But the ambiguous concept of *physis* lurks behind the argument. Nature as "the usual" legitimates the class structure of Athens: it is natural because it exists. *Physis* is a sophisticated way to say, "Whatever is, is just."

Aristotle's implicitly "natural law" defense of social stratification hints at sinister archaic concepts of nature that remain operative in his metaphysics and politics. In its earliest appearances, *physis* is a strictly biological concept, summing up the traits, capacities, and qualities of an organism.[15] On this understanding, the natural man is vital, ferocious, spirited, possessed of a wild, animal exuberance. *Physis* thus justifies the superiority of aristocratic warriors who display an exceptional intensity of life and being.[16] Aristocrats perpetuate their status by endogamy and selective breeding that ensures the natural endowment of their vitality is passed on through an intergenerational inheritance of blood. Greek *physis* is closer to Darwinian nature than we often imagine.

---

12. Aristotle, *Politics* 1.5–6 (slavery), 1.8–10 (money), 1.13 (women), trans. C. D. C. Reeve (Indianapolis: Hackett, 1998).

13. Aristotle, *Politics* 7.7.

14. As Annas points out; "Aristotle on Human Nature," 748–49. For the contrary view, see Fred D. Miller Jr., *Nature, Justice and Rights in Aristotle's Politics* (Cambridge, MA: Clarendon, 1997), 240–45.

15. The following paragraphs sum up the eccentric but penetrating analysis of Costin Alamariu's *Selective Breeding and the Birth of Philosophy* (self-published, 2023).

16. Later, Alamariu argues, tyrants and philosophers lay claim to natural superiority on a similar basis.

284 • Natural Law

This archaic understanding of *physis* persists after heroic Greece into what Jacob Burkhardt called the "Agonal Age" and from there enters surreptitiously into philosophical ethical and political discourse.[17] As Nietzsche observed, the Greek polis, like aristocratic Venice, as "an organization, whether voluntary or involuntary, for *breeding*."[18] Aristotle's ideal man is, MacIntyre insists, not a warrior but a gentleman, but the *arete* of Aristotle's magnanimous man retains heroic elements: he strives for public acclaim, forgets his benefactors and remembers his benefactions, and holds himself back in disdain from those beneath him. Aristotelian virtue is quasi-heroic excellent and "effectiveness" in an agonistic setting.[19] What matters to Aristotle in the ethical realm of *praxis* is control, reason's power to check passions so as to achieve the mean between excess and defect. For Aristotle as much as for Homer, the life of *arete* is a life of combat, no longer against Trojans but against the raging, chaotic urges within and, somewhat less violently, against rivals in polis. A domestication rather than a renunciation of heroic virtue, Aristotelian *arete* incorporates the heroic *agon* into the heart of ethics. As John Milbank argues, Aristotle's ethics and politics of *physis* are ultimately rooted in a pagan ontology of violence that, knowing no Eden or new Jerusalem, cannot imagine a peaceable kingdom or an ethics of peace.

In short, just as Augustine unmasked Roman virtue as disguised *libido dominandi*, so too can one unmask Aristotelian *arete* as refined heroic virtue. Scratch Aristotle, and you will find Achilles. Scratch Achilles, and you will discover Nietzsche lurking within.

When Thomas elevates charity rather than magnanimity as the leading virtue, he disassembles much of the Aristotelian apparatus. Relying on the Spirit who is poured on all flesh, all sorts and conditions of men *and women*, not just wealthy aristocrats, are capable of Christian *arete*. The primacy of charity implies that human action involves relations of mutual dependence, leaving no room for the sniffy detachment characteristic of the magnanimous man. Taking Jesus as model, the charitable man lives out an inherently excessive virtue, a virtue of passionate outpouring rather than one

---

17. Burkhardt, *The Greeks and Greek Civilization*, trans. Sheila Stern (New York: St. Martin's, 1998), 160–213.

18. Nietzsche, *Beyond Good and Evil* §262. Translation by Walter Kauffman (New York: Vintage, 1966).

19. Milbank, *Theology and Social Theory: Beyond Secular Reason* (Oxford: Blackwell, 1990) 352.

of controlled accumulation and retention.[20] Christian virtue is cruciform, displaying God's truth and goodness in vulnerable powerlessness. Charity depends on grace, yet charity is man's natural end. Jesus, love incarnate, provides the "natural" *telos* and standard of human being and action.

Nature, including even the refined nature of Aristotle, is too red of tooth and claw to provide a genuine alternative to nihilism. The real choice is Christ or nothing, and if Aristotle plays any role at all, it will be not the raw Aristotle of ancient Athens but the transfigured, evangelized Aristotle of Christendom. Put it in terms Nietzsche would understand: On the basis of nature, is an ethics or a politics that valorizes weakness conceivable?

---

20. Milbank, *Theology and Social Theory*, 359–62.

Conclusion

RYAN T. ANDERSON AND ANDREW T. WALKER

The last twenty years have seen a renaissance in the development of natural law thought among Protestants. Catholics, of course, have continued their work in natural law. But Protestant engagement has reappeared, and fruitful Catholic-Protestant collaborations on natural law theory have emerged. We see this as an unquestionably positive development and an inevitable result of Western secularism's near-total conquest of society.

As a *positive* development, the continuation of natural law by Catholics and renewed interest in it by Protestants demonstrates a maturing moral ecumenism. As a general observation, Catholics bring philosophical vigor to the moral enterprise, while Protestants base the bulk of their ethics on exegesis. Both sides need the other. This volume can be profitably read as a continuation in the now ecumenical project of natural law theory that takes both philosophy and revelation seriously. Catholics can appreciate Protestantism for its biblical rigor in complementing the natural law, while Protestants can appreciate Catholicism for offering philosophical accounts of natural law that parallel biblical revelation's testimony about general revelation. Even anecdotally, we see a widening enthusiasm for natural law considerations among rising Christians.

We can both recall the halcyon days of the initial release of The Manhattan Declaration in 2009, which brought together luminaries from the Protestant, Catholic, and Orthodox traditions to affirm the values of life, marriage, and religious liberty. Fast forward fifteen years, and while America's moral landscape is in a doubtlessly far worse-off place, we would wager that Christian moral thinking has undergone a helpful maturing. Rather than playing on defense, many Christians are taking up the cause of

288 • Natural Law

the Christian natural law tradition as a way to play offense, to make secularism answer for its baseless swagger. More importantly, both biblical and philosophical approaches to ethical thought, especially on contested moral questions, are helping everyday Christians in the pews better understand and appreciate the truth of Christian morality in a culture that has rejected it.

As a matter of *inevitability*, we believe that secularism's victory also sows its demise and explains natural law's retrieval and resurgence. Western culture's moral revolution has had a deracinating effect on the moral ecology of the West. Materially, we are abundantly well-off. Morally, we are in a state of free fall. The ravaging effects of secularism and its denaturing of human existence are producing an emotionally unwell society. Loneliness, declining marriage rates, declining fertility rates, skyrocketing opioid addictions, growing acceptance of euthanasia, gender ideology, and abortion have produced a society that is aimless, wandering, and at war with itself. When things are at their most dark, the light is most evident. We believe that the Christian natural law tradition provides a matchless account of human flourishing to which our society must return.

We have devoted the early portion of our careers to staking out positions largely hostile to the ambient culture. That has not always earned us accolades from our peers. Still, it does reaffirm an underlying truth of the natural law: If morality is what we believe it is—universal, objective, intelligible, and obligatory—then a moral position's rightness or wrongness is not dependent upon majorities, convention, or consensus. Natural law provides a comprehensive account of human flourishing that is timeless and averse to shifting moral zeitgeists.

We hope those who made it through this volume will see themselves invigorated by the relevance of the Christian natural law tradition to address many areas of cultural tumult, not out of self-righteous vindication but motivated by a concern for the principles of human flourishing that we believe the natural law tradition is unrivaled in articulating and embodying. We also hope that individuals who read this volume would carry the torch of the natural law tradition forward and proceed with considerations about how the natural law relates to their own ecclesiastical body.

Contributors

Ryan T. Anderson (PhD, University of Notre Dame) is the president of the Ethics and Public Policy Center. He is the author or coauthor of five books, including most recently *Tearing Us Apart: How Abortion Harms Everything and Solves Nothing* and *When Harry Became Sally: Responding to the Transgender Moment*. His research has been cited by two US Supreme Court justices, Justice Samuel Alito and Justice Clarence Thomas, in two Supreme Court cases. In addition to leading the Ethics and Public Policy Center, Anderson serves as the John Paul II Teaching Fellow in Social Thought at the University of Dallas and is the founding editor of *Public Discourse*.

Joel D. Biermann (PhD, Concordia Seminary) is the Waldemar A. and June Schuette Professor of Systematic Theology at Concordia Seminary, St. Louis. He is the author of several books, including *Wholly Citizens: God's Two Realms and Christian Engagement with the World*; *A Case for Character: Towards a Lutheran Virtue Ethics*; and *Day 7: For Work, Rest, or Play*.

Brad Littlejohn (PhD, University of Edinburgh) is the founder and president of the Davenant Institute. He also works as a fellow at the Ethics and Public Policy Center and has taught for several institutions, including Moody Bible Institute–Spokane, Bethlehem College and Seminary, and Patrick Henry College. He is the author or coauthor of several books, including *Richard Hooker: A Companion to His Life and Work, The Two Kingdoms*; *Why Do Protestants Convert?*; *Called to Freedom*; and *For the Healing of the Nations*.

Melissa Moschella (PhD, Princeton University) is associate professor of philosophy at the Catholic University of America and author of *To Whom Do*

289

Children Belong? Parental Rights, Civic Education, and Children's Autonomy. She is also a McDonald Distinguished Fellow in the Center for the Study of Law and Religion at Emory University School of Law.

Peter J. Leithart (PhD, University of Cambridge) is the president of Theopolis Institute and serves as teacher at Trinity Presbyterian Church in Birmingham. He is the author of several books, including *Defending Constantine*; *Delivered from the Elements of the World*; *Creator*; *The End of Protestantism*; and *Traces of the Trinity.*

Michael Pakaluk (PhD, Harvard University) is a professor of ethics and social philosophy in the Busch School of Business at the Catholic University of America in Washington, DC, and a member of the Pontifical Academy of St. Thomas Aquinas. He is the author of several books, including *Mary's Voice in the Gospel according to John*; *The Memoirs of St. Peter*; and *Aristotle's Nicomachean Ethics: An Introduction.*

Andrew T. Walker (PhD, Southern Baptist Theological Seminary) is associate professor of Christian ethics and public theology at the Southern Baptist Theological Seminary. He is an associate dean in the School of Theology and the executive director of the Carl F. H. Henry Institute for Evangelical Engagement at Southern Seminary. Walker is also a fellow at the Ethics and Public Policy Center and serves as the managing editor of WORLD Opinions. He is the author of several books on Christian ethics and public theology. His analysis has been written or cited in such outlets as *The New York Times*, *The Wall Street Journal*, *The Atlantic*, *Los Angeles Times*, and many others. He resides in Louisville, Kentucky, with his wife and three daughters. You can follow him on X at @andrewtwalk.

Scripture Index

Genesis
2. 110
2:8, 15 251
2:15–17 251
2:19–20 251
2:23 251
3. . . . . 157, 158, 166
3:6 . . . . 124, 157, 235
3:22 235
4:19–24 237

Exodus
3:16 82
20 131
20:1 63
20:4–6 235
20:8–11 235
22:21 235
23:9 235

Deuteronomy
5:12–15 . . . . .37, 235
6:5 247
10:17–19 235

Psalms
1. 142
73. 109
119:105 139

Jeremiah
31:33 158

Matthew
4:19 236

5:8 141
5:17 142
5:17–20 99
5:21 52
5:22 52
5:23–24 52
5:26 52
5:43–48 236
5:48 142
7:12 183
8:22 236
15:18–20 141
18:3–5 141
18:15 51
19:3–9 255
22:37–39 xiii
22:37–40 2

Mark
1:14–15 100
12:31 51

Luke
1:75 140
5:8 258
6:31 . . . . xiii, xv
22:29–30 225

John
6:70–71 142

Acts
15. 258
16:6–10 82
17:23 125

Romans
1. . . . . .243, 245
1:18 220
1:18–20 . . . . . . 220, 227
1:18–32 . . . . .158, 235
1:19 123
1:20 . . . . .123, 219
1:22–23 220
1:23 125
2. 158
2:14 245
2:14–15 . . . . 59, 121, 158,
166, 269
2:14–16 . . . x, xiv, 84, 227
2:27 158
3:8 xv
3:23 227
6:1–14 236
6:14–15 99
7. . . . . . . 124, 158, 159, 166
7:12 120
7:19 124
7:23–25 239
8:2 239
8:29 144
11:24 158
11:33–36 119
12:1–2 258
12:2 139

1 Corinthians
6:9–10 141
6:12–13 141
6:20 257
9:20–21 99

291

292 • Natural Law

11:14 236	**2 Thessalonians**	4:17 100
13:12 226	1:8 100	
15:58 . . . . 226, 277		**2 Peter**
	1 Timothy	1:16–21 257
Galatians	2:4 228	3:13 225
2:15 158	2:5 228	
4:8 158	4:2 235	
4:21 99		
5. 220	**2 Timothy**	
5:18 99	3:16–17 99	
Ephesians	**1 Peter**	
4:17–18 129	2:17 247	
5. 110	3:15 228	

Subject Index

abortion
    classical natural law and, 3–4, 43, 51
    new natural law and, 38–39, 171, 200
Althusius, Johannes, 128n41, 131, 134, 135, 149
anti-natural law. *See* natural law, anti-
Aquinas, Thomas
    and divine command, 118, 151–54, 158, 241, 243
    and eternal law, 238, 239–42, 265
    and the four orders, 172–73
    and grace, 227, 228n7, 239, 245, 247
    and inclinations, 122, 238–39, 241
    and insufficiency of natural law, 242–48, 265
    and natural friendship of humans, 21
    and natural law as component of larger concept of law, 237–48
    and natural law as knowable and binding, 151, 154, 244, 245
    and natural law as ordinance of reason for common good, 151, 240–41
    and natural law as unchanging, 242–43, 246
    and primary and secondary principles of natural law, 122, 124, 229, 241, 242–43
    and revelation, 235, 236, 237–38, 241, 244, 245, 246
Aristotle, 21, 24, 115, 124–25, 180, 208, 249–50, 253–54, 281–85
artificial contraception, 52–53
Augustine, 2, 24, 125, 127, 141n4, 215, 284
Barth, Karl, 72, 143
Bavinck, Herman, 113
biblicism, 111, 139, 148, 156, 159

Bonhoeffer, Dietrich, 75–77, 108
Boyle, Joseph, 169, 177n28, 185n47, 187n52
Calvin, John, 90, 121, 124–25, 128, 135, 138, 156, 216, 273
cardinal virtues, 12, 188, 191
charity, 2, 22, 91, 186n48, 221, 247, 284–85
Cicero, xvii, 2, 21, 24, 84
concupiscence, 83, 85, 239, 240, 243, 244
courage, 12, 190
creational law, 30, 80–82, 91–92, 106, 110, 148, 163, 263
Daneau, Lambert, 121
debitum, the, 13, 14, 15, 36, 45
Decalogue, the
    authority of, 60, 64–67, 70, 235
    as built into creation from the beginning of the world, xviii, 66–67
    biblical setting of, 47
    as divine moral law, 60, 64, 66
    first table of, 7, 8, 21–23, 28–29, 33–34, 36, 37, 45, 120, 132, 149
    as knowable through reason alone, 225
    Luther's view of, 64–71
    Melanchthon's view of, 60, 83, 84n8
    and the new natural law, 206, 225
    and piety, 7, 28, 29, 34, 36–37
    purpose of, 68
    as restatement of basic principles of natural law, 2, 6–7, 33–34, 36–37, 40, 52, 68–69, 71, 79, 90, 130–32, 148–49, 236
    second table of, 6, 13, 17, 22–23, 29, 33–37, 120, 132, 149, 236
    as setting down duties, 142

293

294 • Natural Law

depravity, total, 116, 121–26, 137, 141, 162
discrimination, 214
double effect, principle of, 182–83
double predestination, 142, 142n5
due, the, 13–16, 20, 36, 41, 45
duty, 15
Eighth Commandment, the, 35–36
eternal law, 94, 119, 237–42, 247, 248, 265, 270
fairness, xv, 183, 197
faith
   as aid in grasping natural law, 28, 31, 52, 143, 218, 276–77
   and grace, 49, 52, 228n7, 265
   justification through, 69, 143, 143n9, 265
   and moral principles, 206, 231, 276, 278
   and reason, 257, 157n1, 278
   and scholastic theology, 83
fall, the
   anti-natural law view of, 157, 235
   effect of on natural law, 121–26, 127
   natural law as knowable despite, xiii, xiv, 115
   Reformed natural law view of, 121–26, 127, 157, 166
Finnis, John
   and basic human goods, 175–76, 237
   and freedom, 179n33
   and God, 225, 234n2
   and the kingdom of God, 185n47
   and moral truth, 187–88n52
   and natural law as necessary for our flourishing, 151, 164
   and political authority, 196n80, 197, 198n87
   and self-evidence, 229, 237
first principle of morality, the, 181, 188n52
first principle of practical reason, 41, 169, 174, 176–78, 180, 186–87, 229, 230, 240, 241
first table, the. See Decalogue, the: first table of
free will, 171, 209
friendship
   as basic human good, 151, 169, 175, 177, 178, 184, 197, 198, 214
   civic, 198, 214

   marriage as fostering, 86
   natural law as fostering, 20, 21, 23, and "other selves," xvii, 24–26
   and right, 16
   with God, 48, 213, 215, 218
Gaston, Lloyd, 158n5
Golden Rule, the, xiii, xv, 42, 51, 183, 187, 191, 193, 196
grace
   and charity, 285
   common, 106, 116, 127–29, 149, 160
   divine, 186n48, 209, 220, 221, 228n7, 254, 267
   justification by, 60, 69, 265, 266
   middle, 160
   nature as born of, xx
   as necessary for acting in a morally upright way, 52, 143, 227–28, 228n6, 245, 247
   as necessary for fulfilling the commandments, 49, 143, 222, 245
   as necessary for the attainment of eternal life, 156–57n1, 228n7, 265–67
   as perfecting rather than replacing nature, 33, 114, 221
   special, 127, 156–57n1, 160
Grisez, Germain
   and God, 170n3, 180, 185, 218, 219
   and Jesus as example, 193–94n74
   and insufficiency of natural law, 225, 226, 276
   and integral human fulfillment, 231
   and the kingdom of God, 185n47
   and limits of emotional motivation, 193–94, 195n79, 231
   and modes of responsibility, 187–88, 187n51, 190–91, 190n60, 204, 206, 231
   and moral truth, 187–88n52
   and the new natural law, xix, 3, 169
   and revelation, 225, 276–77
   and universality of basic goods, 237
happiness
   as becoming like God (theosis), 11, 46, 248, 254
   difficulty defining, 10, 46
   humans created for end of eternal, 246, 246n54, 248, 254

Subject Index • 295

natural law as side-constraint on pursuit of, 17
pursuit of as aim of human action, 10, 46, 204, 213, 246
virtuous life as requirement for, 11, 12, 46
harm principle, the, 35
Hauerwas, Stanley, 73n27, 74–75, 88
Heidegger, Johann, 120
Hodge, Charles, 112, 120, 143, 144n13
Hooker, Richard, 114, 117, 119, 122, 129, 133, 134, 161, 167
hymns, use of in worship, 143, 143–44n13
images, use of in worship, 143, 144
imperium, 152, 153, 164
integral human fulfillment, 96, 97, 181–83, 181n38, 184–86, 198, 211, 225–26, 230–31
intellectualism, 117
intelligible acts, 181
Junius, Franciscus, 119
justice
Aristotle and, 253
Augustine and, 125
as cardinal virtue, 12, 188, 191
and the Decalogue, 35, 37, 40
definition of, 5
friendship and, 24, 198
God's, 54, 220, 240, 243
and the Golden Rule, 191, 196
substantive requirements of, 196–97
yearning for as evidence for a moral order, x
justification, 60, 69, 76, 112, 265, 266
Karlstadt, Andreas, 62
Kuyper, Abraham, 127, 128–29
law
biblical perspective of, 237–49
ceremonial, 132–33
civil, 129–31, 134–37, 149, 165
of concupiscence, 240, 243, 244
creational, 80–81, 82, 91–92, 106, 148, 163, 263, 265
divine, 129–33, 136–37, 237, 246–49, 246n54, 263, 264–65, 276
eternal, 94, 119, 237, 239–42, 247, 248, 265, 270
judicial, 132–33
of love, 135, 247

moral, 97–98, 103, 132–33
of Moses, 62–64, 66, 67, 71
natural. *See* natural law, Anglican; natural law, anti- view of; natural law, classical view of; natural law, Lutheran view of; natural law, new view of; natural law, Reformed view of
New, 246, 247, 247n61, 248, 266
Old, 246, 247, 247n61
partly vs. purely human, 134, 163
as performative, 22–23
positive, 97–98, 166, 196–97
requirements of, 22
scientific, 101, 102, 103
lawgiver
God as, xii, xiv, 33, 125, 144, 154, 164
as required for existence of law, 22, 106, 116, 124, 125, 150–51, 154, 164, 242
Leiden Synopsis, the, 115–16, 122
leisure, 9, 29, 283
Lewis, C. S., xii, xiii, 4, 138, 143, 213, 237, 250, 258
LNC. *See* noncontradiction: law of (LNC)
logic, 173
logos, 82
Lord's Supper, the, 49
Luther, Martin, 62–69, 83, 91, 99–100, 107, 109, 142, 209
market, the, 8–9, 29, 46
marriage
adultery as harm against, 6, 10, 44, 70, 85, 88, 97, 101, 102, 147
as basic good, 177, 177n28, 178–79, 184
and fostering friendship, 86, 214
and polygamy, 85–86
and procreation, 86, 171,
pursuing family prospering as strengthening, xv, 184
purposes of, 85–86
same-sex, 44, 281
Marsilius of Padua, 130
Melanchthon, Philip
and classical thought, 83–84, 109
and human virtue, 84
and justification by grace, 69
and marriage, 86n12
and natural law, 58–61, 67, 83–85

296 • Natural Law

mental prayer, 48–49
moderation, 12
modes of responsibility, 187–91, 190n60, 204, 206, 231
morality, objectivity of, xi, xii, xiv, xx, 95
moral truths, 96, 123, 187–88n52, 227, 228, 230, 275–79
Moses, law of, 62–64, 66, 67, 71
Müntzer, Thomas, 62
natural law, Anglican, 114
natural law, anti- view of
  and atheological natural law, xix, 233–34, 234n2, 238, 242, 242n33, 249, 256, 264, 271
  and the Bible, 156–60, 233, 235, 237, 242n33, 247, 248, 255, 268, 272–73
  and Christianity, 233, 248, 256
  and ethics as grounded by events, 235–36
  and the Fall, 157, 235
  and the first principle of practical reason, 240
  and grace, 245, 247, 248, 254, 255–56, 259
  and Jesus as source, justification, and model for human life, 236, 267, 285
  and history, 159–60
  and law, 233, 237–49, 264, 265
  and the lawgiver, 242
  and natural law as changeable, 242–43, 244–45
  and natural law as collection of fragments of a coherent theology, xx, 233, 256, 256n99
  and nature, 233, 249–56, 280–85
  overview of, xix–xx
  and revelation, 158, 234–36, 244, 245, 246, 254, 255, 257–58, 274–77, 280
  and sin, 243–44, 273, 275
  sufficiency of, 236–37, 242, 273, 274, 276
natural law, classical view of
  authority issuing, 5, 7, 12, 22–23, 28, 33, 45
  and the cardinal virtues, 12
  claim of existence of, 5–8, 44
  as constraint on pursuit of self-love, 8, 10, 17, 31, 34–35, 36, 39–40
  and the Decalogue, 2, 6–7, 17, 21–23

  and the human will, 21–22
  importance of virtue in, xvii, 5, 10–12, 40, 46, 140
  and justice, 12, 24
  lawfulness of, 8, 9, 17–20, 22
  and leisure, 9
  and natural setting of humans, xvii, 5, 8–9, 13, 29, 46, 47
  negative vs. positive obligations of, 36–37, 40–42
  obligation to harm no one within, 5, 13, 16, 20, 21, 26, 30, 35, 40, 41, 42, 51
  obligation to honor God within, 2, 7, 12, 22, 23, 28–29, 37, 40, 43, 45, 51
  obligation to love neighbor as oneself, 2, 22, 24, 51
  obligation to honor mother and father within, 7, 12–13, 23, 28–29, 37, 40, 45
  and "other selves," xvii, 24–26
  overview of, xvii, 1–3
  as permissive, 35, 166
  and practical vs. speculative reason, 17–20
  precepts of, 5–6, 12–13, 30, 40, 45
  and procreation, 5, 11, 40
  promulgation of, 5, 12–20, 22–23, 33
  and prudence, 12, 17
  purpose of theory of, 3–4, 32–33, 38, 43, 47, 140
  and pursuit of happiness, 10–11
  and right, 16
  and self-love, xvii, 8, 10–12, 16, 22, 24, 31, 34–36, 39–40, 51
  and sin, 49
  sources regarding, 2–3
  strictly vs. merely due in, 13–16, 36–37, 41–42, 45
natural law, Lutheran view of
  as applicable to all people, 68, 76, 79, 80, 89, 146–47
  as based on Scripture, 59–60
  Bonhoeffer's views on, 75–77, 108
  as creational law, 80–81, 82, 91–92, 106, 148
  and death of self in service to the other, 208
  and the Decalogue, xviii, 64–71, 79, 83–84, 90, 120

definition of, 58, 59, 62, 64, 67–68, 69, 93, 106
doctrine of Melanchthon, the, 58–62, 67, 69
as eternal, 67–68, 71, 72, 76, 79, 96, 106
existence of, xvii, 70, 96
and Jesus, 79–80, 211, 267
lack of guidance of on moral questions in the public arena, 74, 80, 81, 88, 90, 100, 106
Luther's views on, 62–69
opposition to, 72–75
overview of, xvii–xviii, 69–72
as paving the way for the gospel, xvii, 60–61, 67, 68, 81, 88, 91
power of to convict sinners, xvii–xviii, 60–61, 68, 79, 81, 88, 91, 109
purpose of, 60–61, 68, 69, 77, 78–79, 81, 88, 91, 109
source of, 64, 68, 76–77
as the will of God, 64, 67–69, 71, 75, 77, 81–82, 93, 106, 108, 147, 208
Wingren's views on, 78–79
natural law, new view of
and abortion, 38–39
applying to humans as rational creatures, 94, 96
and basic human goods, xix, 169, 171, 176–80, 177n28, 184, 204–6, 214–16, 241
and the Bible, 215–16, 219, 264, 278
bindingness of, 150, 151, 152, 153–55, 186
and Christianity, 209–11, 218–19, 220, 228, 276–77
definition of, 94, 96
developers of, 169
as eudaimonistic, xix, 109, 204
and first principles of practical reason, 177–78, 180, 229, 230, 241, 242
and the four orders, 150, 172–76, 213, 230
and free choice, 171, 209
and friendship with God, 213, 215, 218, 225
and God as the author of the natural law, xix, 170, 185, 199, 212–13, 218–19, 227

and human nature, 171–72, 175, 208, 213
and integral human fulfillment, 181, 181n38, 182, 183, 186, 198, 225–26, 230–31
and Jesus as example of moral living, 193–94n74, 209, 211, 264
and the lawgiver, 154, 170
and liberalism, 213–14
and liberty, 199
metaphysical and anthropological presuppositions of, xix, 170–72
and modes of responsibility, 187–91, 190n60, 204, 206, 231
and moral norms, xix, 169, 171, 181–87, 204, 208, 209, 213, 229–31
and the moral order, 95, 173
and natural law as natural, 172
and the natural order, 173
negative vs. positive duties of, 40–41
overview of, xix, 3
as participation in God's wisdom, 154
political implications of, 195–99
as positive, 187, 191–92, 215
and practical reason vs. speculative knowledge, xix, 40–41, 150, 173–76, 186n49, 199, 210, 213, 230, 274
precepts of, 40–41
purposes of, 277–79
sufficiency of, 225, 226
and religion, 171, 180, 185, 218, 225, 226, 276
and revelation, 216–17, 219, 220, 224–25, 275–79
ultimate end of, 276
and utilitarianism, 39
as universal and unchanging, 186
and virtue, 169, 187–95, 199, 220–21, 227
and the vocation principle, 184–85, 184n43, 187, 215
natural law, Reformed view of
and Anglican natural law, 114
and the Bible, 138–39, 148, 156, 159, 166–67, 268, 270, 272–73
bindingness of, 146, 150, 151, 152, 153–55, 164, 270

298 • Natural Law

as both metaphysical and
epistemological reality, xix, 115, 150
and civil law, 129–30, 132, 134–37,
149, 153, 165
and common grace, 116, 127–29, 149,
160
and the Decalogue, 130–32, 149
definition of, xviii, 114–15, 117, 120
and divine law, 129–33, 136–37
as eternal, 120
and eternal law, 117, 119
and the Fall, 121–26, 127, 157, 166
and grace, 114
as guiding believers in living wisely, 91,
147, 273
and history, 167
and the lawgiver, 116, 124–26, 150–51,
153, 154, 164, 273
nature vs. law in, 115–16, 117–18, 150,
156
negative vs. positive duties of, 36, 91
and the Noahide precepts, 131–32
overview of, xviii–xix
precepts of, 36, 122, 123, 132
and predestination, 162–63
purpose of, 137–39, 146, 273
realist-voluntarist debate in, 116,
117–20, 151–52, 164
rejection of idea of, 111–12
and revelation, xviii, 112, 271
sin and, 125, 129, 166, 273
sufficiency of, 273
and total depravity, 116, 121–26, 137,
141, 162, 268
and the will of God, 118, 119–20, 126,
147, 165, 270
and will vs. intellect, 150–51
natural law theory, xii–xvi
natural order, the, 173
natural religion, 72
natural science, 114
natural teleology, 202–3
natural theology, 114
nature
anti-natural law view of, 233, 249–56,
280–85
and artifice, 251, 271–72, 274
definition of, 249–50, 255
and grace, xx, 33, 114, 221

and human practices, 253
and language, 252–53, 252n85
mere vs. ethical, 253
as oppositional concept, 250
pure, 254, 254n97, 255
as theological, 251–52
vs. law, 115–16, 117–18, 150, 156
negative principle of worship, 137
new natural law theory, the (NNLT). *See*
natural law, new view of
Noahide precepts, the, 131–32
nominalism, 71, 72, 88, 118
noncontradiction
law of (LNC), 18–19, 19n11
practical law of (P-LNC), 20, 42
practical principle of (P-PNC), 20
principle of (PNC), 17, 18, 19
numen supremum, 7
Ockham, William of, 118, 130
other selves, xvii, 24–26
P-LNC. *See* noncontradiction: practical
law of (P-LNC)
P-PNC. *See* noncontradiction: practical
principle of (P-PNC)
Paul
and fallen humans as without excuse,
138, 227, 244, 245
and the gift of the Spirit, 159, 220n4,
239, 245
and humanity no longer under the
law, 99
and natural law as condemning
sinners, 88, 158n5, 159
and natural law as written onto human
hearts, 59, 71, 84, 112–13, 158,
158n3
and necessity of rapprochement
between biblical faith and Greek
inquiry, 82
and wicked customs of humans as a
result of the fall, 122, 124
prohibition of against evil deeds even
for good ends, xv
Philip of Hesse, 85–86
physis, 281, 282–84
piety, 5, 7, 12, 23, 28–29, 37, 40, 45, 47
Plato, xv, 11, 33, 71, 125, 143, 249
PNC. *See* noncontradiction: principle of
(PNC)

Subject Index • 299

political authority, 196, 197, 197n85, 198
political common good, 197, 198, 198n97
political community, 196, 197
polygamy, arguments for and against, 85–86
practical reason
    first principle of, 41, 169, 174, 176–78, 180, 186–87, 229, 230, 240, 241
    integral directiveness of, 181, 184, 185, 187–89, 191, 195, 208, 230, 231
    knowledge of human goods and moral norms through, xiii, xv, 95, 150, 169, 173–76, 178–79, 181, 213
    new natural law view of, xix, 40–41, 150, 173–76, 186n49, 199, 210, 213, 230, 274
    and the principle of noncontradiction, 17–20
    and prudence, 12, 192
    range of, 17
    speculative knowledge as prerequisite to, 41, 95, 171, 173, 175, 210
practical reasonableness, 177, 179n32, 185, 198n87
precepts
    articulable, 6
    of classical view of natural law, 5–6, 12–13, 30, 40, 45
    definition, 5–6
    of new natural law, 40–41
    of Reformed view of natural law, 36, 122, 123, 132
    specifiable, 6
procreation, 5, 6, 11, 40, 86, 171, 237
predestination, 62–63, 142, 142n5
prudence, 12, 17, 188, 189, 191–95
prudential reasoning, 52–54
Pufendorf, Samuel, 234n2, 269
rationalism, 107, 112, 117
reason
    as defining aspect of humanity, 108
    Lutheran skepticism of, 107–8
    practical vs. speculative, 95
    vs. will, 123–25
Reformed, definition of, 113–14
re-inscription, 127, 128
revelation
    anti-natural law view of, 158, 234–36,

244, 245, 246, 254, 255, 257–58, 274–77, 280
    divine, 216–17, 219–20, 224–25
    natural, 114, 127, 166, 167
    new natural law view of, 216–17, 219, 220, 224–25, 275–79
    Reformed natural law view of, xviii, 112, 271
    special, 127, 158, 160, 166, 167, 216–17
    supernatural, 32, 167, 172, 217, 219, 220, 227
salvation
    as addition to human nature, 254–55
    assurance of, 143, 143n9
    as a right rather than a gift, 254–55n97
scope, 6, 15, 16, 17, 21
Scotus, Duns, 118, 164
second table, the. *See* Decalogue, the: second table of
self-evident, 229, 237
self-love
    classical view of, xvii, 8, 10–12, 16, 22, 24, 31, 34–36, 39–40, 51
    and imitation of Christ, 49
    love of neighbor in relation to, 51
    as a movement of the will, 22
    natural law as constraint on pursuit of, 8, 10, 17, 31, 34–35, 36, 39–40
    nature of, 10–12
    as a result of the Fall, 124
    and virtue, 40, 49
sin
    anti-natural law view of, 243–44, 273, 275
    classical view of, 49
    common grace as restraint on, 128
    mortal, 50
    natural law and, 34, 46–47, 100, 106, 125, 129, 220
    Reformed view of, 125, 129, 166, 273
slavery, 253–54
Smith, James K. A., 73
sola scriptura, 83, 84, 85, 112
standing, 25
strictly due, the. *See debitum*, the
Suarez, Francisco, 118, 151–53, 164, 165
subsidiarity, principle of, 197
telos, xiii, 115, 117

300 • Natural Law

theonomy, 136
theosis, 11, 46
unintegrated emotions, 187–95
virtue
   as becoming like God, 11, 84
   cardinal, 12, 188, 191
   importance of in classical view, xvii, 5, 10–12, 40, 46, 140
   Melanchthon's views on, 84
   new natural law view of, 169, 187–95, 199, 220–21, 227
   requirement of for happiness, 11, 12
   and self-love, 40, 49
vocation principle, 184–85, 184n43, 187, 215
Way, the, 50–51

will, of God
   as arbitrary, 120
   as divine law, 264–65
   Lutheran view of, 64, 67–69, 71, 75, 77, 81–82, 93, 106, 108, 147, 208
   Reformed view of, 118, 119–20, 126, 147, 165, 270
will, human
   effects of the Fall on, 124
   natural movements of, 21–22
Willard, Samuel, 120
Wilson, James, 213, 270, 271
Wingren, Gustaf, 78–79
works, as fruits of faith, 142
Yoder, John Howard, 73n27, 88
Zanchi, Girolamo, 125, 127–28